NEW YORK NEW YORK

NEW YORK NEW YORK
MARIE TOMANOVA

Thomas Beachdel

Foreword
Kim Gordon

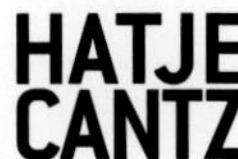

Foreword

Kim Gordon

In the beginning of the twentieth century, posters could be seen around Boston that said, “For a good time go to New York.” I believe in the DNA of a city, NY has always been about money and good times!

The portraits in Marie’s book are also a picture of the promise of freedom. That’s what I felt when I first moved there in 1980. You take what you want from the city, people leave you alone. The diversity of the people in this book is a mirror of that thirst for freedom. Despite the shopping mall aspect of lower Manhattan, it still feels like a safe haven from “AMERICA.” Your friends become your family, the family extension is a community that you give back to because you live there; you’re not a distant investor buying a condo you’ll never live in.

Marie’s book is a celebration of that young community. You don’t mind struggling for rent and food because you feel alive in the city. This was not really my early ’80s NY, I was already old, twenty-seven. I had anxiety about the art world. I felt way too middle class. Discovering the downtown music scene was a hunt; it was work, or my kind of fun. I wasn’t looking for that. I was looking for becoming . . . new ideas and weird music and art spaces to check out. I would scour the over-postered building walls for flyers that looked interesting.

I felt like an outsider wanting to get in. How does one get to show in a gallery? I slowly met artists and musicians, but I still always felt like an outsider. The city was dense and crowded with space around me. The characters in No Wave bands like Lydia Lunch and James Chance were intriguing but intimidating and “cool.” They would fit right into this book. The music was exciting. They had style, something I hadn’t yet figured out. Lo-fi glamour. Basically, everybody wore black (it didn’t show the dirt and looked chic) and eyeliner, Manic Panic hair dye of screaming reds and purples or simply bleached out.

The downtown scene was messy, the Pyramid Club (recently closed) would have dancers on the bar, straight and trans. Bands played and people smashed into the small space all nite long. In this collection of exuberant photos Marie captures the inside look, as it is now, being “cool” is accessible to all, a New York kind of democracy.

Introduction

Thomas Beachdel

The Pull of Mythic Space: Marie Tomanova's Downtown New York City

> Place is security, space is freedom: we are attached to the one and long for the other. There is no place like home.
>
> — Yi-Fu Tuan, *At Home in the World*, 1995

Marie Tomanova's *New York New York* is a landscape of youth and a portrait of place—entwining person and environment. New York City is an almost mythic entity, a place of both coming to and becoming in. Depending on one's point of view, it has been—and perhaps still is—a gateway to "America," to a new life, to a land of vast opportunity. It has been the kernel and the door to a future for those arriving from another country, as well as from other parts of the United States, to find, express, and be themselves. In *New York New York*, Tomanova merges the genres of portrait and landscape to effortlessly bounce off one another, revealing a social landscape inextricably linked to place, a portrait of a certain New York City, one that is a picture of her world, a landscape of her life.

Tomanova left her family farm in the small border town of Mikulov in the Czech Republic and came to the United States in 2011 and to New York in 2012, alone, knowing no one. And her world expands. It is a story of dreaming, risking, surviving, and finding one's own way, and it likely mirrors the aspirations and the emotional landscape of the individuals Tomanova has photographed for *New York New York*. It is often easy to look back and not see the struggle, not see the hardship, to forget the moments of pain and difficulty that can loom so large in the process of finding oneself in a new place. The antidote, of course, is to focus on the dream, the motivation; to build a world in which to fit or to find a place of belonging. *New York New York* is that big city of dreams.

Shot in New York City, mostly in 2019 and 2020, *New York New York* is at once vast and specific, intimate and outgoing. It is about deep truth and superficial moments, the range of what it means to be human. It is honest and forthright—it is real. Tomanova's images are direct and speak to the essence of an instant. They are about emotions and space, place and identity. Perhaps the most visible thread

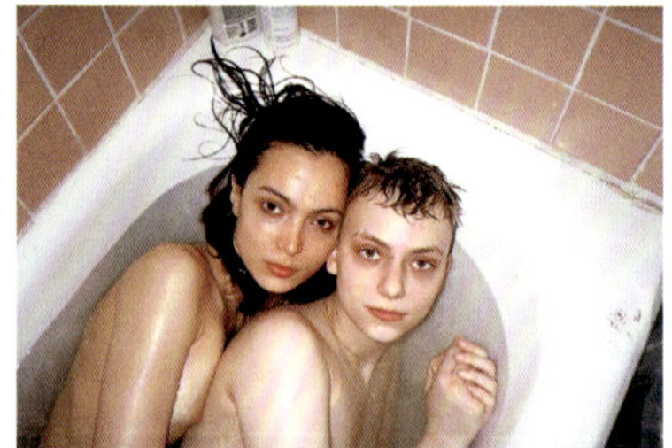

Figure 1. Marie Tomanova, *Kate and Odie*, 2017.

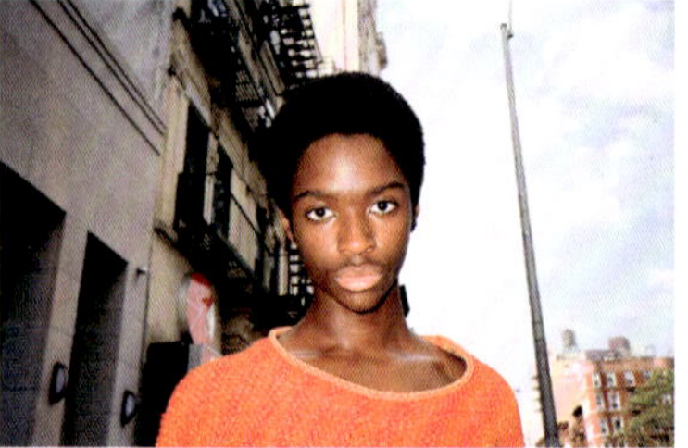

Figure 2. Marie Tomanova, *Alton*, 2016.

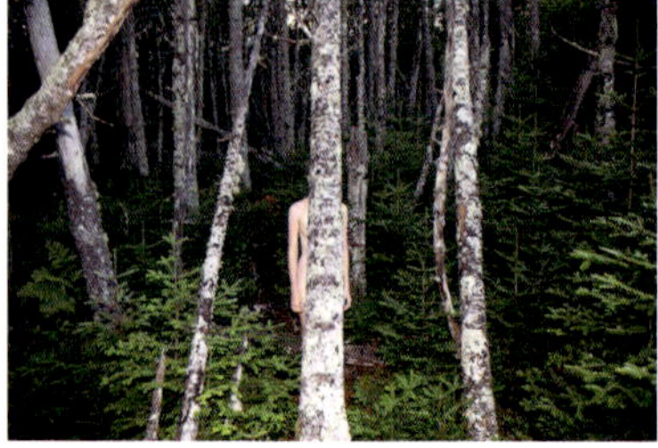

Figure 3. Marie Tomanova, *Trees*, 2016.

running through *New York New York* is a certain intensity of youth experience, often linked to connection, freedom, and individual expression. This can be seen in the book's cover image, *Ayana* (2020), of a gracefully arcing body against the background of low Brooklyn buildings and a setting sun. Eyes gaze outward with a depth of feeling, alive and engaging in the open space on a rooftop. There is a shared moment here, between Tomanova and Ayana, and ultimately with us, as viewers. We are let into a special space. And each image carries a certain preciousness and immediacy. It can be tender, as in *Aheem* (2020), where there is gravitas and profundity against a spray of water. It can be outward and irreverent, as seen in *Makenna & Doe* (2020) and *Kids (Tompkins Square Park)* (2020), photographs of a large group of friends that Tomanova shot in the park over the course of the summer of 2020 during the period when the coronavirus pandemic effectively shuttered New York City, presenting a corner of life and friendship circles that came together. *New York New York* is a document, a picture, a landscape of vibrant life in New York City. Many of the images are of individuals that Tomanova has photographed many times, such as Kate and Odie (fig. 1) or Alton Mason (fig. 2), who appeared on the covers of her first book, *Young American* (Paradigm Publishing, 2019). They also appear in *New York New York* in images such as *Kate & Odie (Laughing)* (2019) and *Jeremy & Alton* (2019), illustrating the longitudinal aspect of Tomanova's practice that traces an individual over time. In *Young American*, we see Kate and Odie in a bathtub at the very beginning of their relationship, whereas in *New York New York*, two years later and now married, they still exhibit a signature closeness and bond that is intensely touching. Alton, against the backdrop of the Lower East Side in *Young American*, is seen on the cusp of breaking into the worldwide fame that is evident in *New York New York* in his swagger at a party for Gucci with the actor and playwright Jeremy O. Harris. Inside and intimate, out and over-the-top, this is *New York New York*.

After receiving her Master of Fine Arts degree in painting in the Czech Republic, Tomanova travels to New York City and turns to photography as a means of being with herself in a new place, connecting with her past, seeing herself in America; literally, picturing herself there in a very different and unfamiliar environment. Her self-portraiture in the landscape, still an active body of work (2012–ongoing), was a way of belonging. All she had was herself, a camera, and the landscape. Tomanova sought out nature at first, as it provided a familiar link to her past, on a farm, in nature, that relationship between body and some primordial space, a geography of human belonging.

Tomanova's self-portraits from this period, *Trees* (2016) (fig. 3), for example, loosely evoke or bring to mind the work of Ana Mendieta, but while Mendieta's work in general brings gender to the fore in relation to nature, Tomanova's is a more personal association, a visceral echo of her past, from where she came, and to where she was now, in a new environment. While the body/gender connection is present in Tomanova's self-portraits, fundamentally, the work is more aligned with individual empowerment, a drive to see herself and to realize herself so far from home. For Tomanova, the empowerment she seeks and expresses in her work is fluid along gender and identity lines; it is not binary or simple. *Trees* connects Tomanova to the landscape, allowing her to envision herself being in a new place, but it also problematizes this space. Her body, mostly obscured by a tree trunk, is present but almost lost in the woods, perhaps indicating a certain difficulty or tension in fully seeing or realizing herself in that place, in the United States. There is a certain lack of visibility that may suggest the struggle brought on by her new environment or in her artistic practice. And yet at the same time, Tomanova's body becomes an analogue for the tree itself, standing as part of many others. While it may be obscured, it is also a testament to strength and flexibility.

This early self-portrait work influences images in *New York New York*, such as *Isabel (East River)* (2020), in which Tomanova enmeshes figure and flowers to effectively override an urban background consisting of a chain-link fence and FDR Drive. Just as importantly, however, is the skinned elbow, brought to the fore of the image, challenging, or bringing into tension, so-called traditional and definitely outdated gender norms and associations, a critical component of Tomanova's practice. Moreover, this presentation of nature in New York City disrupts a vision, or expectation, of the city as an entirely urban space, an aspect reflected in many images in *New York New York* where green space is emphasized in places such as Tompkins Square Park and the East River Park, as can be seen in *Atticus* (2019) and *Lexi* (2020). For Tomanova, New York City is more than just ceaseless activity, consumerism, concrete, and glass; it is a connection to her sense of place, her sense of home, her past. For her, it is connected to nature. Notably, these downtown locations, such as park and river, are close to where she lives in the East Village; they are close to home. In this sense, they almost function as a stand-in for, or an extension of, the earliest substantial body of photographic work that Tomanova created when living in Mikulov and Brno, Czech Republic, in her early twenties, where between 2005 and 2010 she took thousands of photos of friends, relationships, and her environment using only a cell-phone camera, recording her own formative years in the Czech Republic. Gathered together and shown for the first time in 2017 under the title *Live for the Weather*, these images, such as *Nighttime* (2008) (fig. 4), trace the landscape of youth in Mikulov, socially and geographically. They are about being in and out of love, being free, being together, and dreaming. *Live for the Weather* is about restless youth and belonging. It is about being in the moment.

New York New York also reflects and expands on this earlier body of work, particularly in terms of the extended space of social relationships and an expanded sense of home. This can be seen in images such as *Kate & Odie* (2019), which highlights not only Tomanova's bond with others, but also the intimacy or interiority of interpersonal relationships, in this case, the precious closeness of Kate and Odie, a couple with whom Tomanova deeply identifies. Kate and Odie perform an essential role of connecting Tomanova with her new life in New York City, while linking her to earlier experiences in the Czech Republic. As a Czech living in New York, Kate, like Tomanova, mediates between two worlds. Both came to New York City to find and be themselves. It is a shared process of reflection, as can be seen in *Kate (Mirror)* (2019). While Kate looks at herself in a mirror, Tomanova photographs. This gaze upon the self as a means of seeing or placing oneself is a function not only of the mirror but of the film portrait itself, a durable visual record of identity tied to a specific space and time.

Photographs such as *Kate & Odie* or *Massima (Sunlight)* (2016) also emphasize the notion of shared intimate space, or home, that winds through *New York New York*. Indeed, the strength of Tomanova's portraiture is that it reveals a landscape of intimacy, not only through the creation of the empathic, close, connected portrait, as firmly established in her earlier *Young American* work, as can be seen in *Jiggy* (2018) (fig. 5), but also through the process of portraiture that often takes place in the subject's home, or intimate space. Thus, the work becomes both a landscape of a person, in terms of themself and their environment, and a portrait of person and place. These aspects are deftly woven together to create a more complex and revealing whole. It is work that is far from studio or street photography in its unmediated closeness and intimacy. These images are more complete, merging subject and environment, allowing the viewer to see deeply within. In images such as *Alannah* (2019) or *Cameron (Yellow Light)* (2019), Tomanova allows us, as viewers, to know these individuals through this connection to their spaces, their homes, their worlds. This is New York City, too, and as interior space, Tomanova asks us to question how different it is from anyplace else. What determines specificity of place?

As a Czech immigrant living in New York City, this question of specificity of place is a major theme in Tomanova's work, and it is tied to notions of identity, displacement, memory, belonging, and home. After having published her first book, *Young American*, Tomanova began work on two major concurrent projects, *New York New York* (2019–21) and *It Was Once My Universe* (2018–20). At first glance, each seems very different, or even diametrically at odds with the other. *New York New York* focuses on youth in New York City, while *It Was Once My Universe* reflects on Tomanova's return to her family home for the first time after eight long, and sometimes very difficult, years of exile in the United States. On the surface, *It Was Once My Universe* is a project that should be about homecoming. As it has been for many others, emigrating was the most significant decision of Tomanova's life. It was not her choice to stay away from home for so long, but she could not return. And for her, it hurt to be away. During her time in the United States, she relived and idealized home in her mind whenever things were difficult, so when she actually returned home in the winter of 2018 she was unprepared for the deep confusion and conflict she found within herself. She felt alien, yet . . . she still belonged—after all, it is home, . . . but now, so is New York City.

This work is about that. It is about contradictory feelings and disorientation—home, family, memory, distance, and time. These are aspects that the curator Sonia Voss has emphasized in her summer 2021 Louis Roederer Discovery Award exhibition of Tomanova's *It Was Once My Universe*, in Arles, France, for the Rencontres d'Arles photography festival. Voss has treated the work almost as an intimate family album, or snapshots, presenting it in a small format and framing it with a dark wood, mediating the spaces of photography, family, and memory in a way that reverberates with strategies employed by artist Sophie Calle (fig. 6). The time stamp in the photos is important, because it emphasizes a specific time—a moment, an instant. And yet, there is something off-kilter, just as her return to home was—the camera is still set to a New York time zone.

It is important to recognize this connection, this tendril of time stamp in *It Was Once My Universe* to *New York New York.* It is a telling sign that joins the two projects in more than an insignificant way, speaking to a shared sense of place. Tomanova belongs to both worlds, both spaces, both landscapes. There is a link between images such as *My Old Clothes, My Old Room* (2019) (fig. 7), shot in Mikulov as part of *It Was Once My Universe*, and an image such as *Michelle* (2020) in *New York New York*. Although there are considerable differences in these photographs—the former is a self-portrait of Tomanova back in her childhood room with her past, while the portrait of Michelle is set in her apartment in New York City—the images connect in terms of their intimacy of personal space. Each image seems entirely honest and open. And they also speak to the specificity of place or the lack of it. Without explanation or contextualization, either photograph could be in

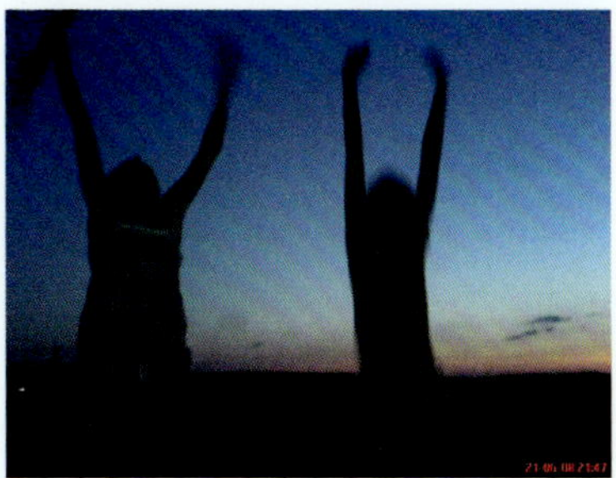

Figure 4. Marie Tomanova, *Nighttime*, 2008.

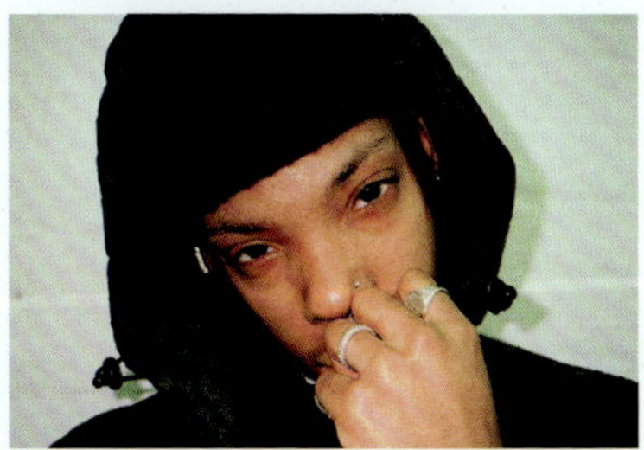

Figure 5. Marie Tomanova, *Jiggy*, 2018.

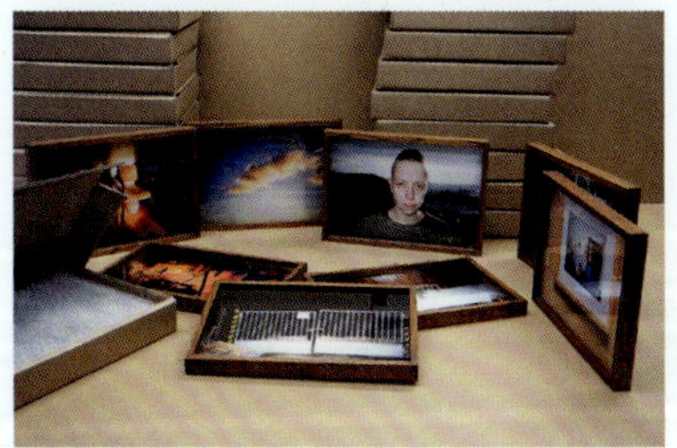

Figure 6. Selection of exhibition prints for *It Was Once My Universe* at Rencontres d'Arles, Arles, France, 2021. Photo courtesy of Milan Brát.

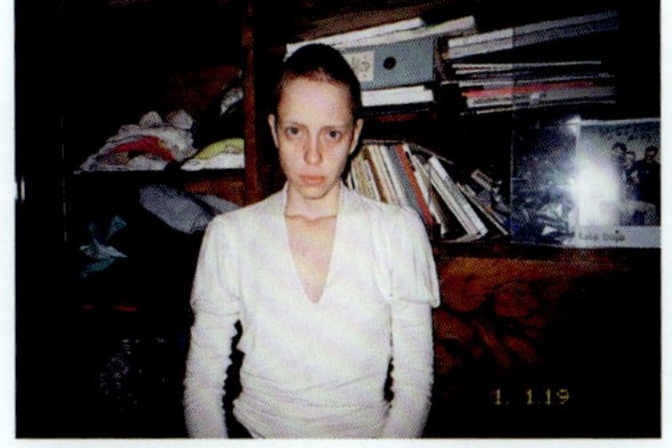

Figure 7. Marie Tomanova, *My Old Clothes, My Old Room*, 2019.

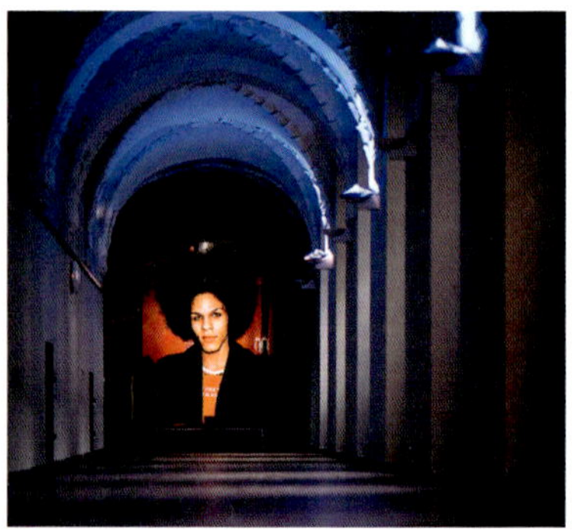

Figure 8. Marie Tomanova, *So Far From Mikulov*, video (29:47), 2018. Site-specific installation, Olomouc, Czech Republic, 2019. Photo courtesy of Jan Andreáš.

either location, Mikulov or New York City—the only thing that would give this away might be a detail or two, such as the flyer for the Tata Bojs band in Tomanova's room or the label on a bottle in Michelle's—subtle indicators or glyphs of a particular cultural and geographical matrix, things that, upon close inspection, tie an image to place.

This connection with place, with a landscape, beginning in the Czech Republic with *Live for the Weather* and then as self-portrait in nature upon moving to New York, expands in 2015 with her *Young American* (2015–18) series in which Tomanova sought kinship not only with a landscape of nature but with an expanded landscape of social relationships. Feeling alone in the United States and apart from the social circles she left in the Czech Republic, Tomanova embarks on a remarkable spree of portraiture of people she identifies with or wants to identify with, needing to connect with people and needing to see the "America" of her dreams and the faces of the America that she has idealized. In short, she is looking for that same sense of belonging that she sought in the natural landscape, but now she is searching for it in the social landscape of New York City. In light of the anti-immigrant sentiment growing in United States politics, Tomanova struggles with where she is, in America, a place that is not seeming at all like what she imagined or hoped for it to be. It is a familiar scenario for many who come to the United States with a dream that is menacingly shadowed by rampant systemic oppression and inequality; the façade of "land of opportunity" and "freedom for all" begins to crack. Tomanova's response is to photograph what *her* America looks like. As Ryan McGinley wrote in his introduction to Tomanova's 2019 book *Young American*, "This is a future free of gender binaries and stale old definitions of beauty. In Marie's world people can just simply be. I wish all of America's youth culture looked like Marie's photos of Downtown, diverse and inclusive."

While Tomanova's *Young American* work was widely shown internationally, perhaps one of its most powerful presentations in realizing its goals of challenging and attempting to dispel all forms of racism, sexism, and colonized perspectives of culture—so as to affirmatively and rigorously embrace multiple perspectives, identities, and voices—was in the showing of her *Young American* series in a site-specific installation. Approximately 15 by 22 feet in size, this installation was projected onto the Baroque architecture of a Jesuit monastery in Olomouc, Czech Republic, during the Academia Film Olomouc (AFO54) festival in the spring of 2019 (fig. 8). With this large video installation, Tomanova strongly asserts the presence and importance of inclusivity, claiming space for all as a response to the history of oppression and colonialism conveyed by this architecture and what it represents. Of course the projection is gone, but the architecture remains standing, a testament to the unfortunately enduring strength and presence of oppression, a force that still needs to be continually challenged and undermined through the increasing visibility, presence, empathy, and inclusion of all. And perhaps Tomanova's latest work, *New York New York*, strongly tied to *Young American*, is a continued testament to this process.

New York New York, in many ways, can be seen as an extension of the *Young American* series, but with several important differences. *Young American* was shot at a very close range in order to emphasize and highlight the sense of human connection and empathy, not only between Tomanova and her subject but also between the subject and the viewer, an aspect reinforced by the large-scale projection and print format at her exhibitions and in the size and formatting of the *Young American* book—where one is viscerally brought face-to-face. Overall, *New York New York* has been shot from more of a distance. Tomanova has stepped back with her camera to open the frame, to include more of the surroundings, more of New York City.

This stepping back and opening up of the image has significant ramifications. While the sense of connection between Tomanova and her subject is still present and vital, that sense of shared empathy is not as overwhelming in the *New York New York* work. Part of this is a function of the increased physical distance between Tomanova and her subject when the photograph is taken (always with a prime lens on film). But more crucially, that physical distancing is also psychological. Simply put, Tomanova—now more comfortable in her surroundings, having been back home to visit her family after eight years apart (during which time she produced the *Young American* images)—seeks less desperately the sense of belonging she sought in the past, first with her landscape self-portraiture and then with the social identification in *Young American*. Indeed, *New York New York* reflects that sense of being more at comfort and ease, after mediating different places and challenges. Tomanova now belongs.

Perhaps most importantly, this stepping back and opening up builds on Tomanova's sense of belonging to the point that it conveys an important sense of freedom, precisely the thing she felt in her hometown of Mikulov, surrounded by friends in *Live for the Weather*, a work that is a visual document, almost a journal of youth, after the immediate shadow of Communism and restricted borders had passed, but one that still bears the weight of that memory. Very significantly, Tomanova's generation is the first to have been able to leave the former Eastern Bloc after the fall of the Berlin Wall. It is this sense of youth and freedom and individual expression that is the most compelling aspect of *New York New York*. It is Tomanova's New York City.

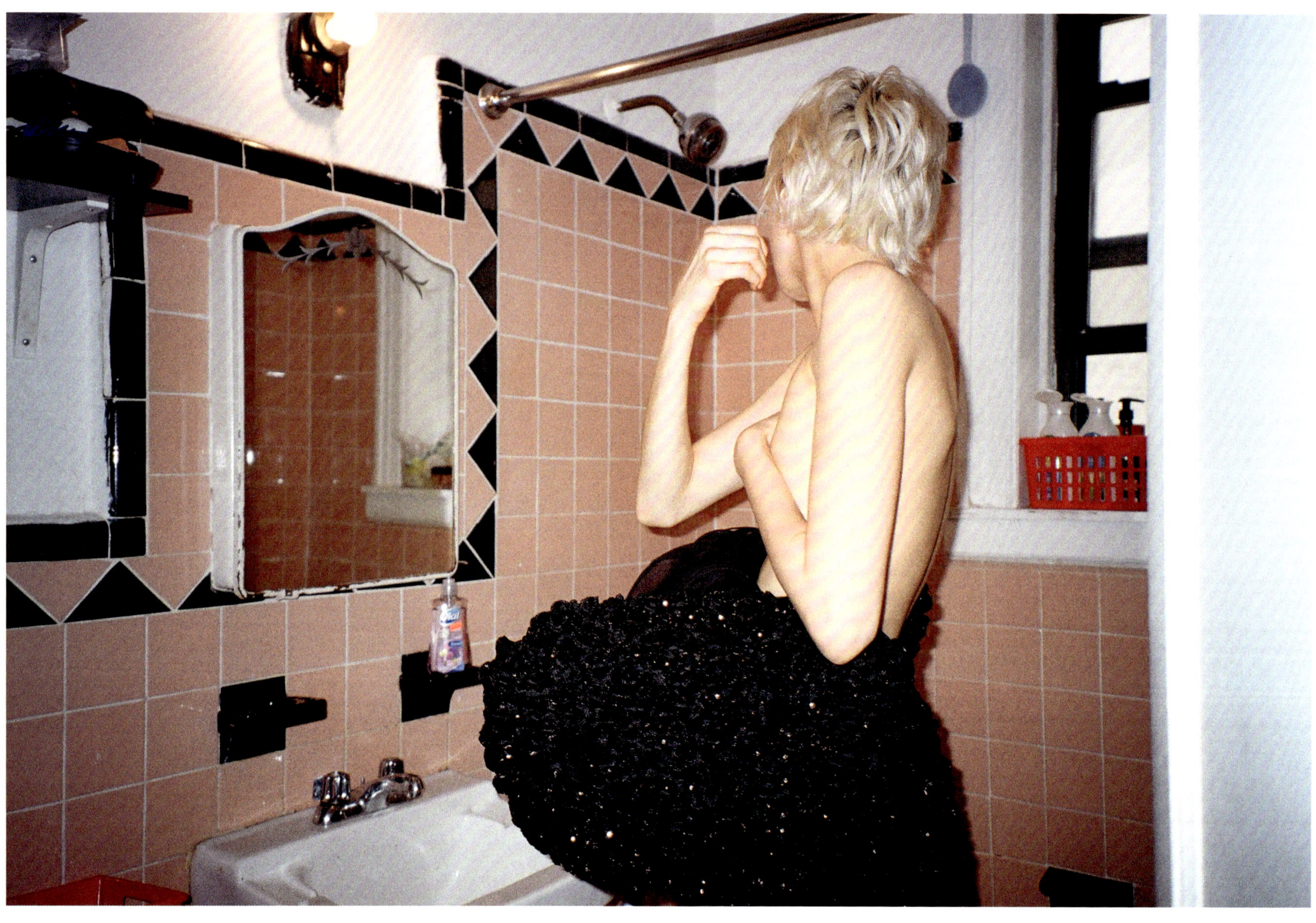

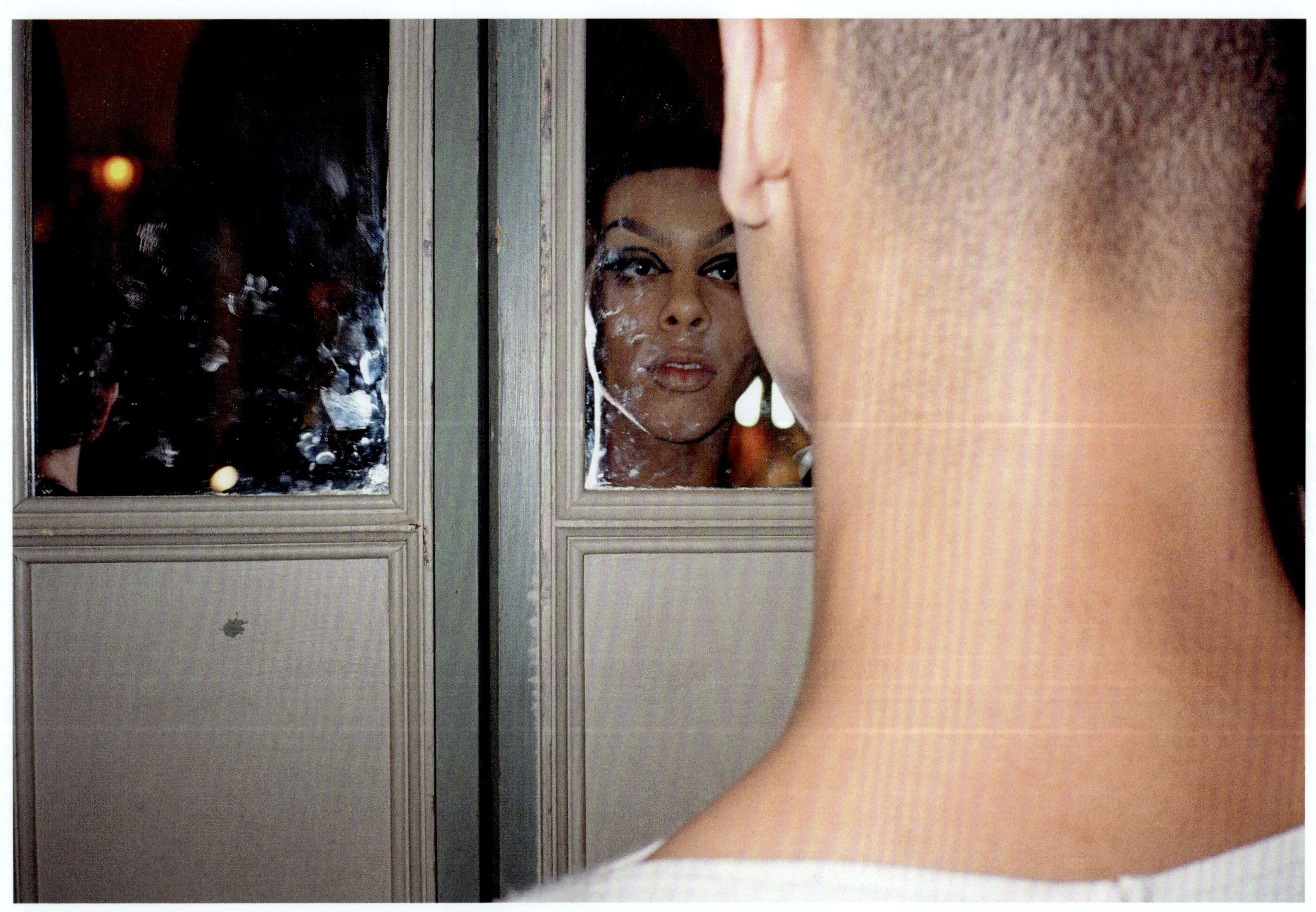

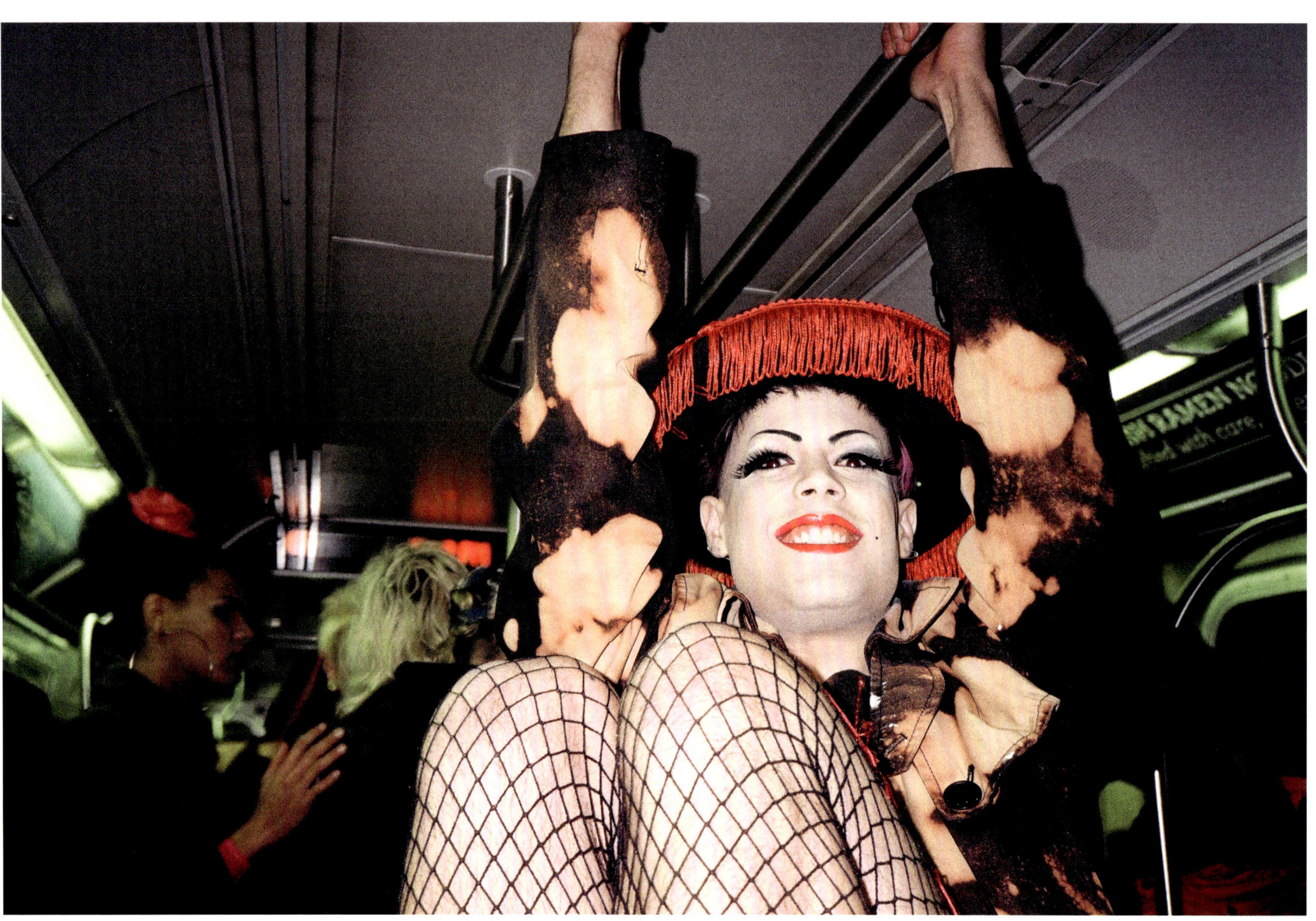

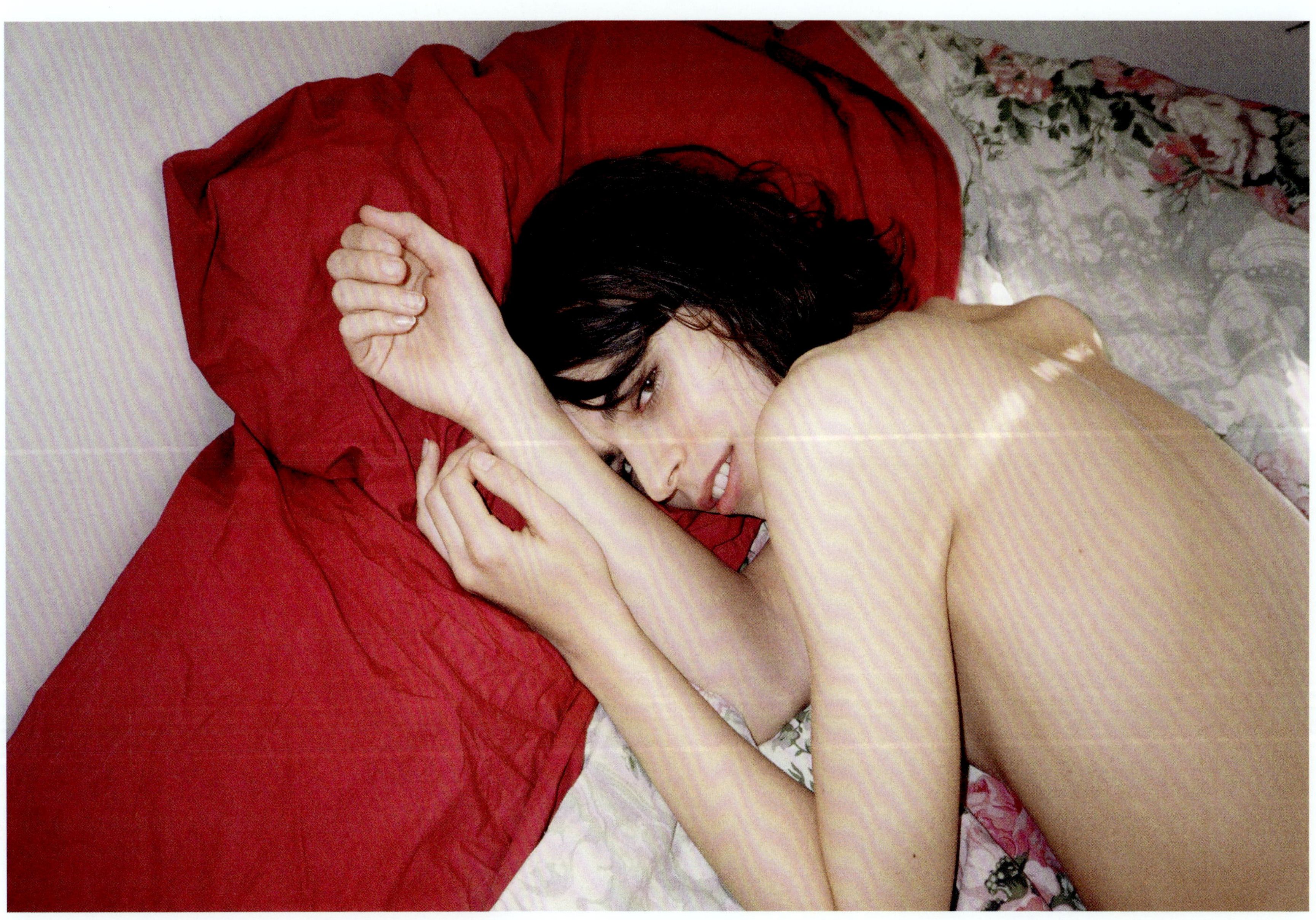

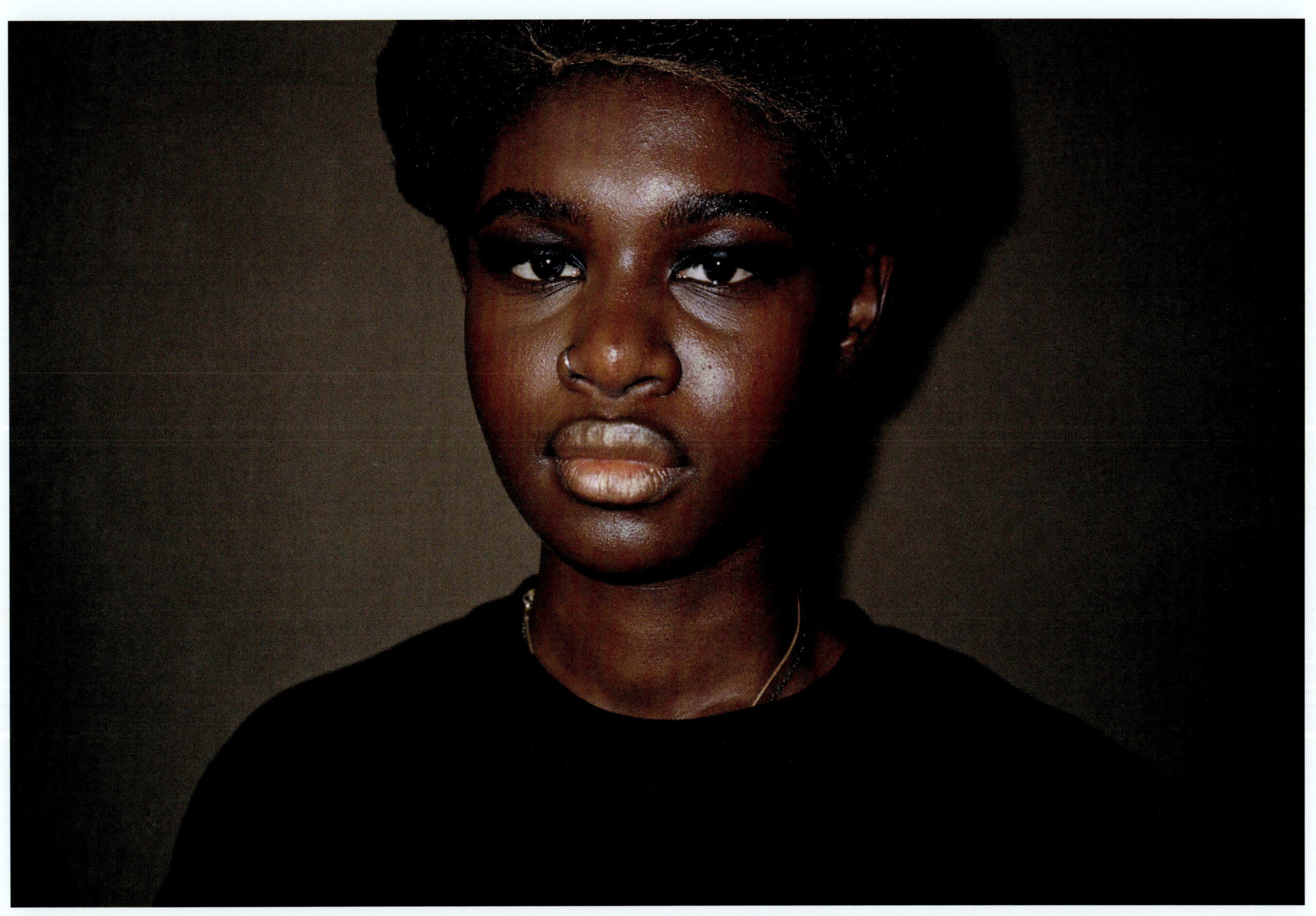

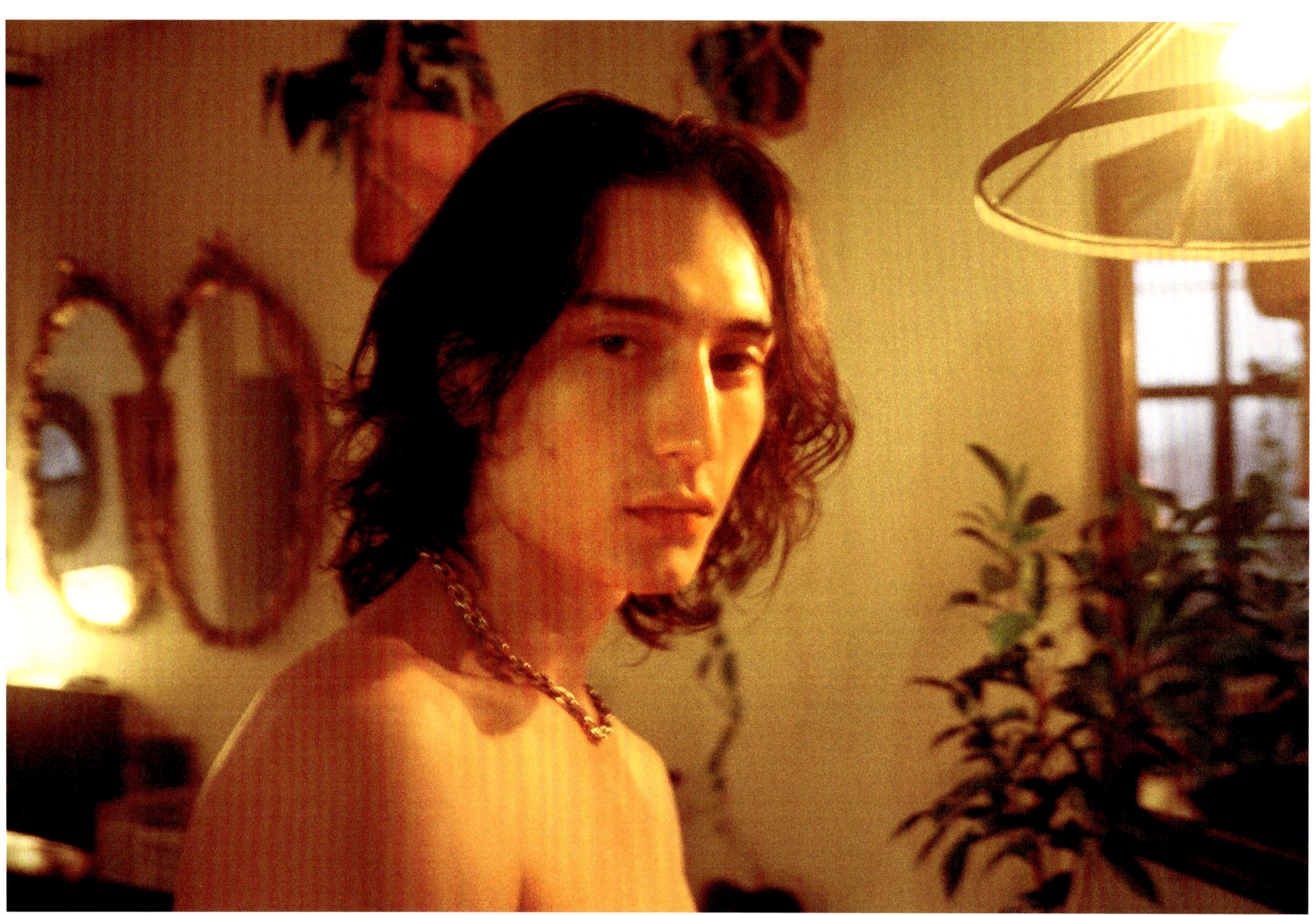

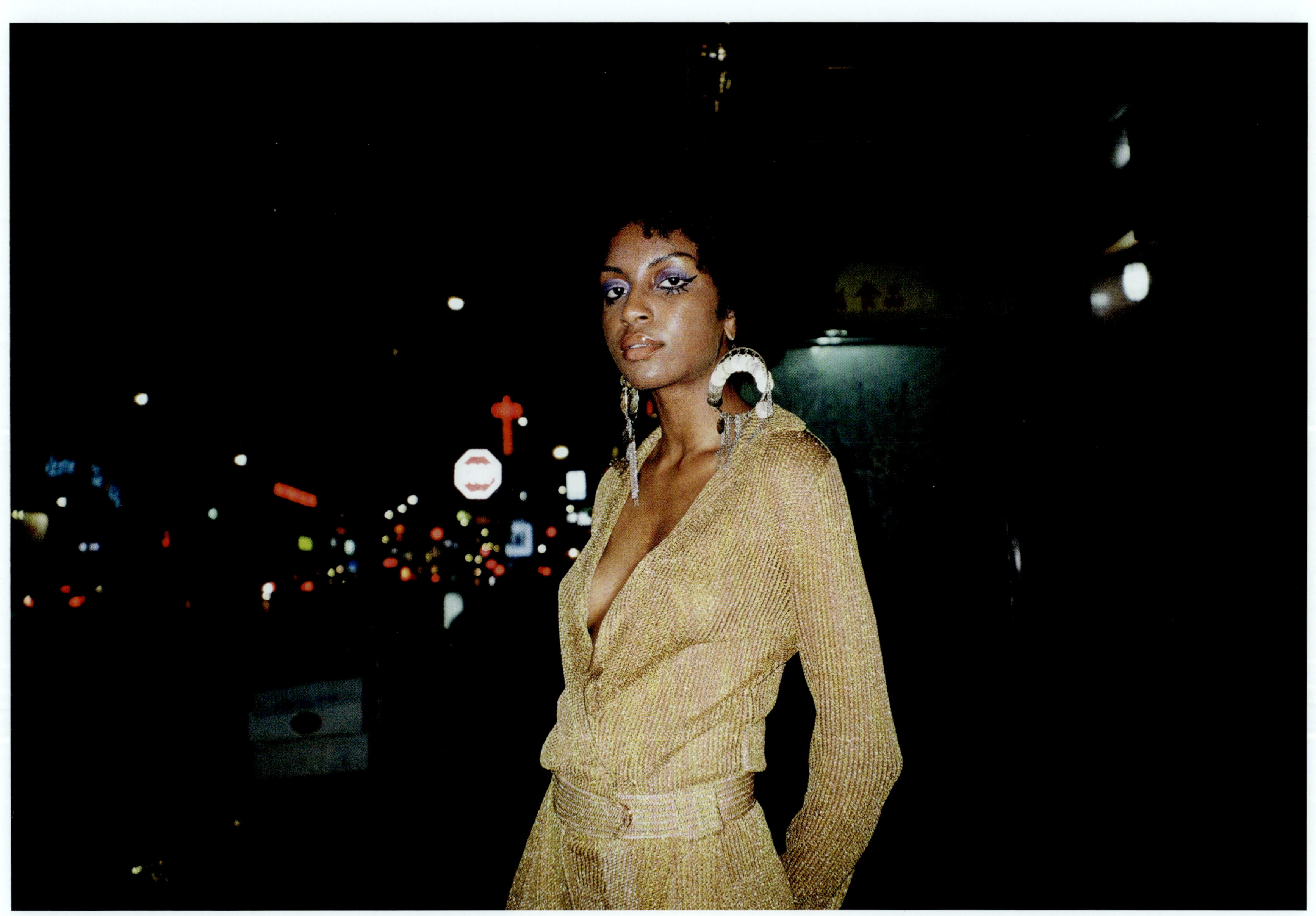

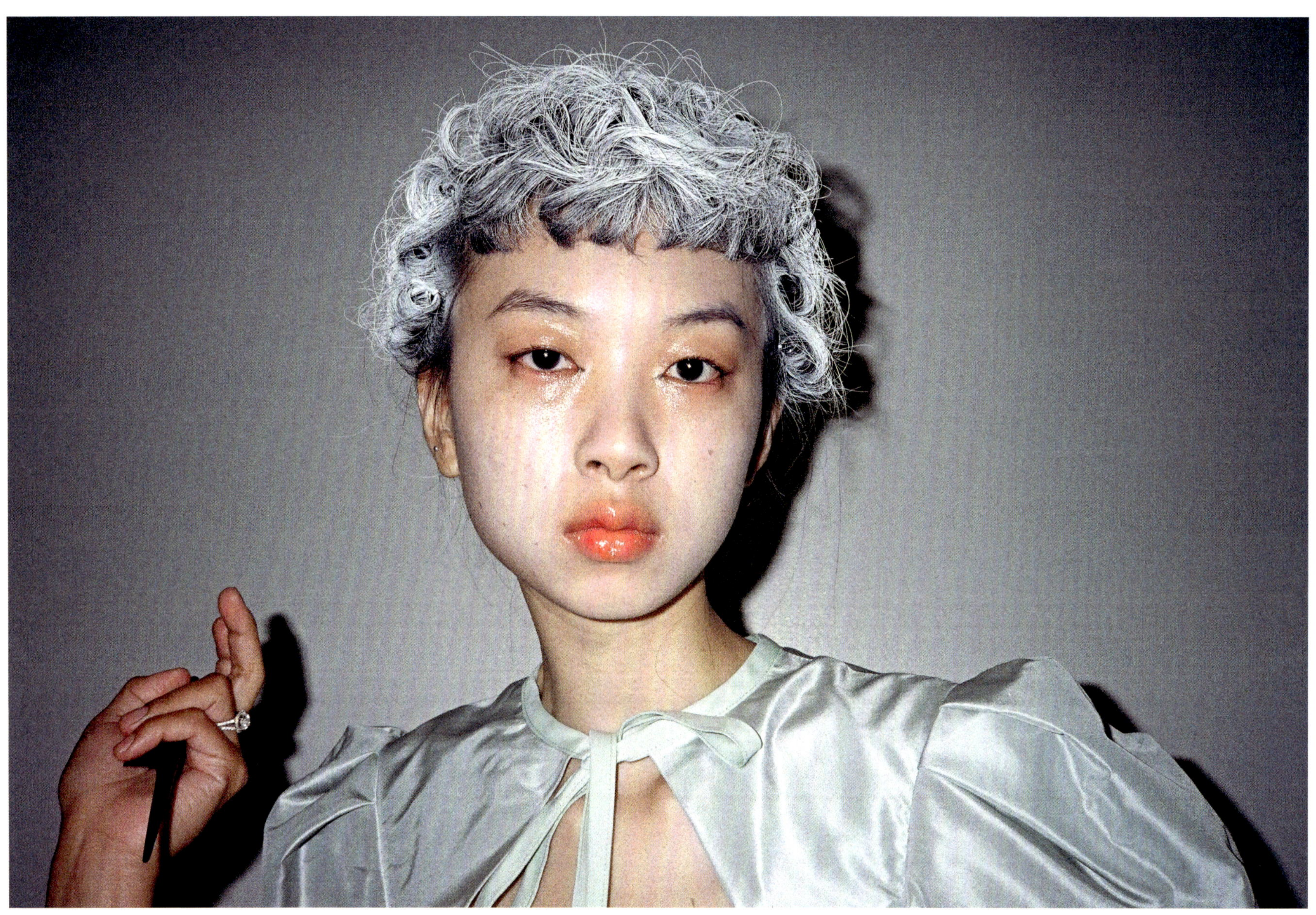

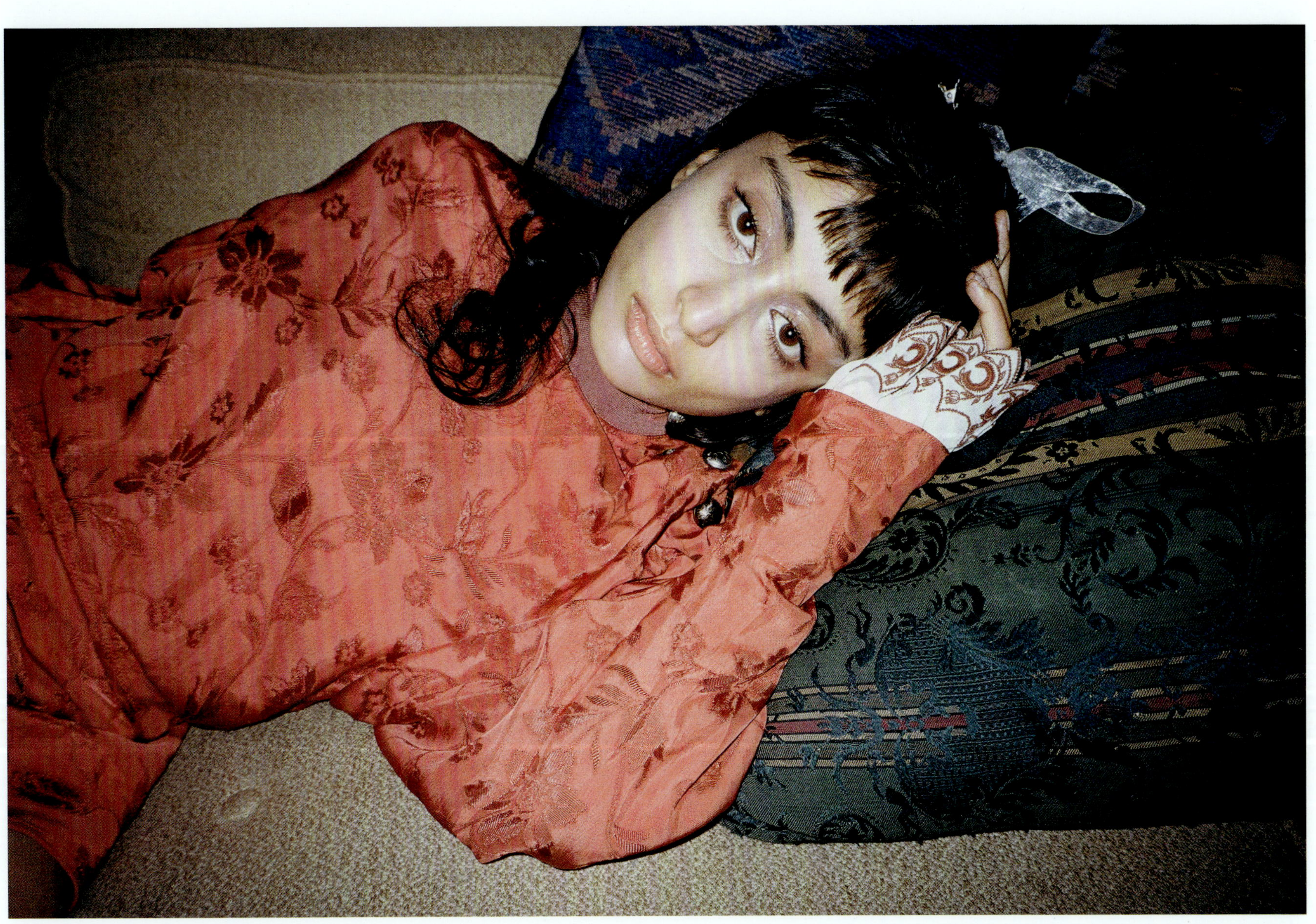

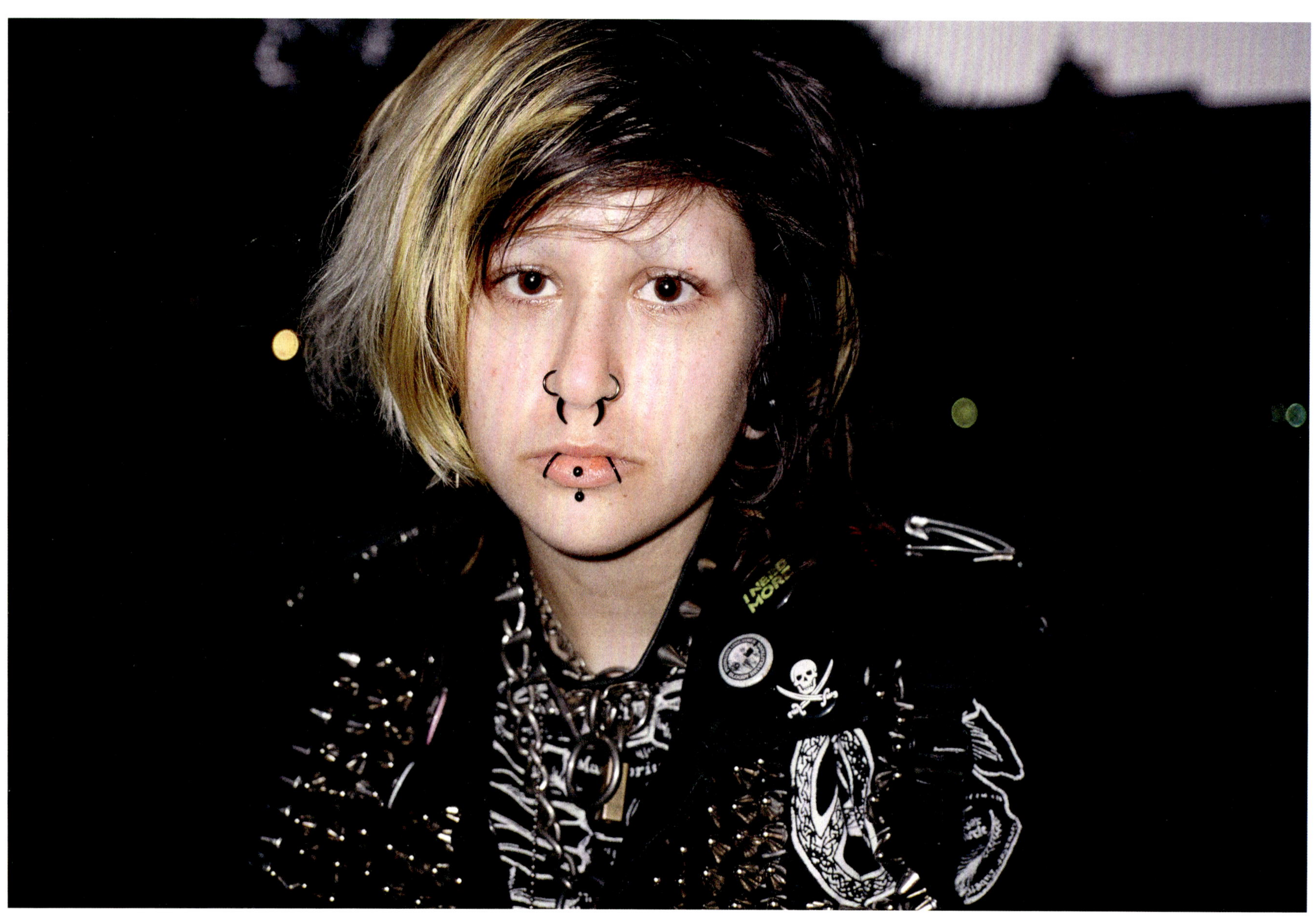

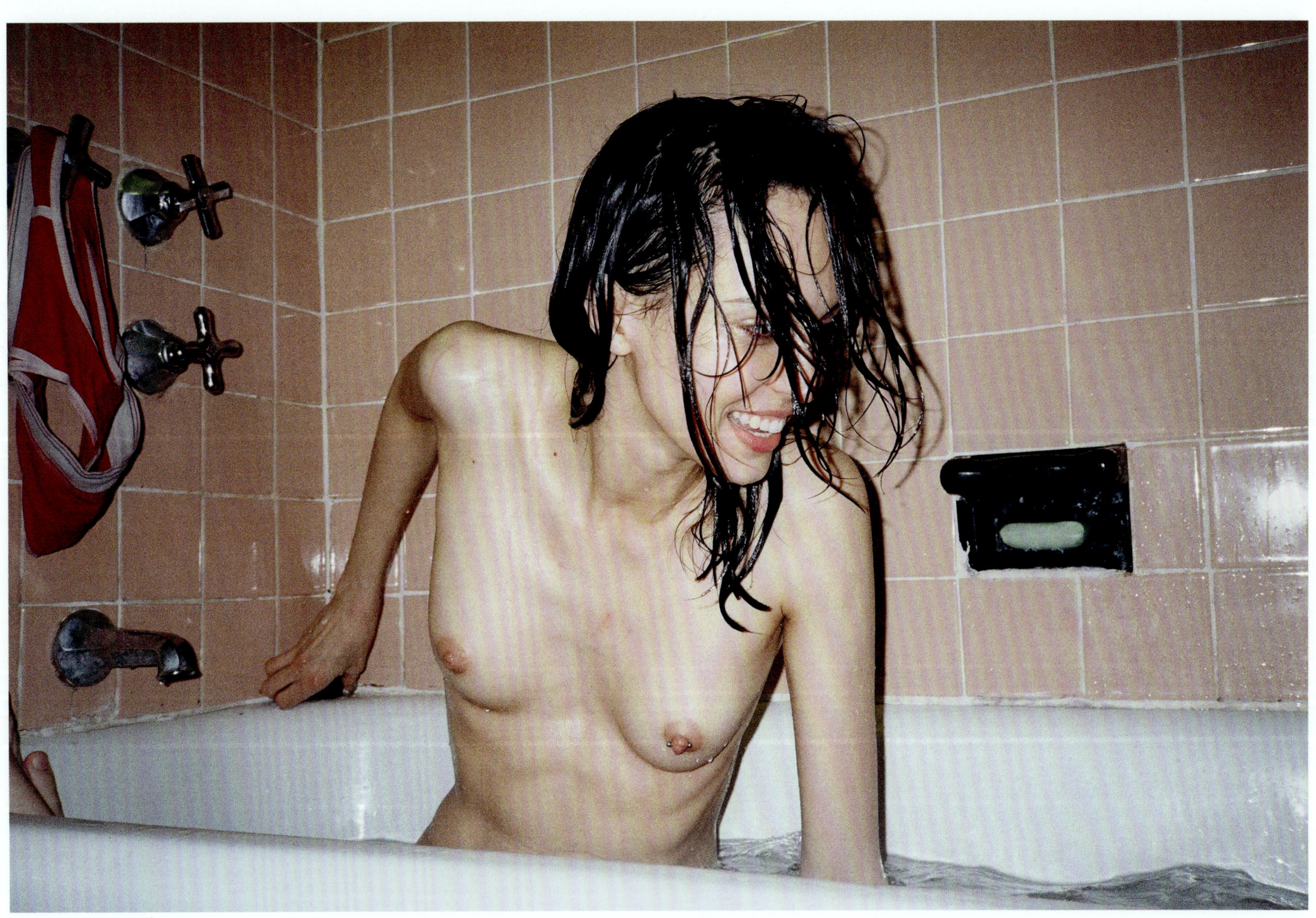

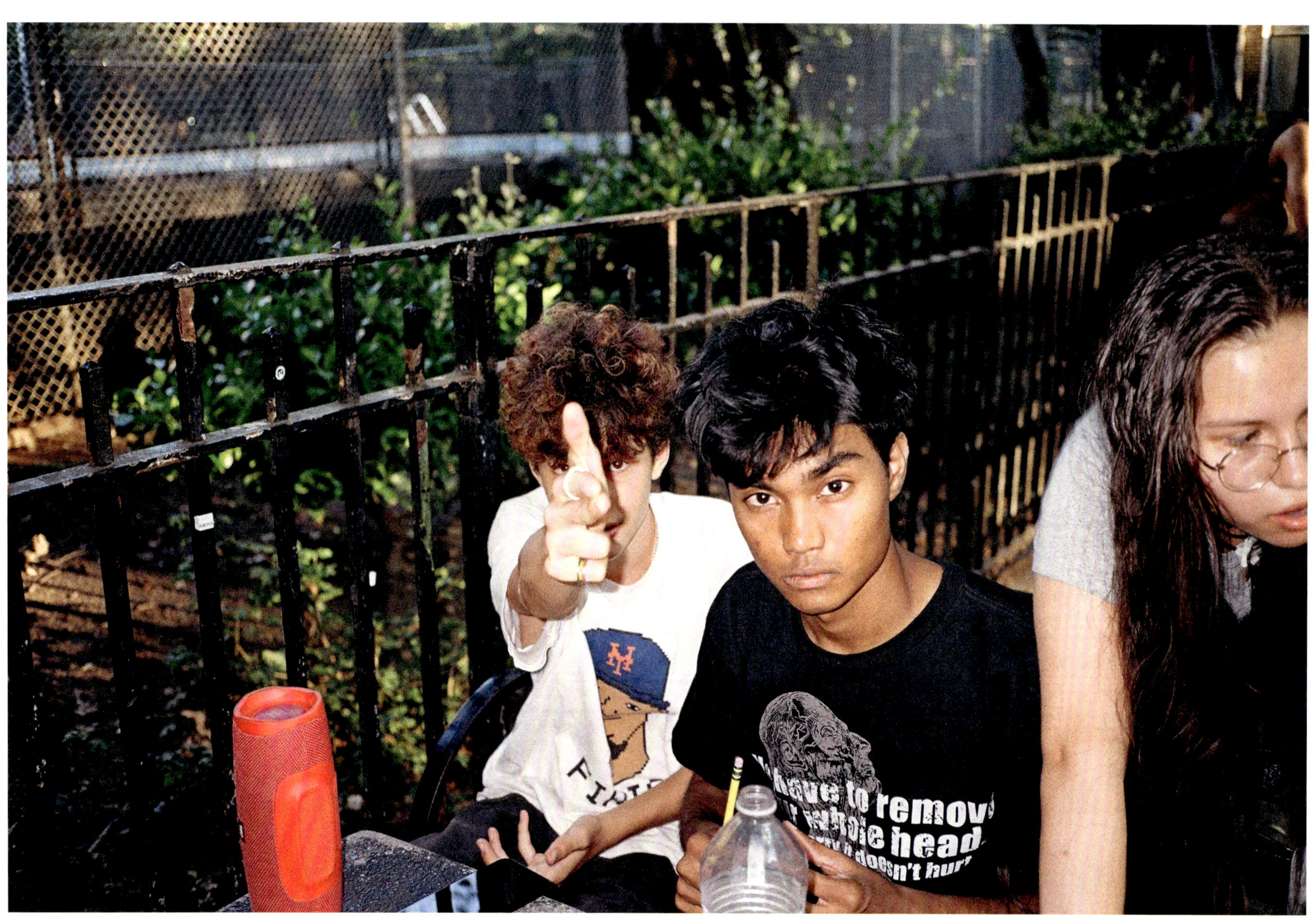

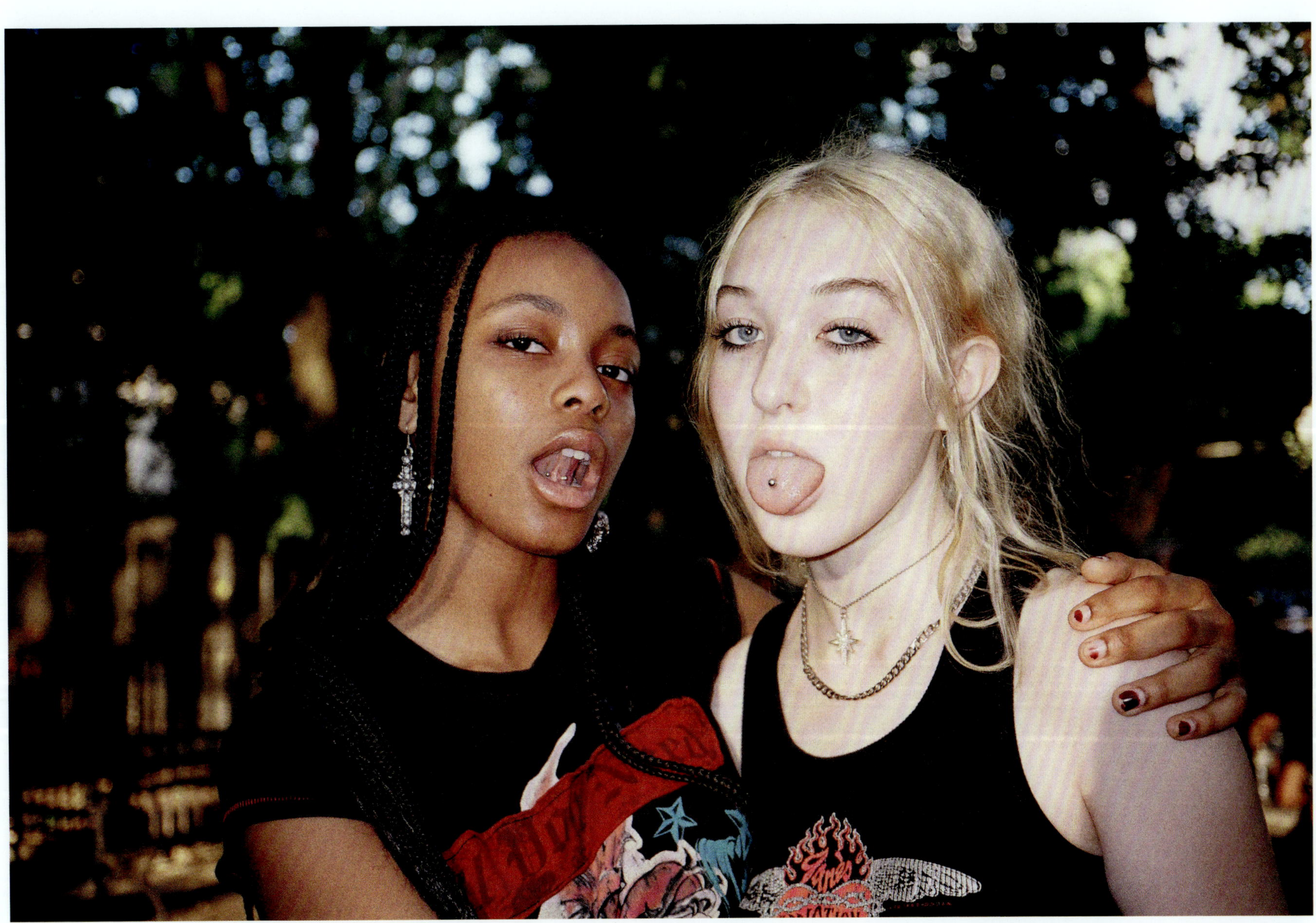

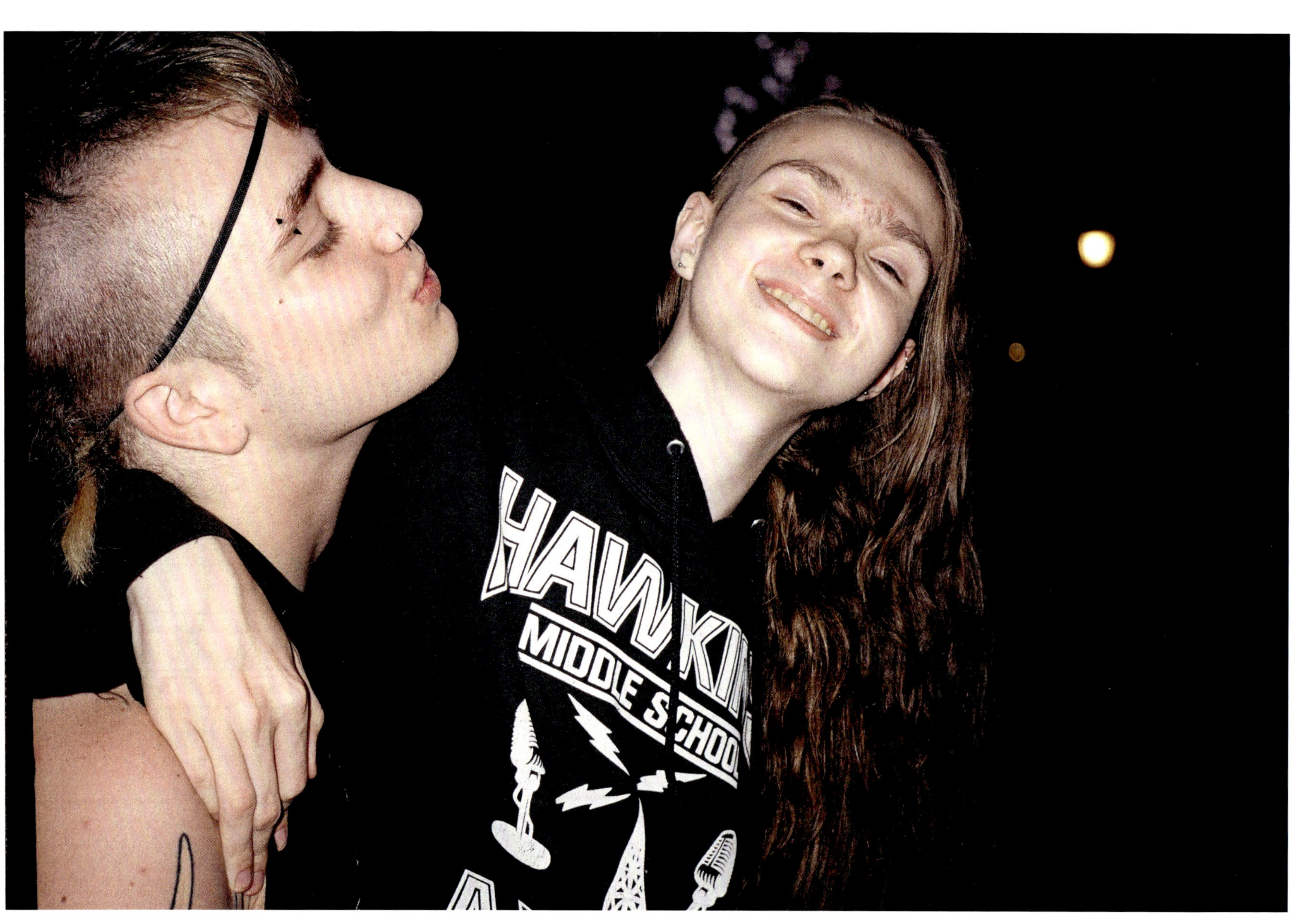
HAWKIN
MIDDLE SCHOOL

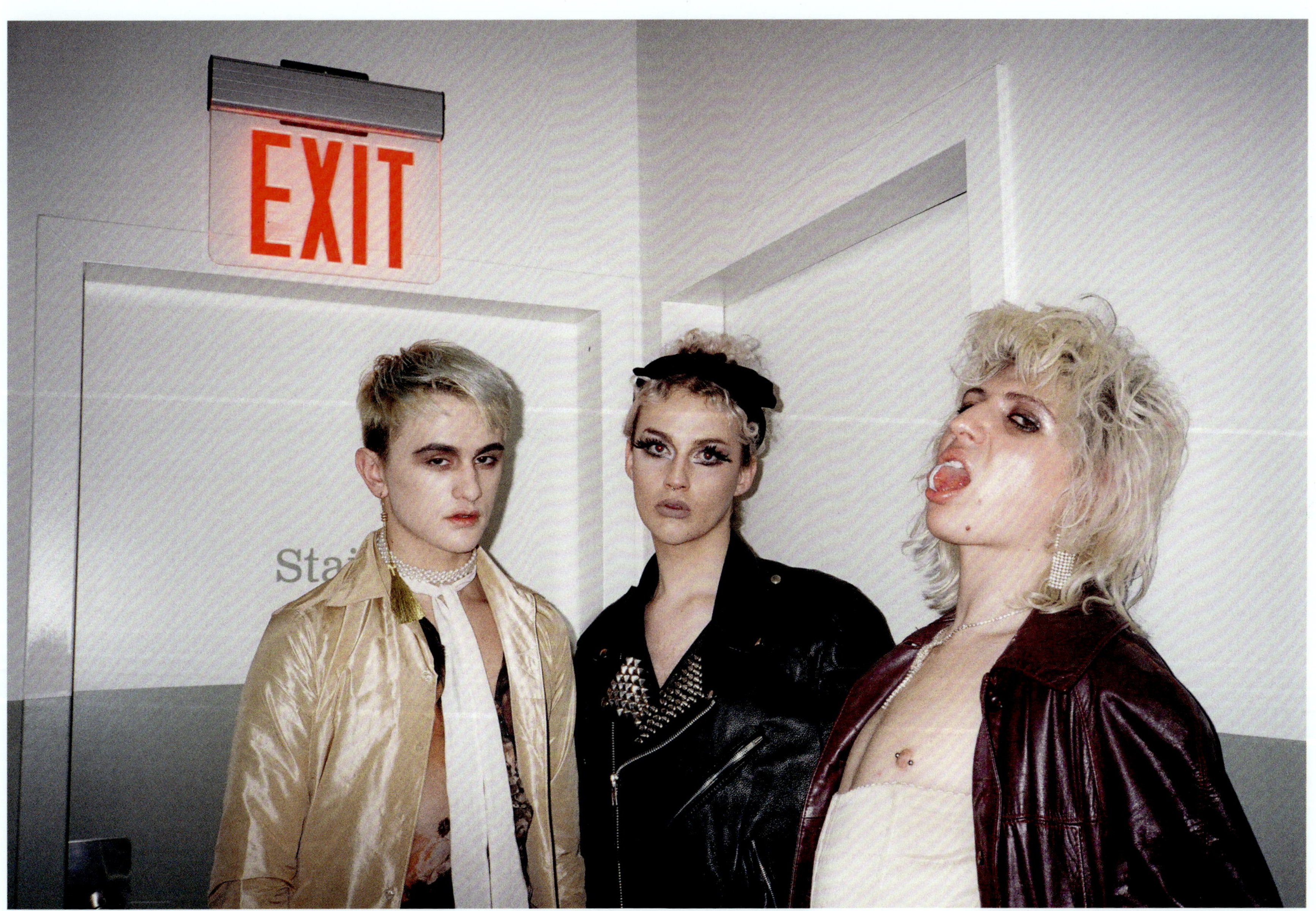
EXIT

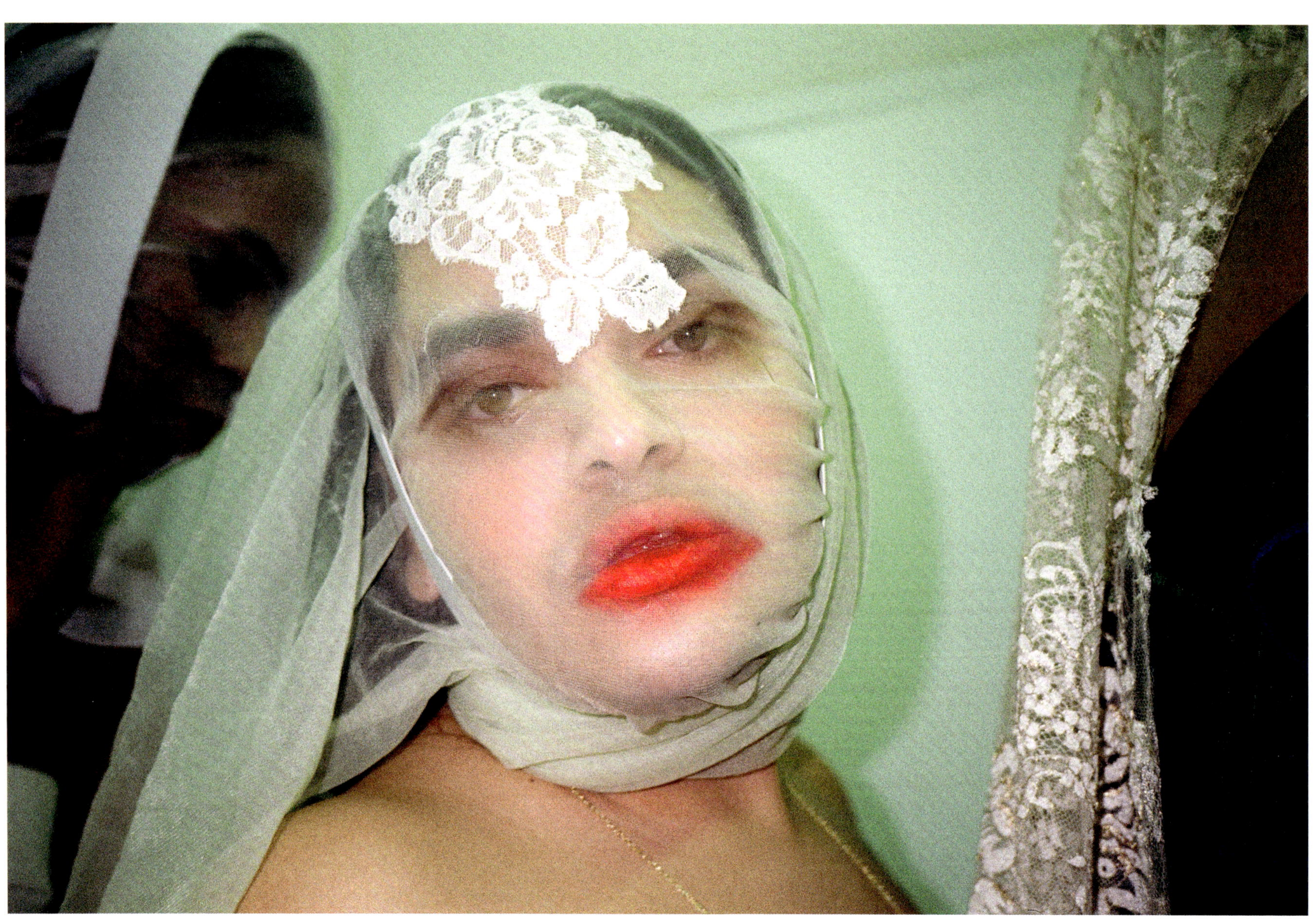

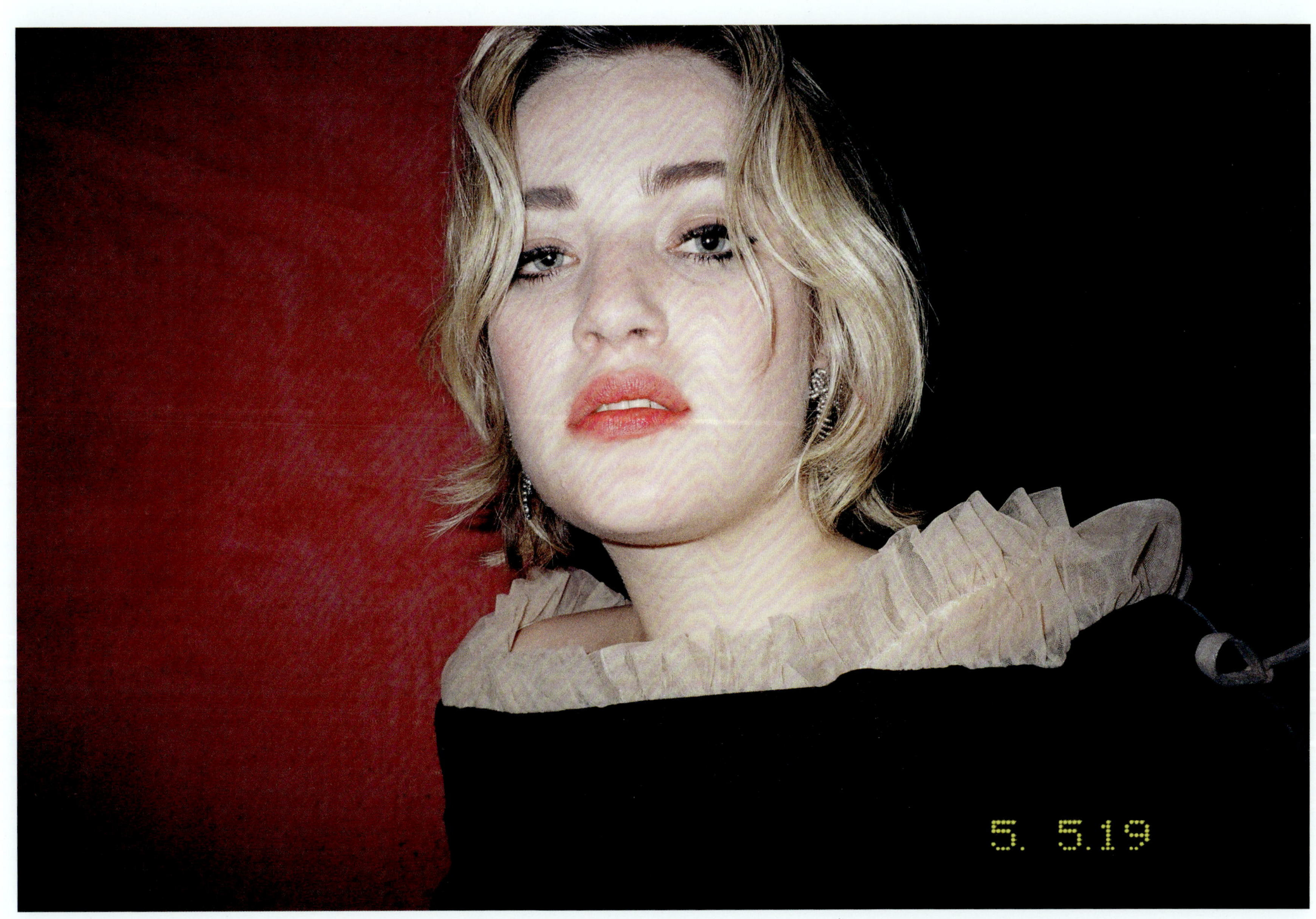
5. 5.19

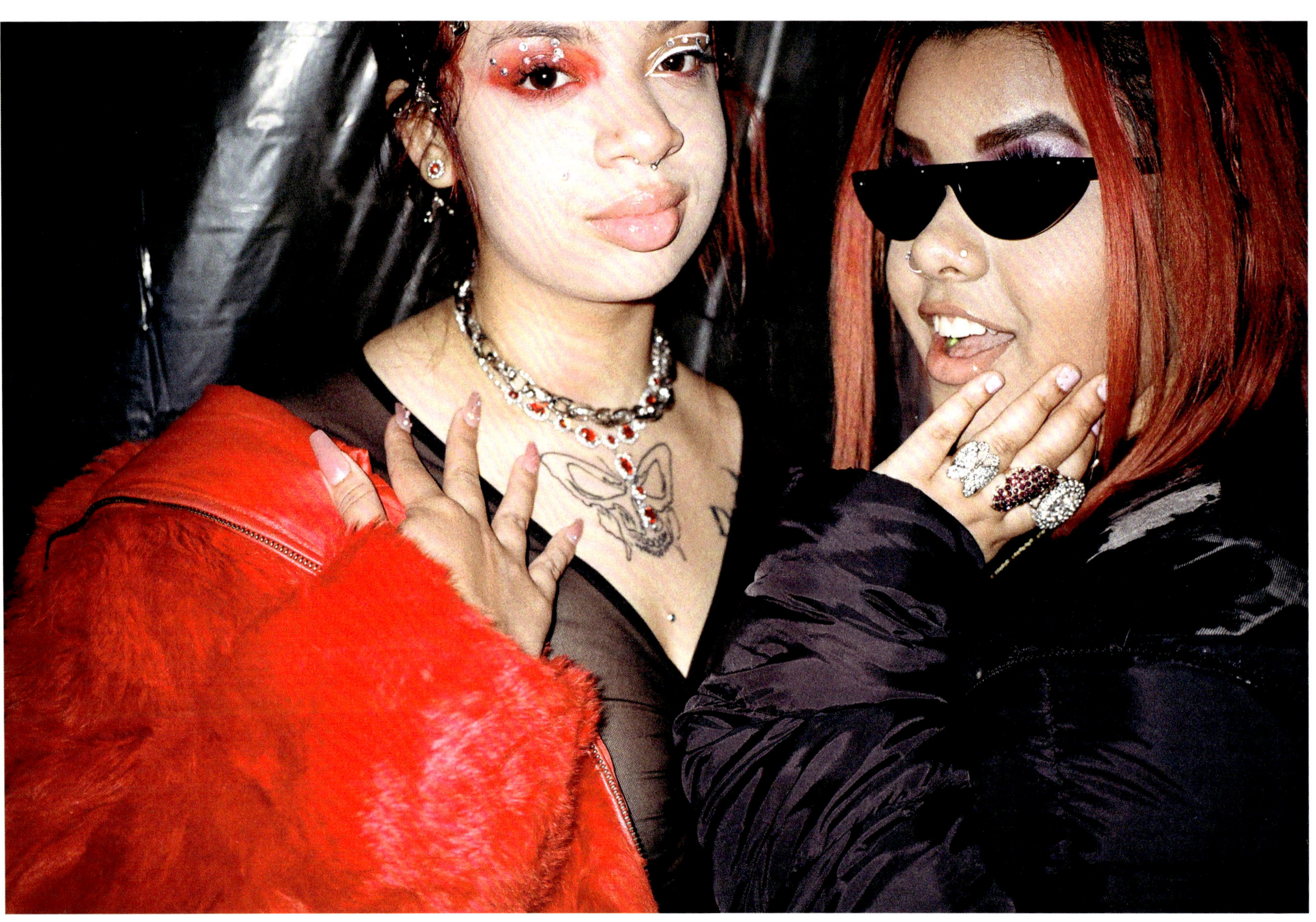

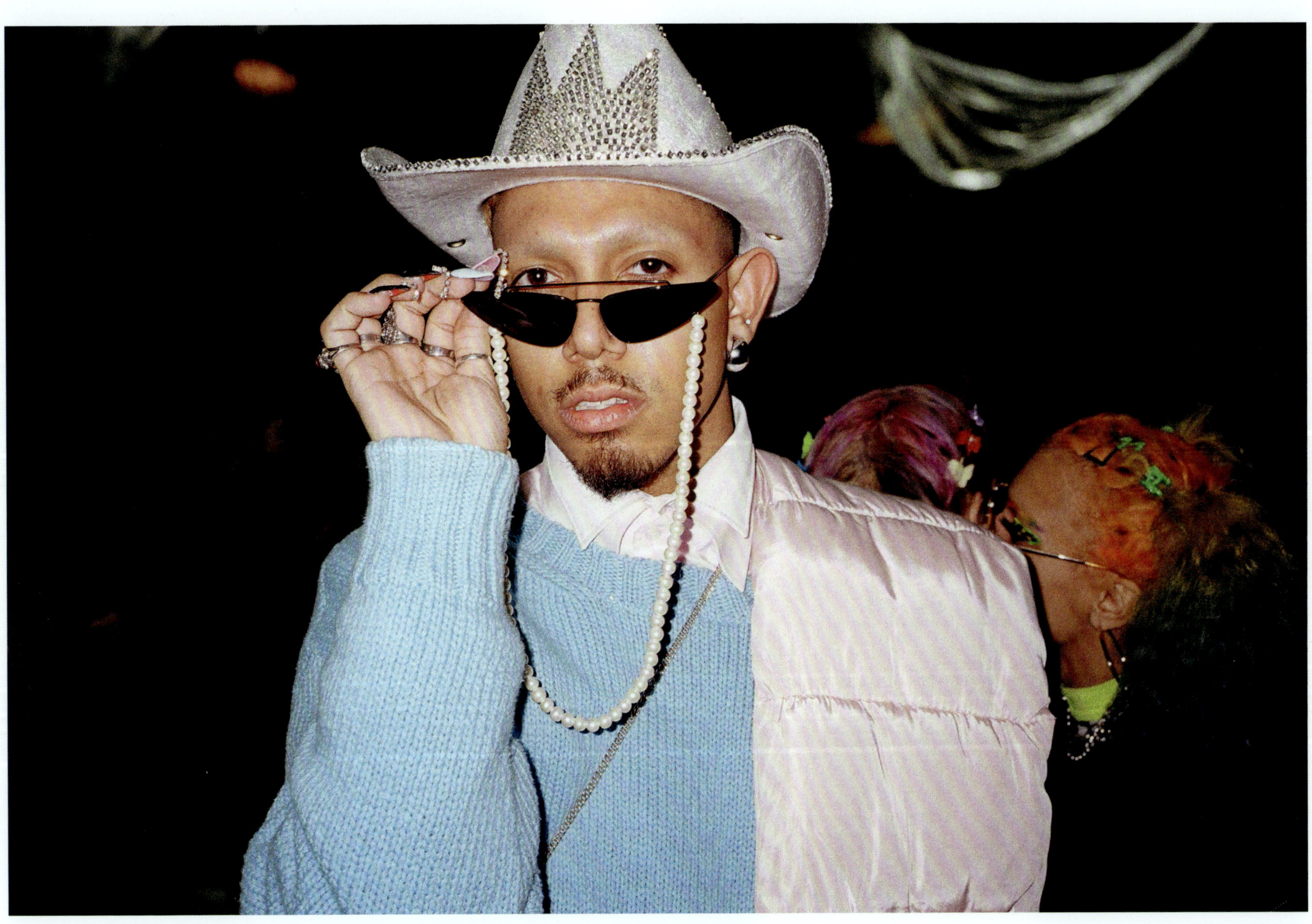

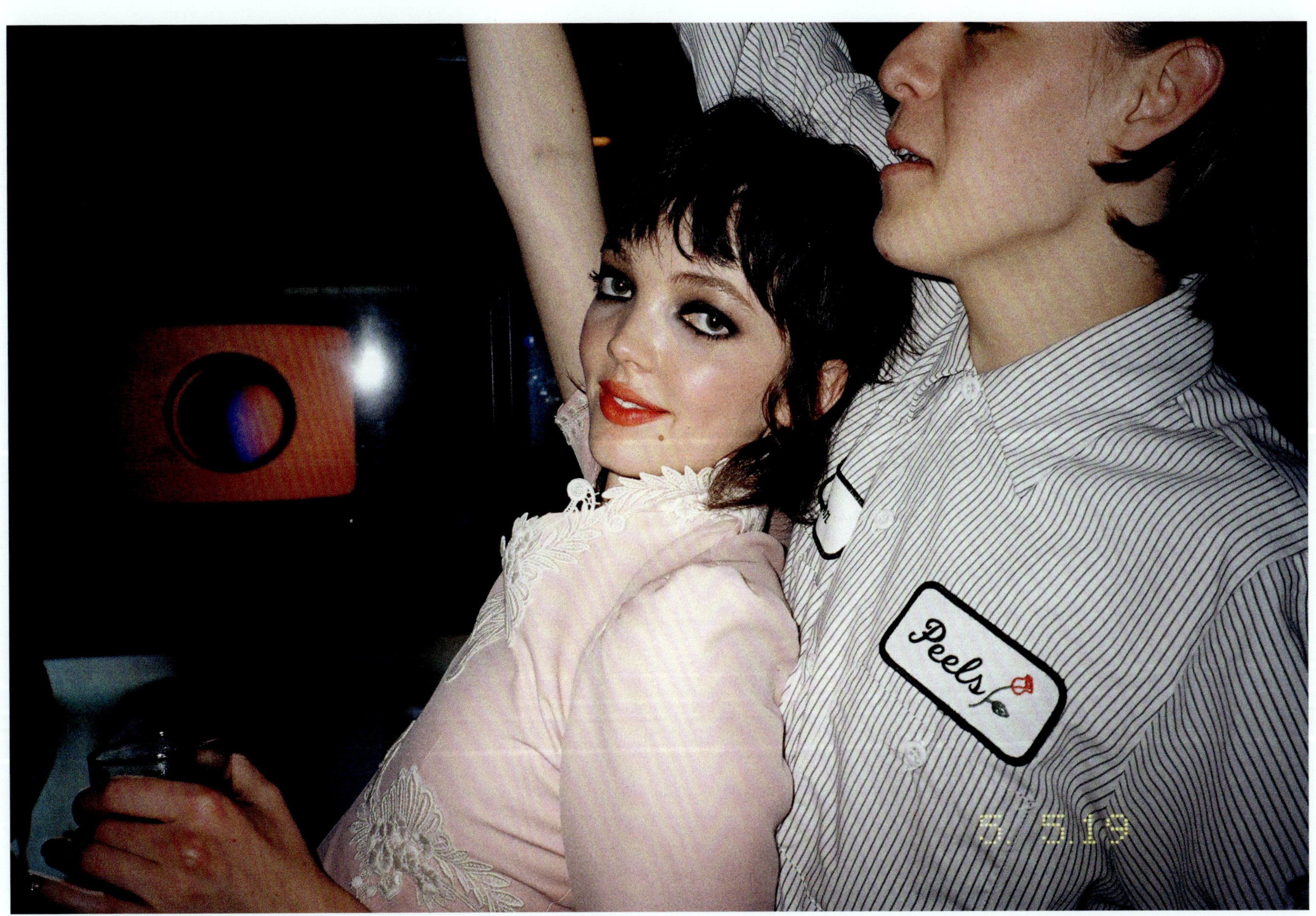
Peels
5. 5.19

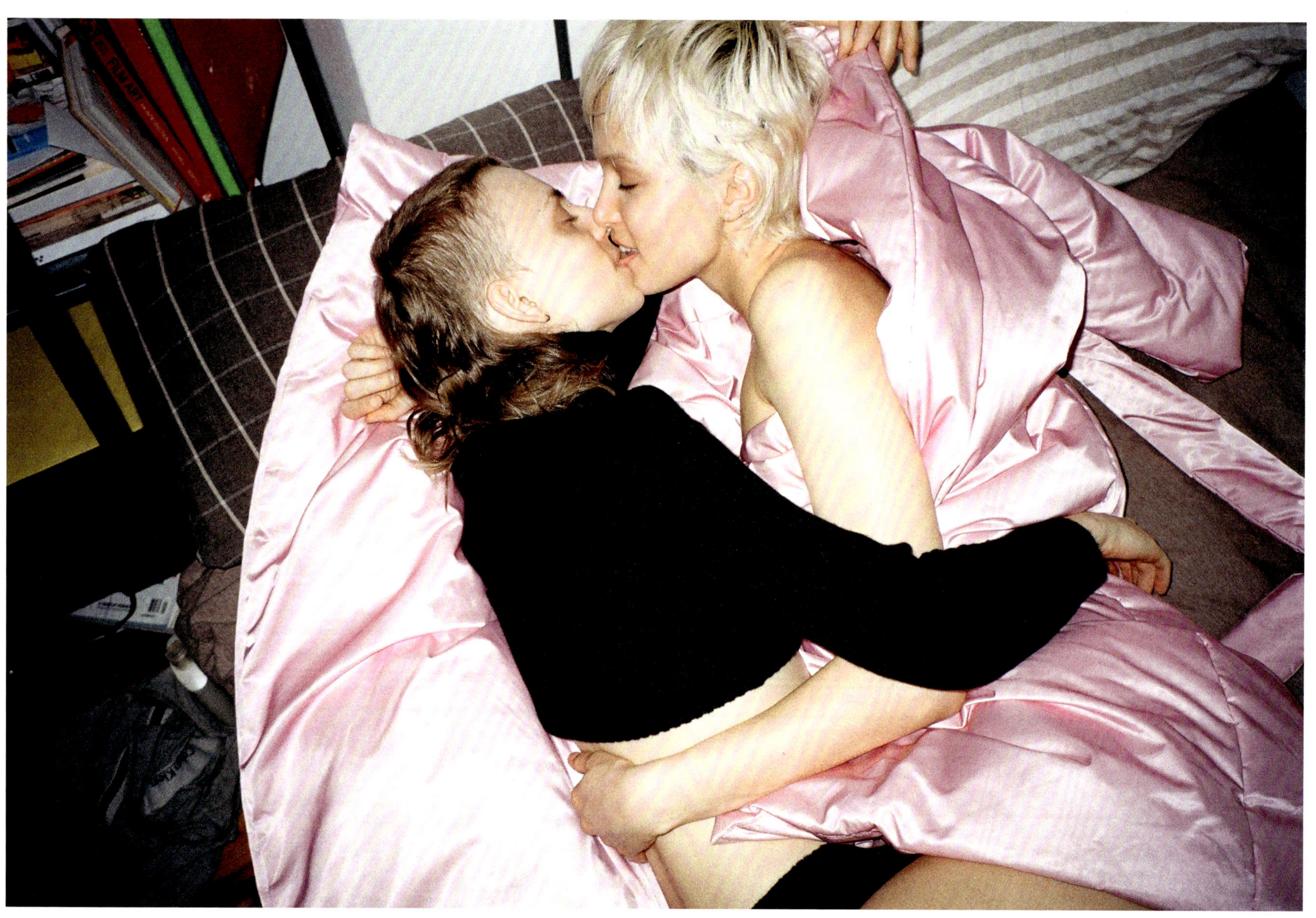

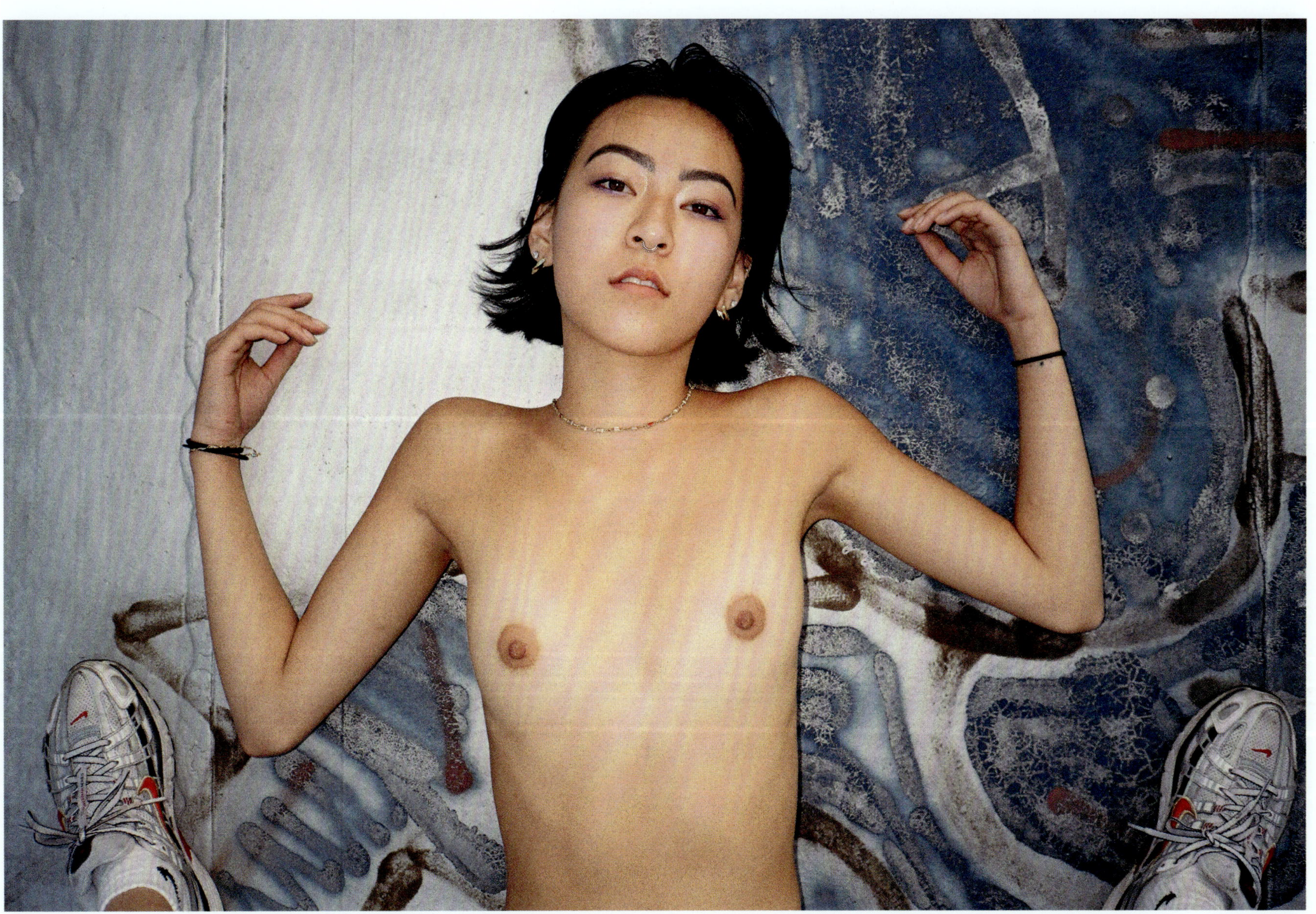

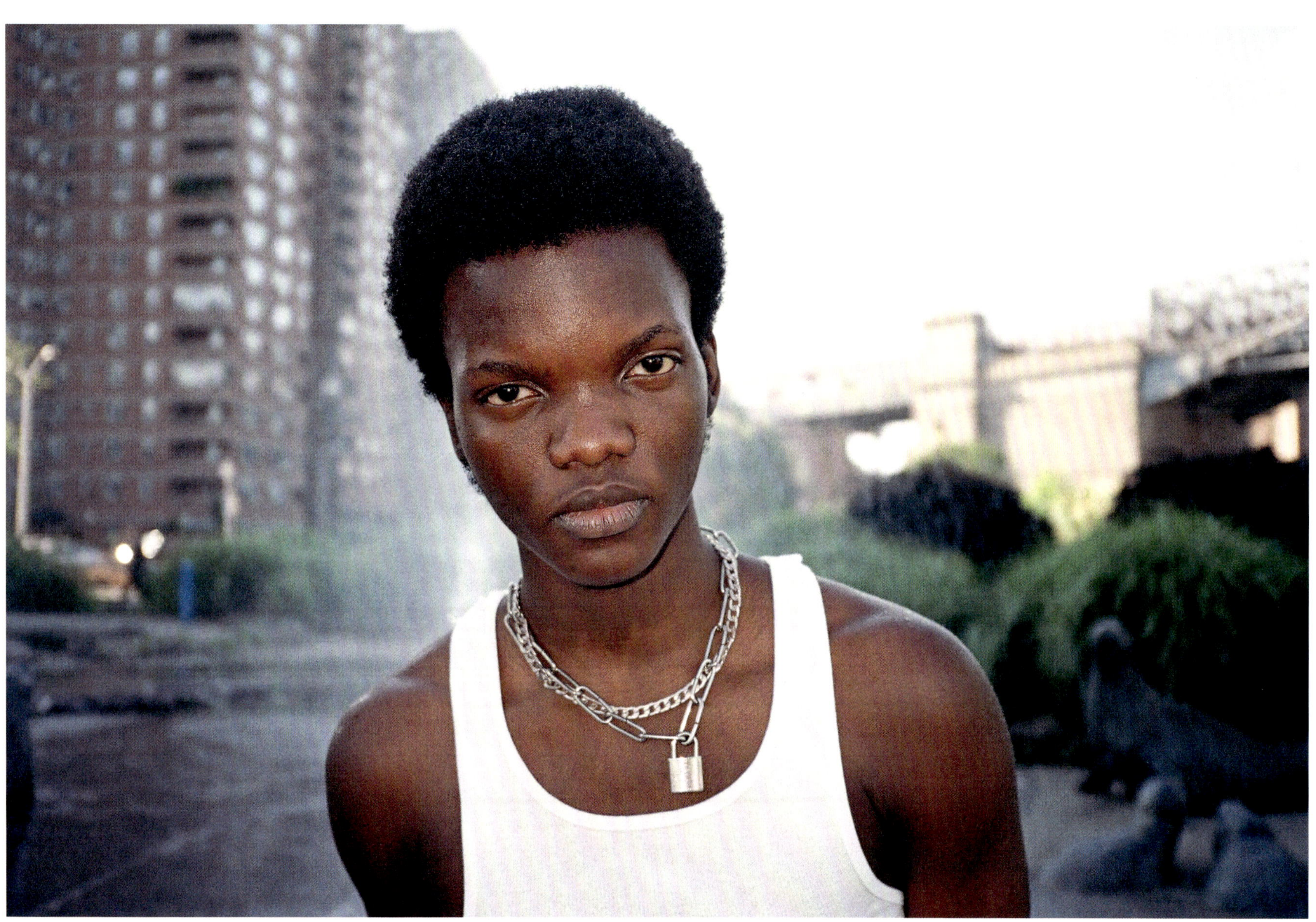

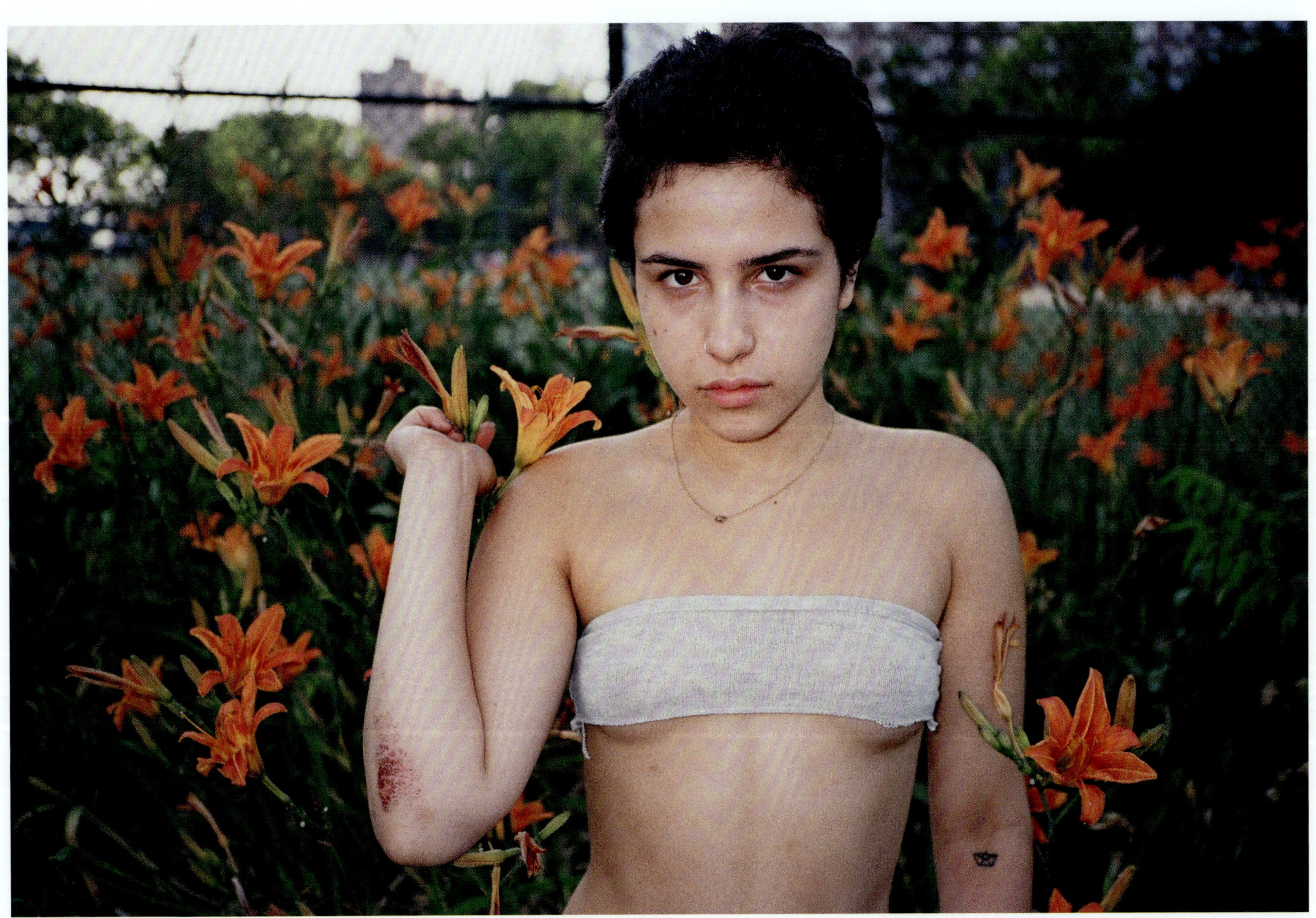

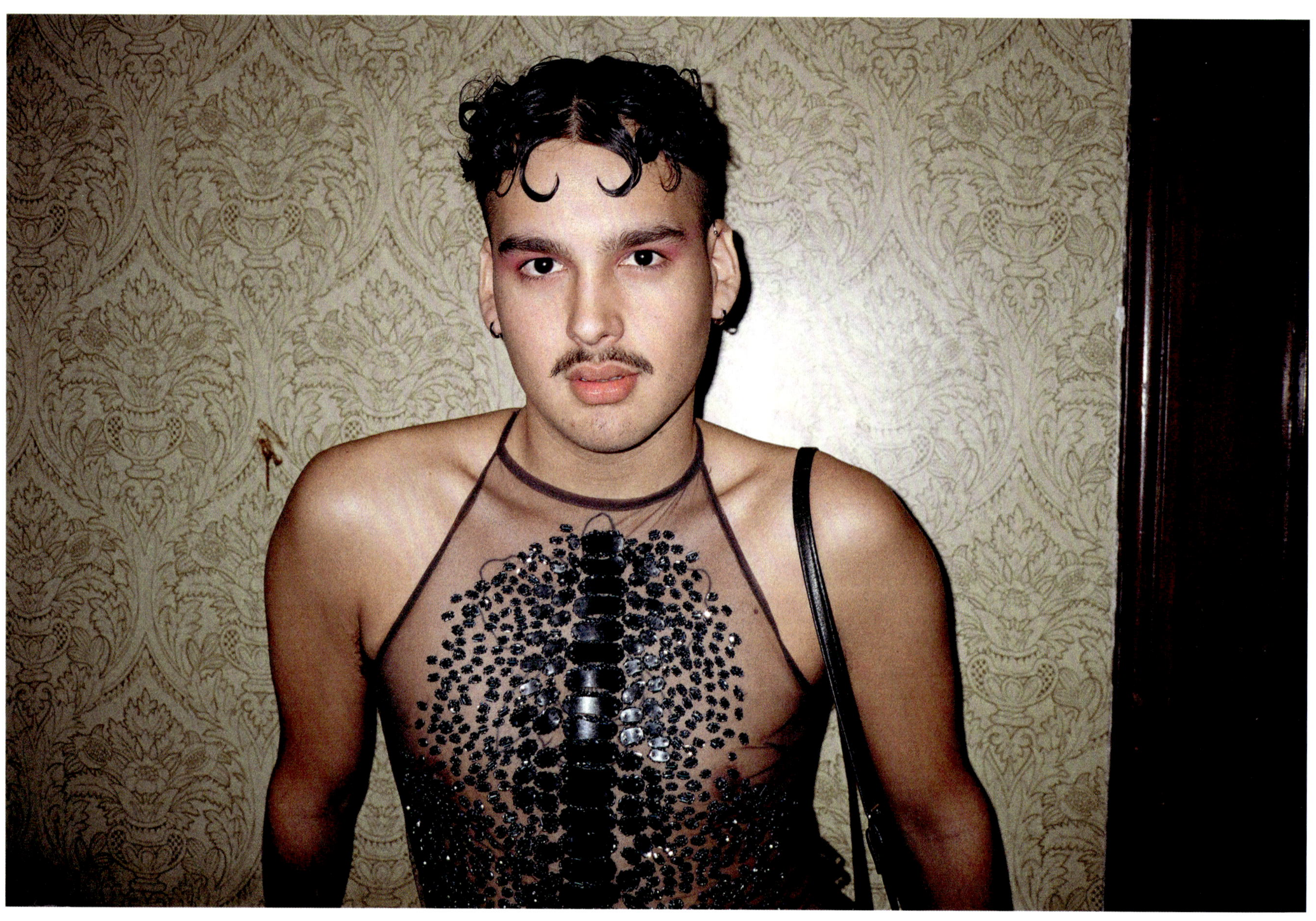

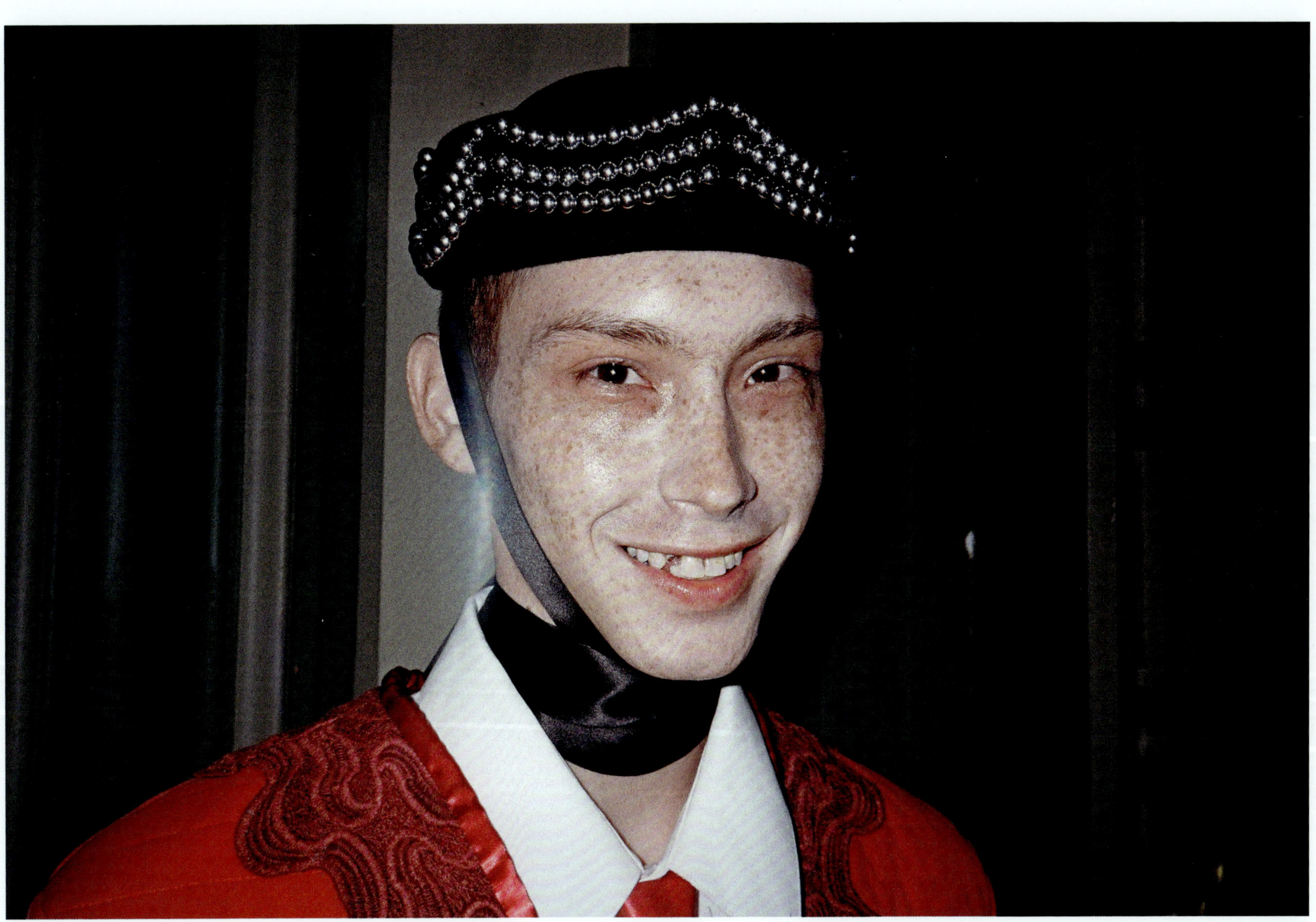

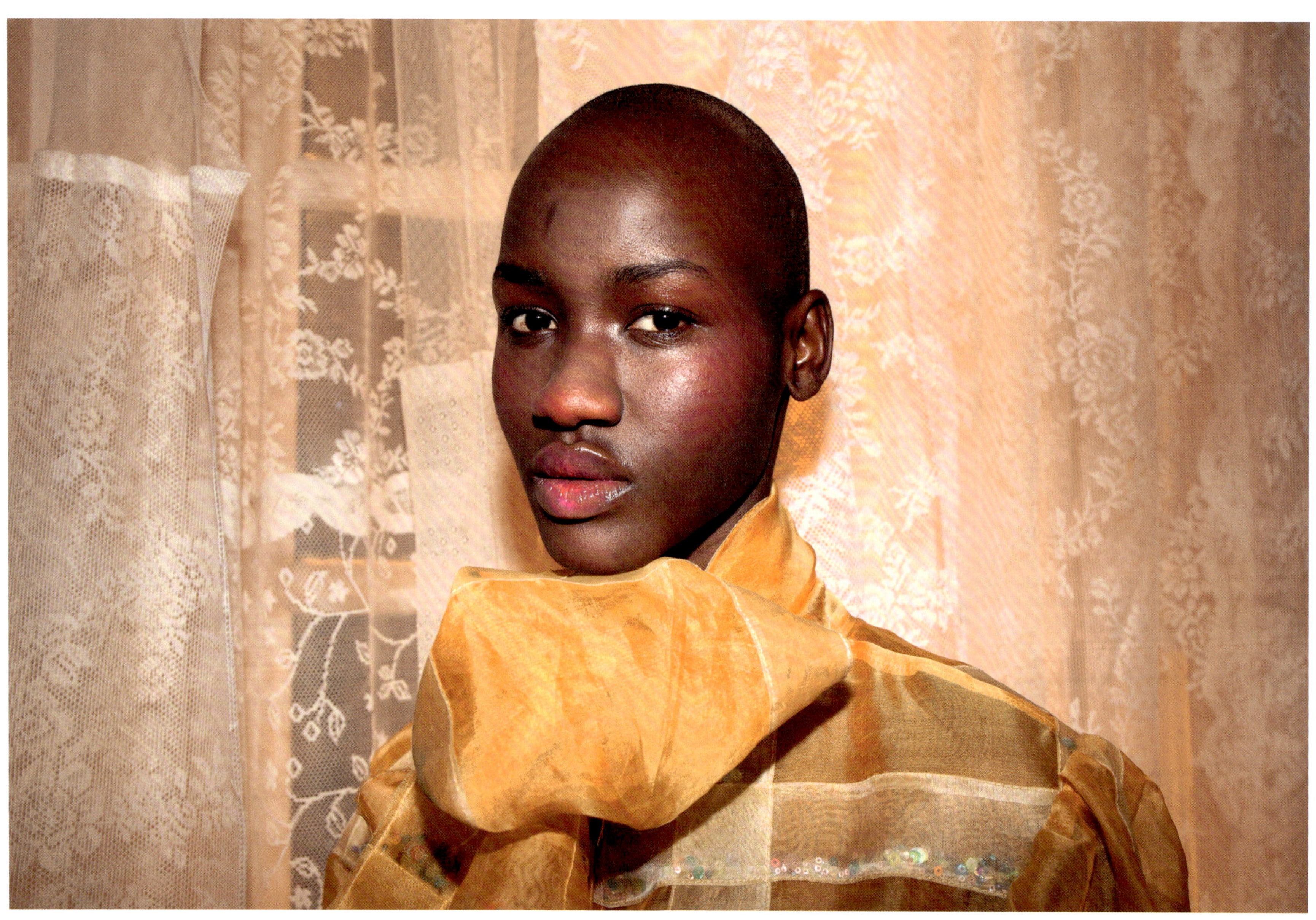

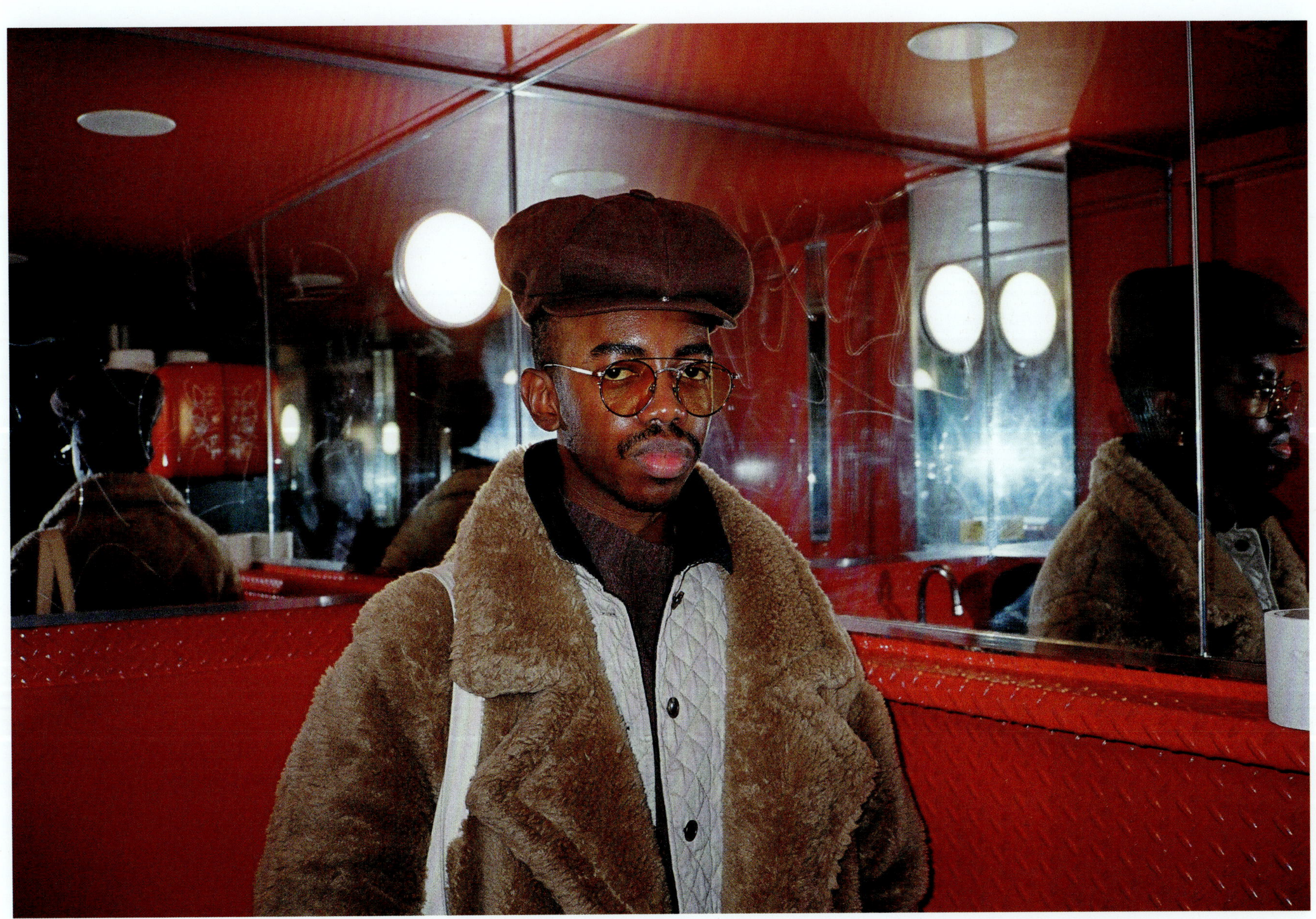

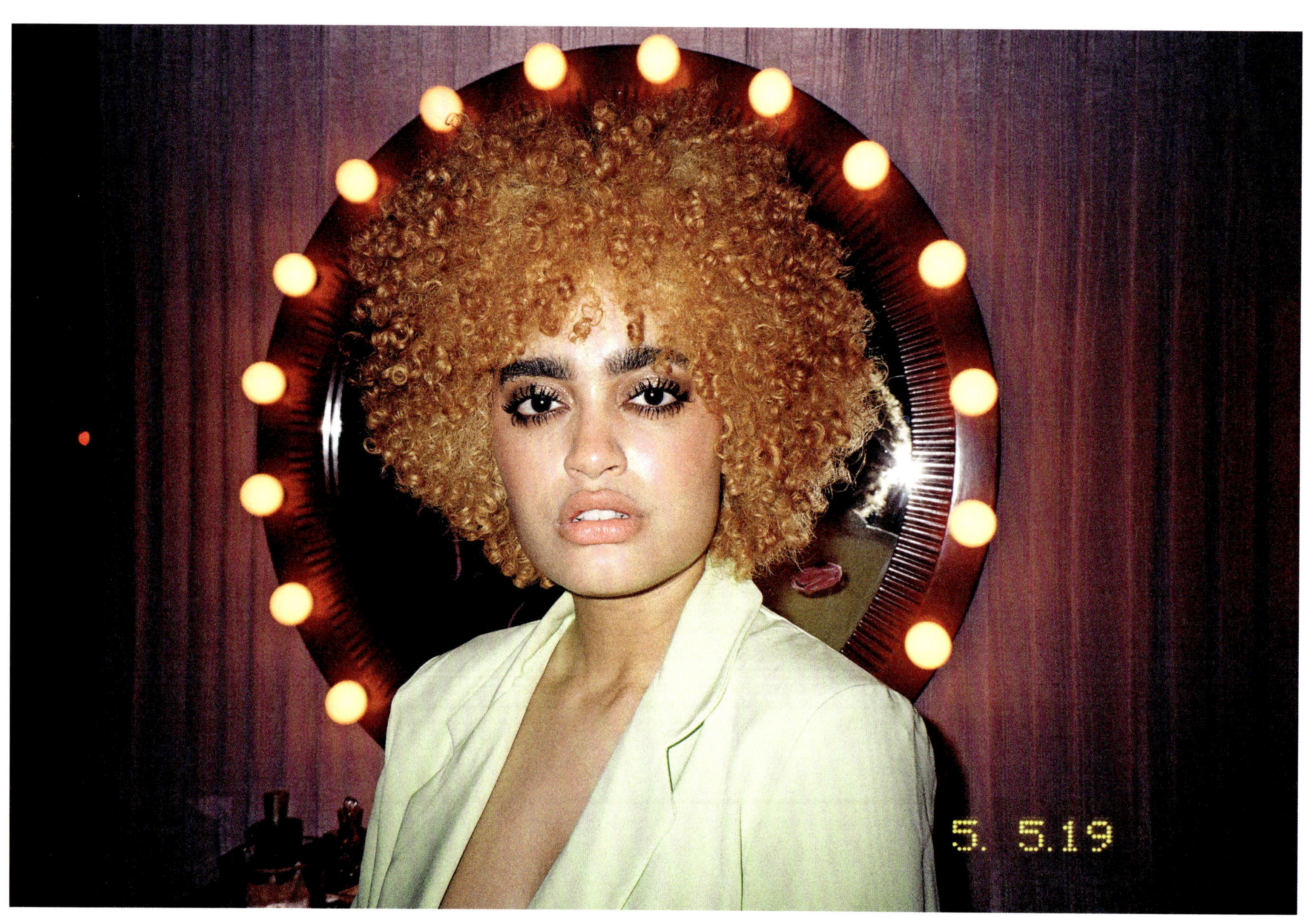
5. 5.19

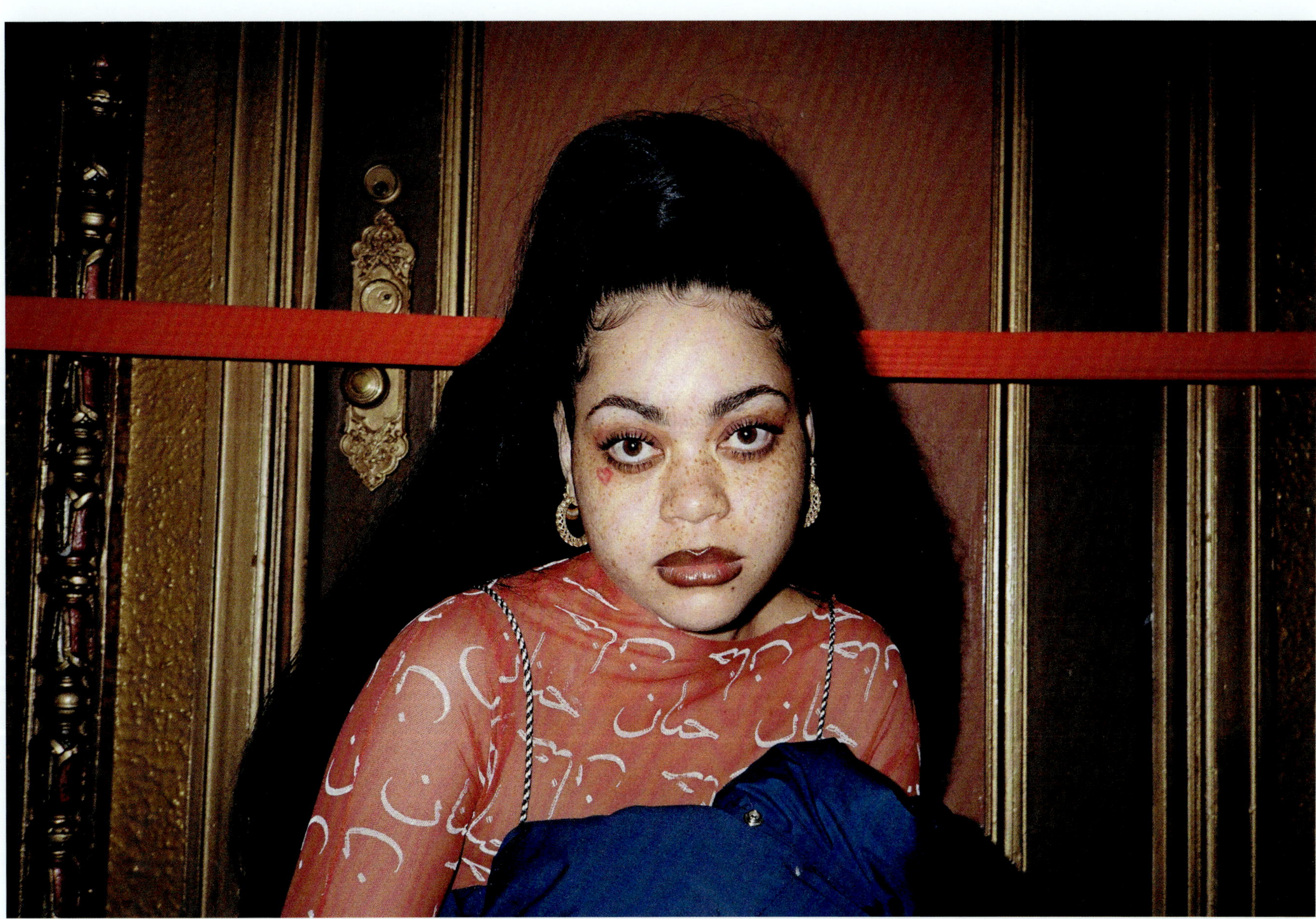

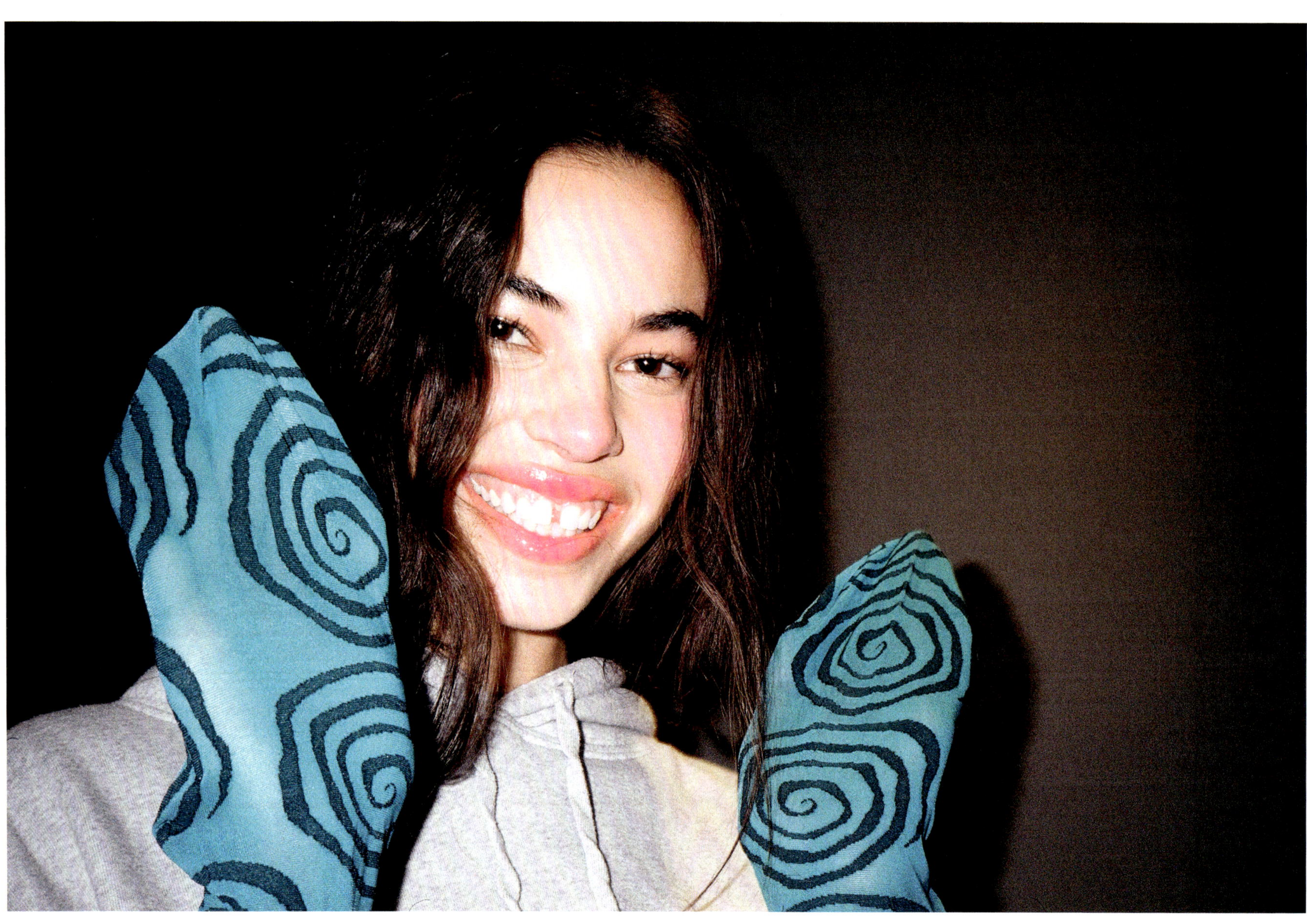

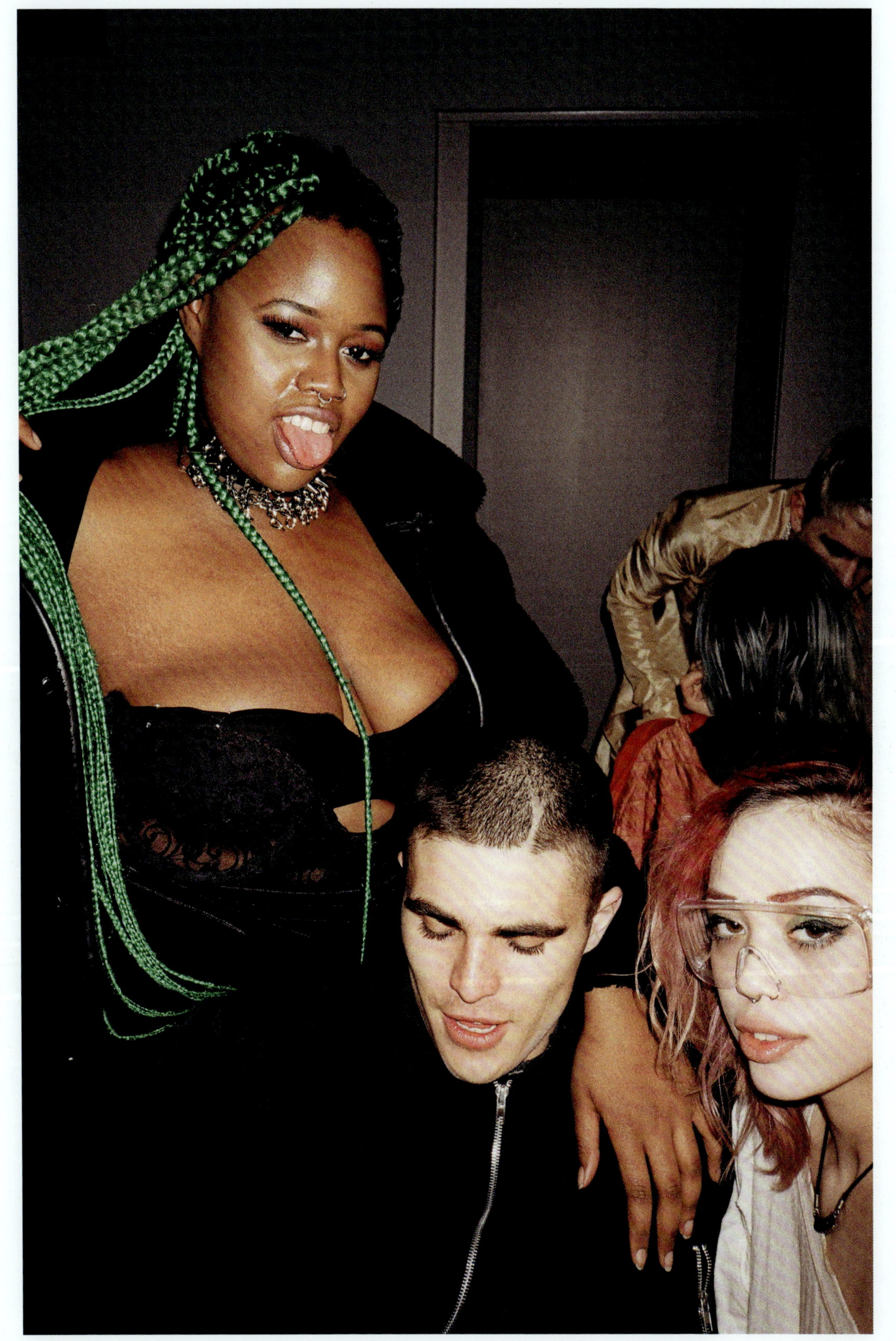

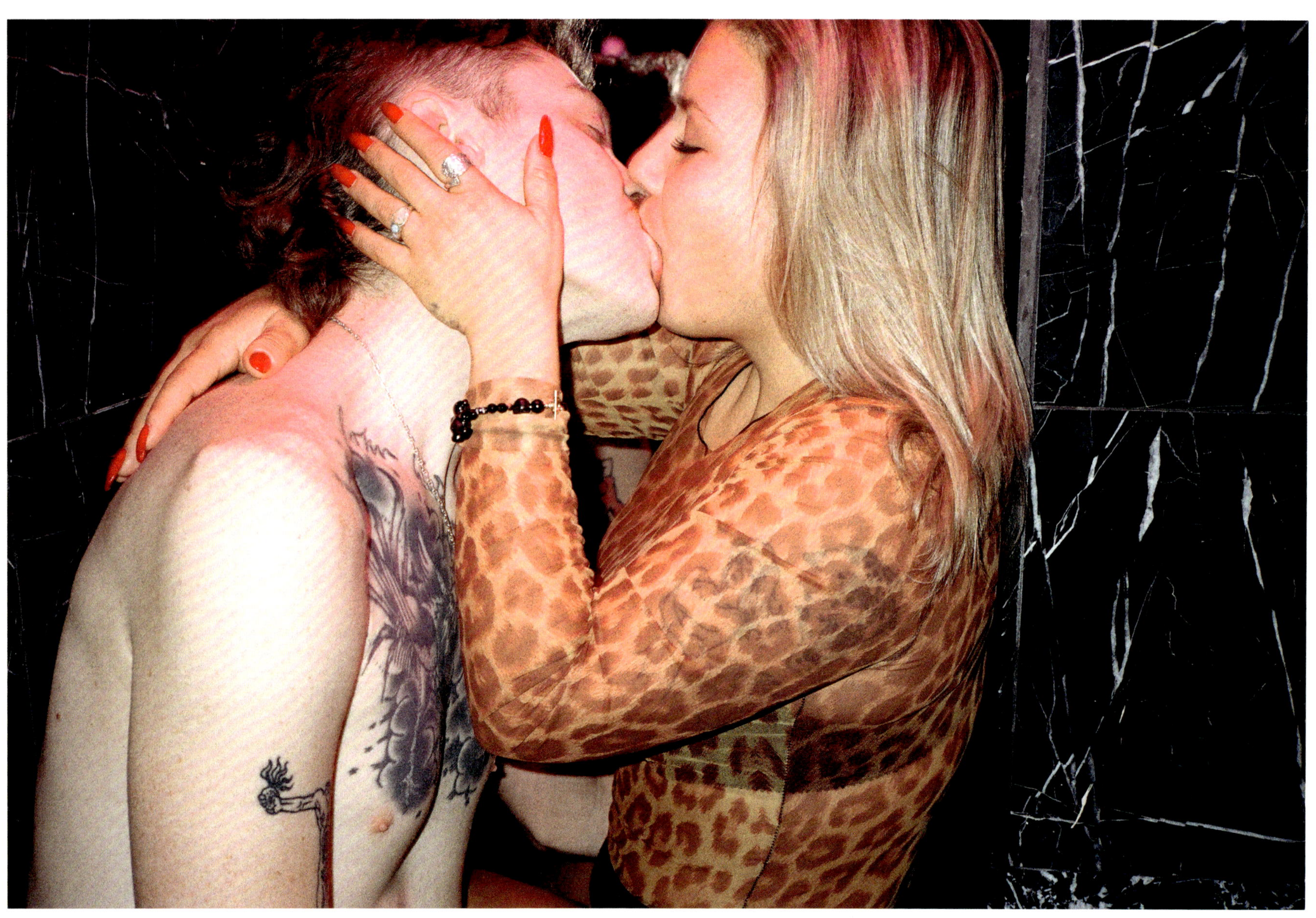

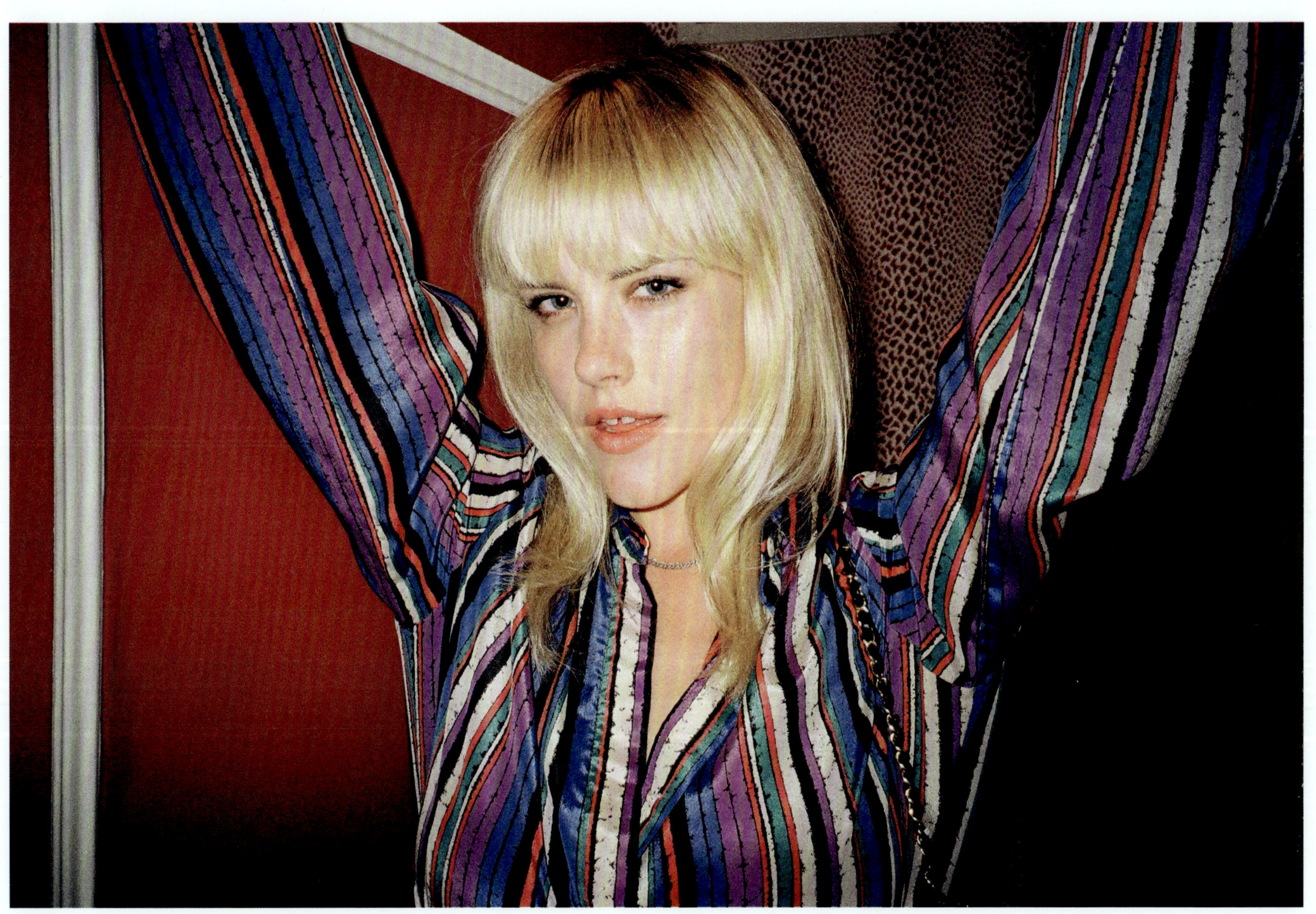

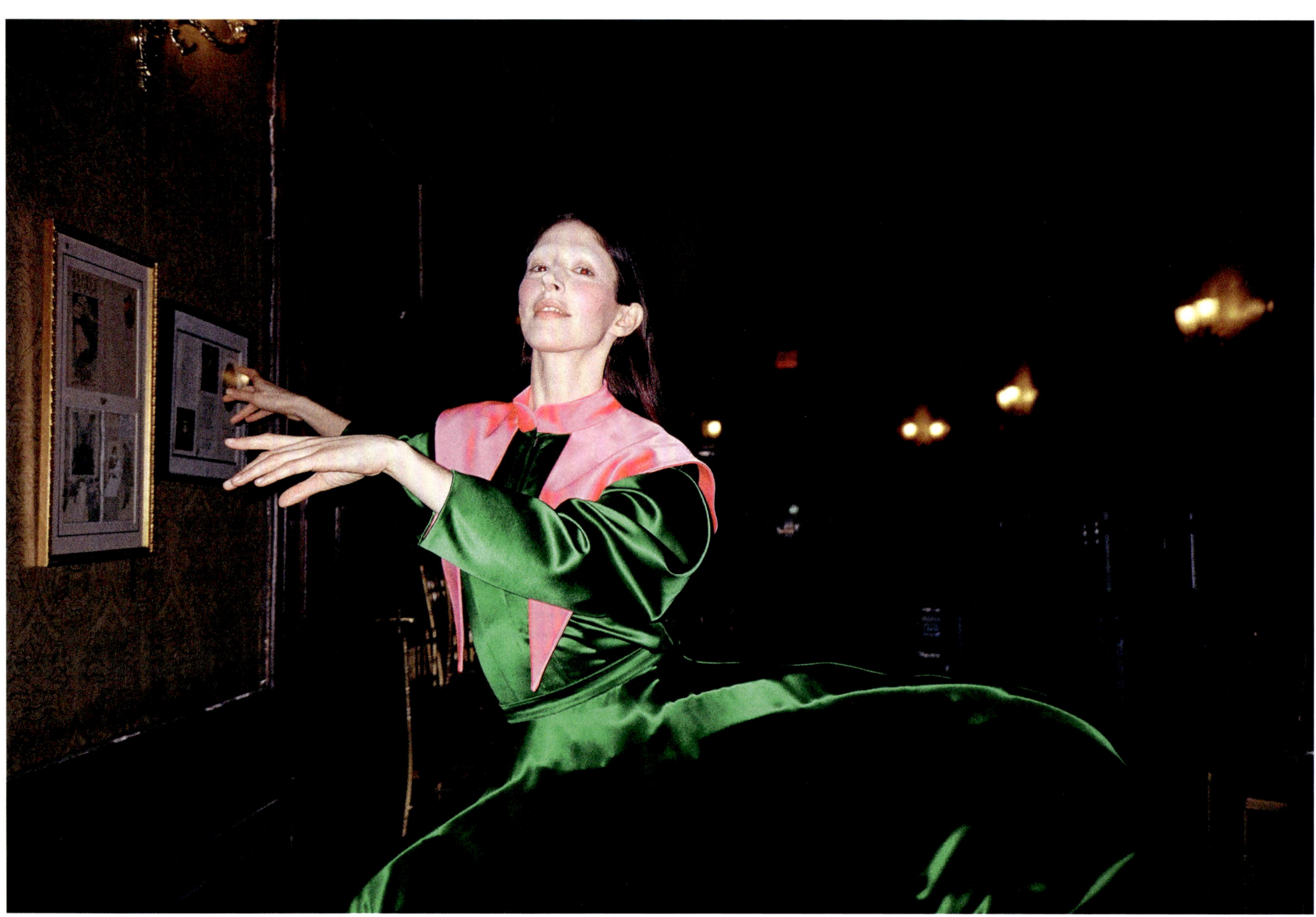

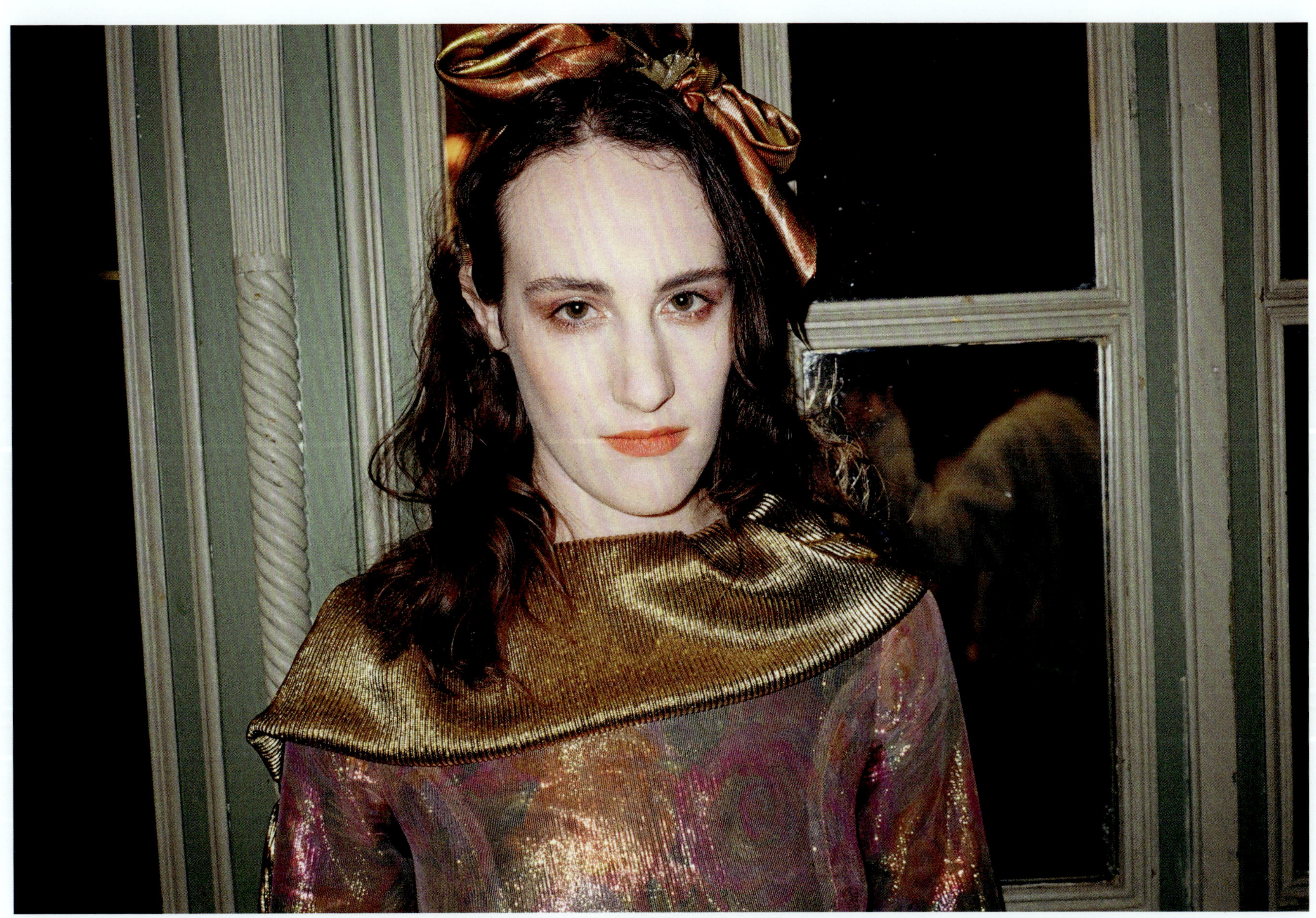

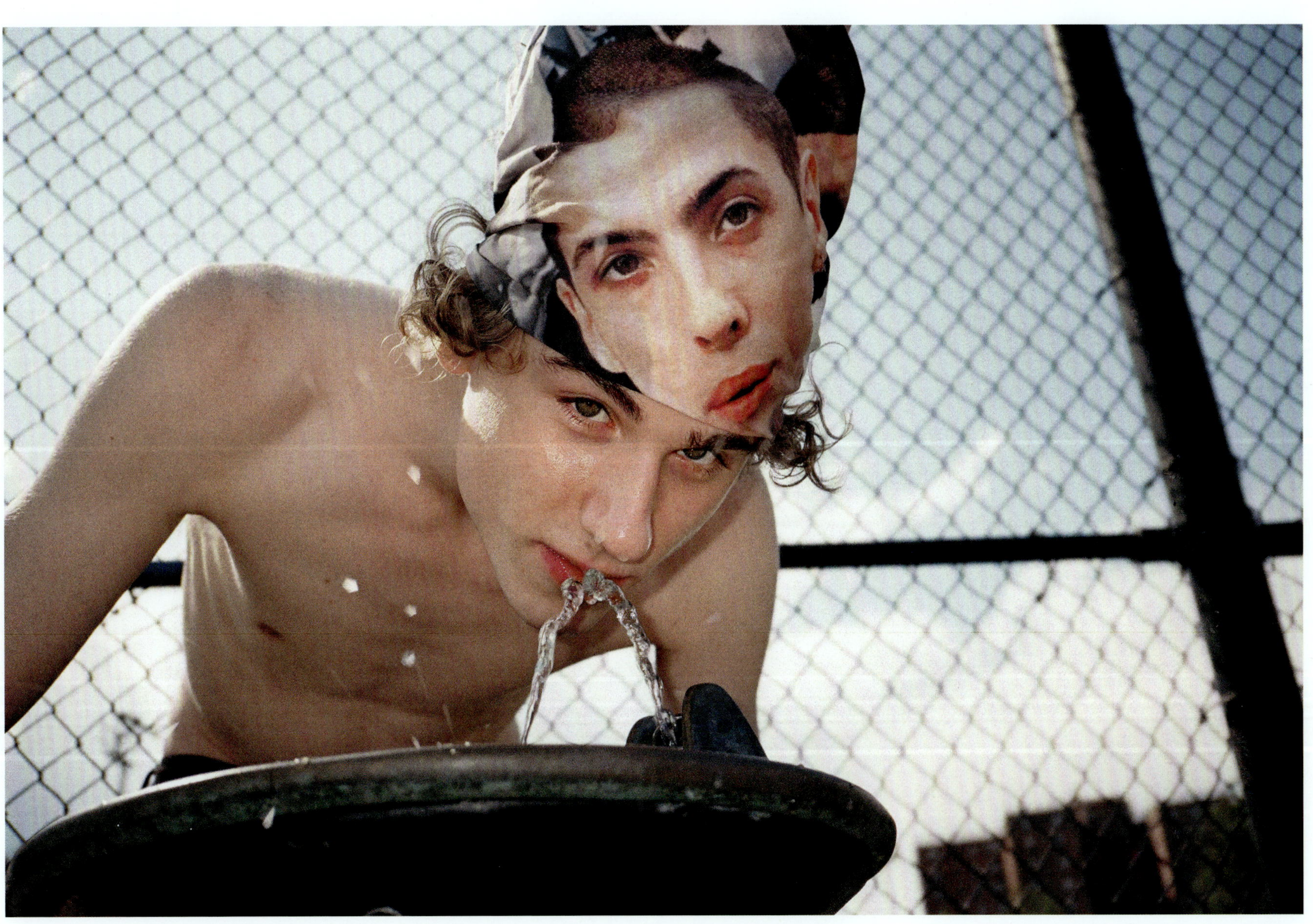

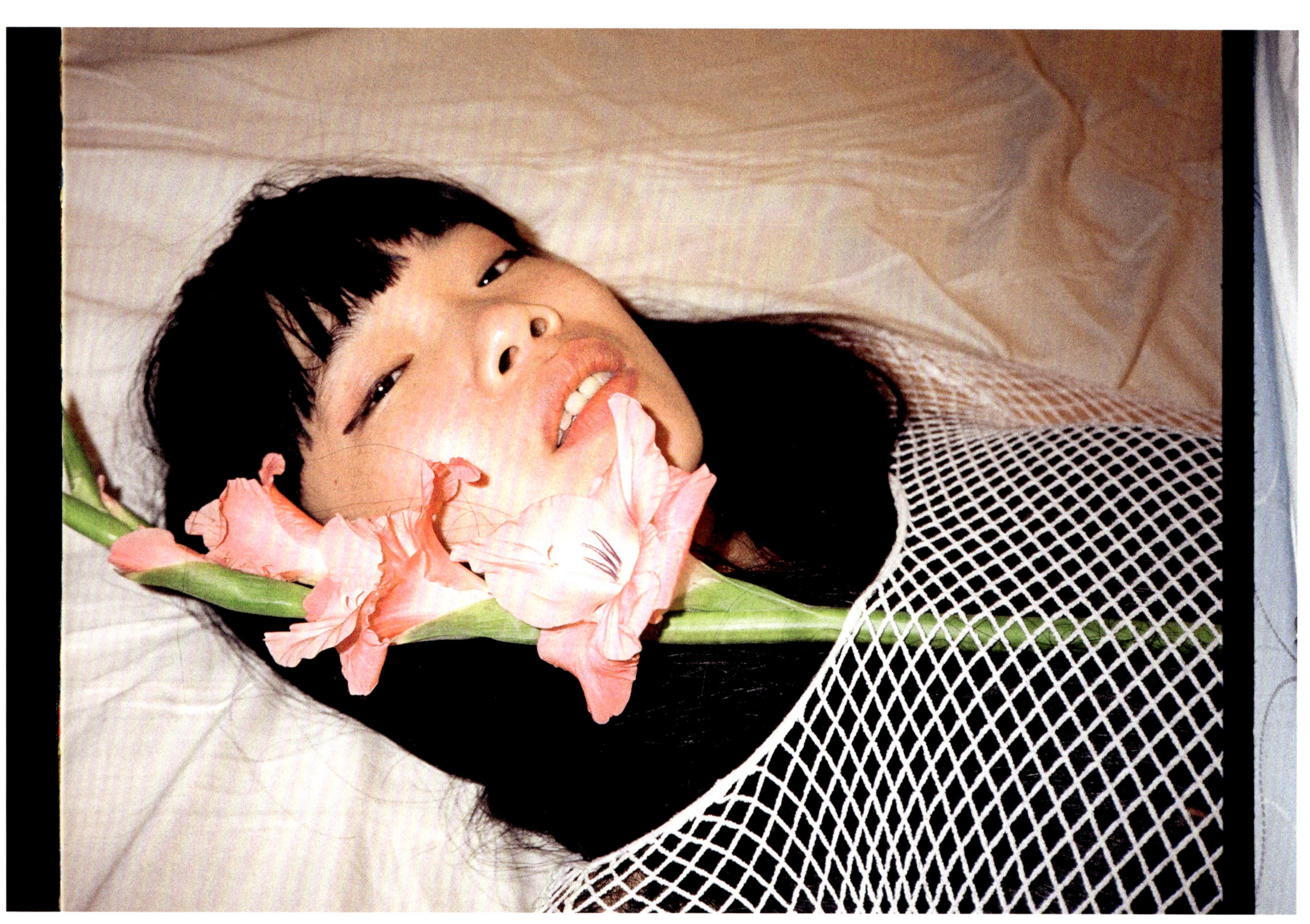

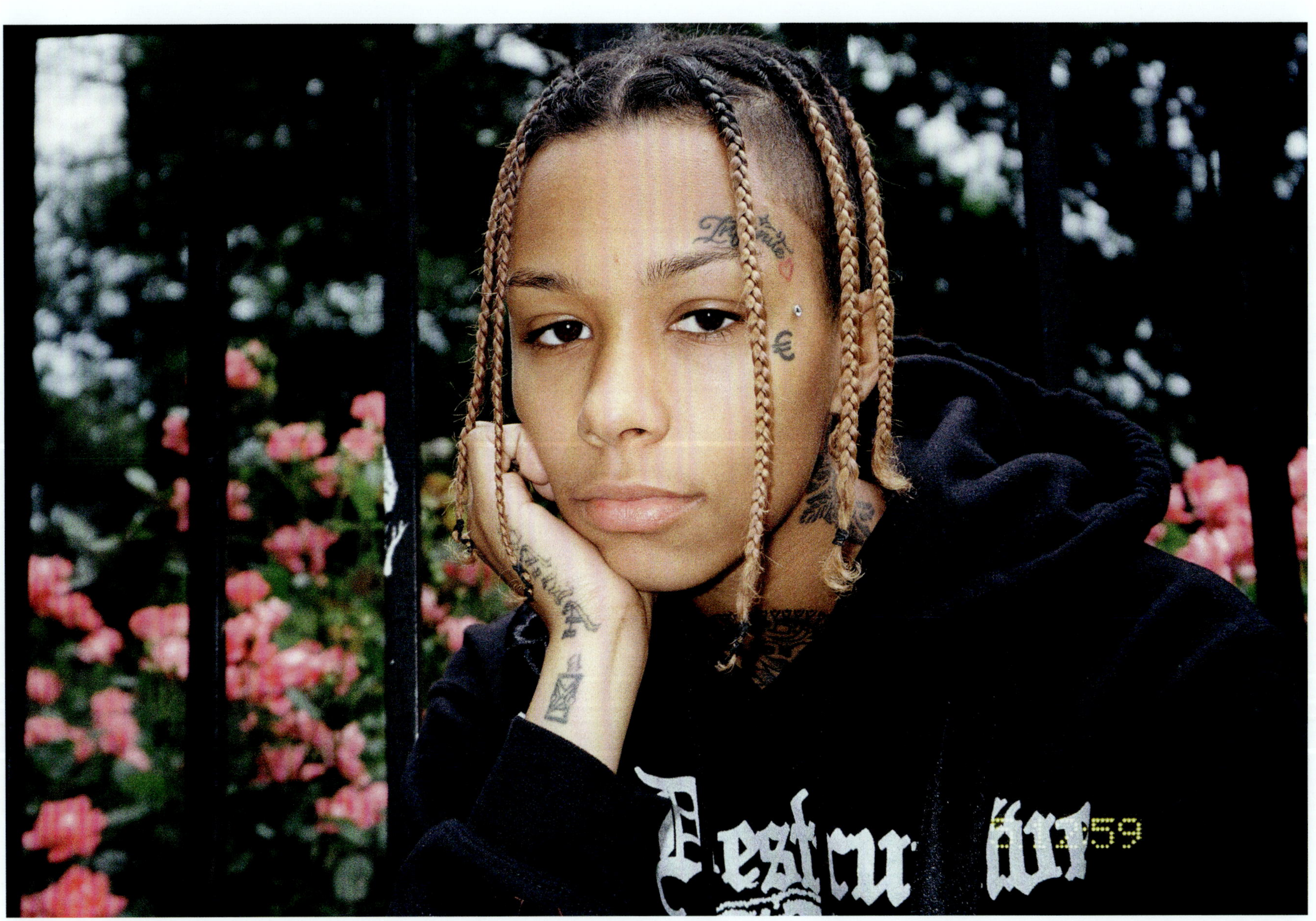

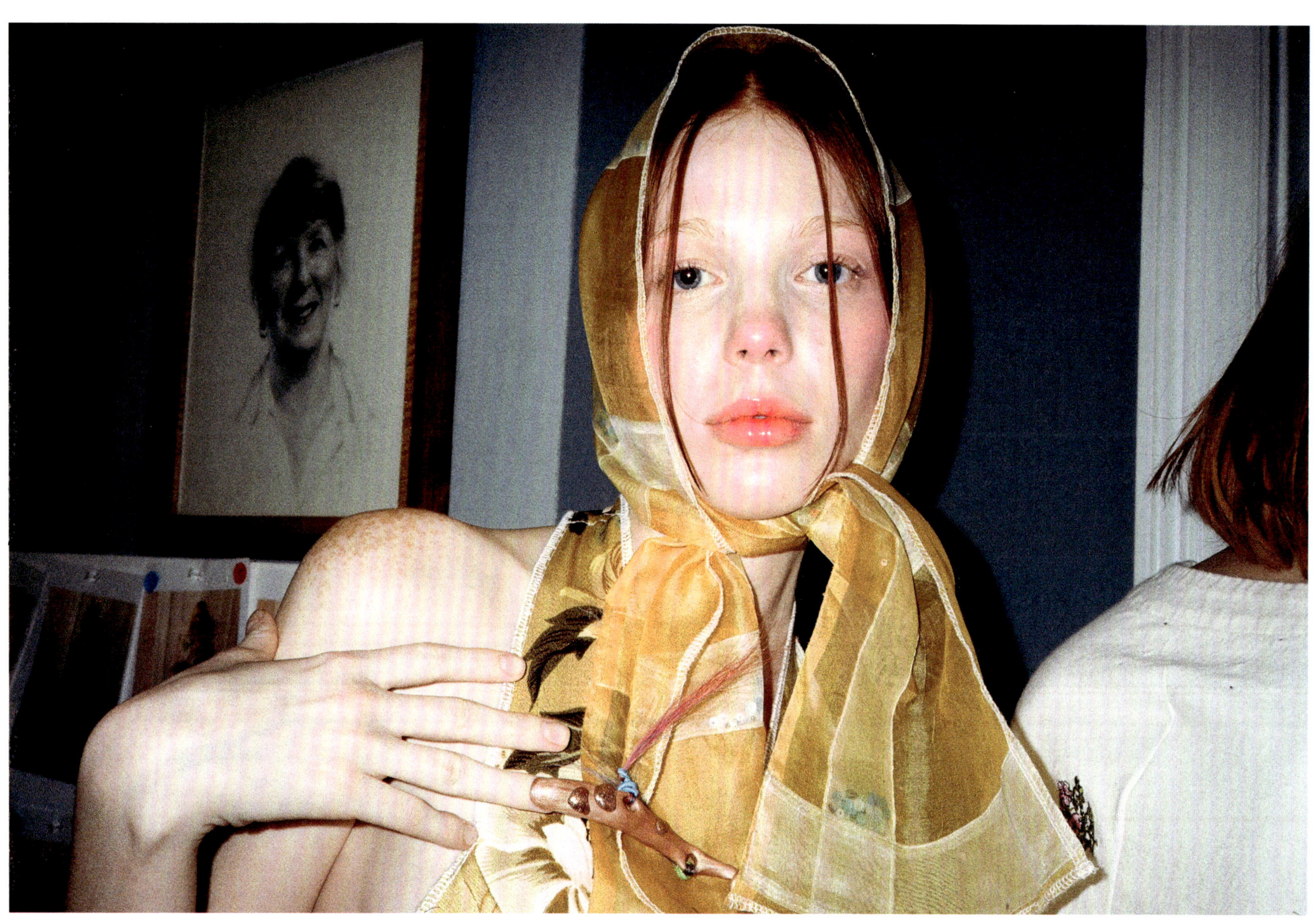

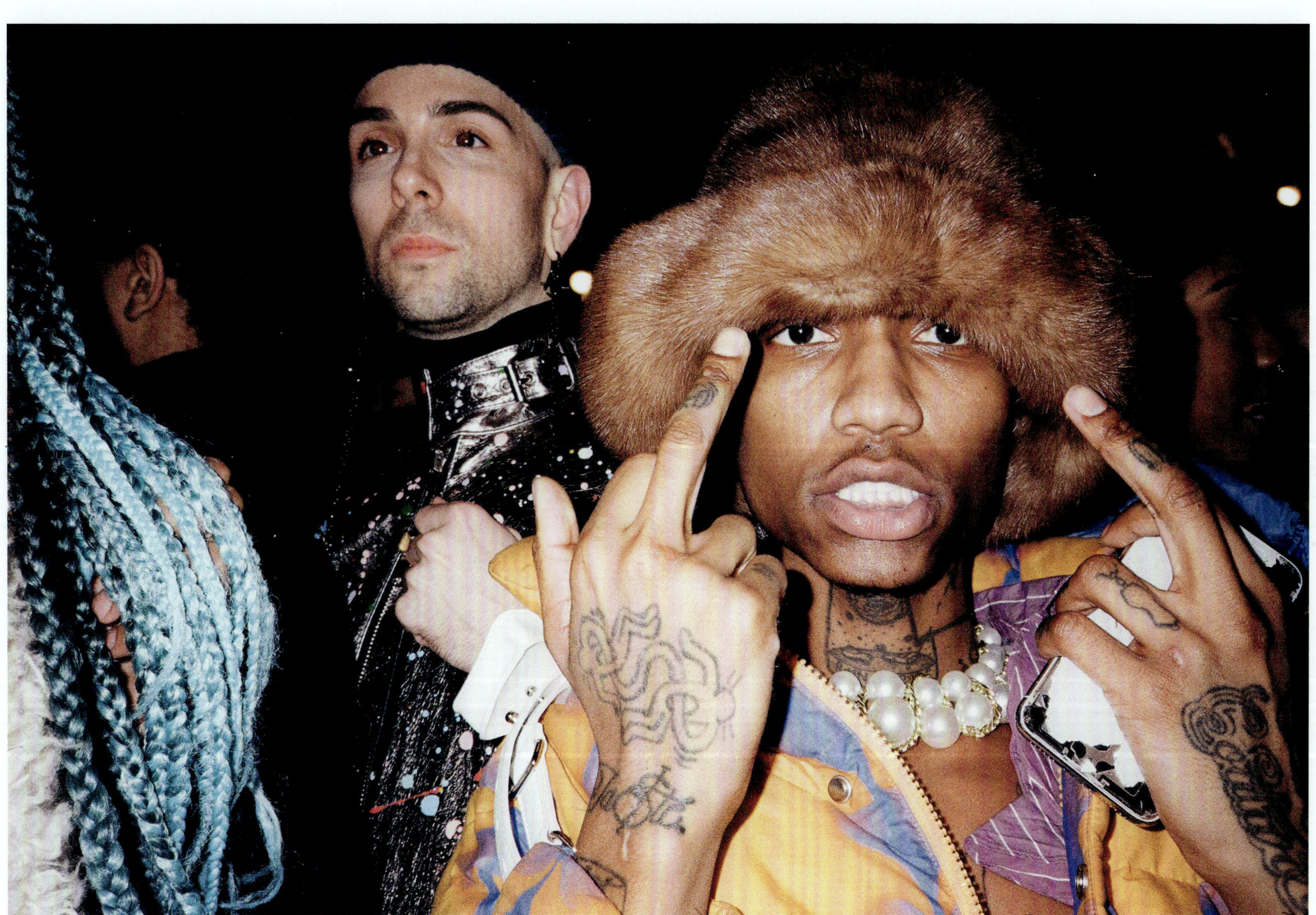

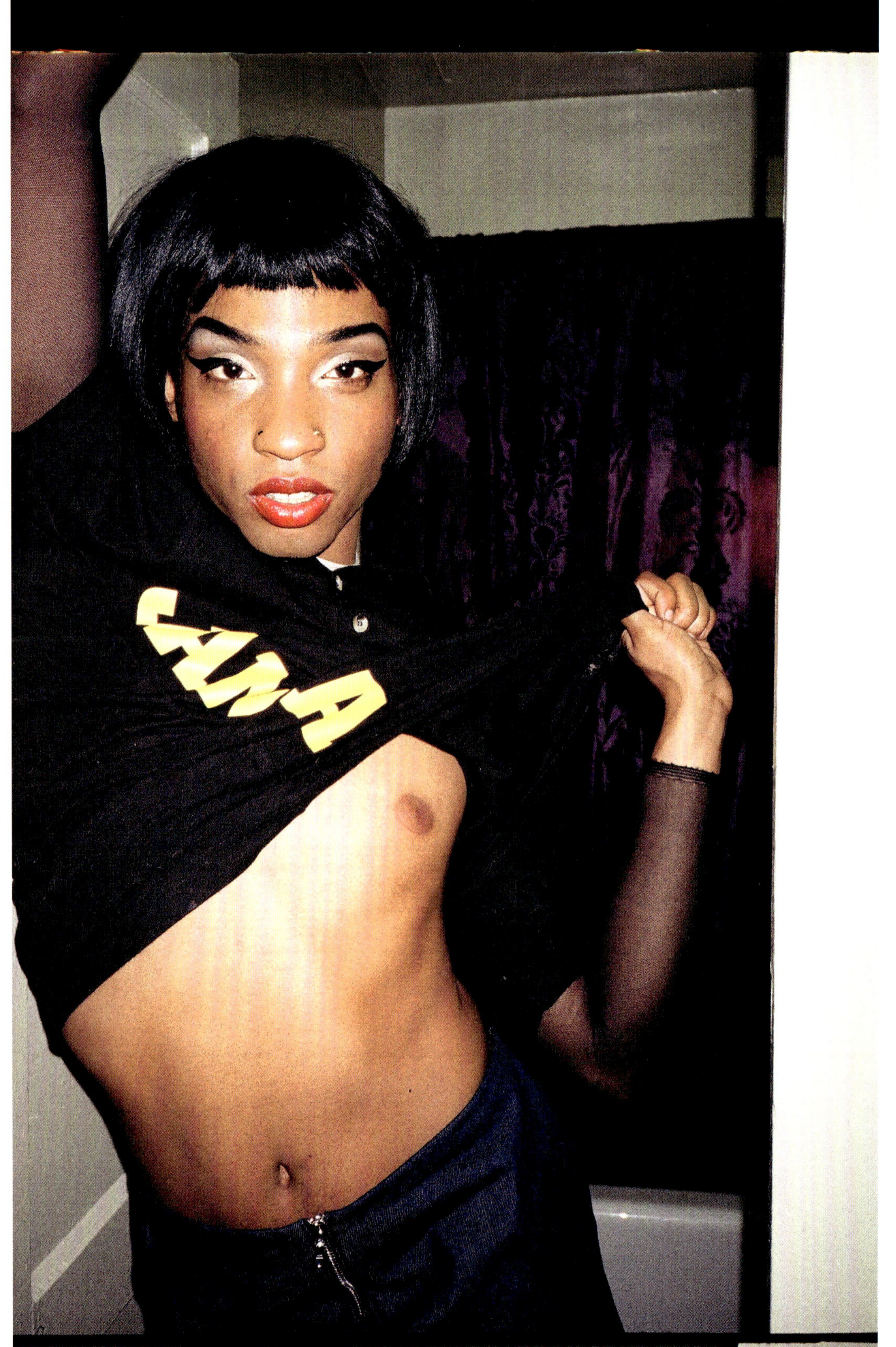

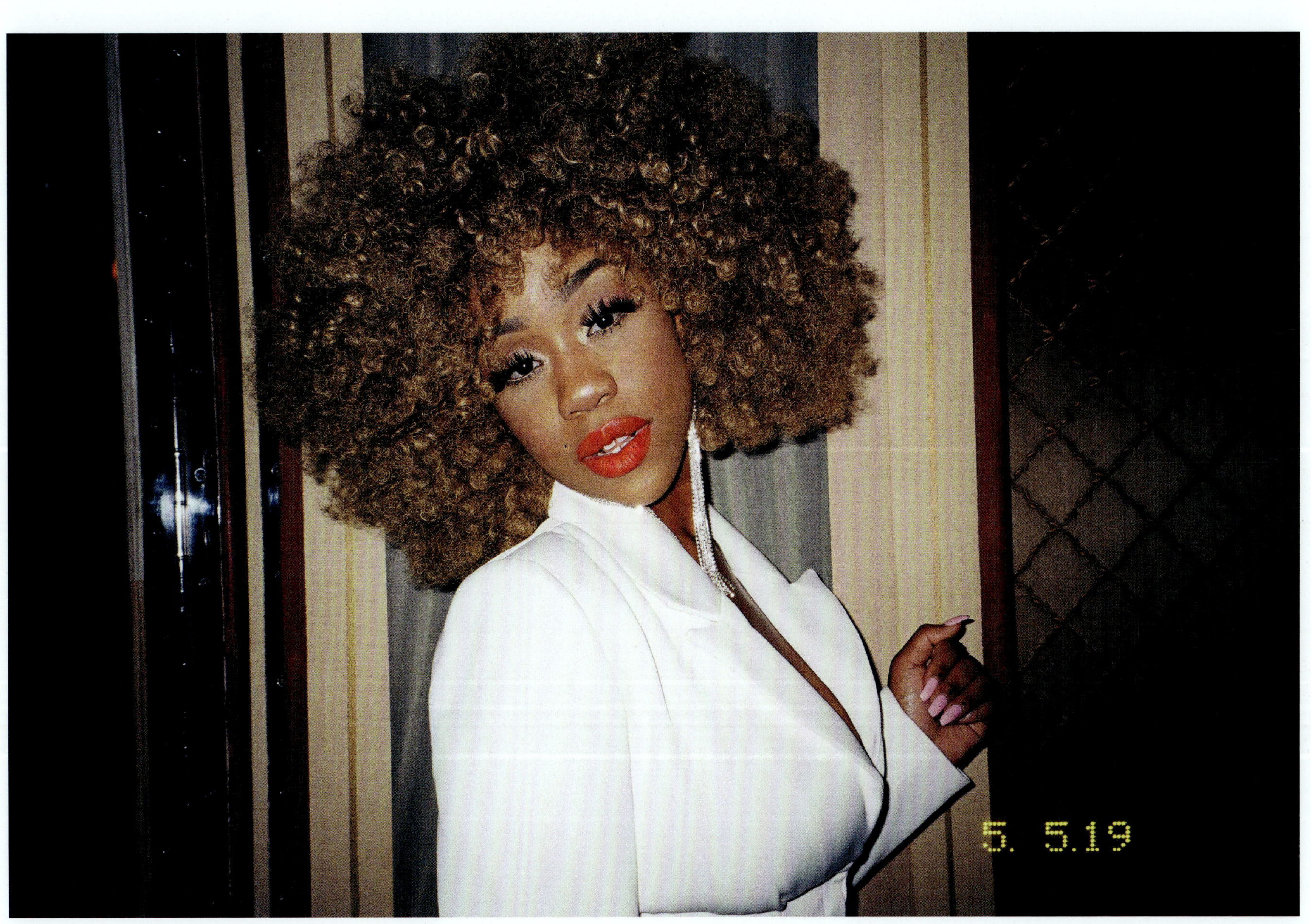
5. 5.19

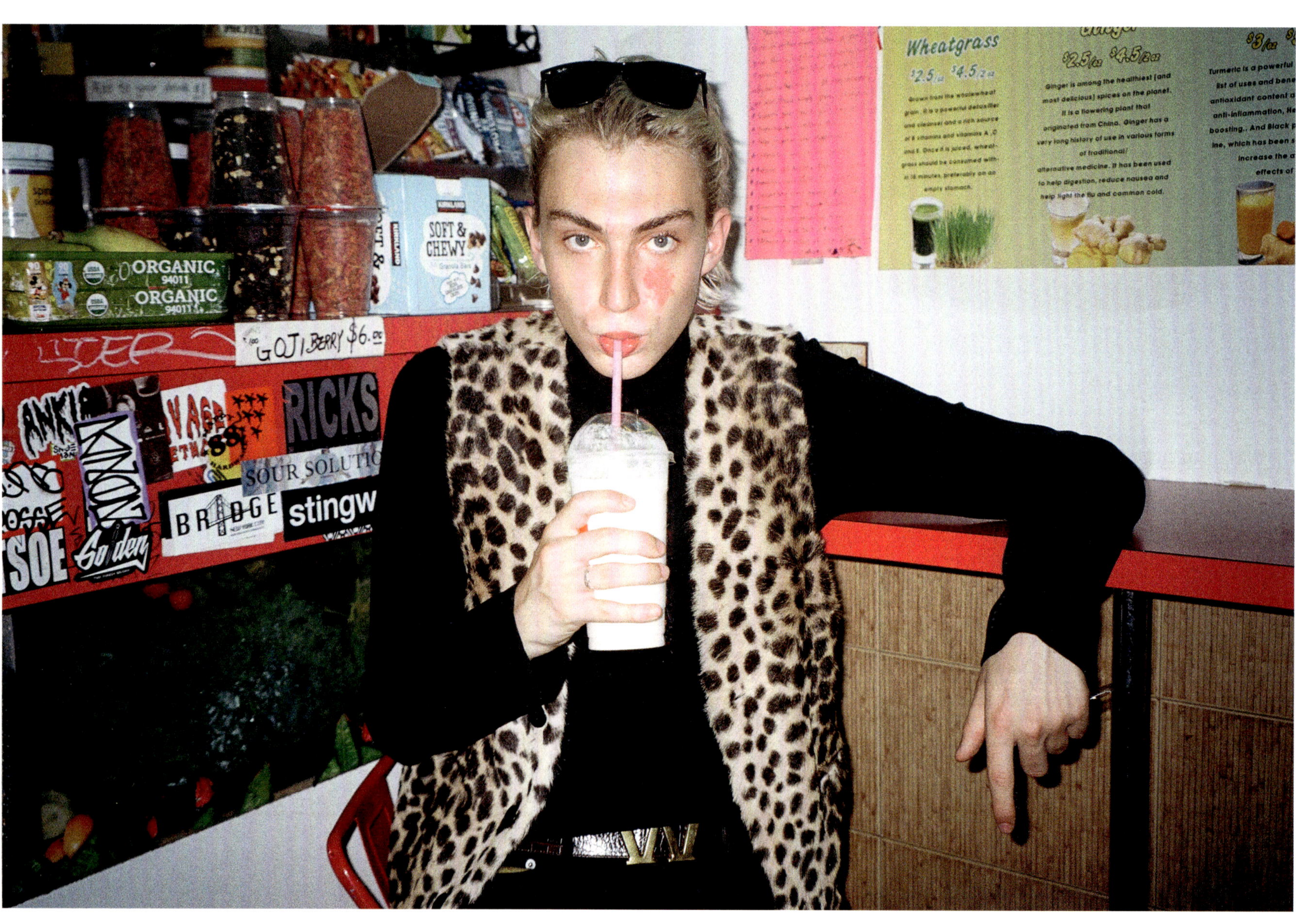
ORGANIC
94011
ORGANIC
94011
SOFT &
CHEWY
GOJI BERRY $6.
RICKS
SOUR SOLUTIO
BRIDGE
stingw
Wheatgrass

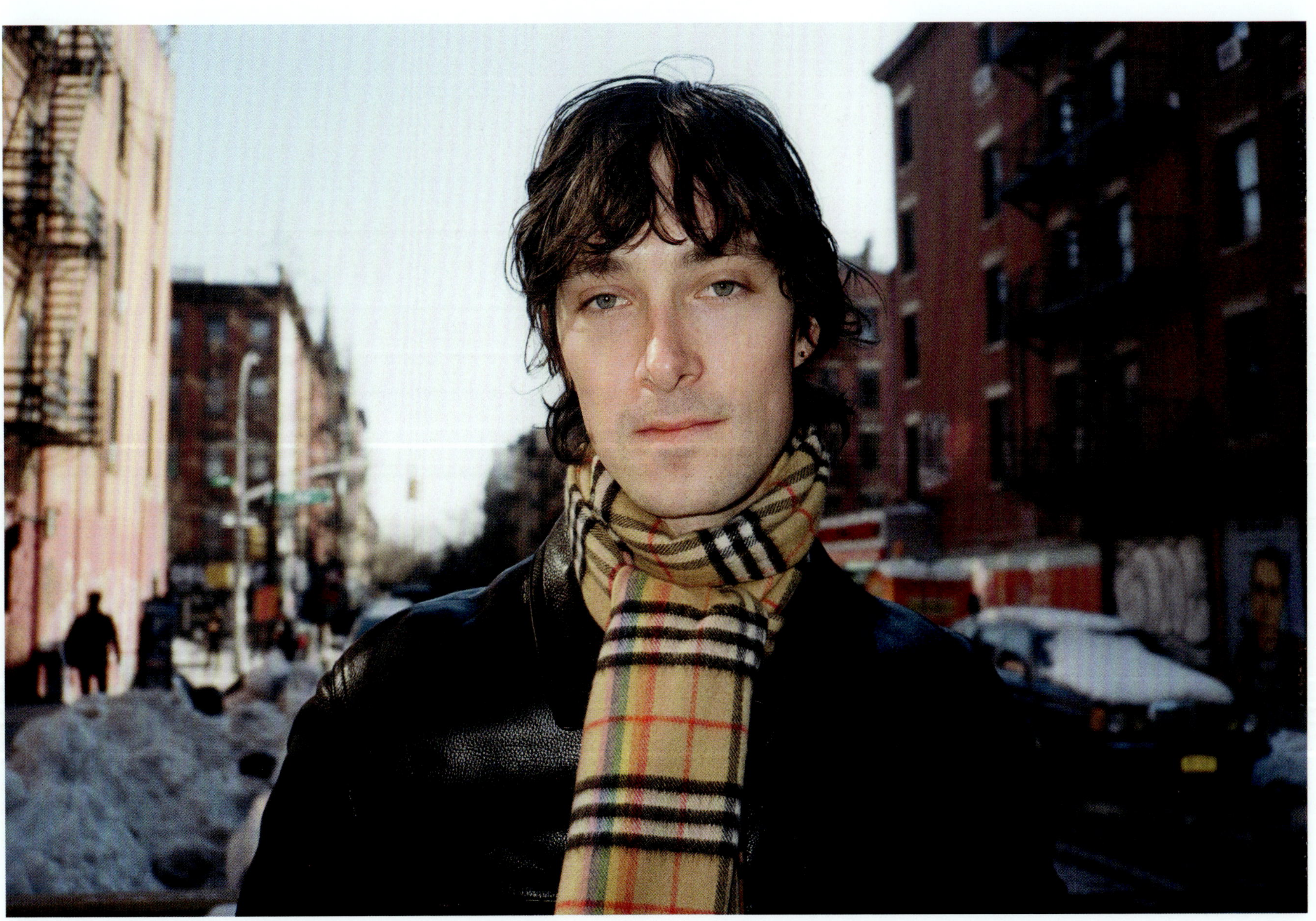

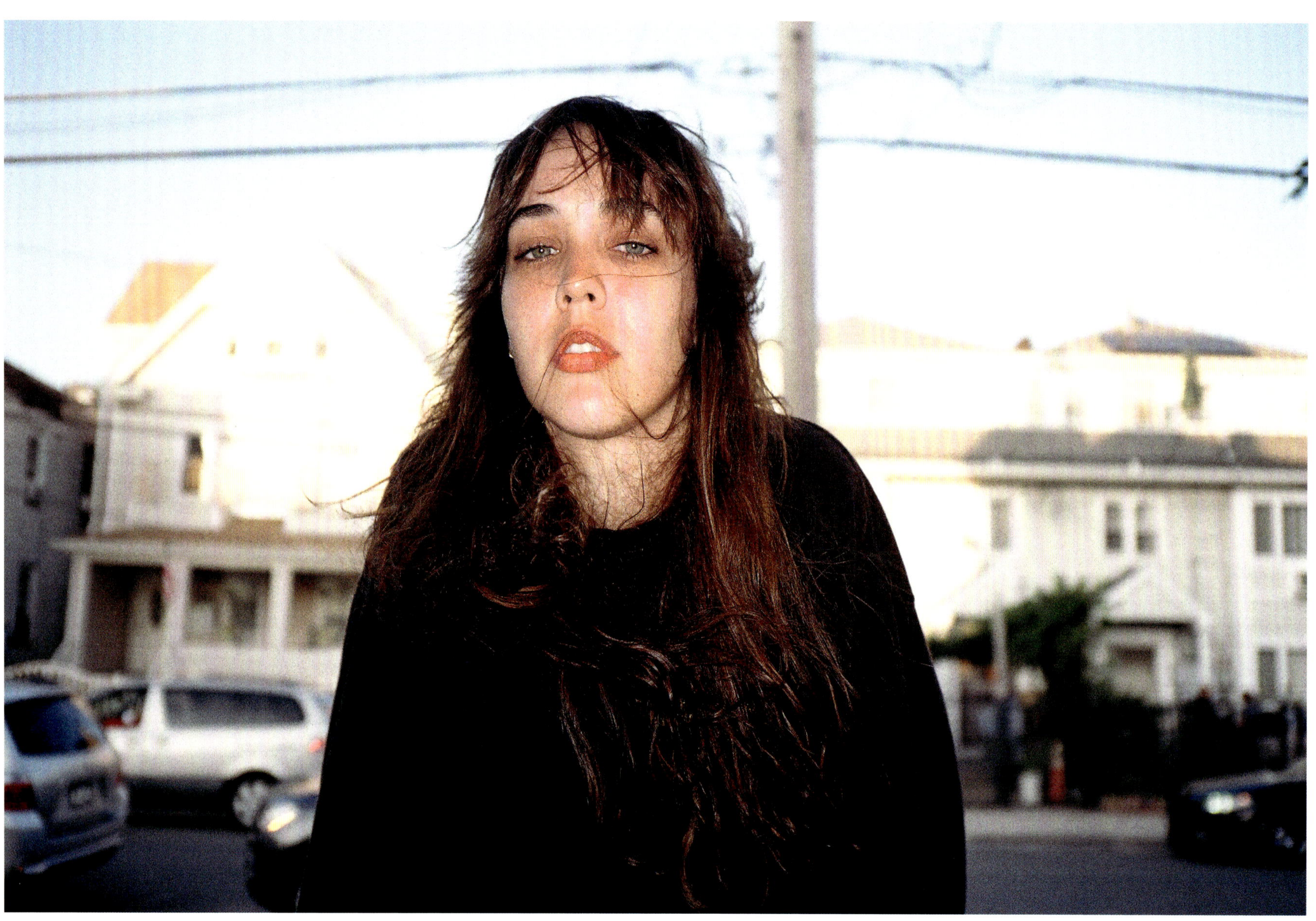

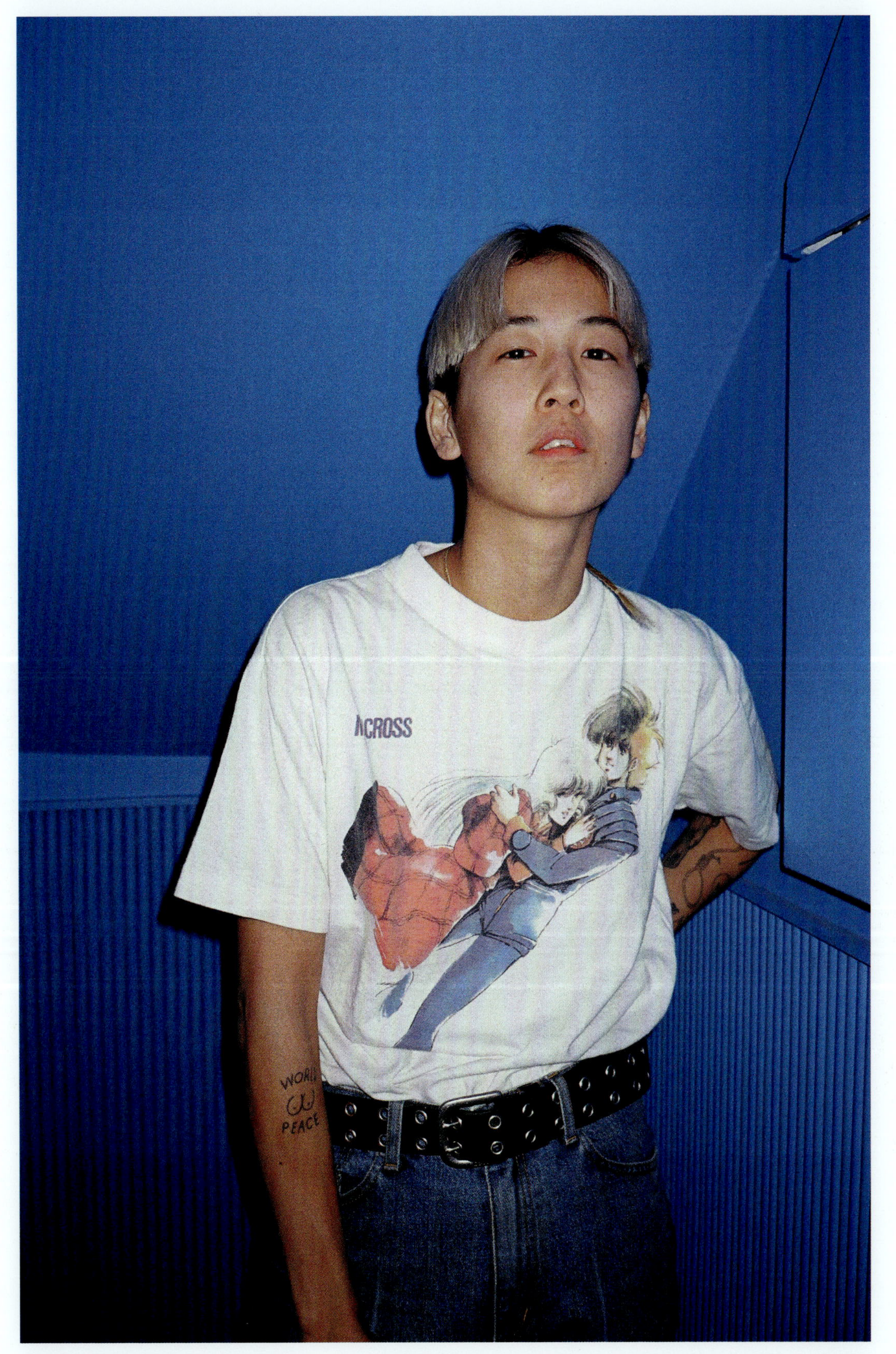
ACROSS
PEACE

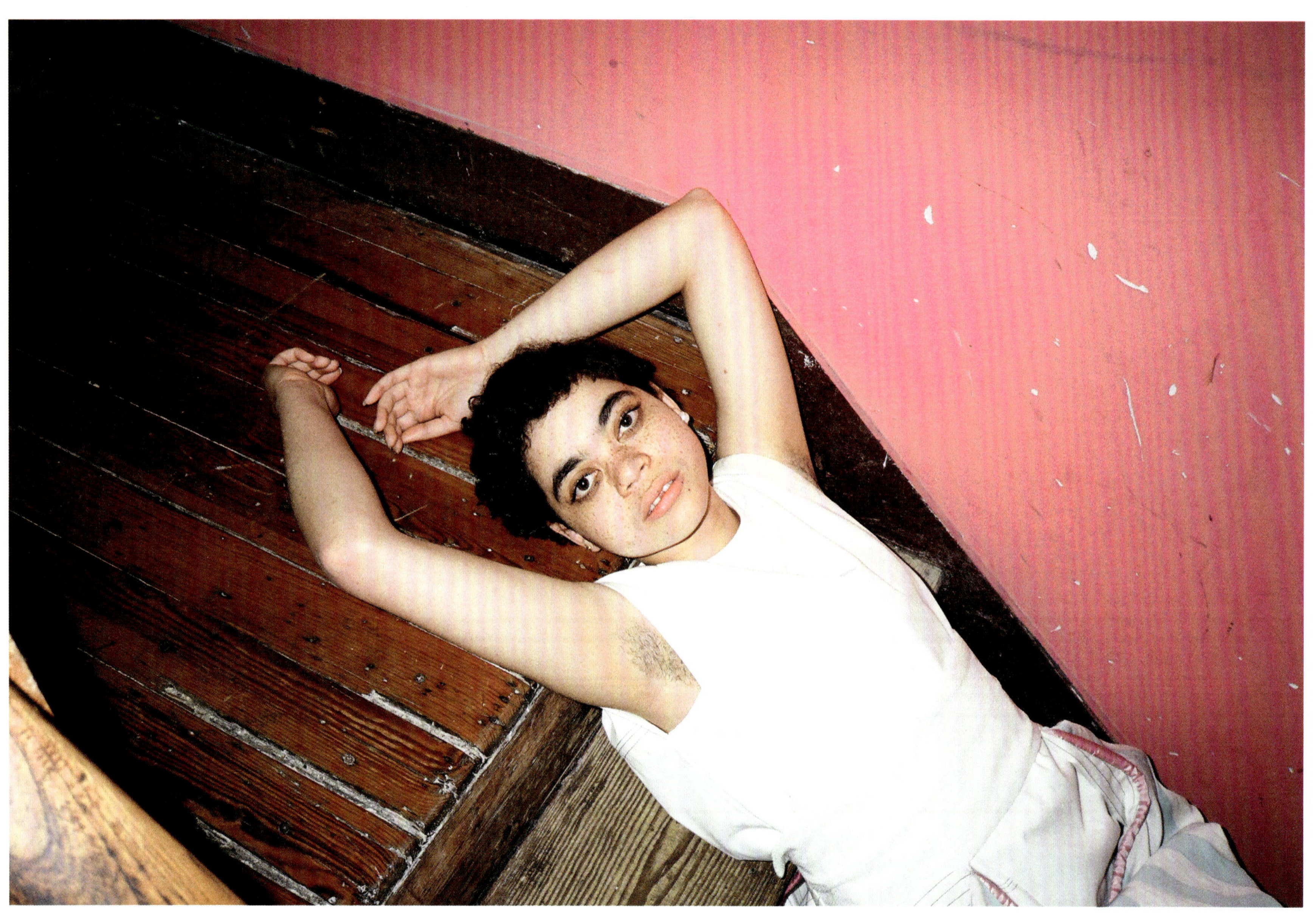

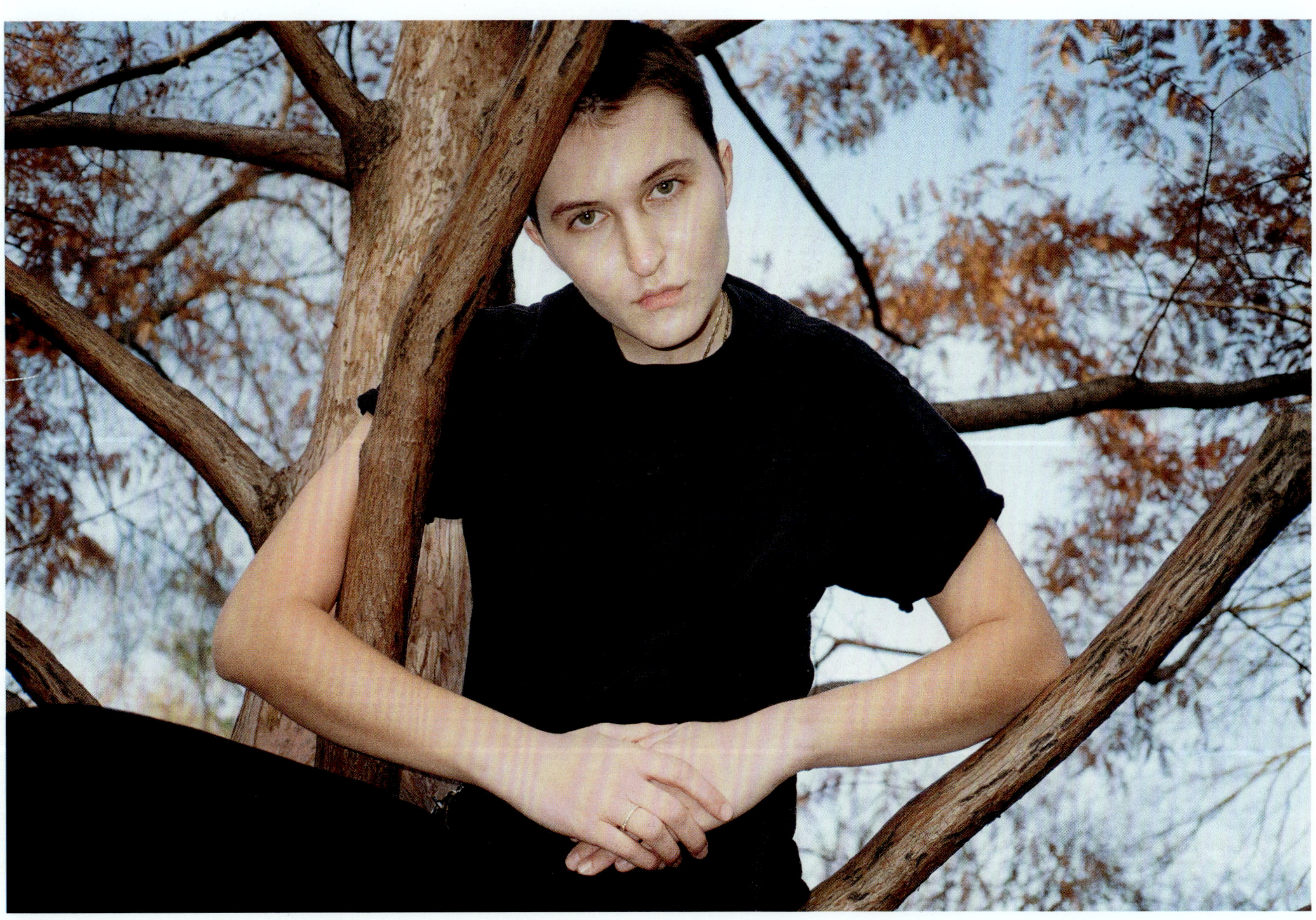

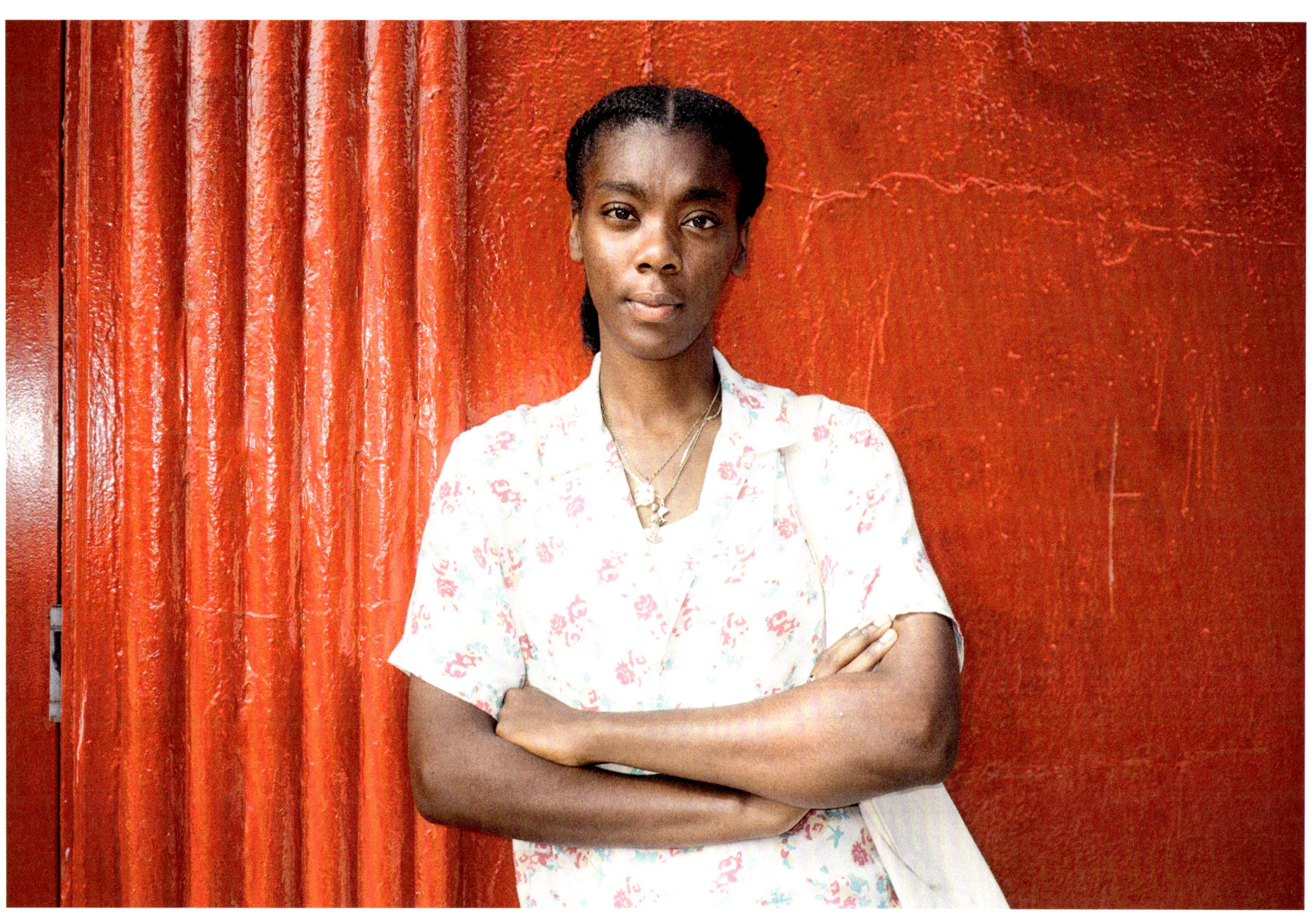

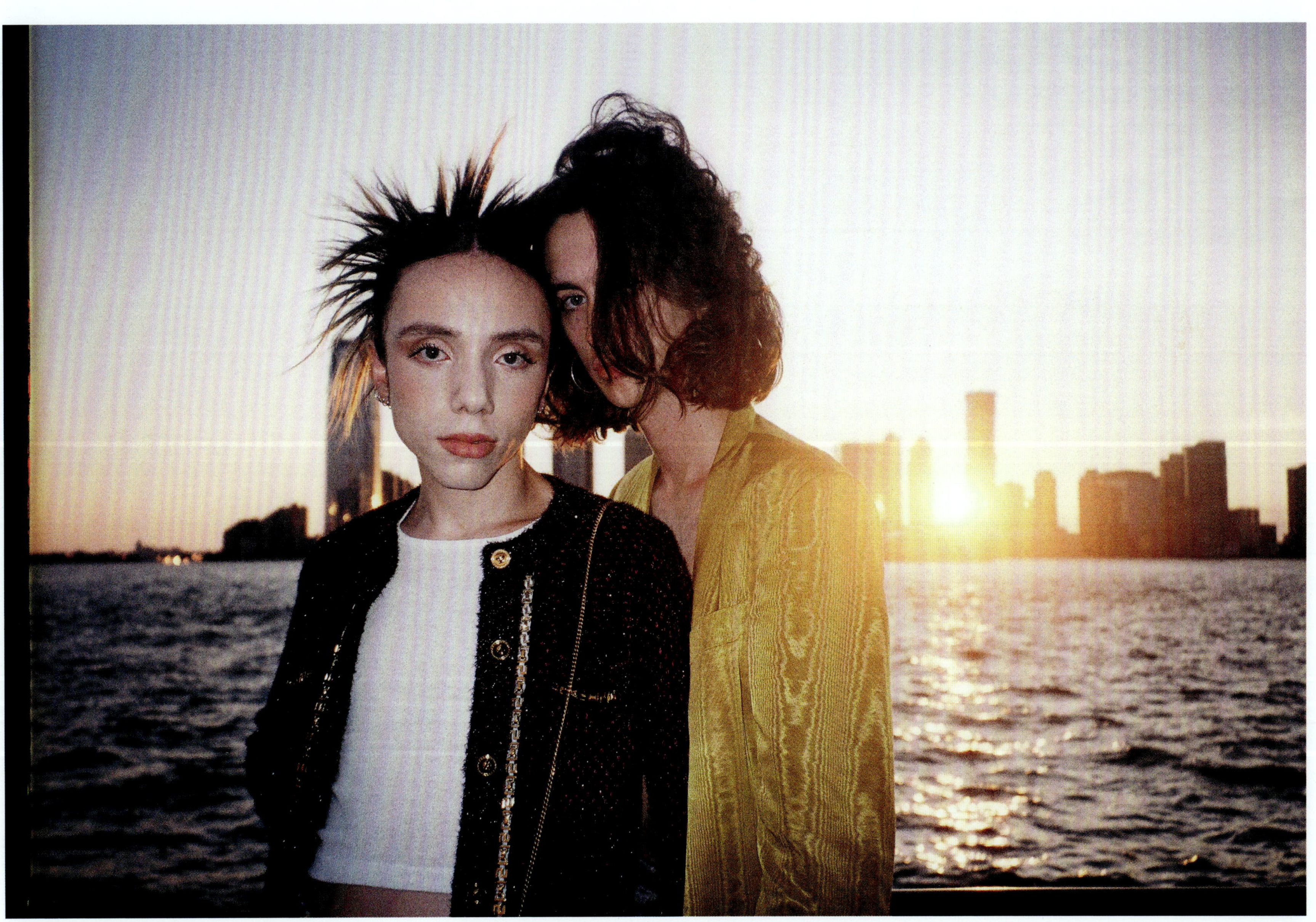

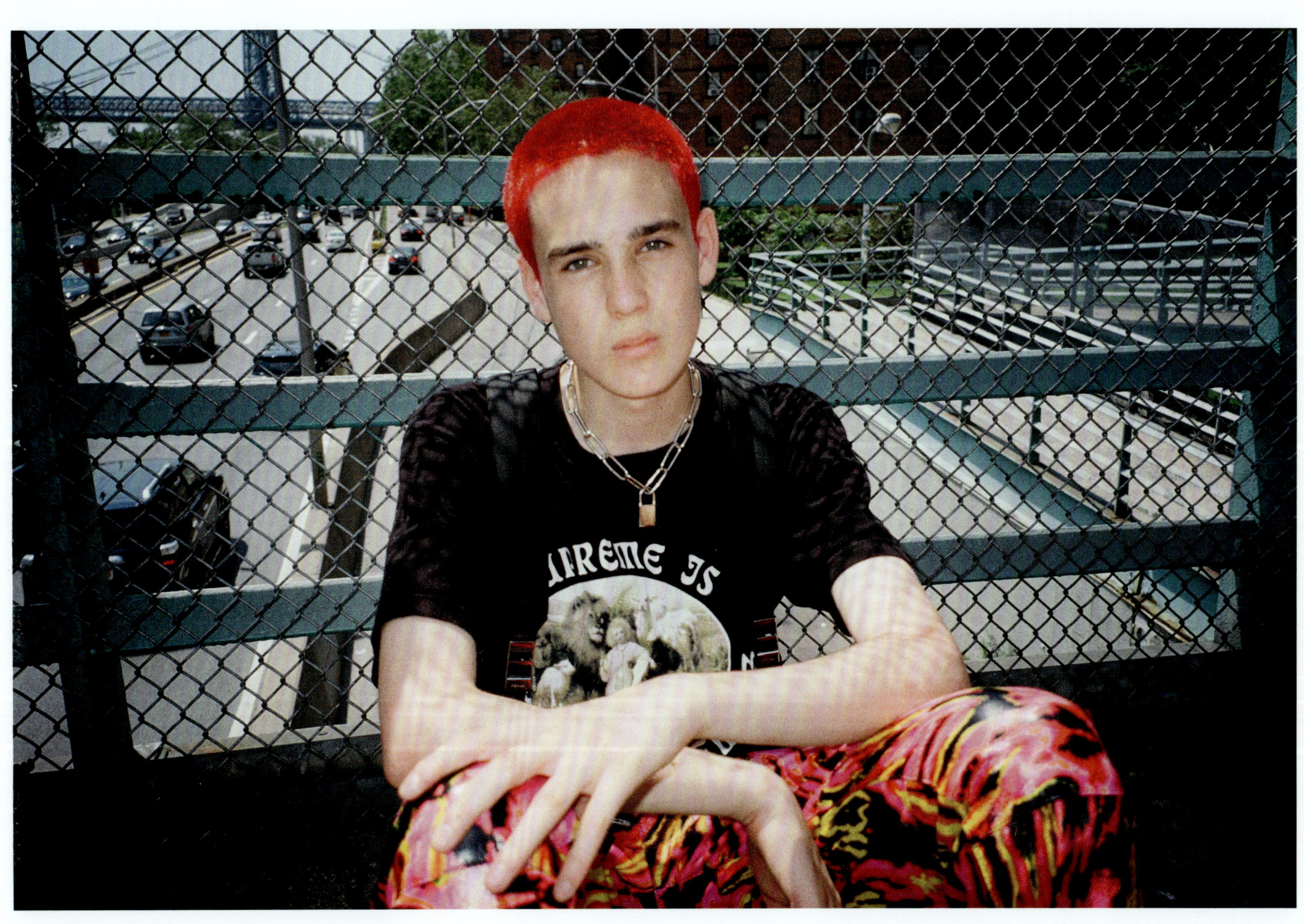

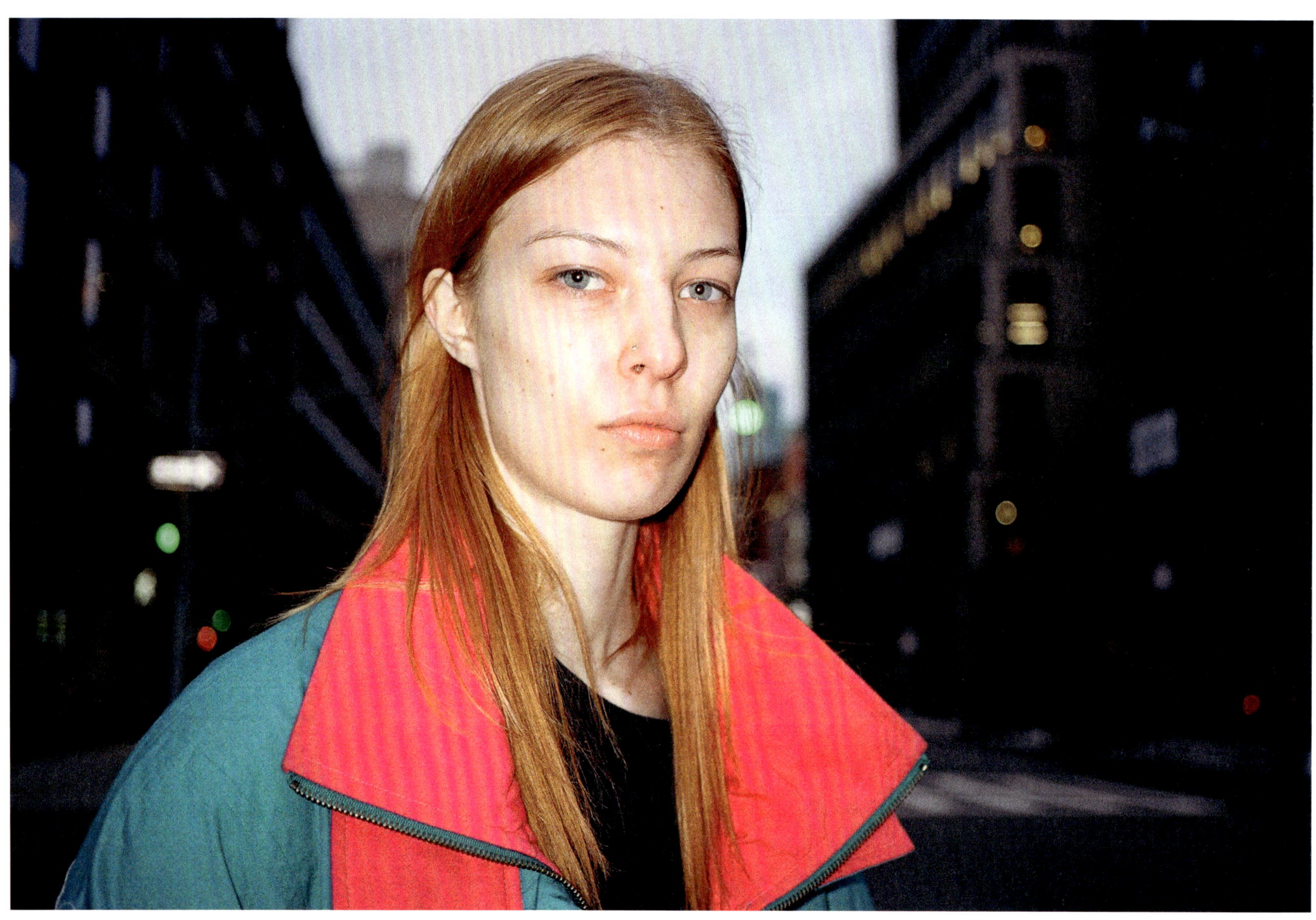

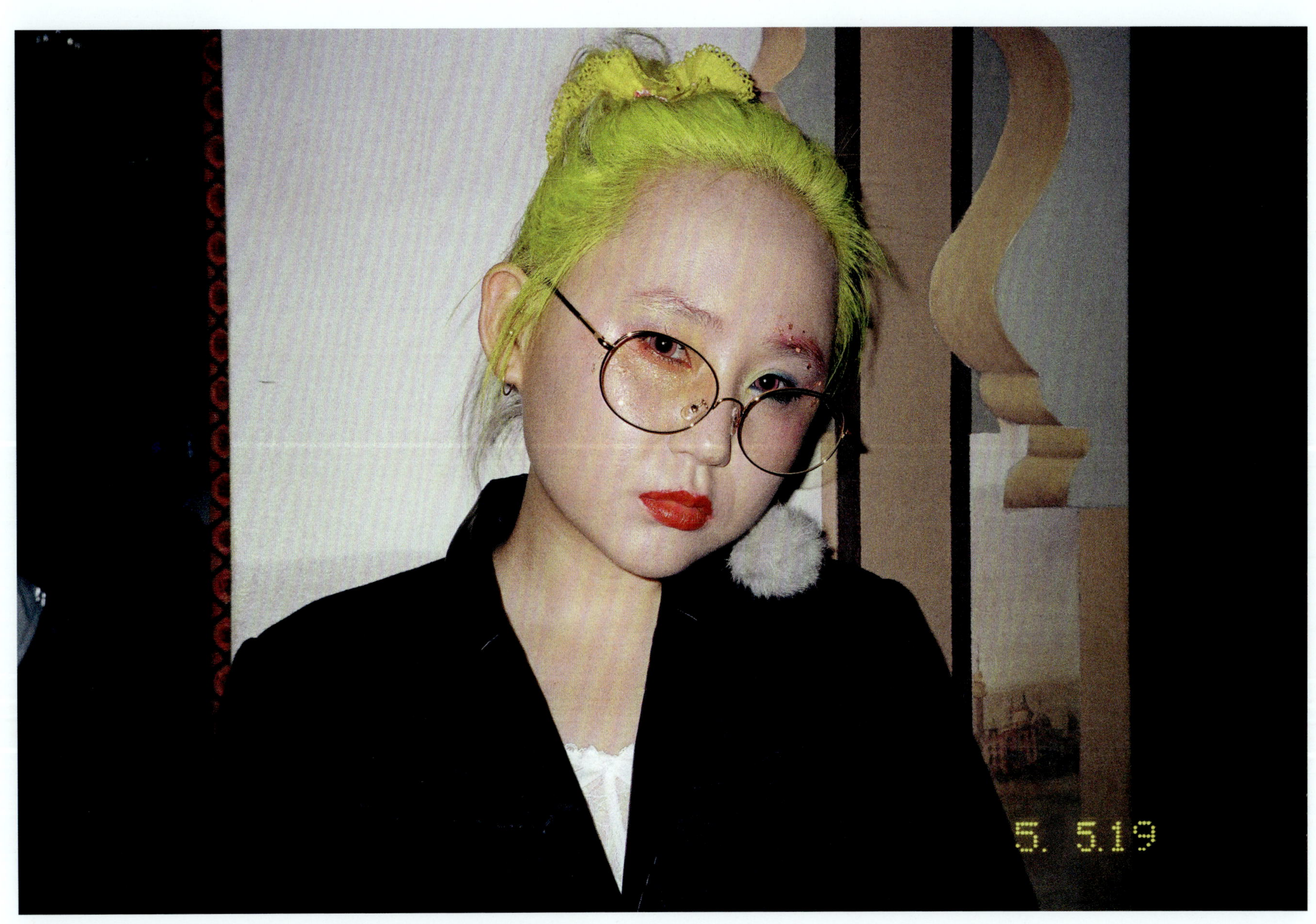
5. 5.19

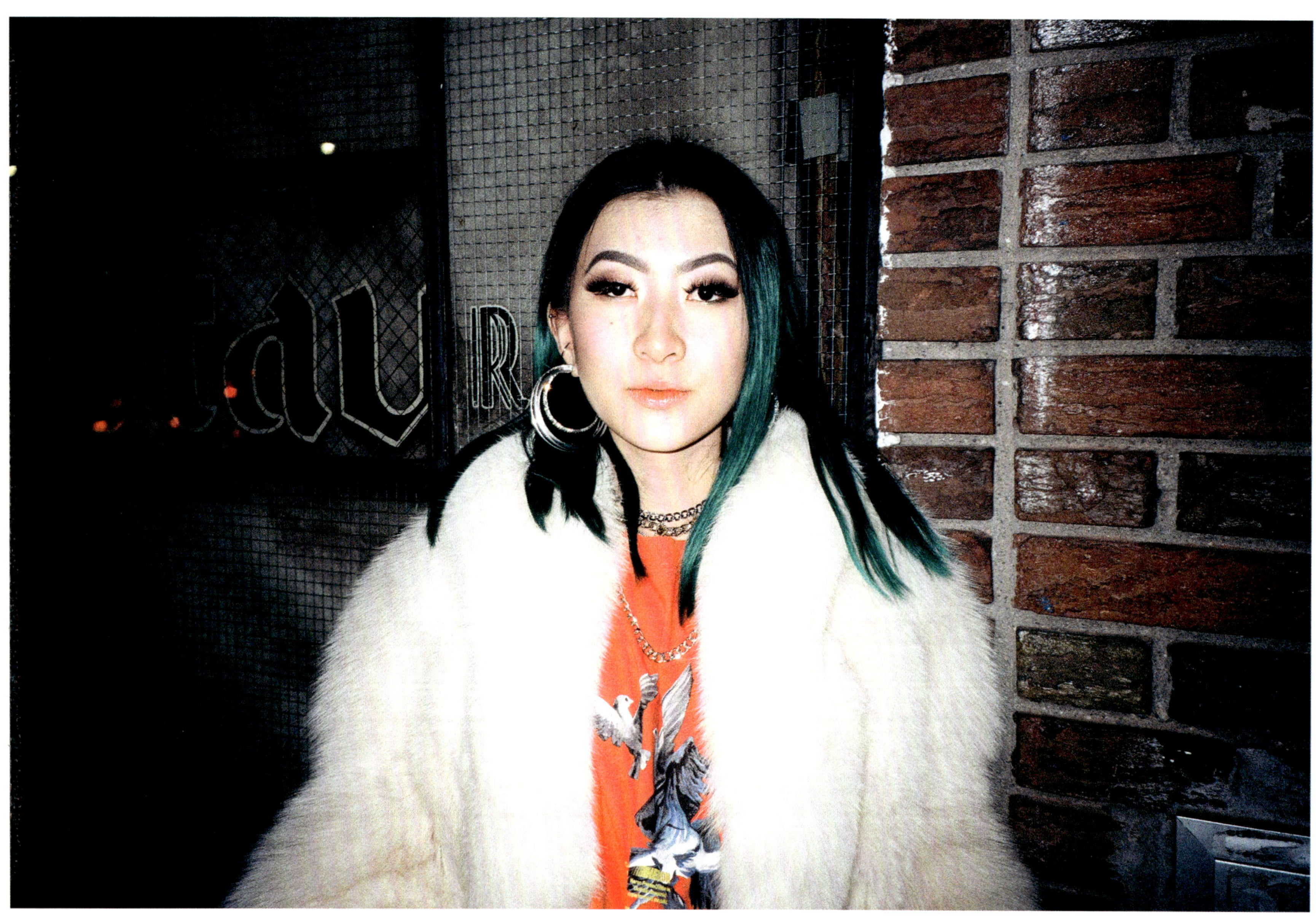

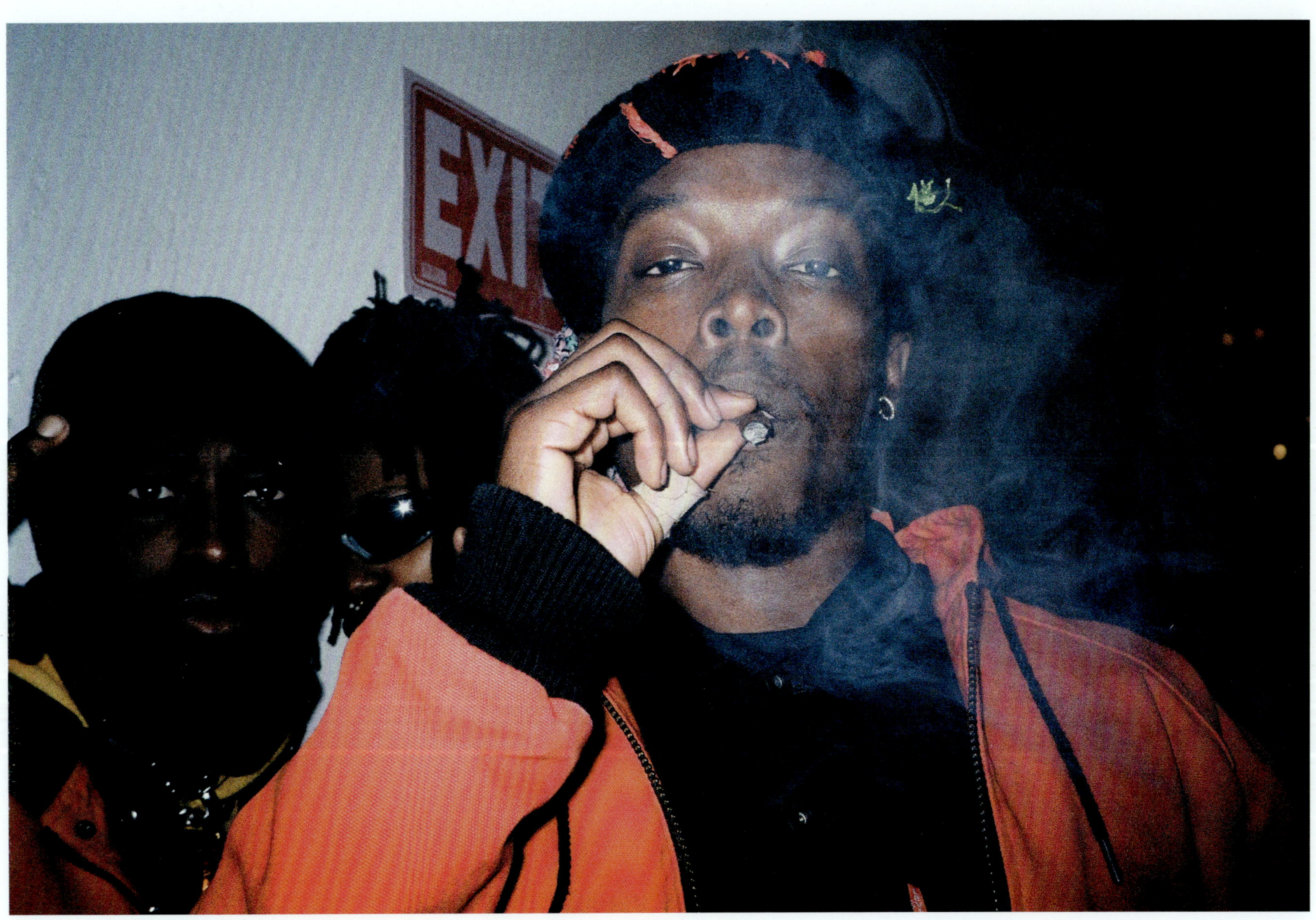

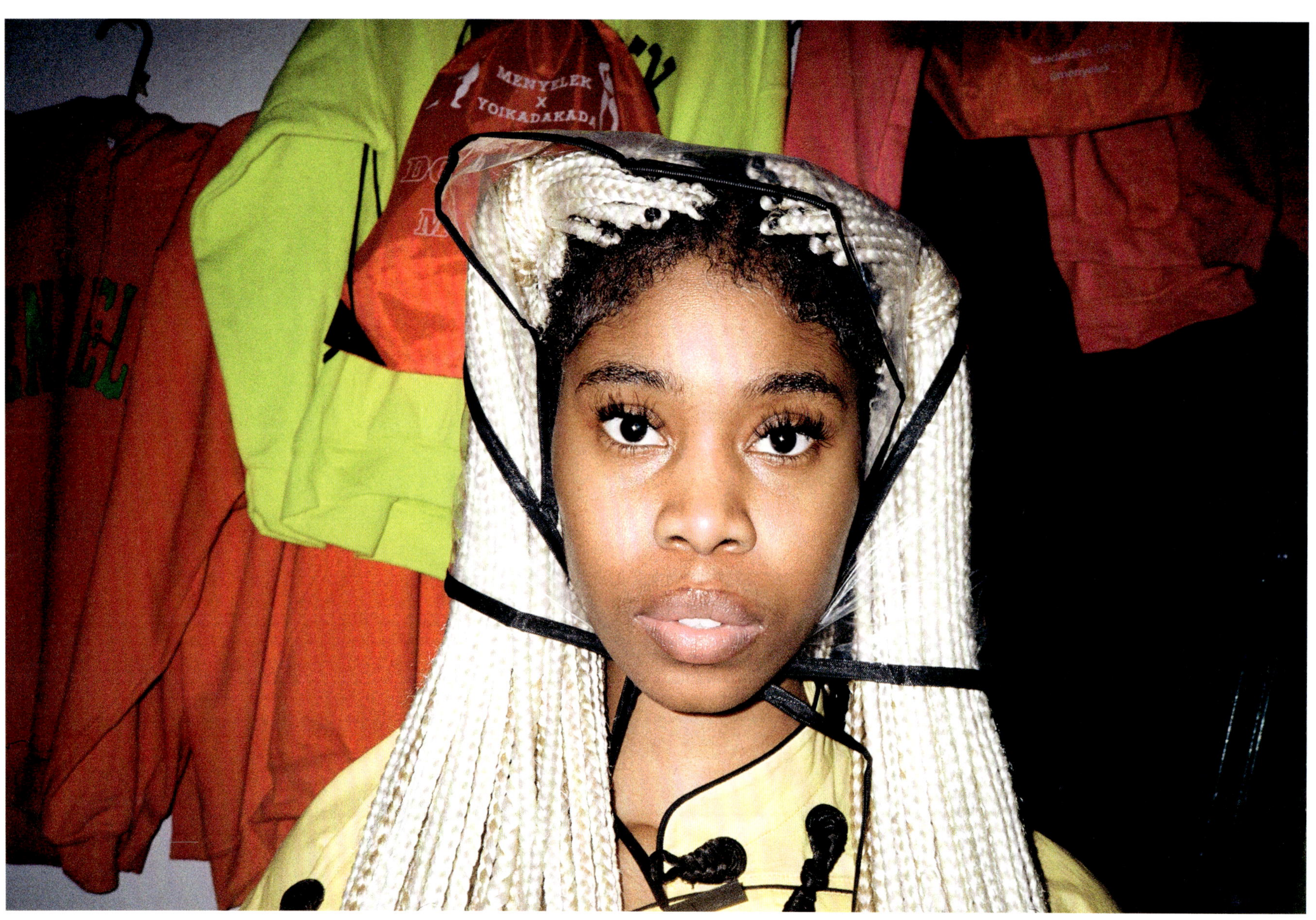
MENYELEK
X
YOIKADAKADA

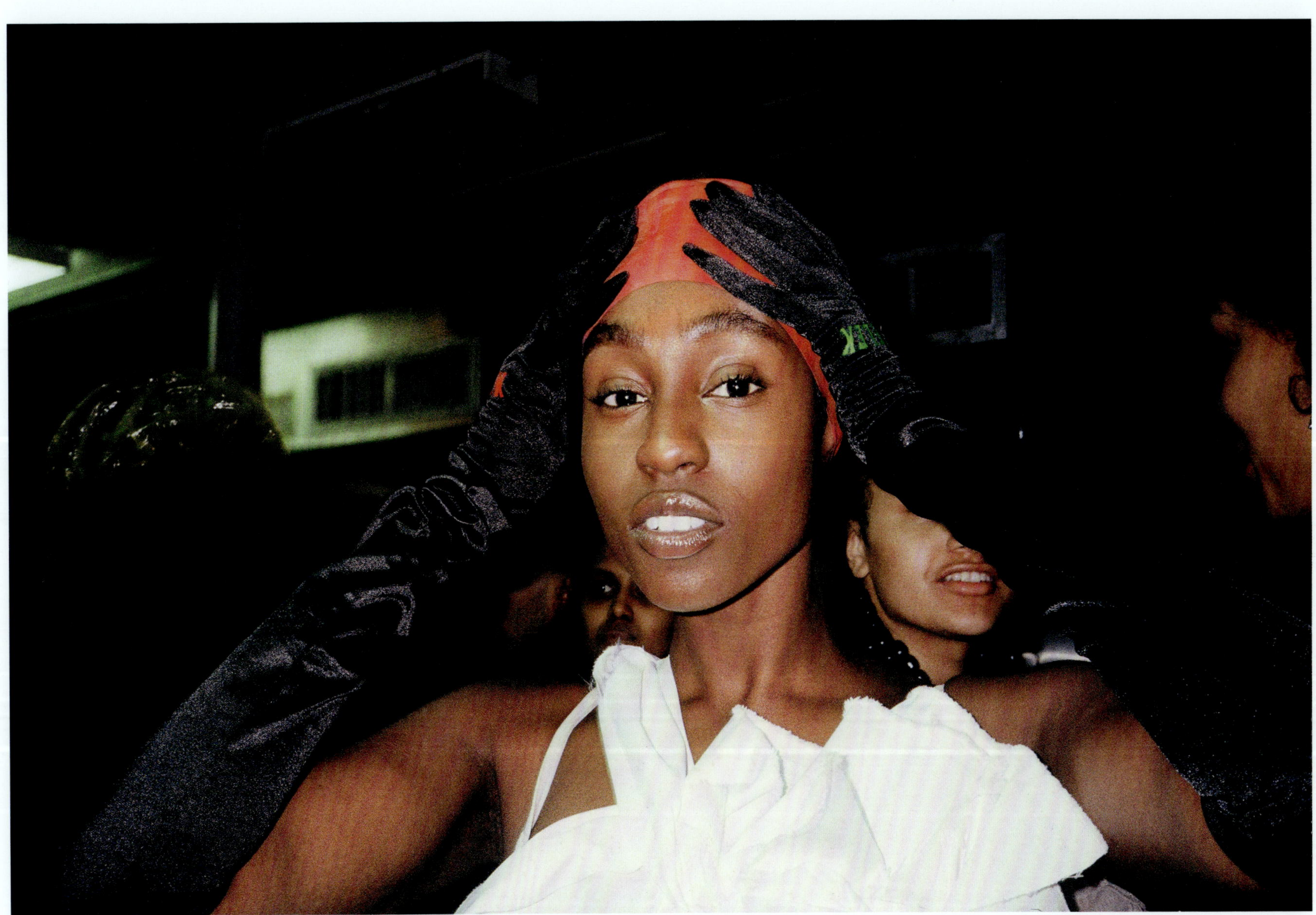

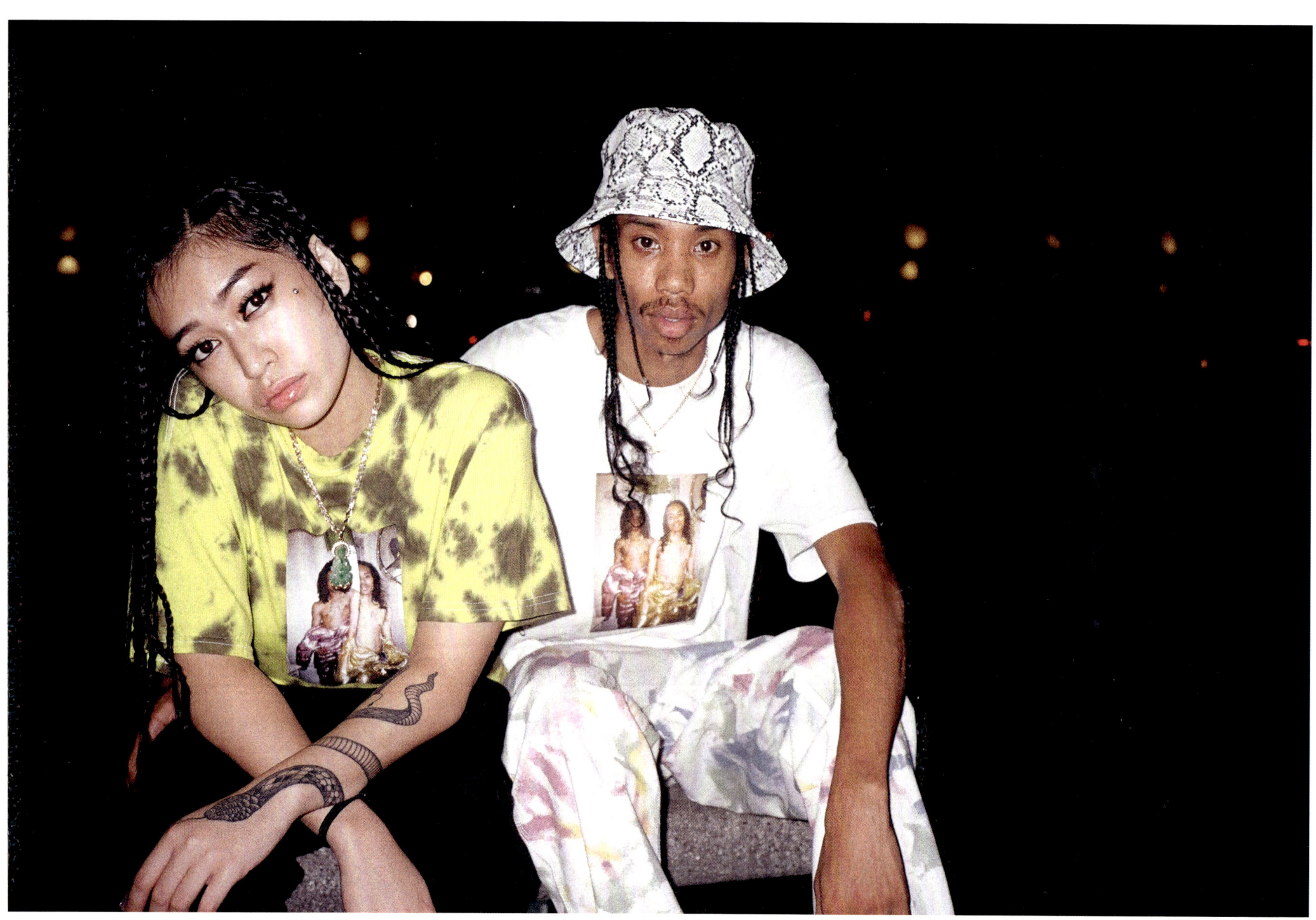

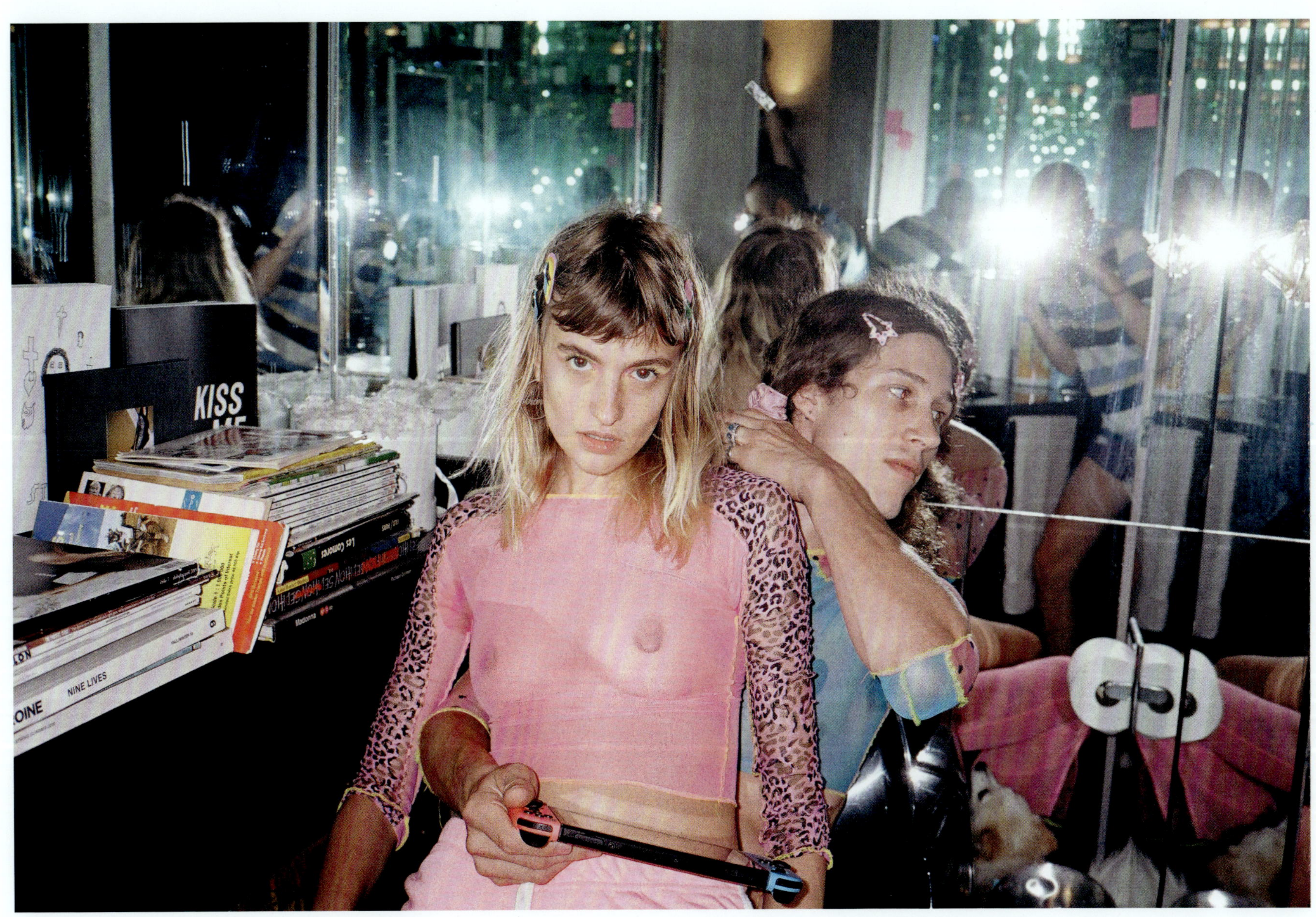
KISS
NINE LIVES

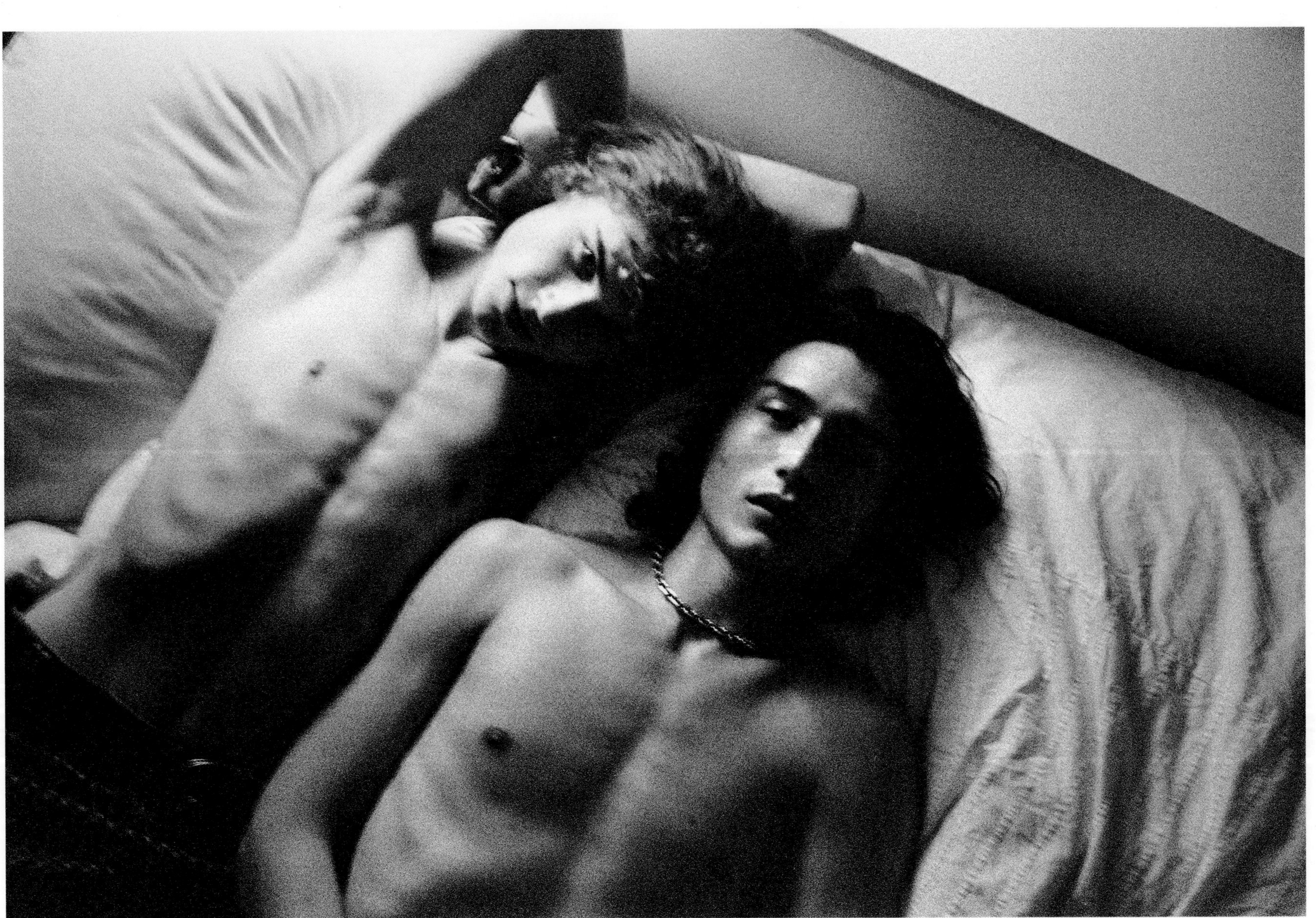

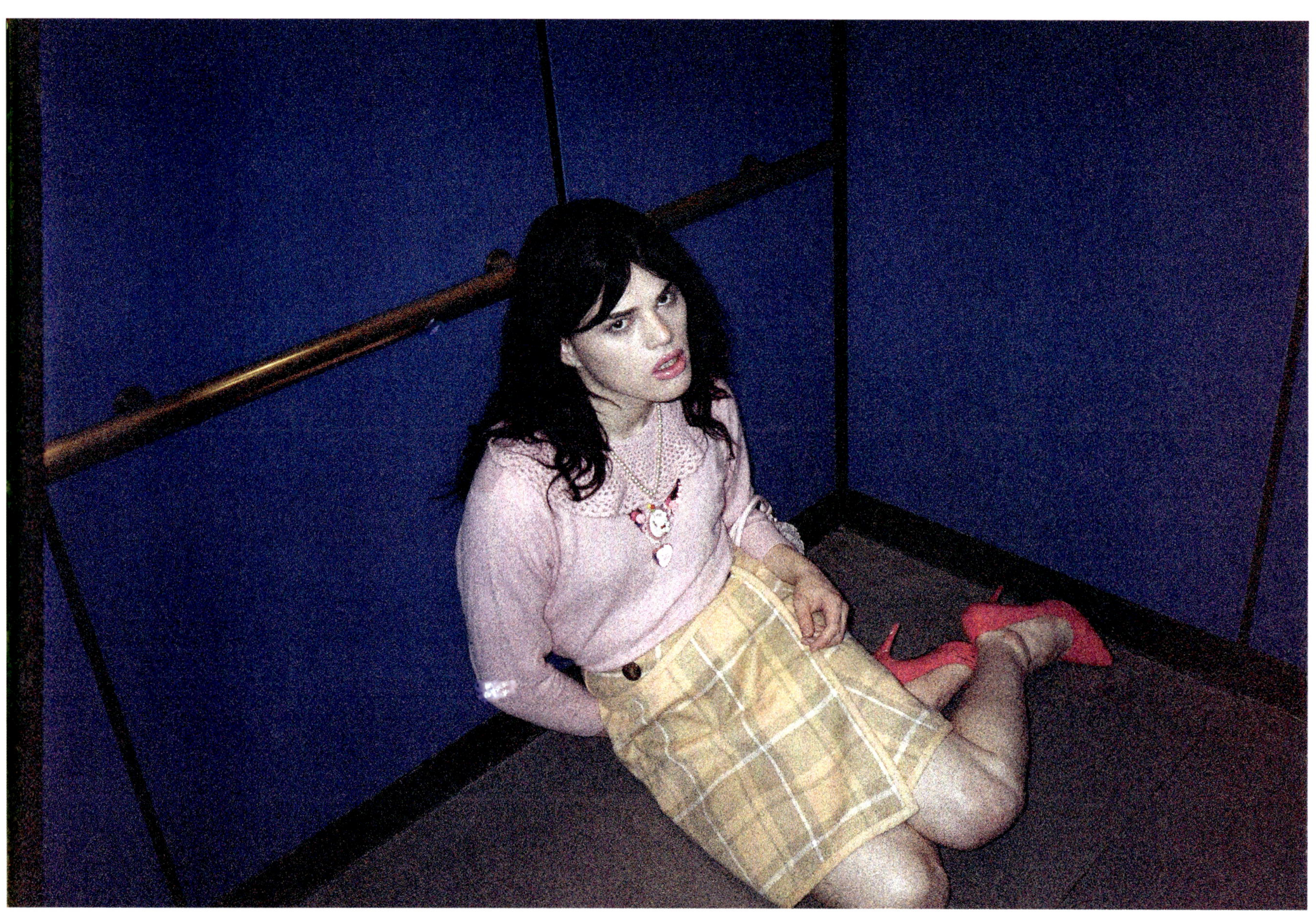

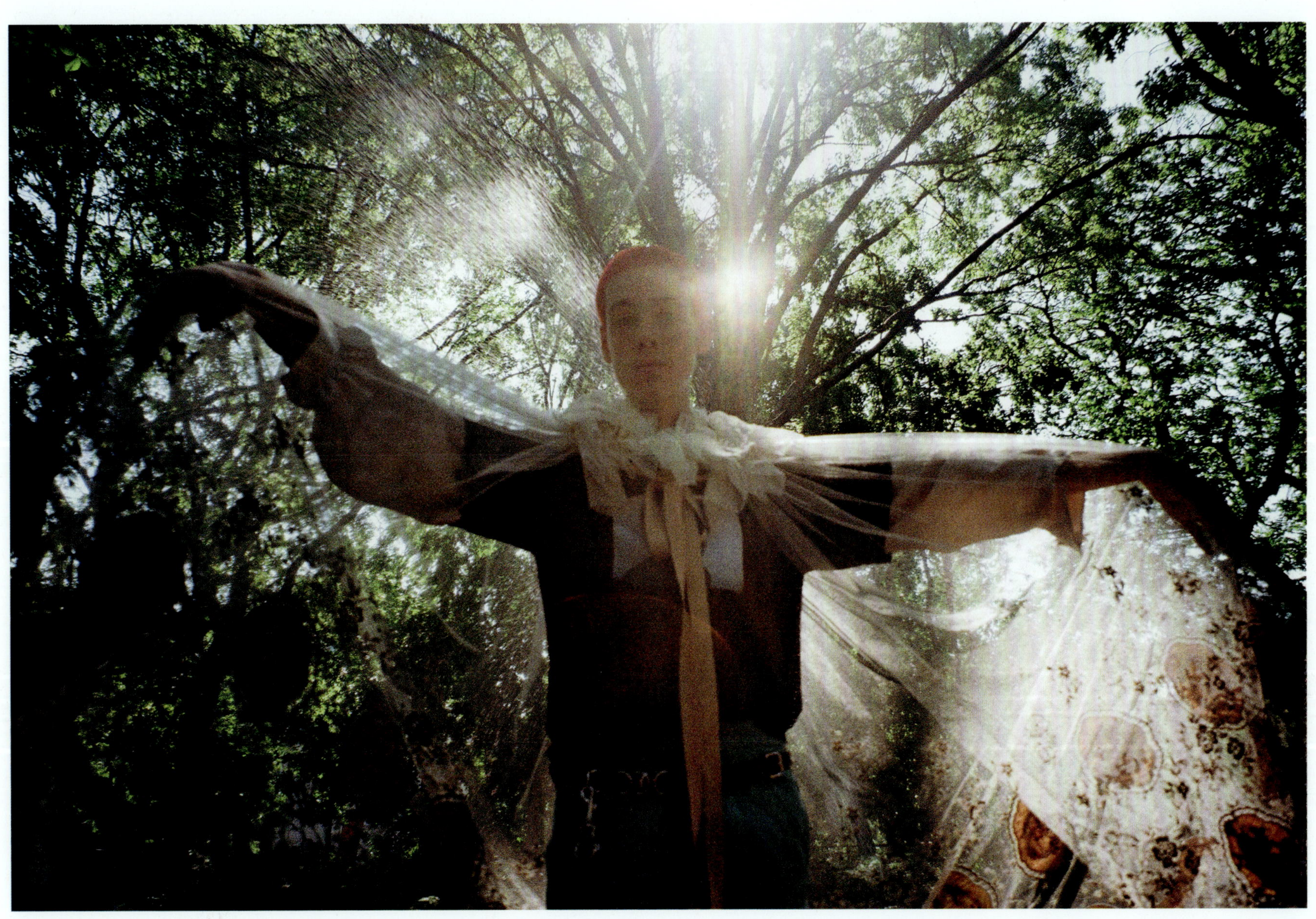

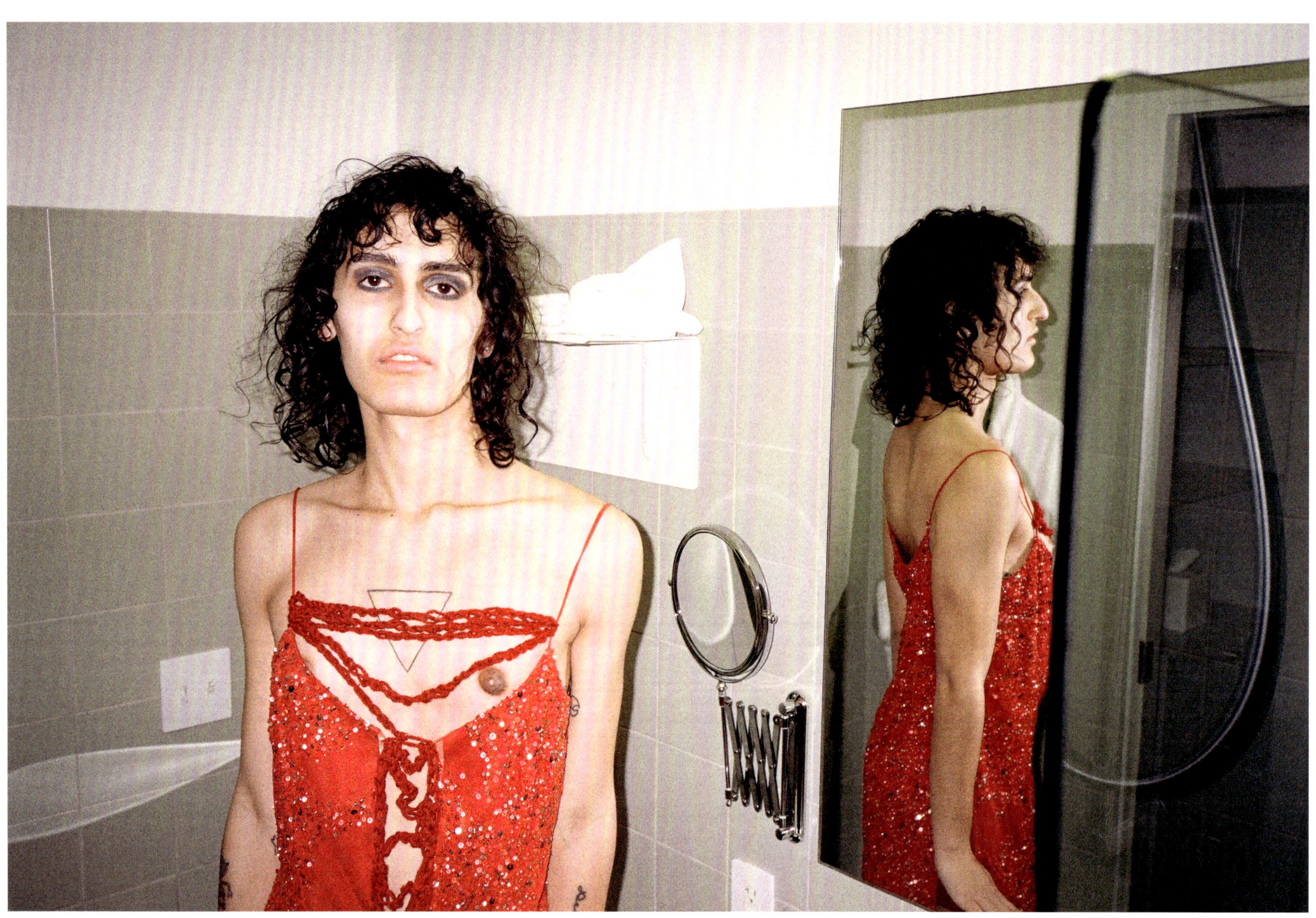

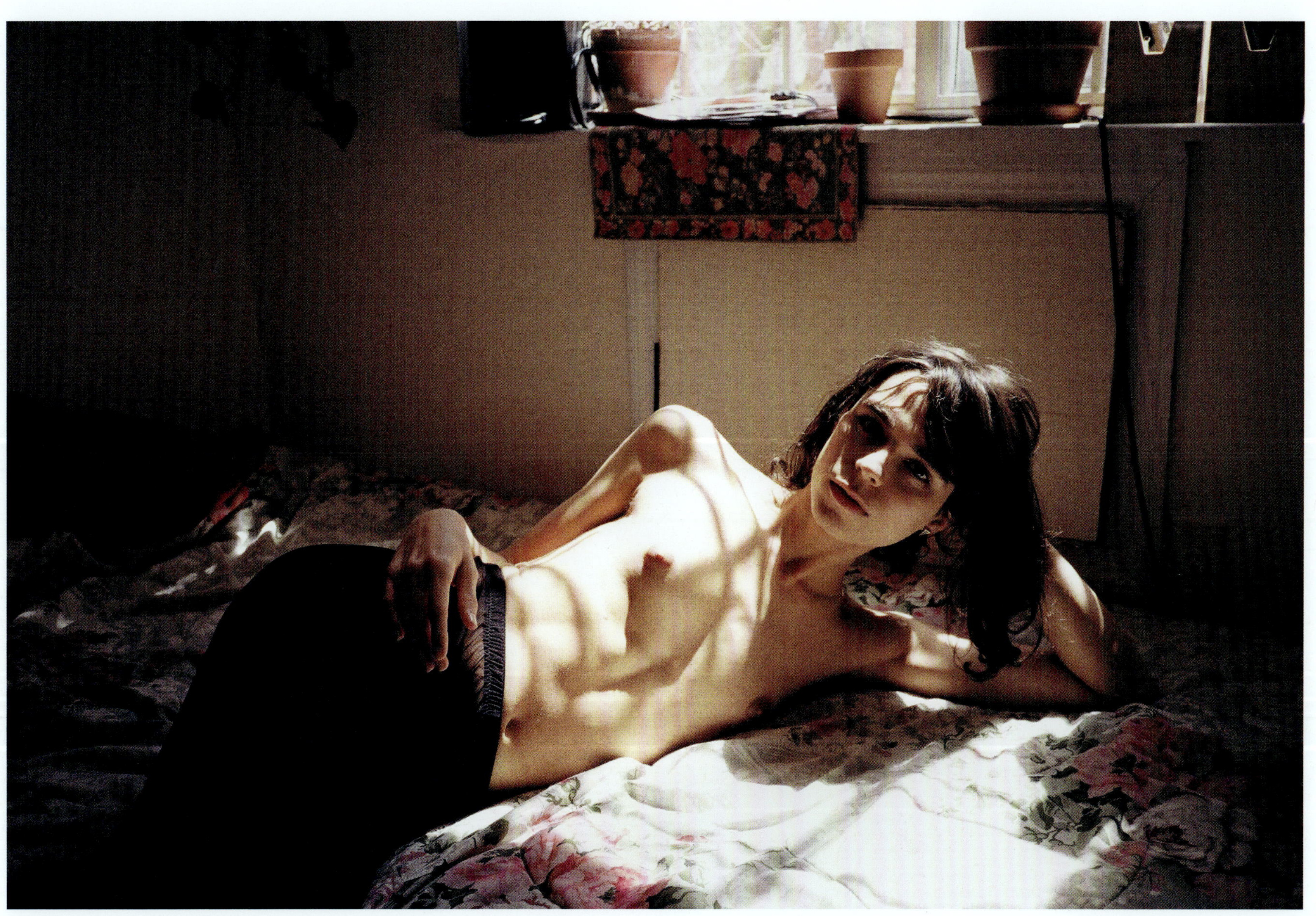

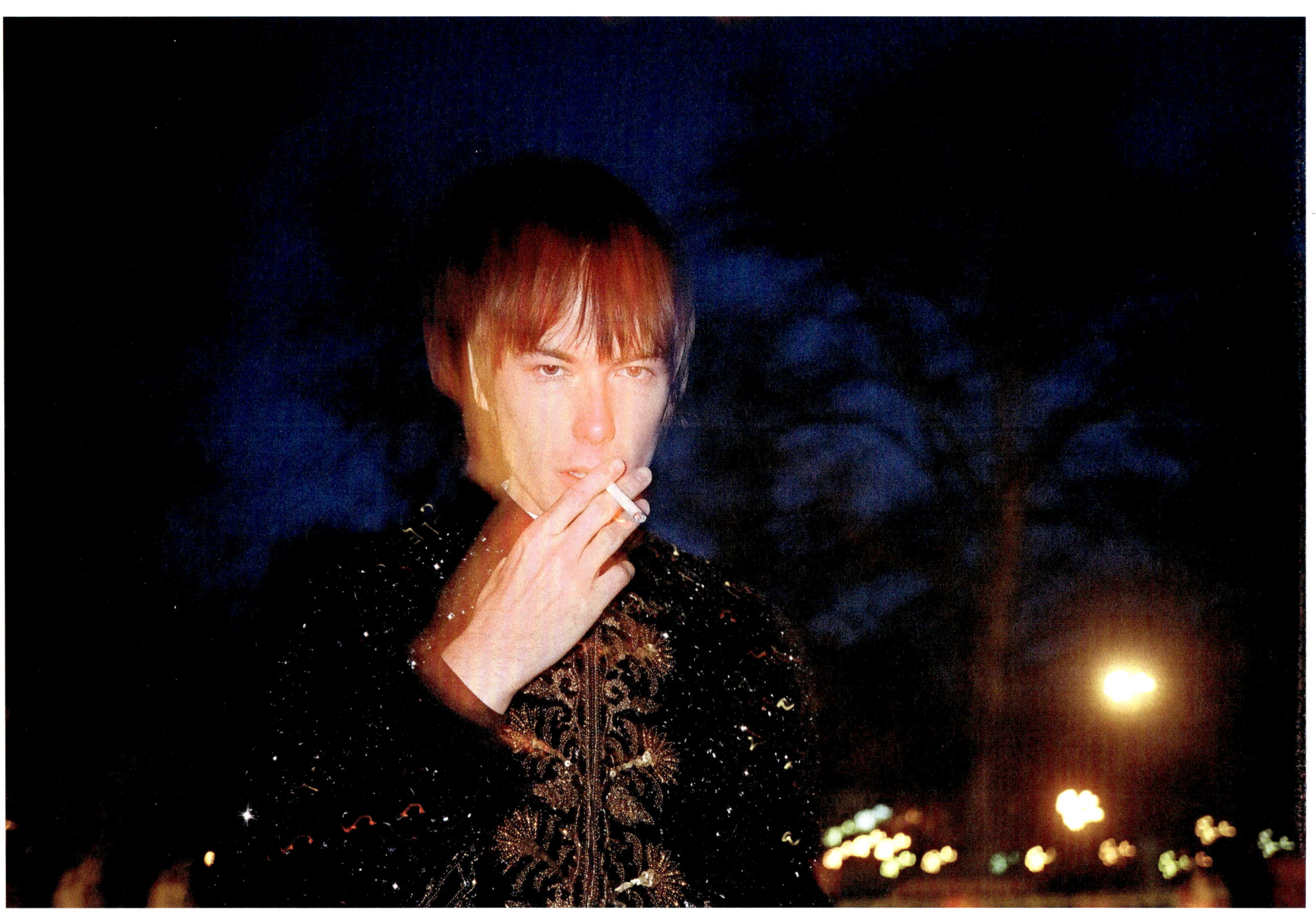

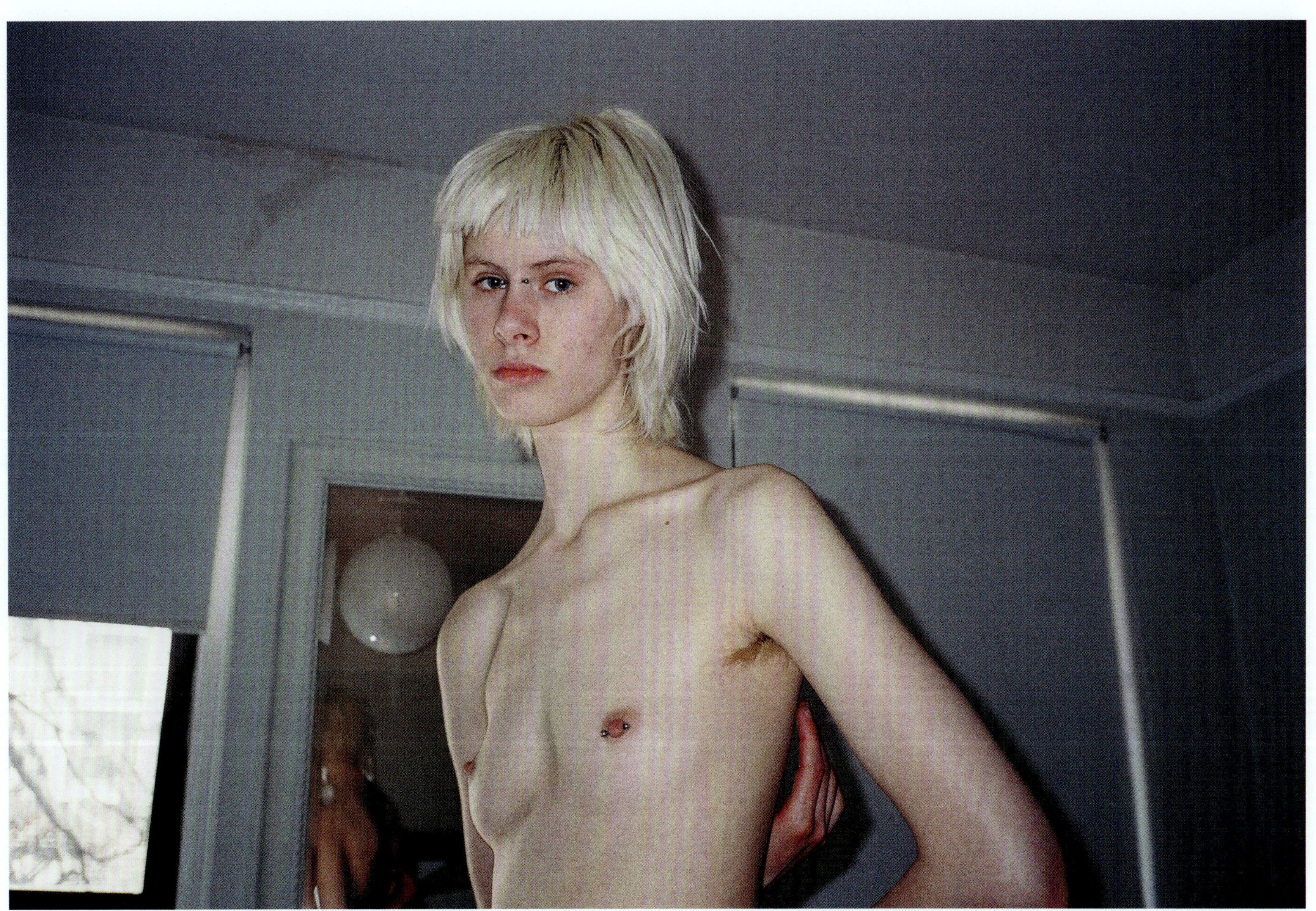

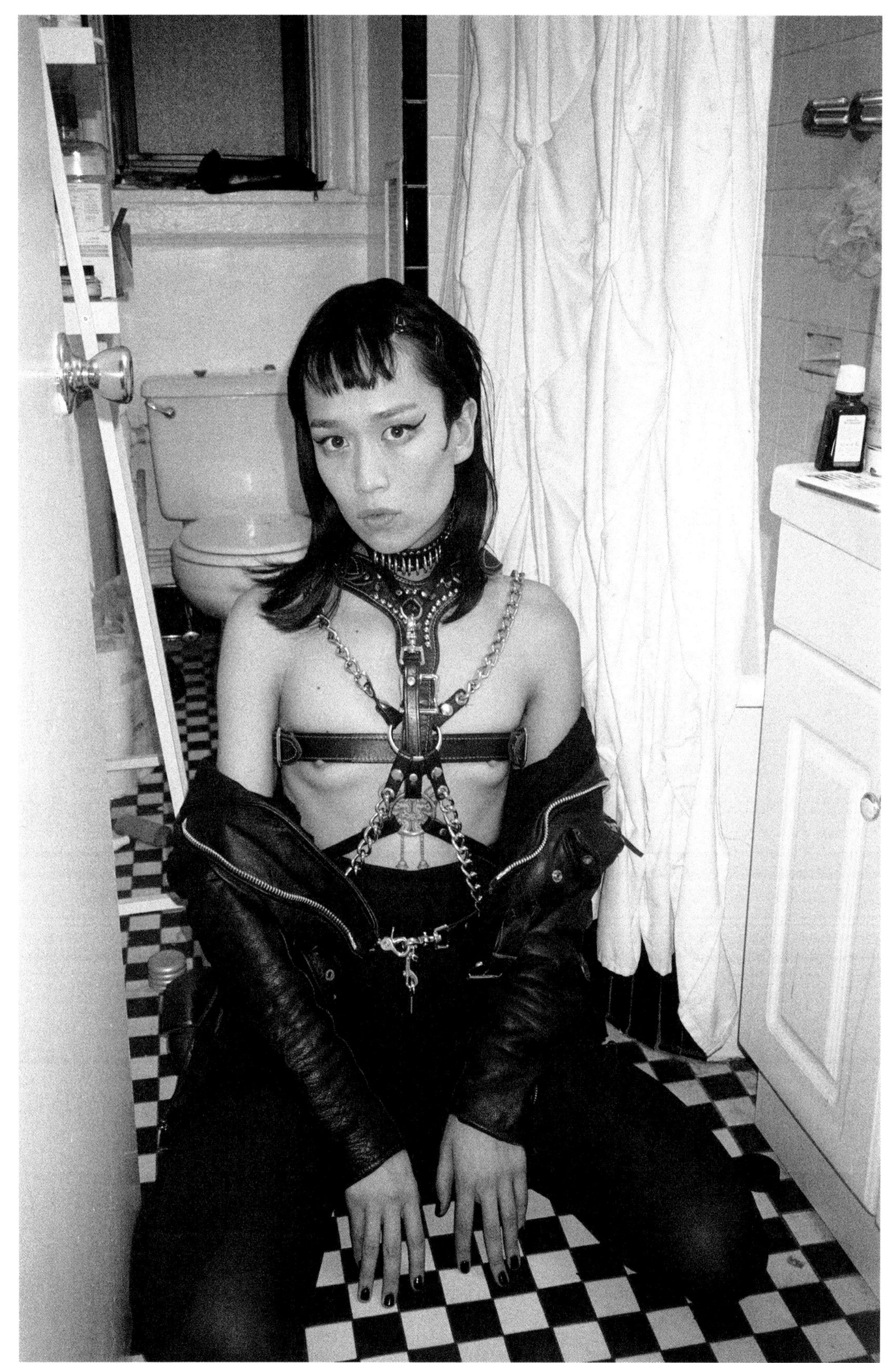

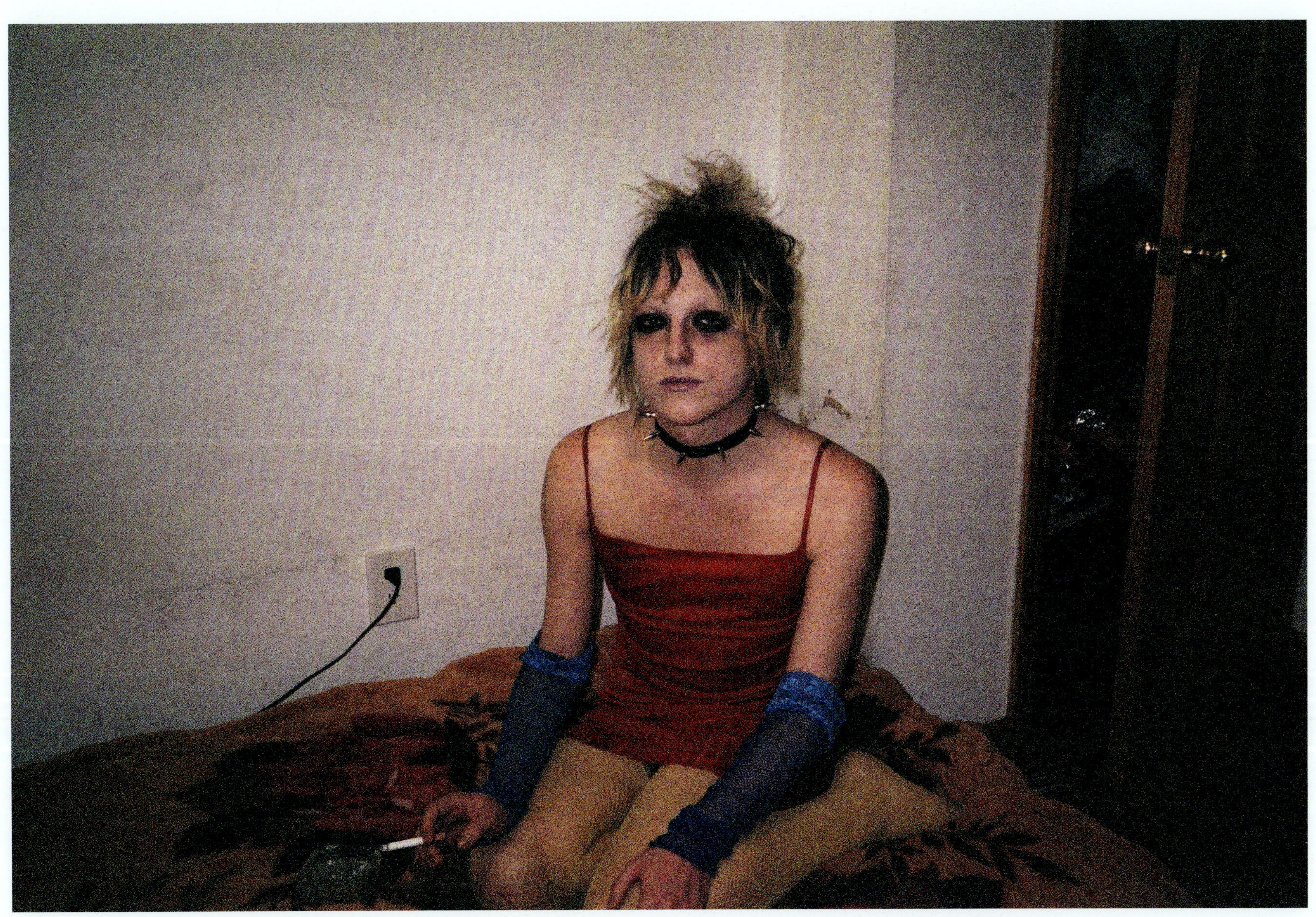

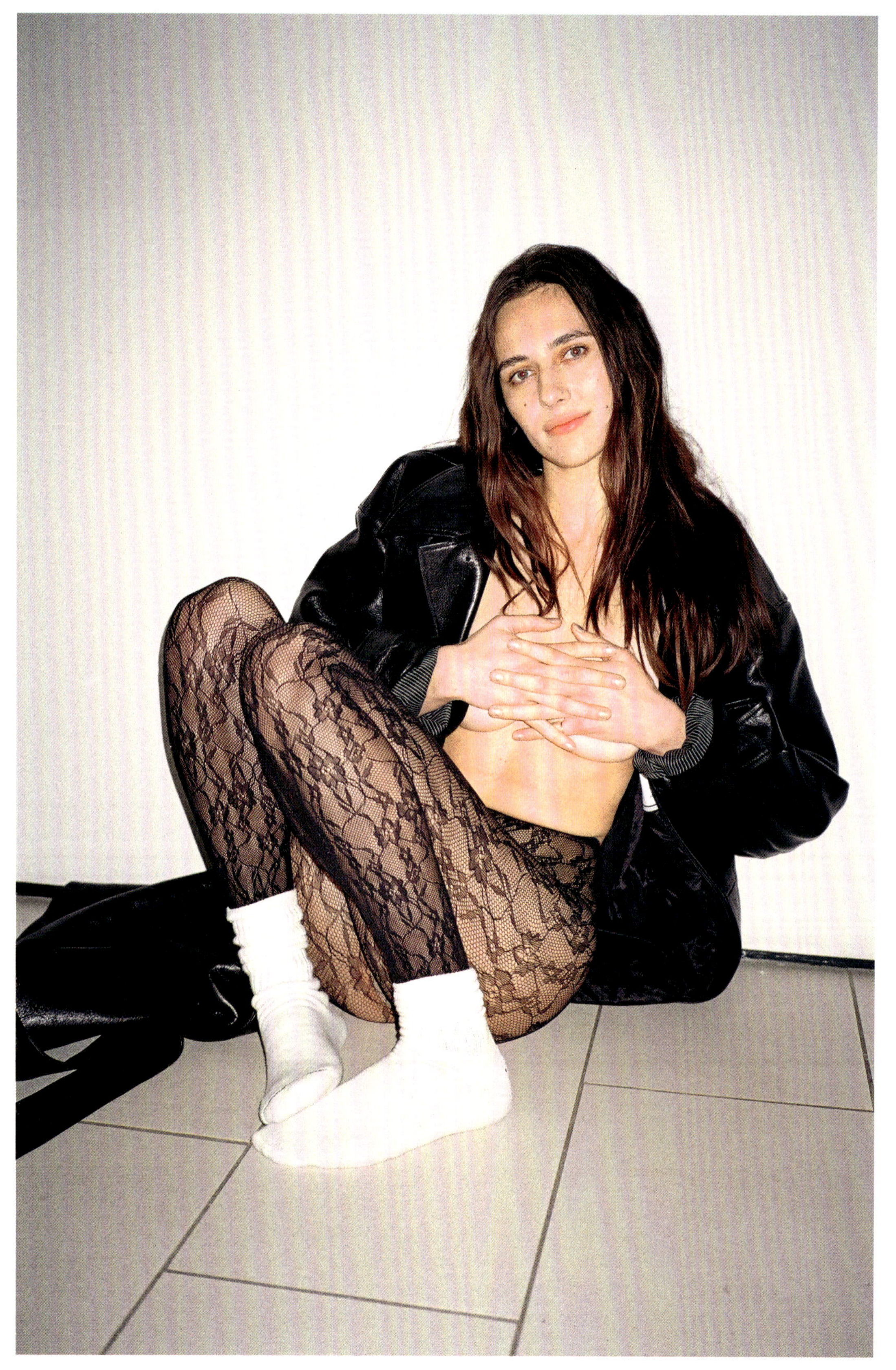

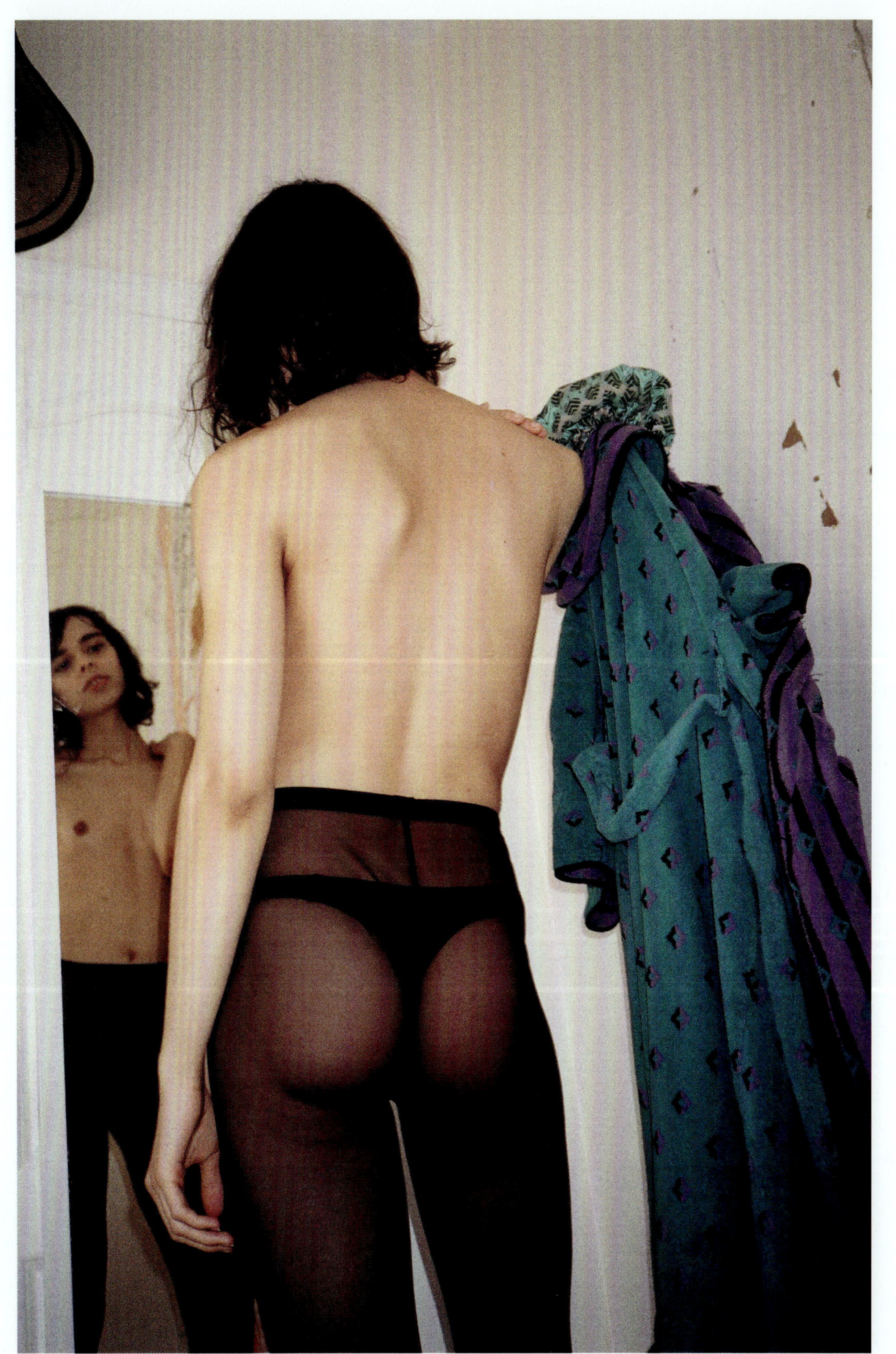

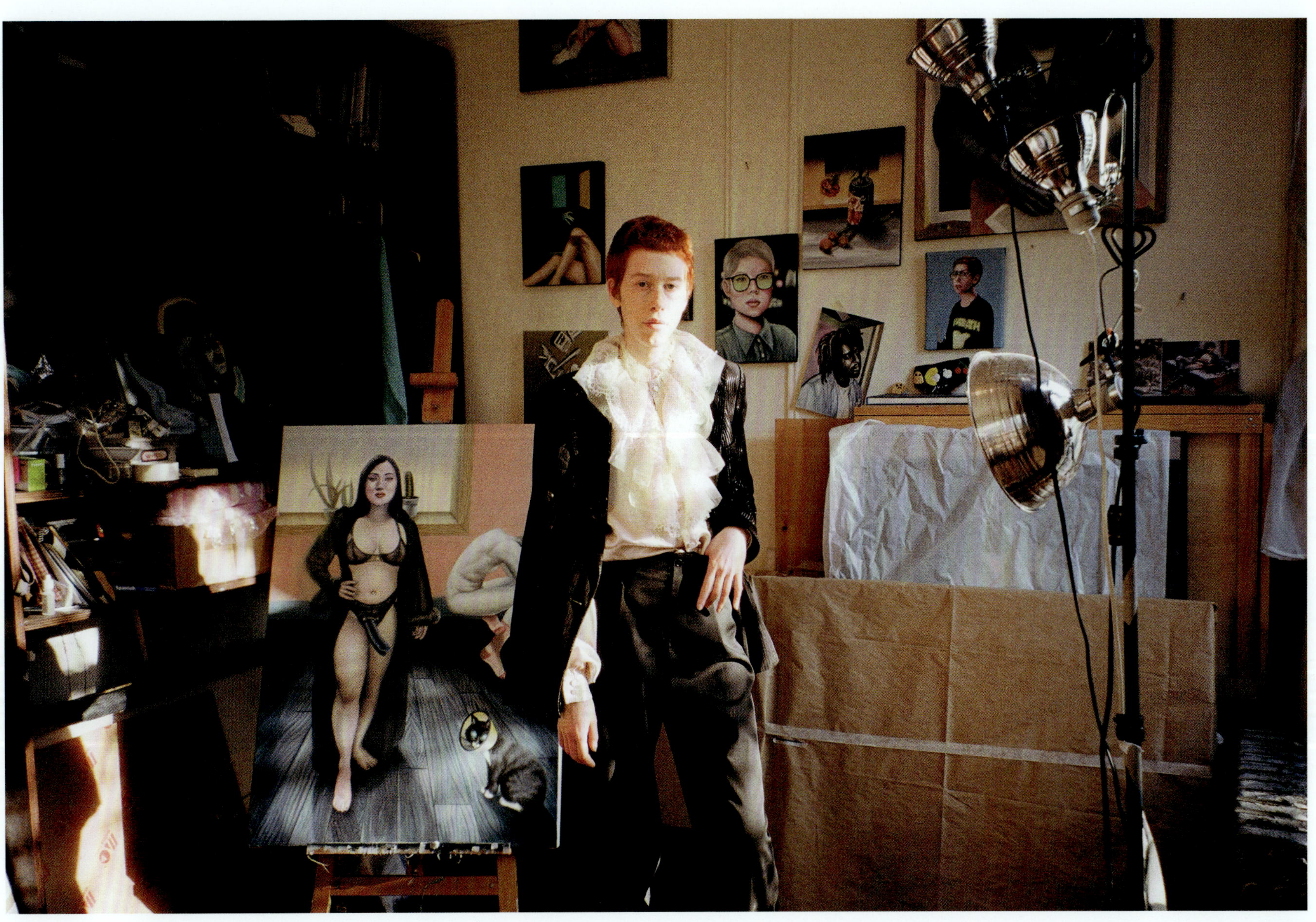

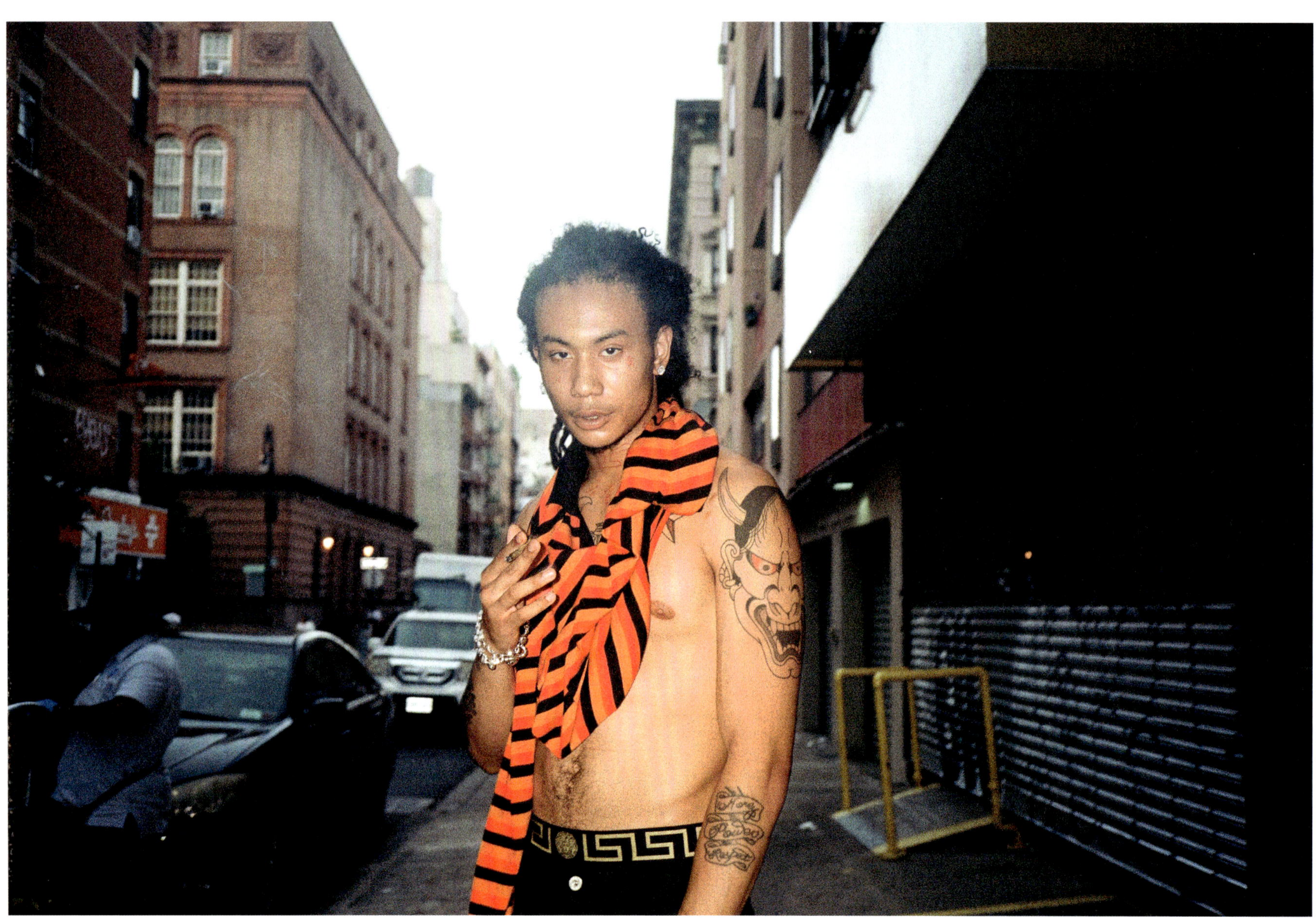

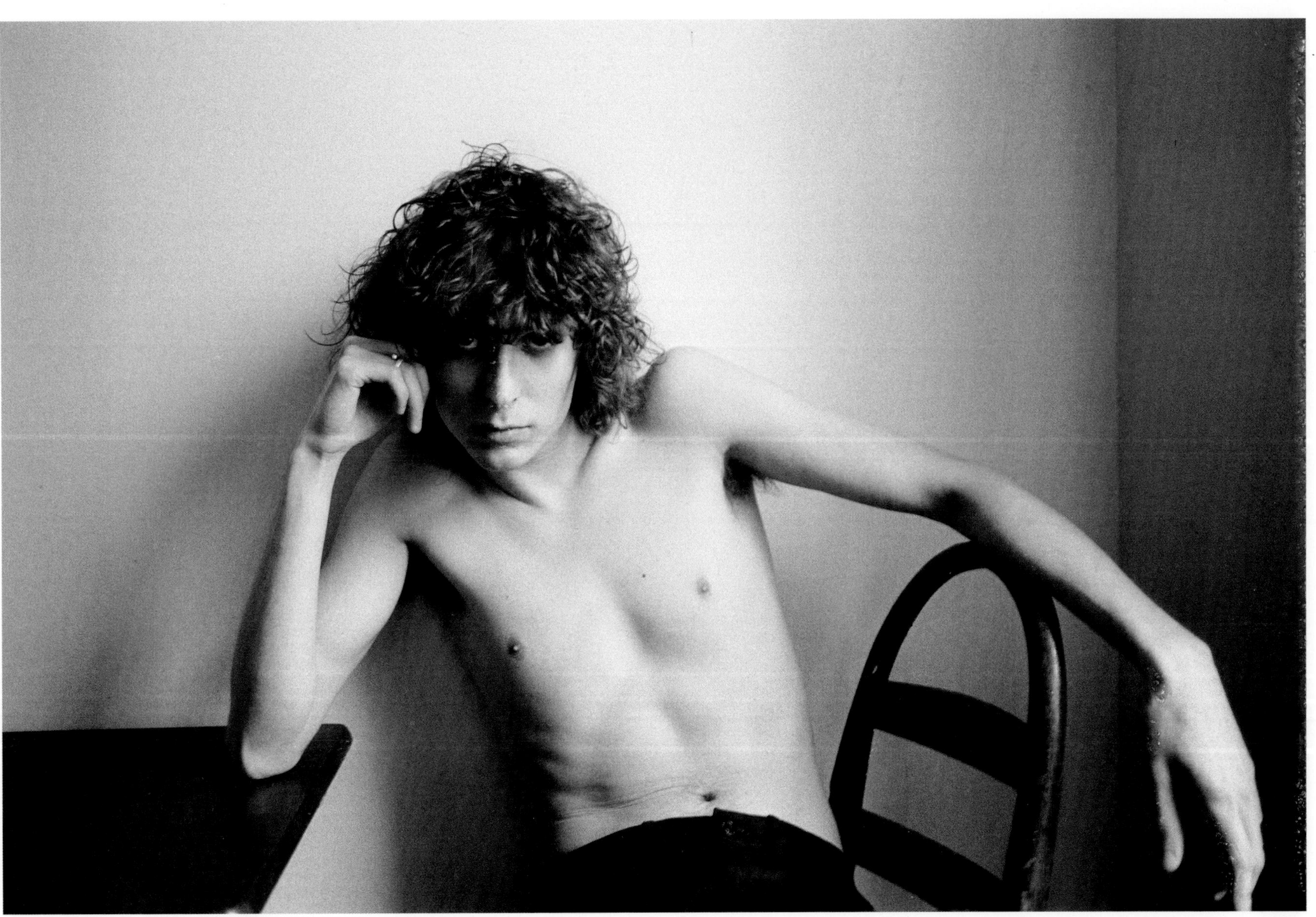

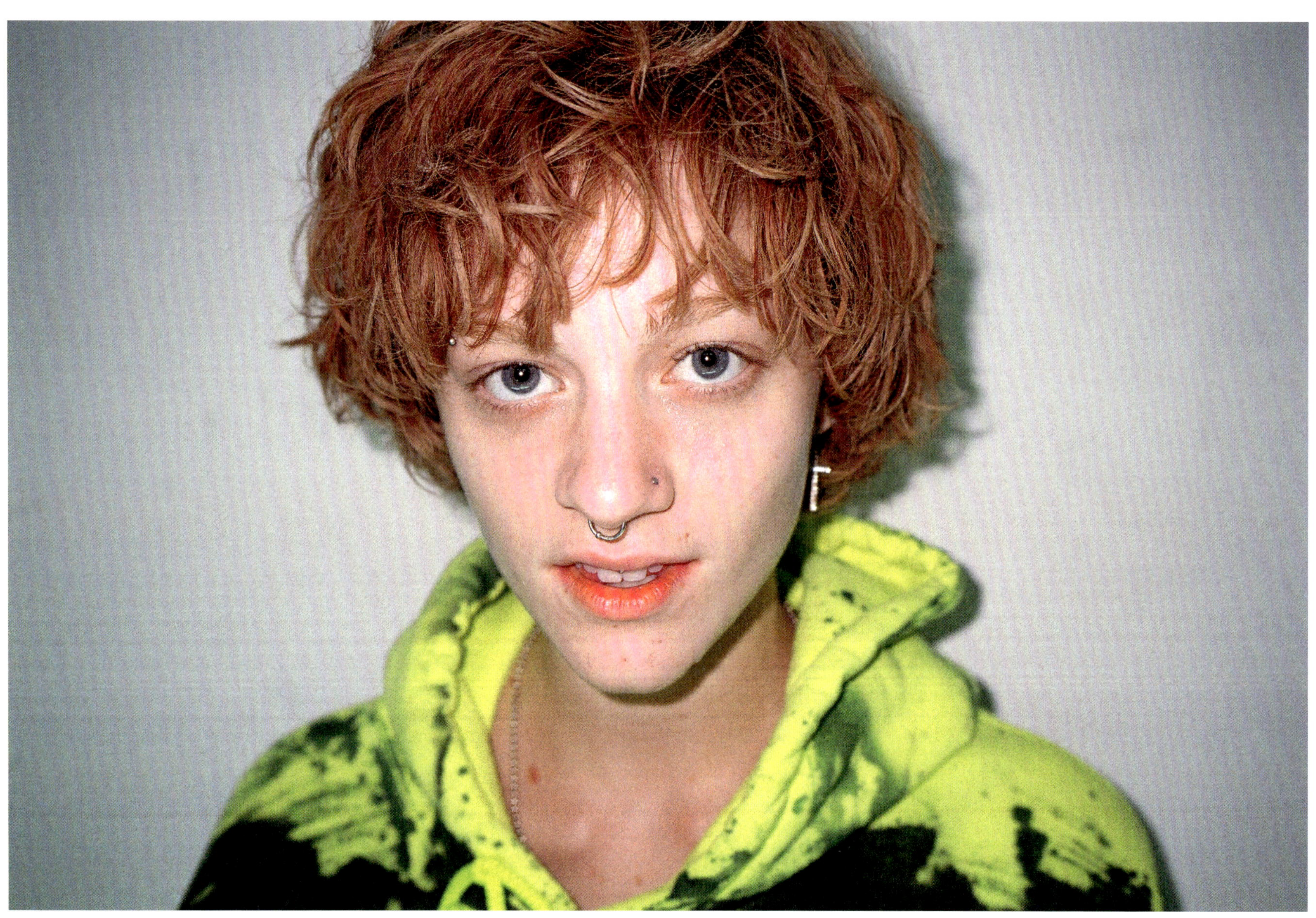

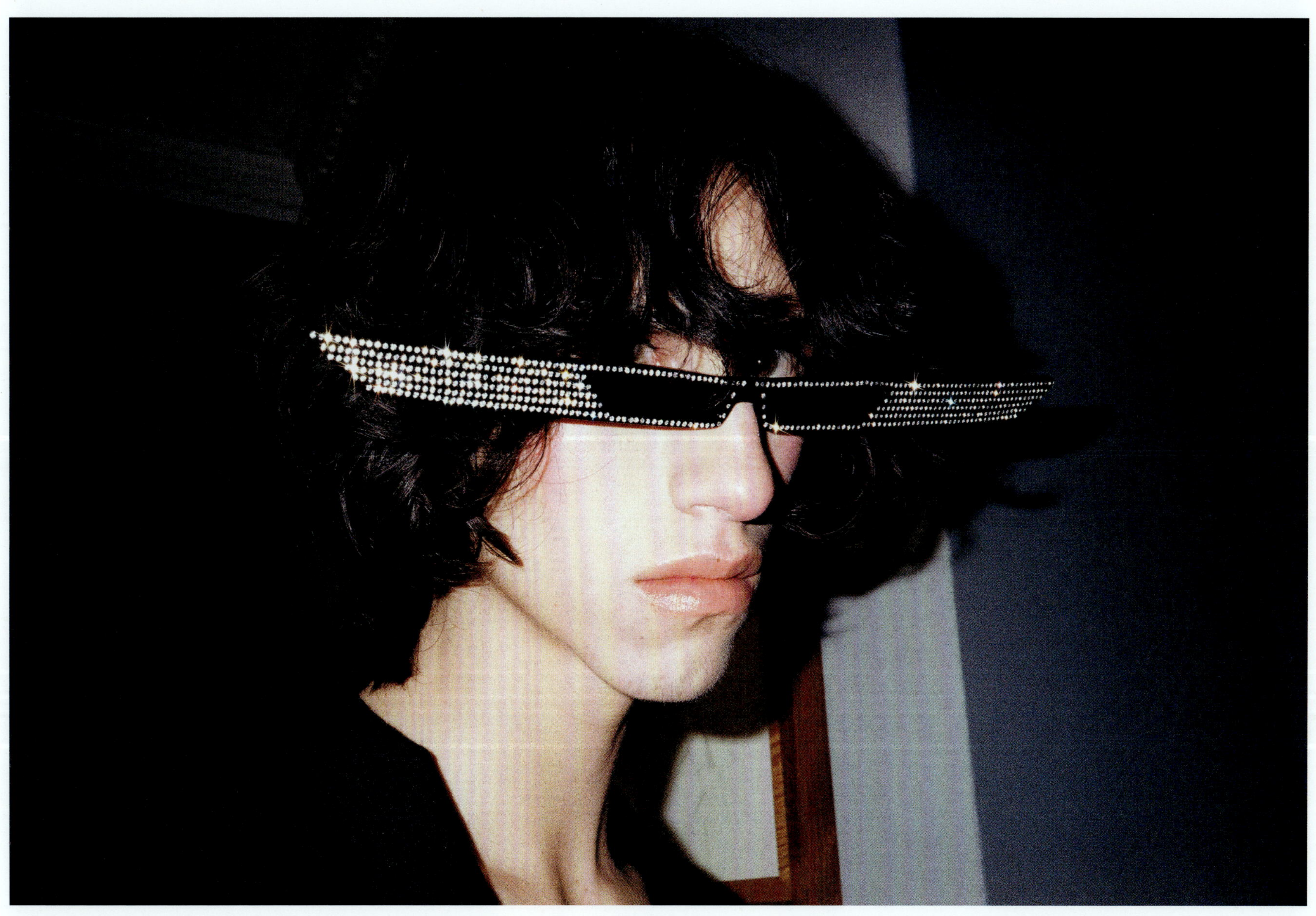

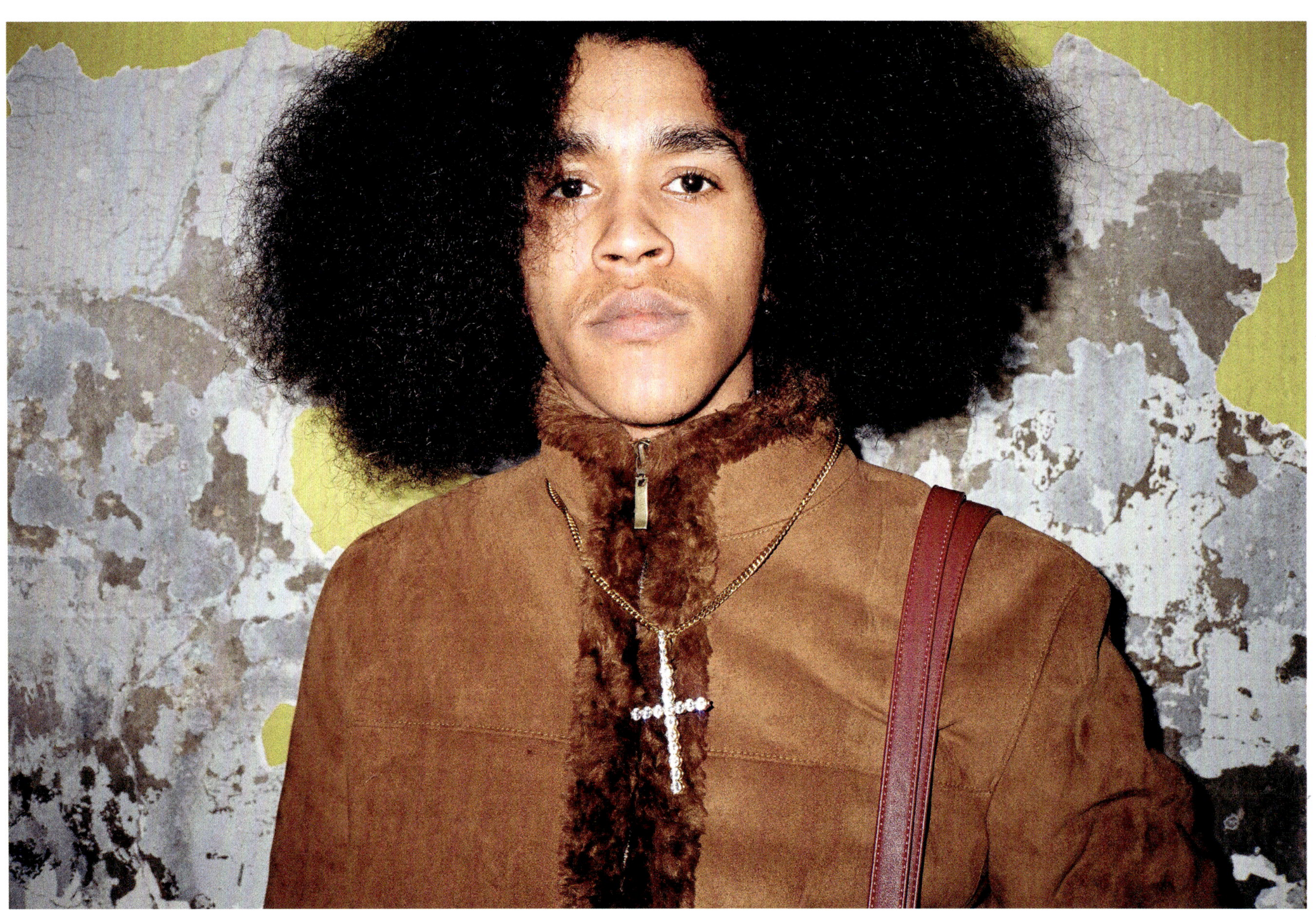

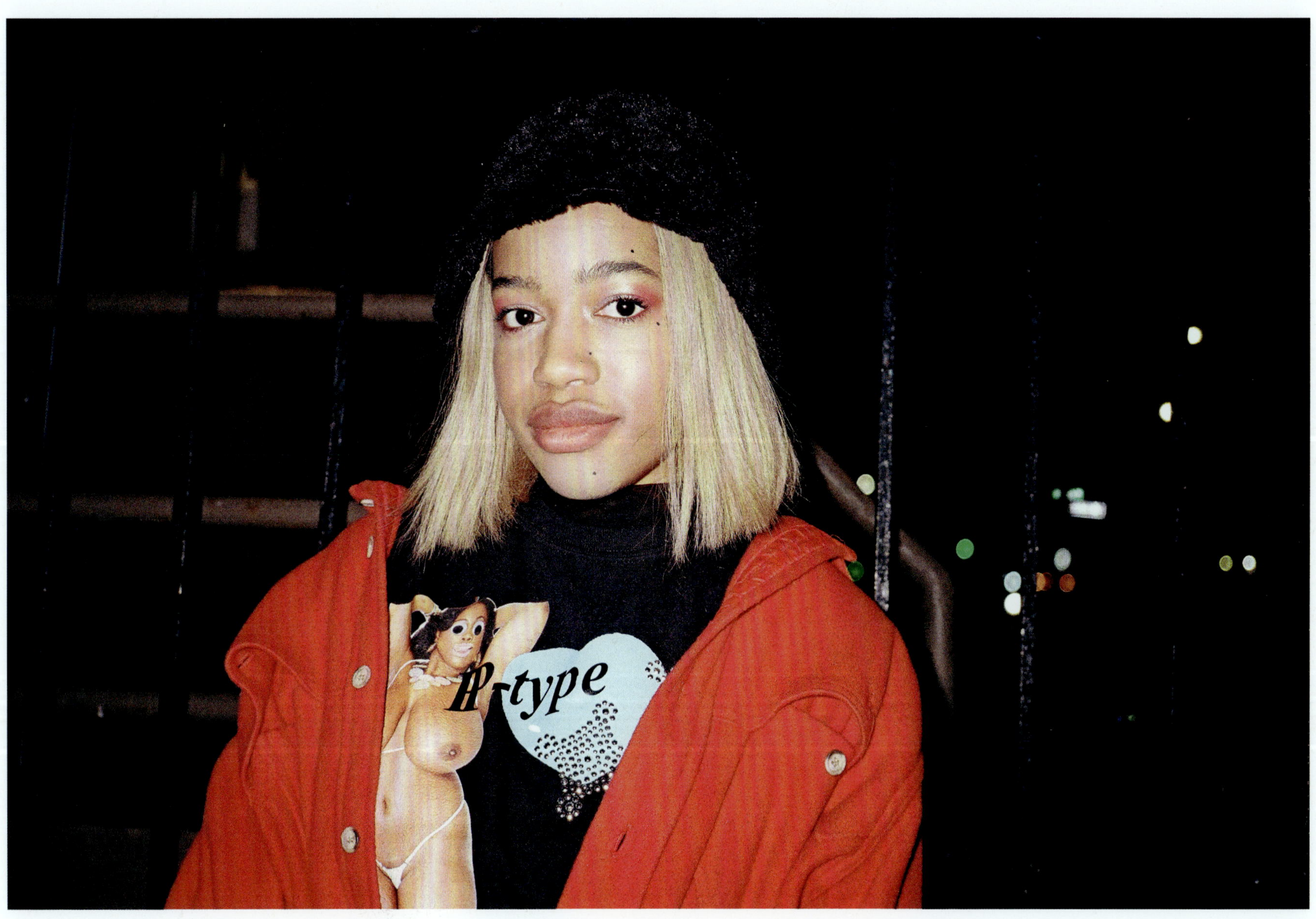
P-type

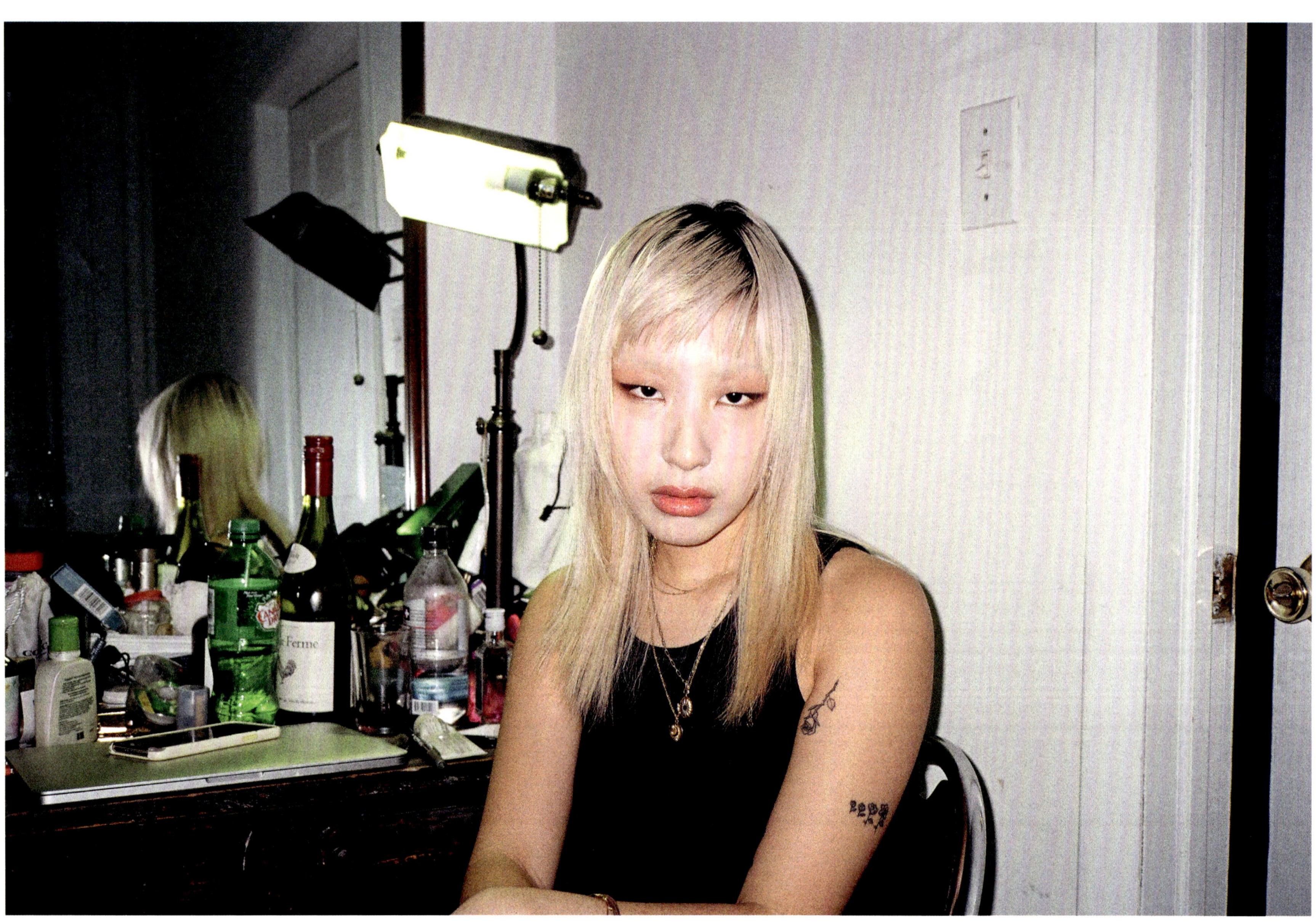

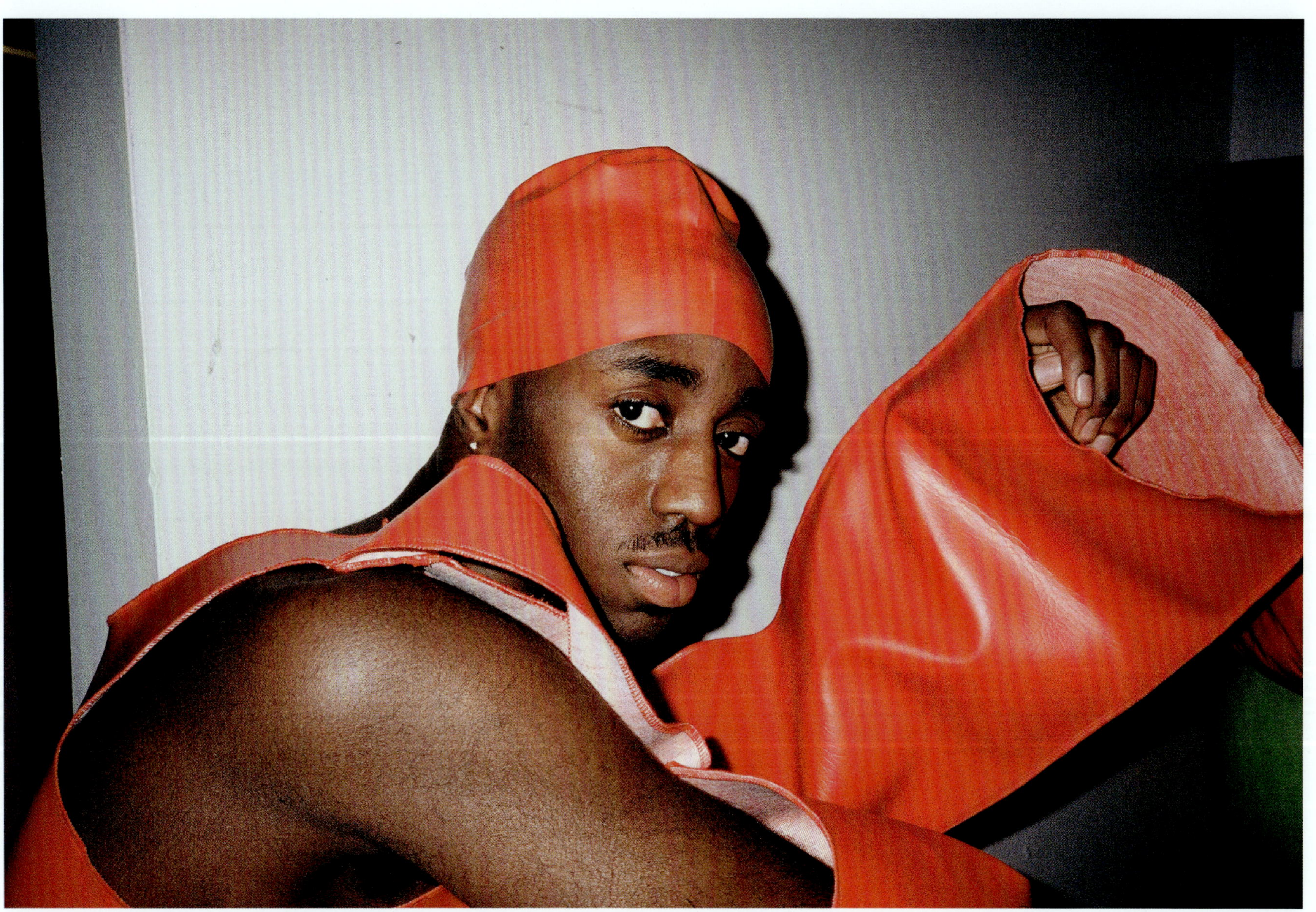

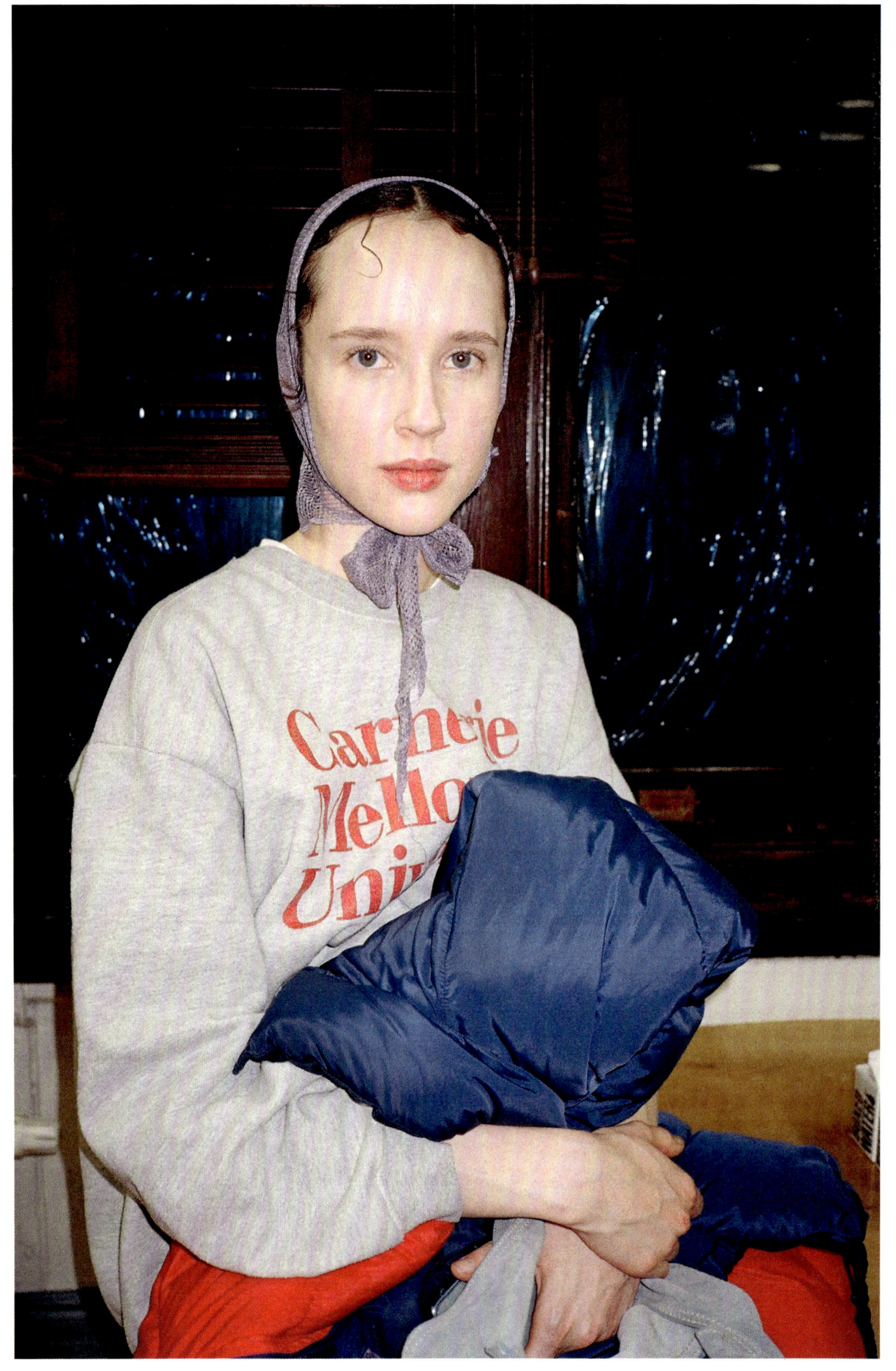

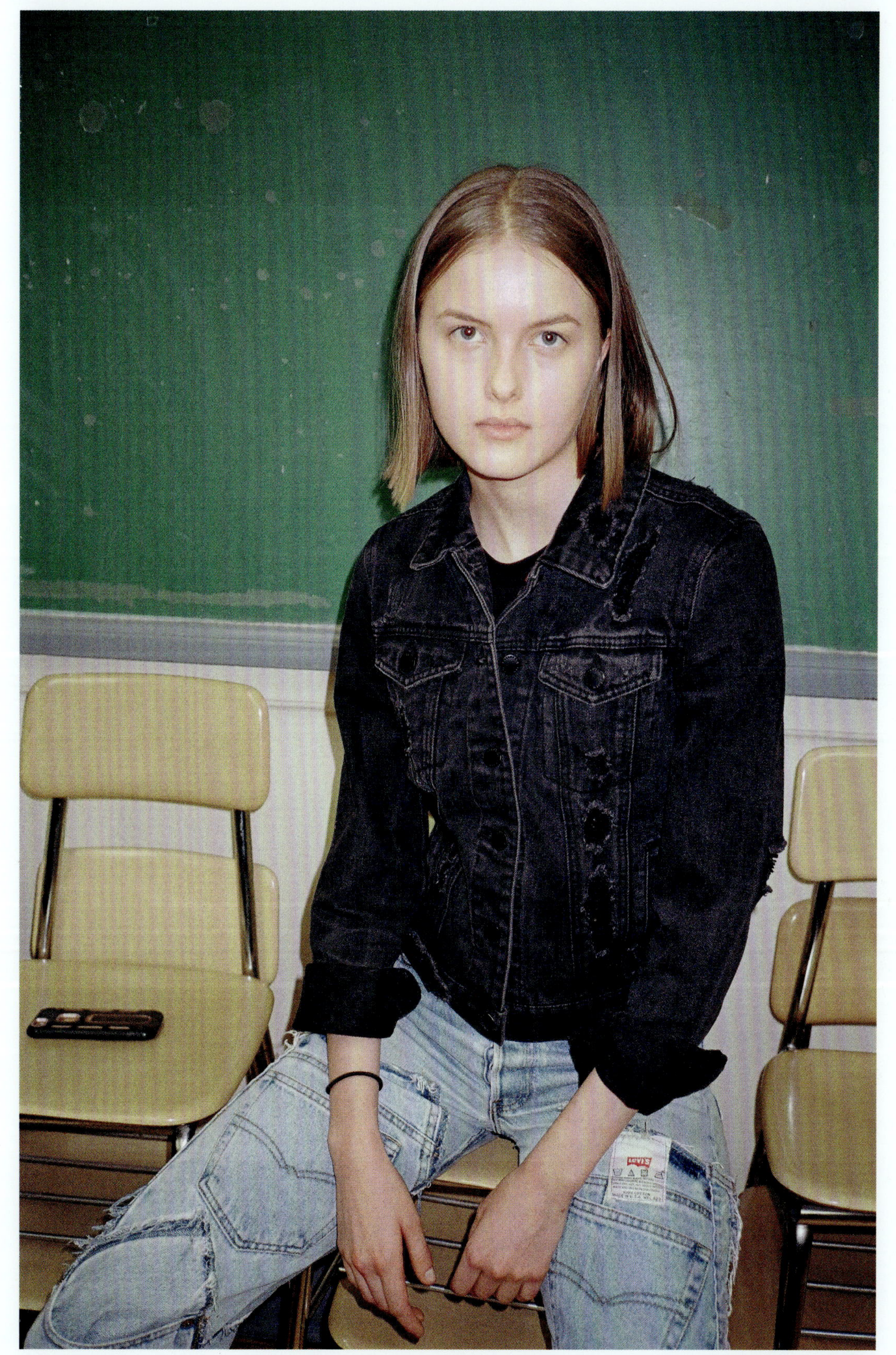

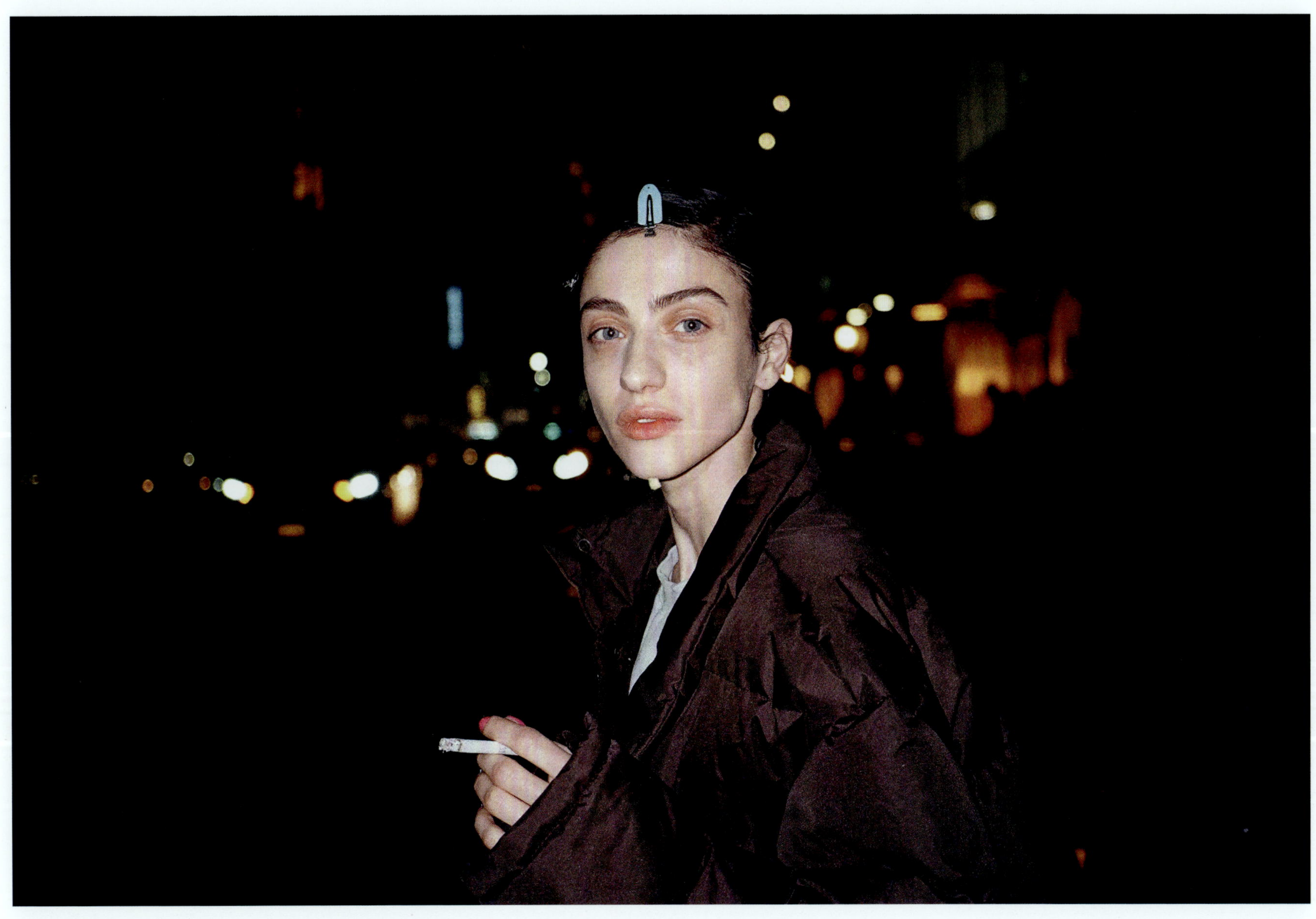

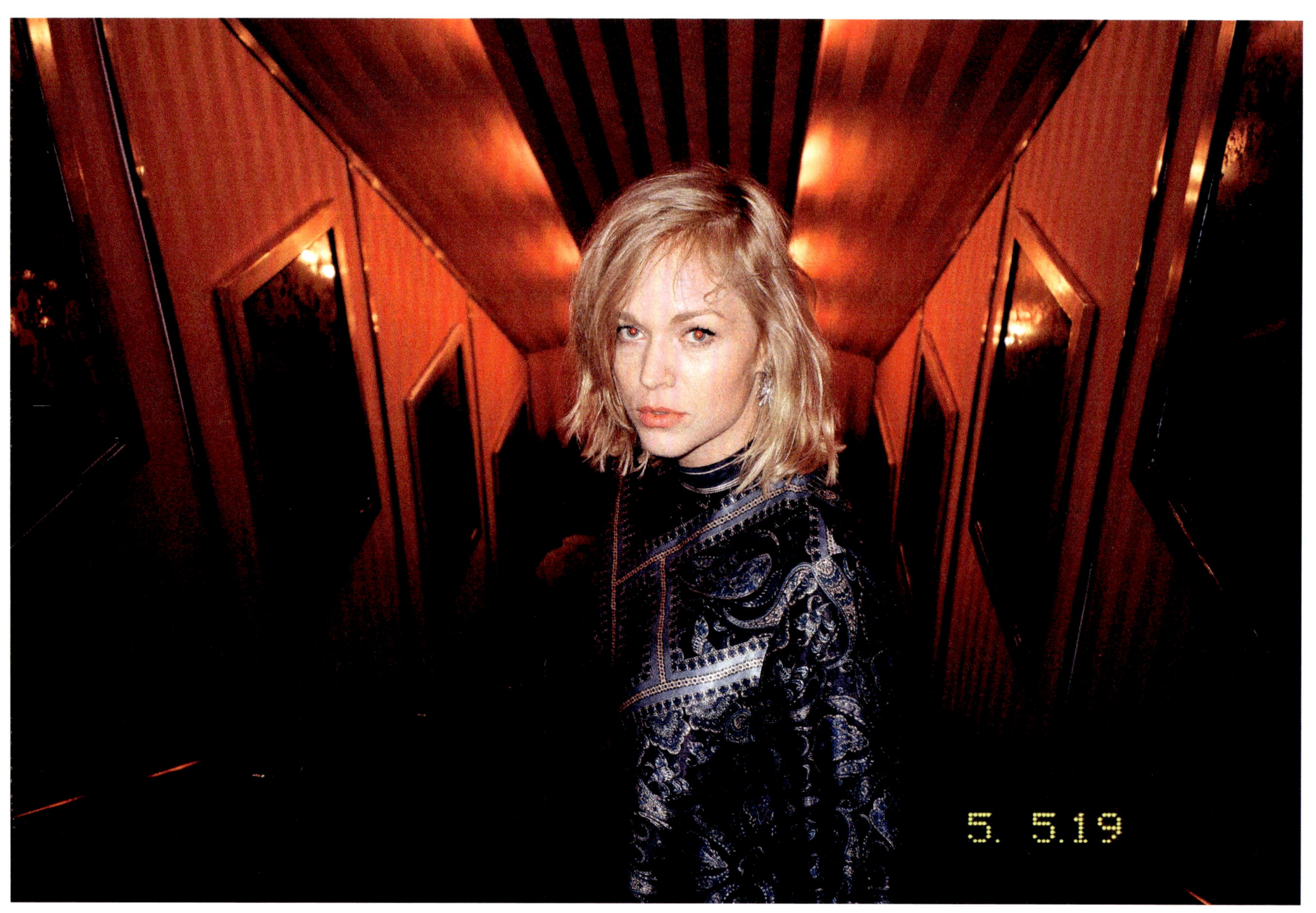
5. 5.19

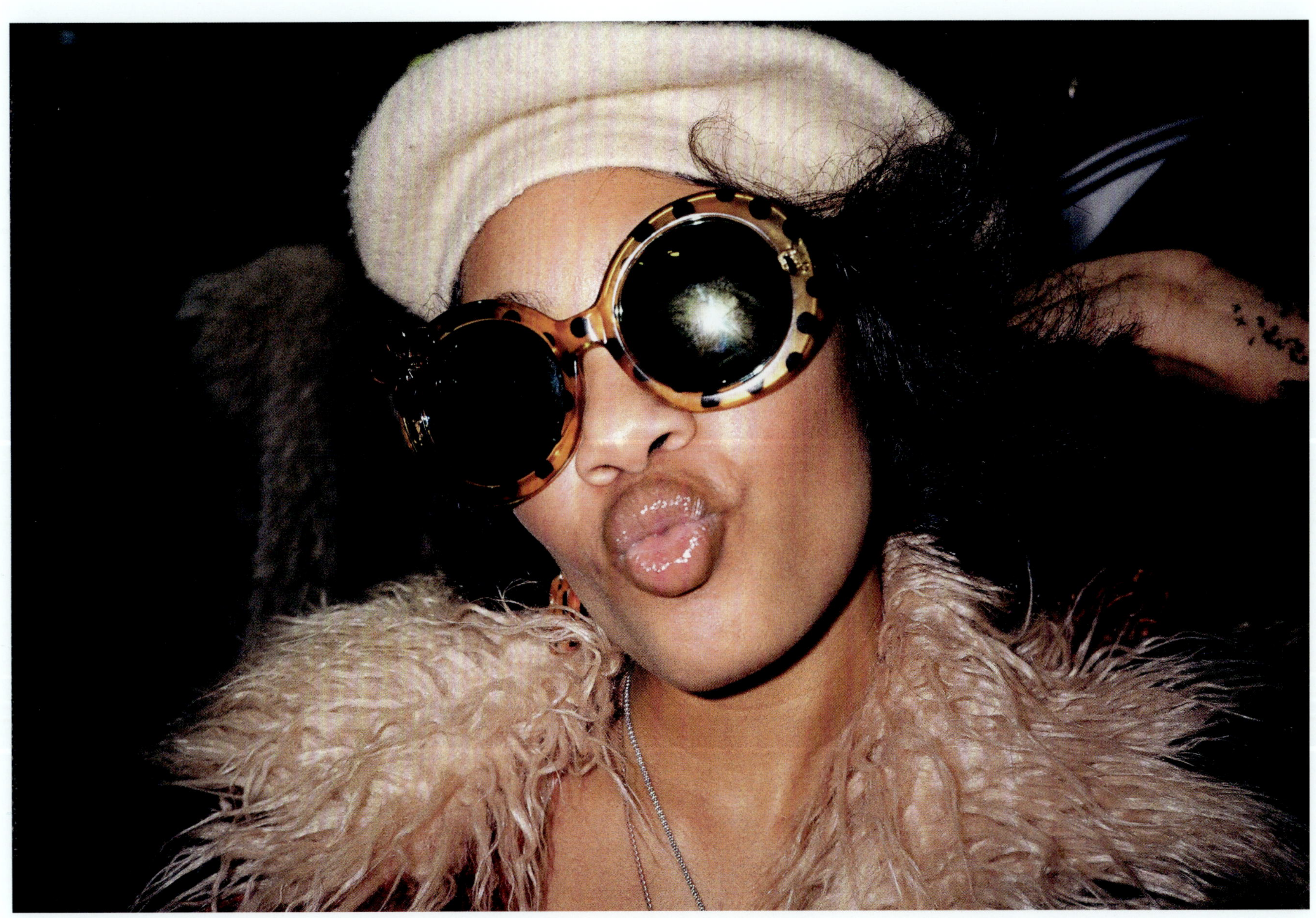

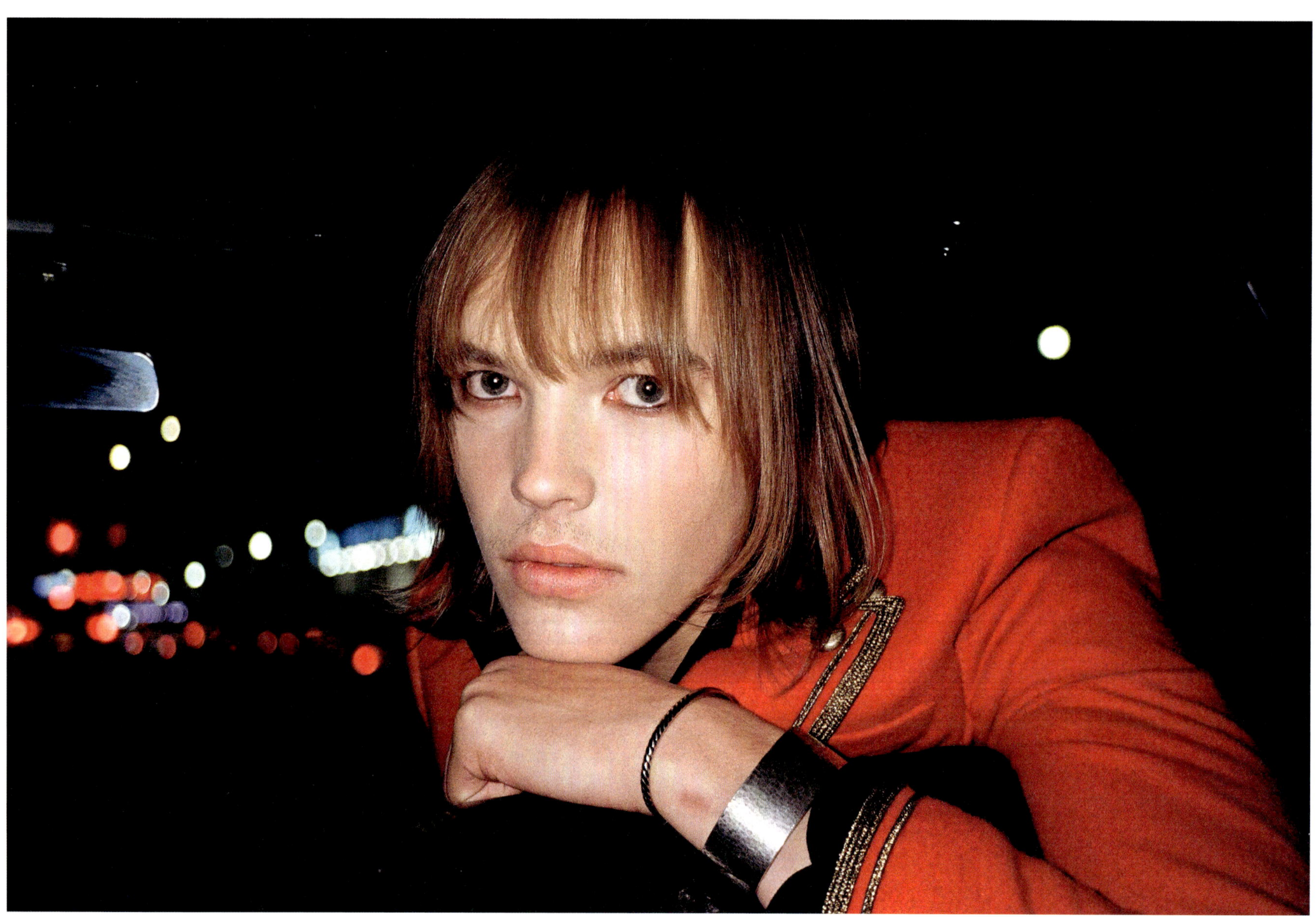

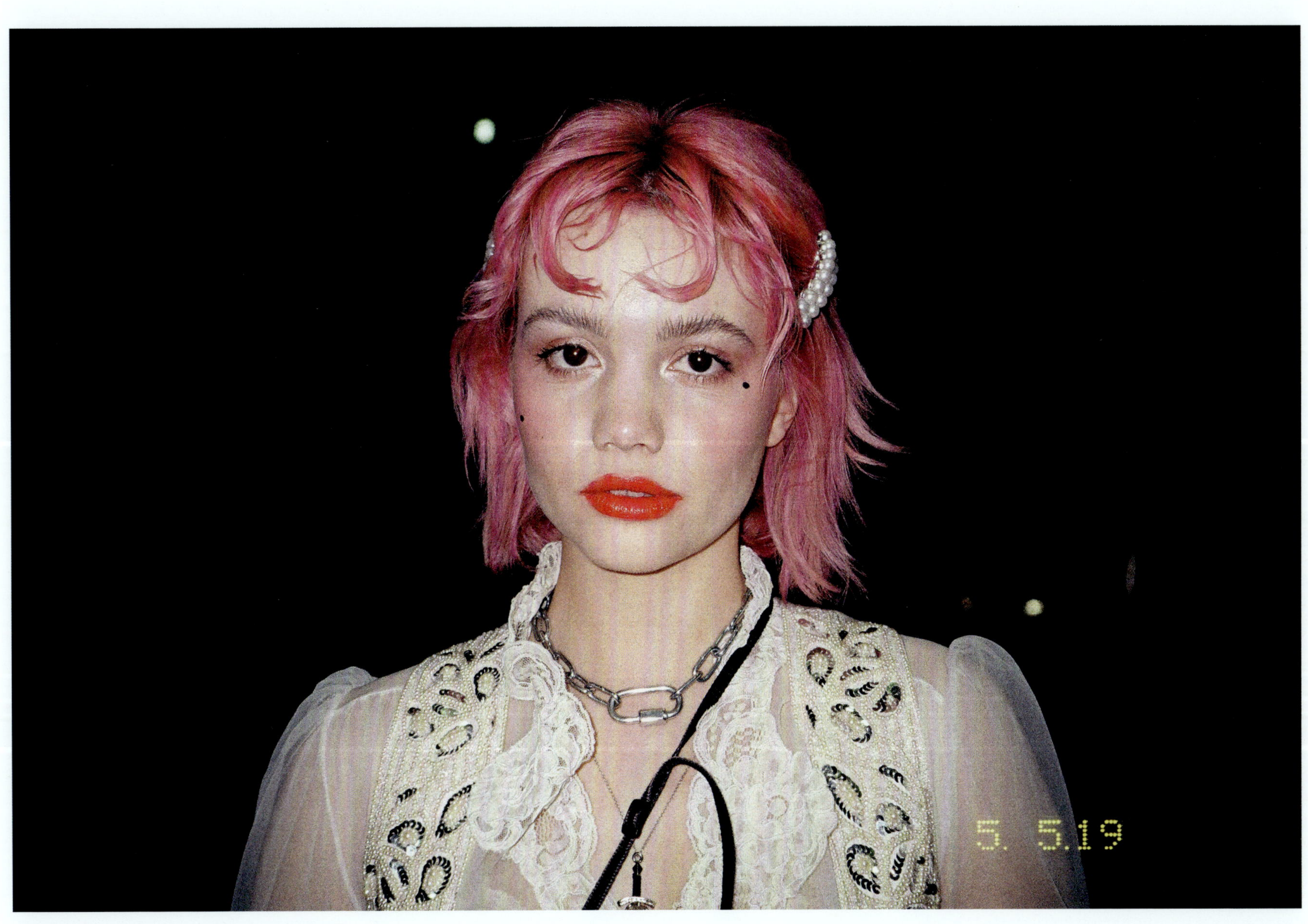
5. 5.19

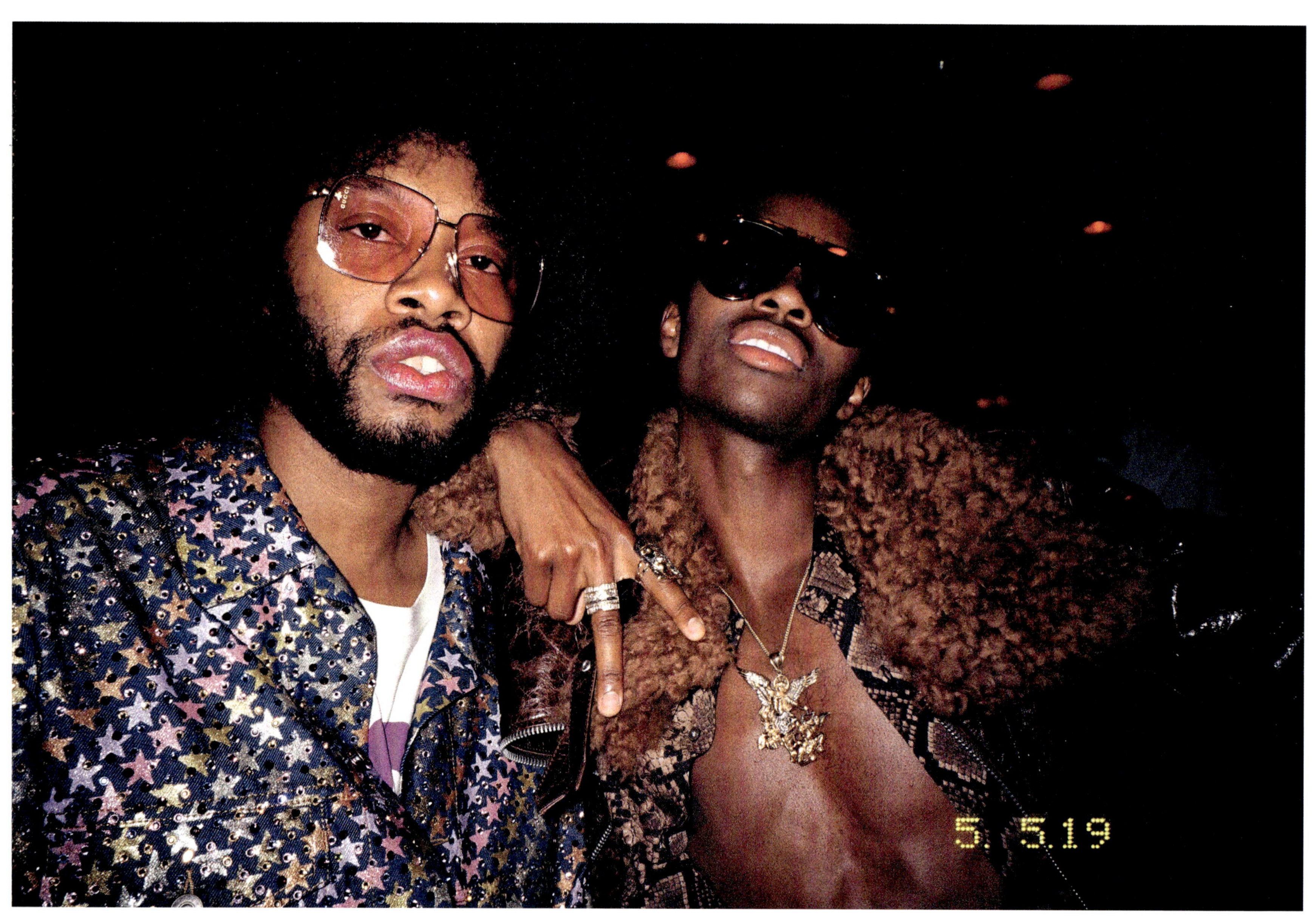
5. 5.19

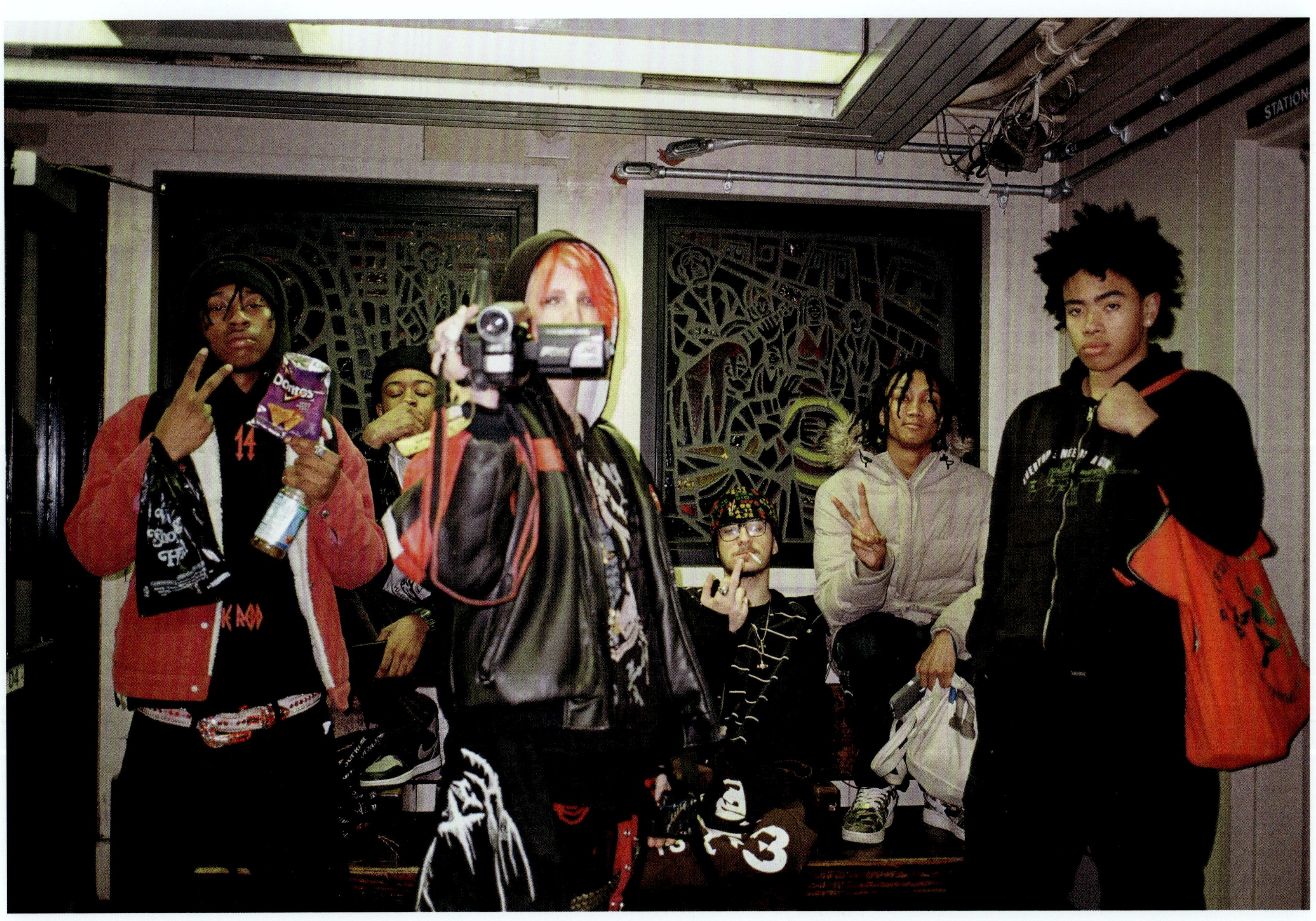
STATION
Doritos
14

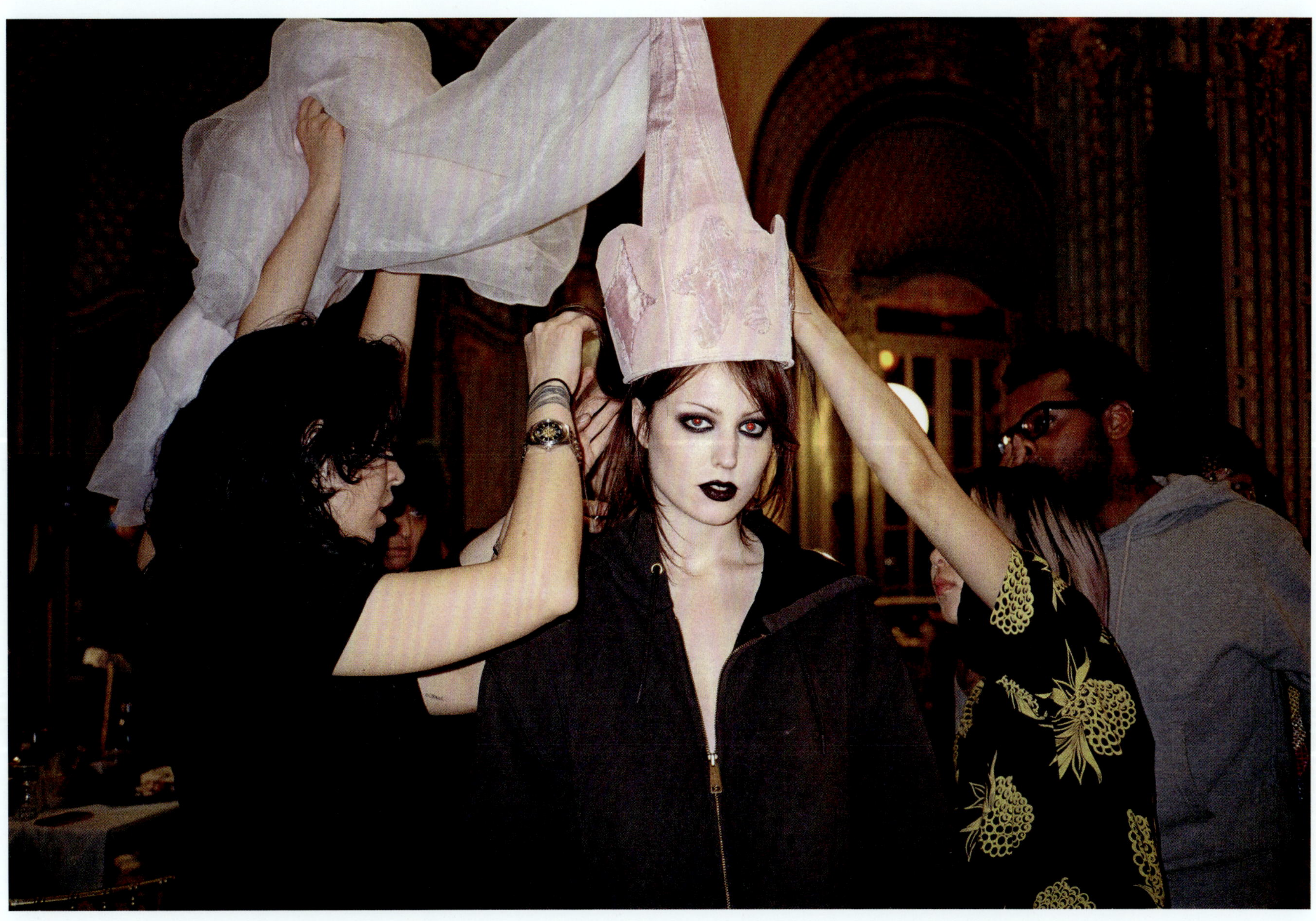

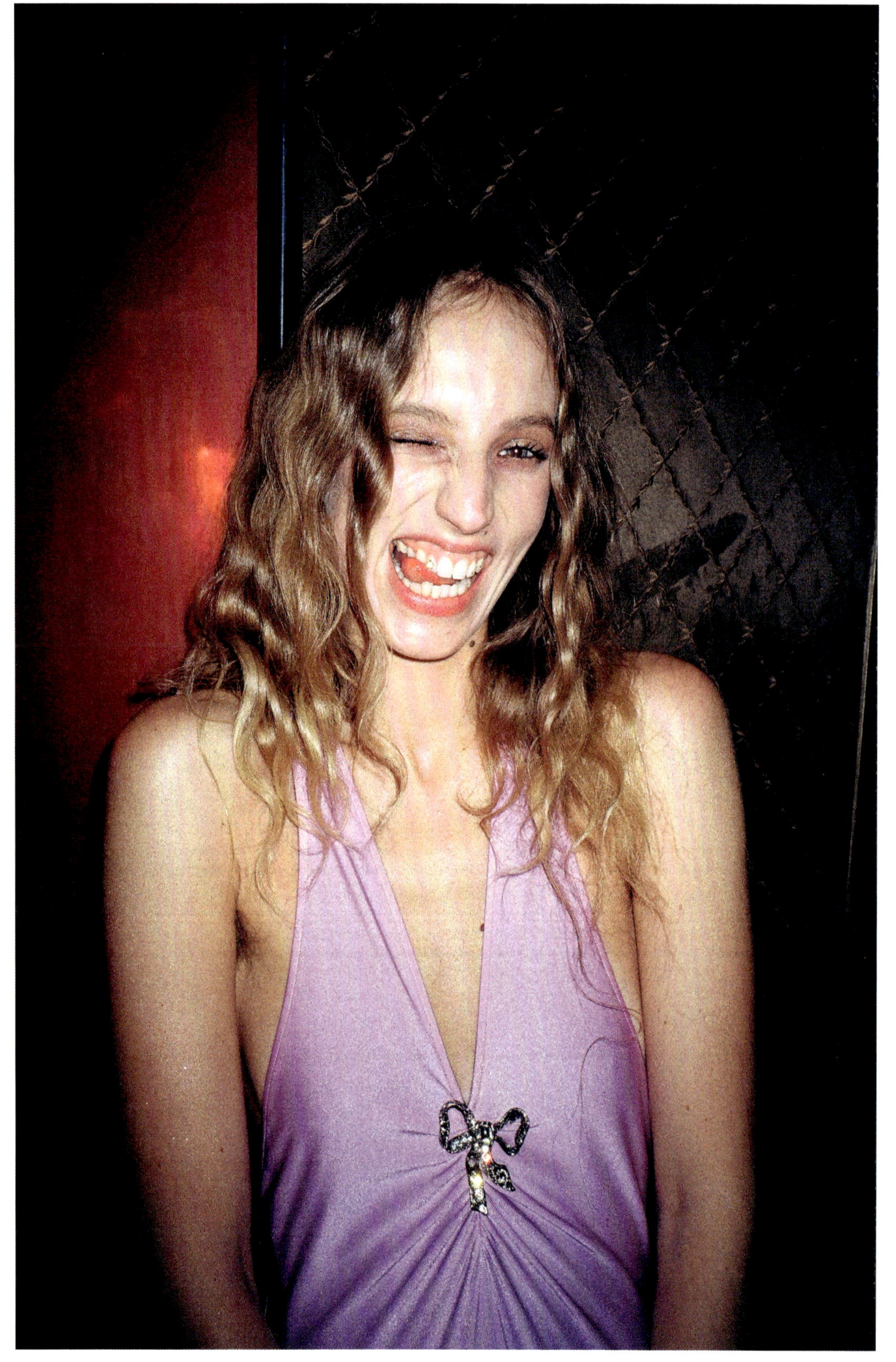

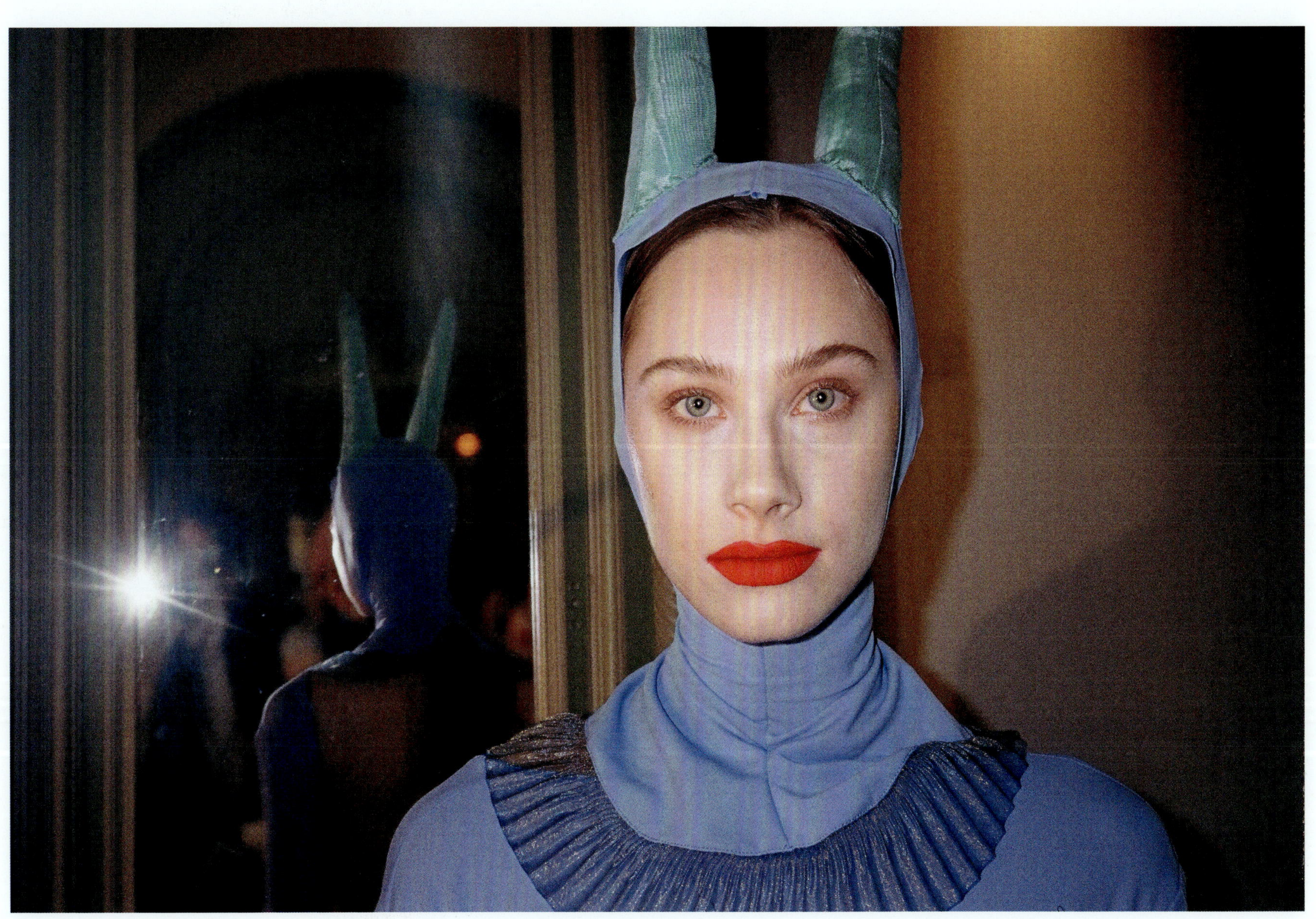

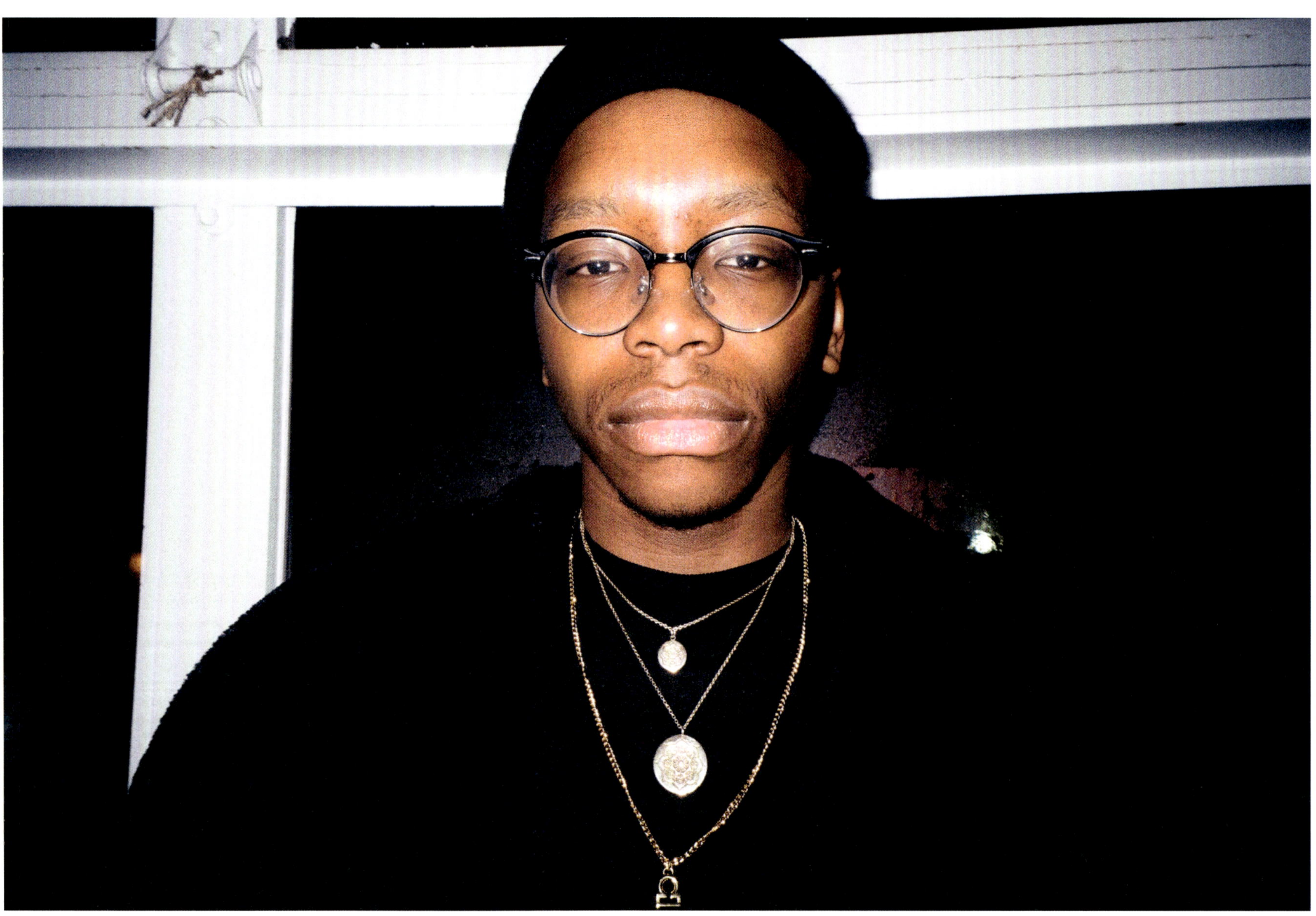

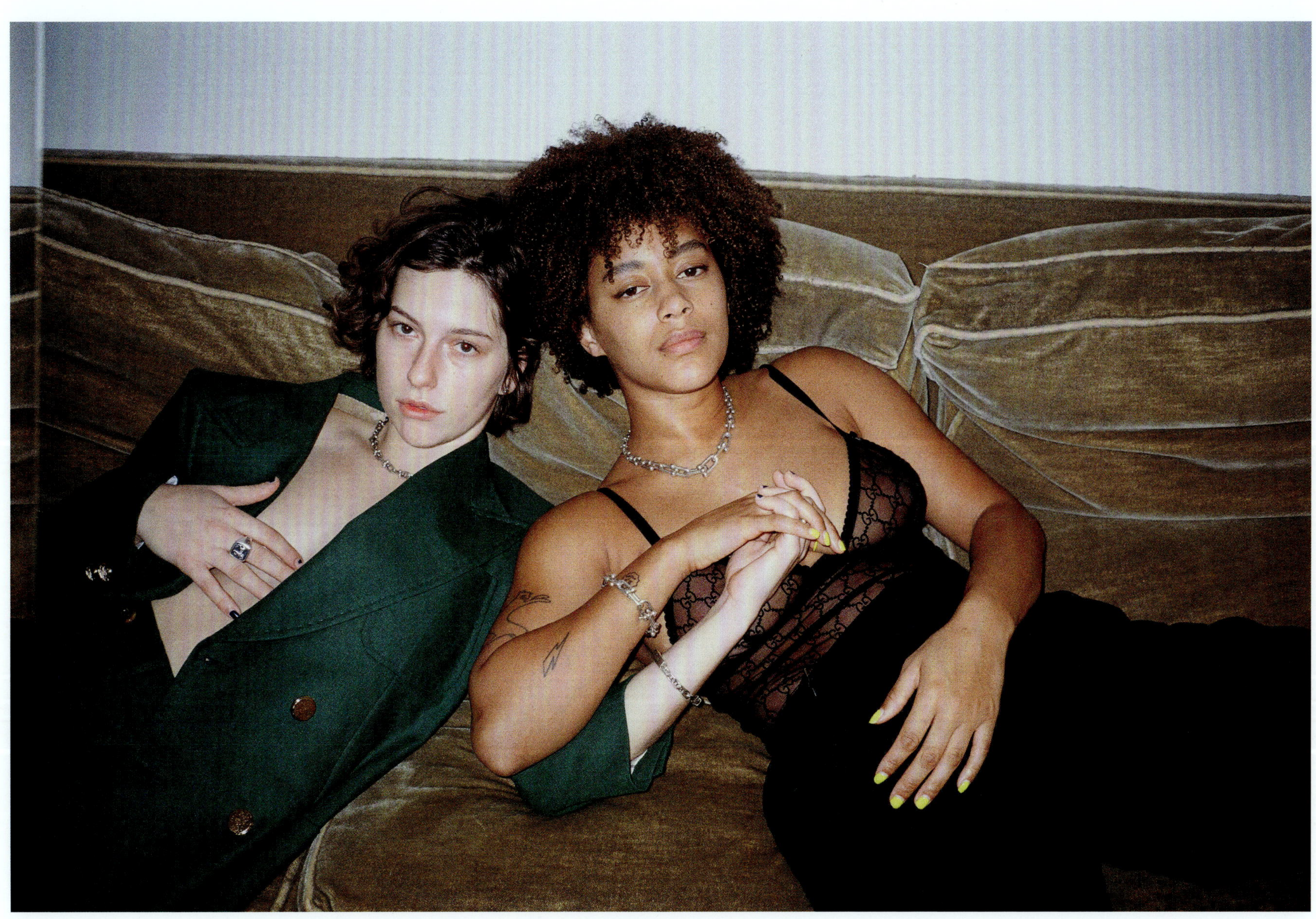

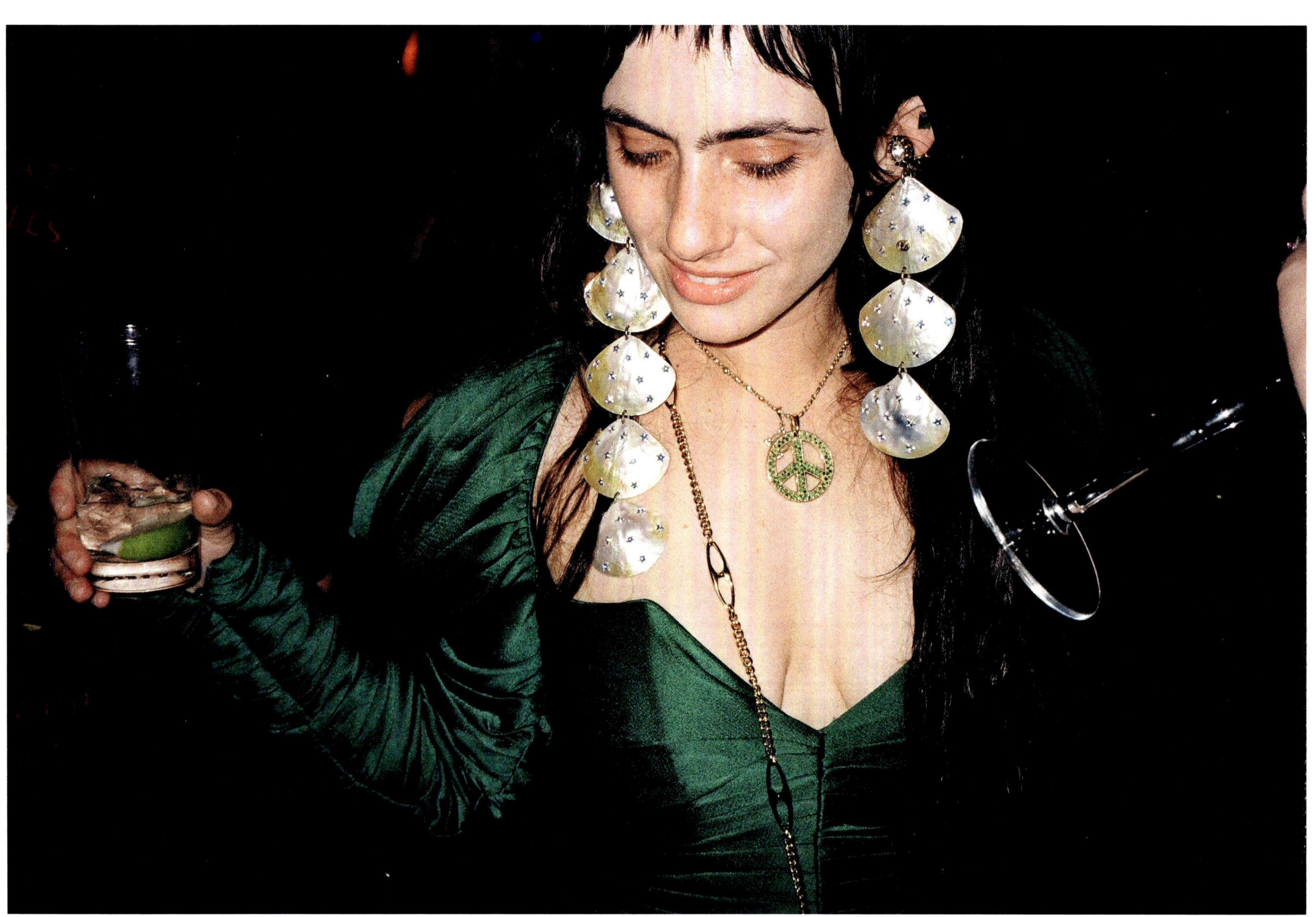

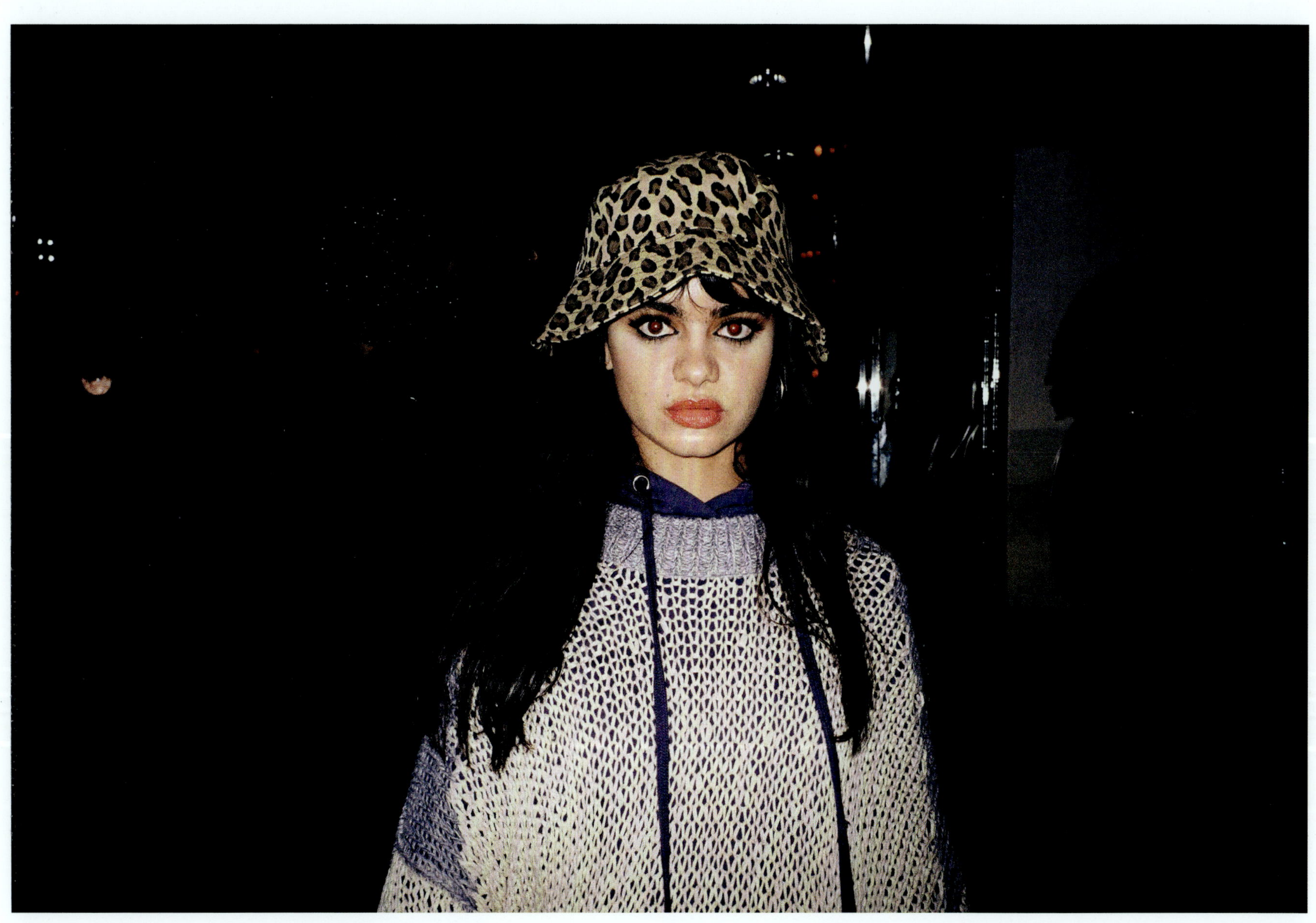

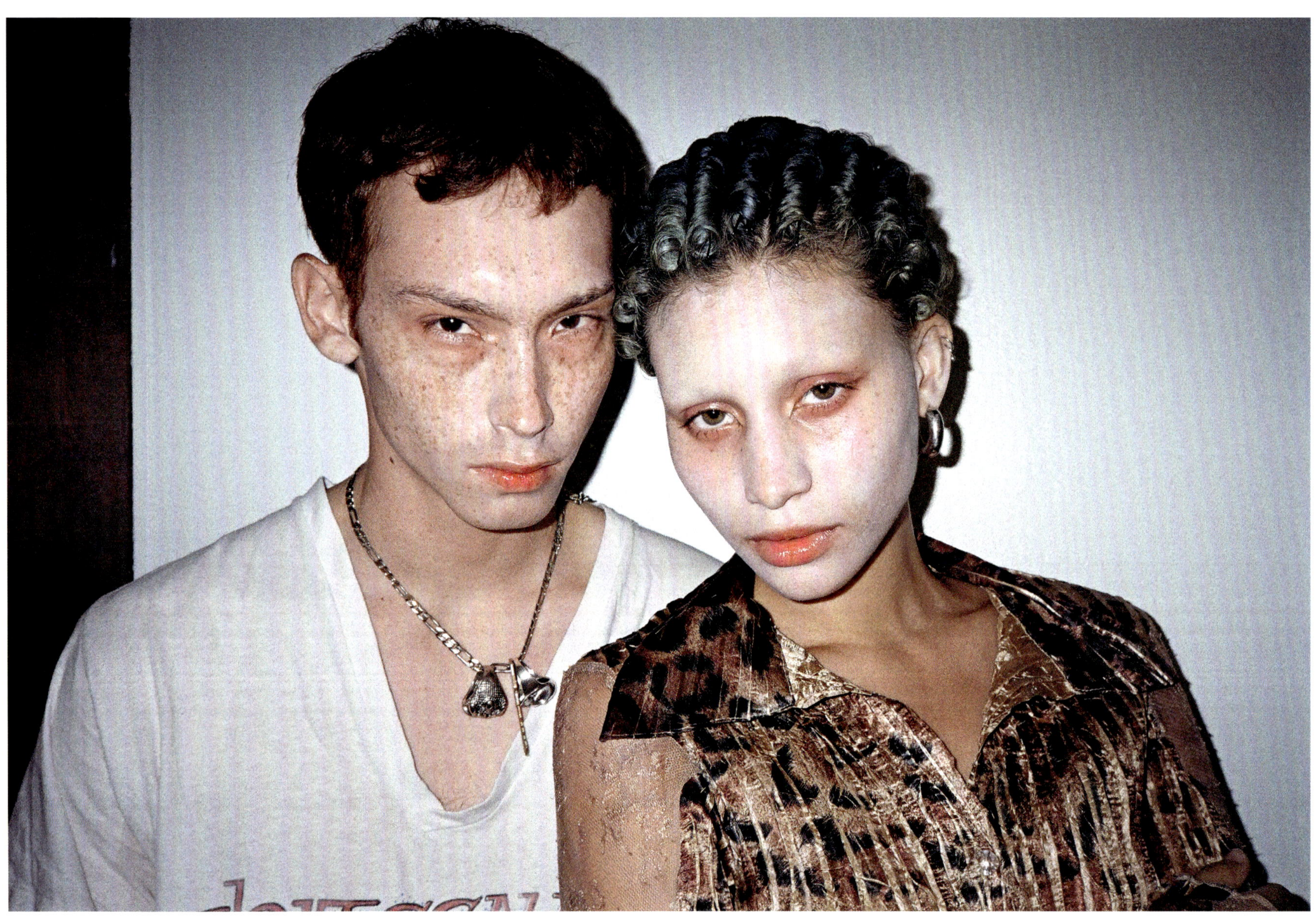

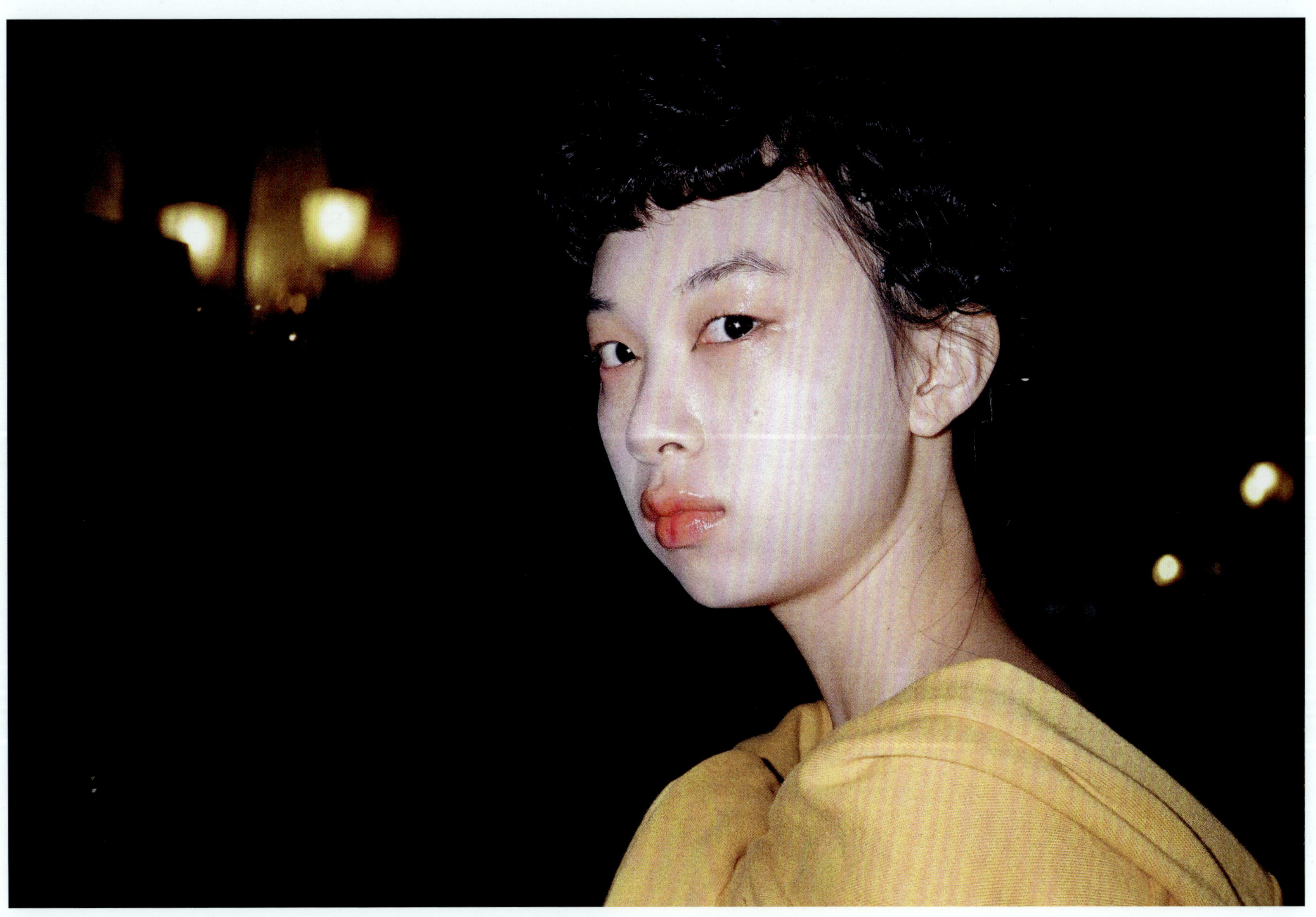

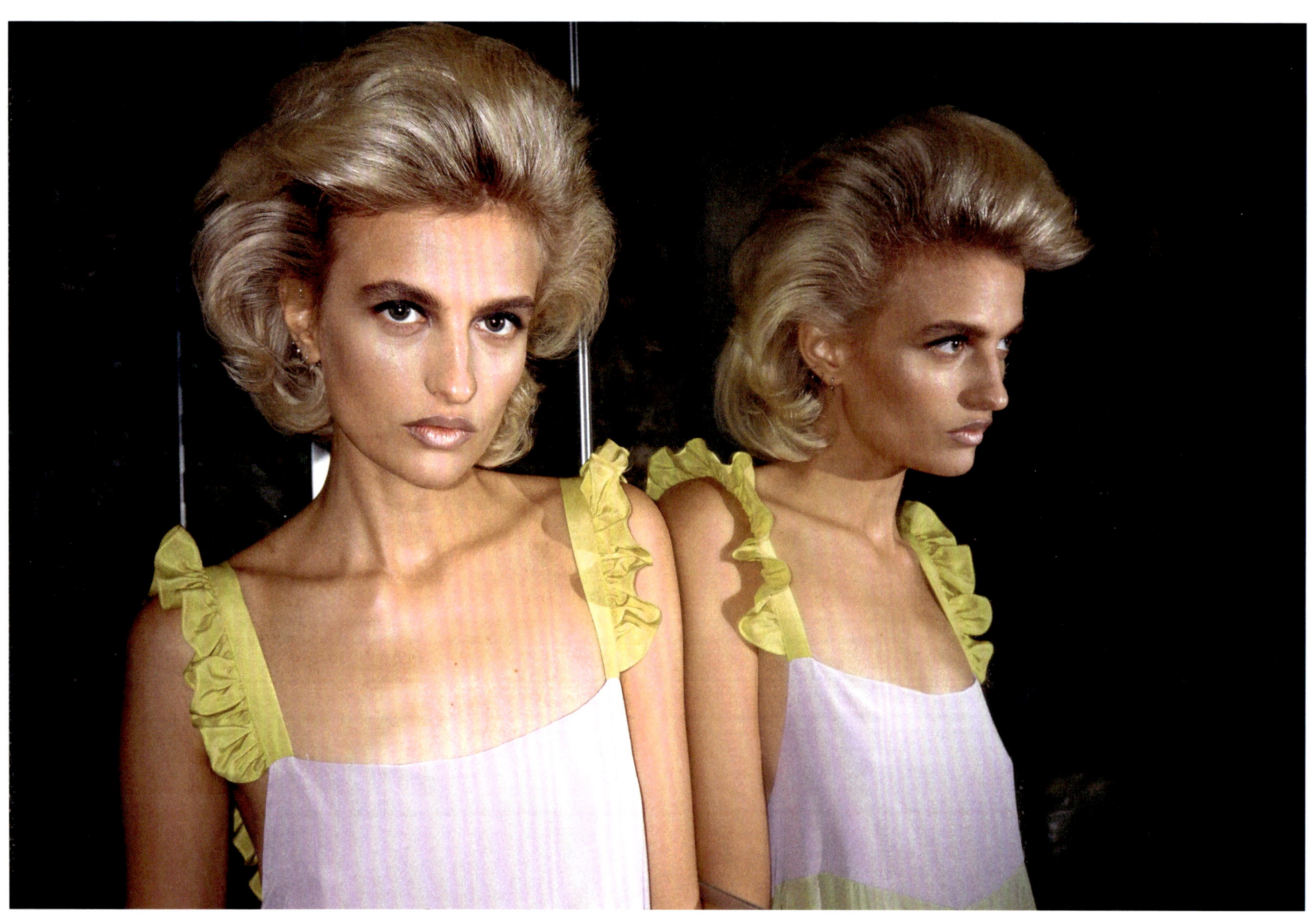

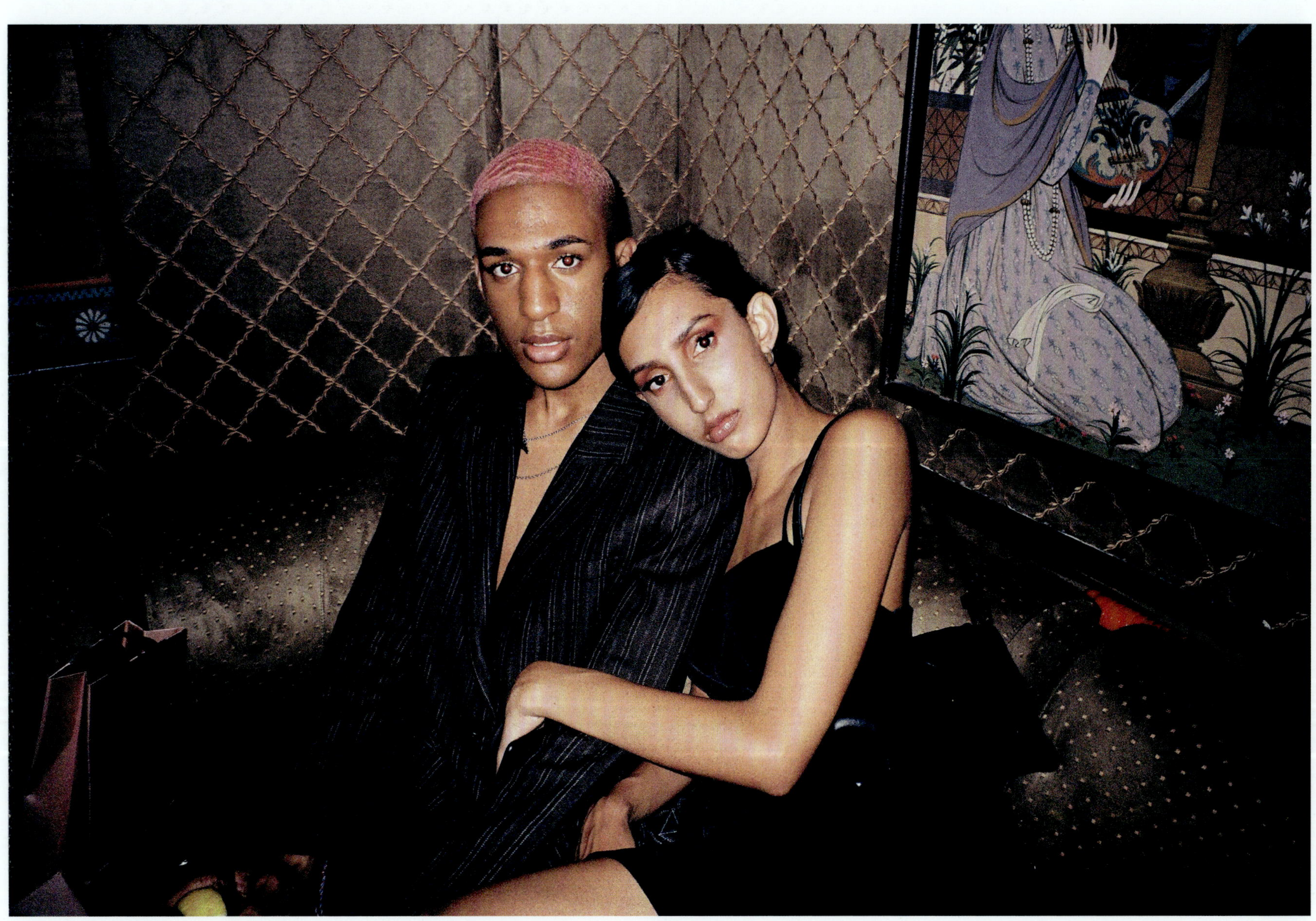

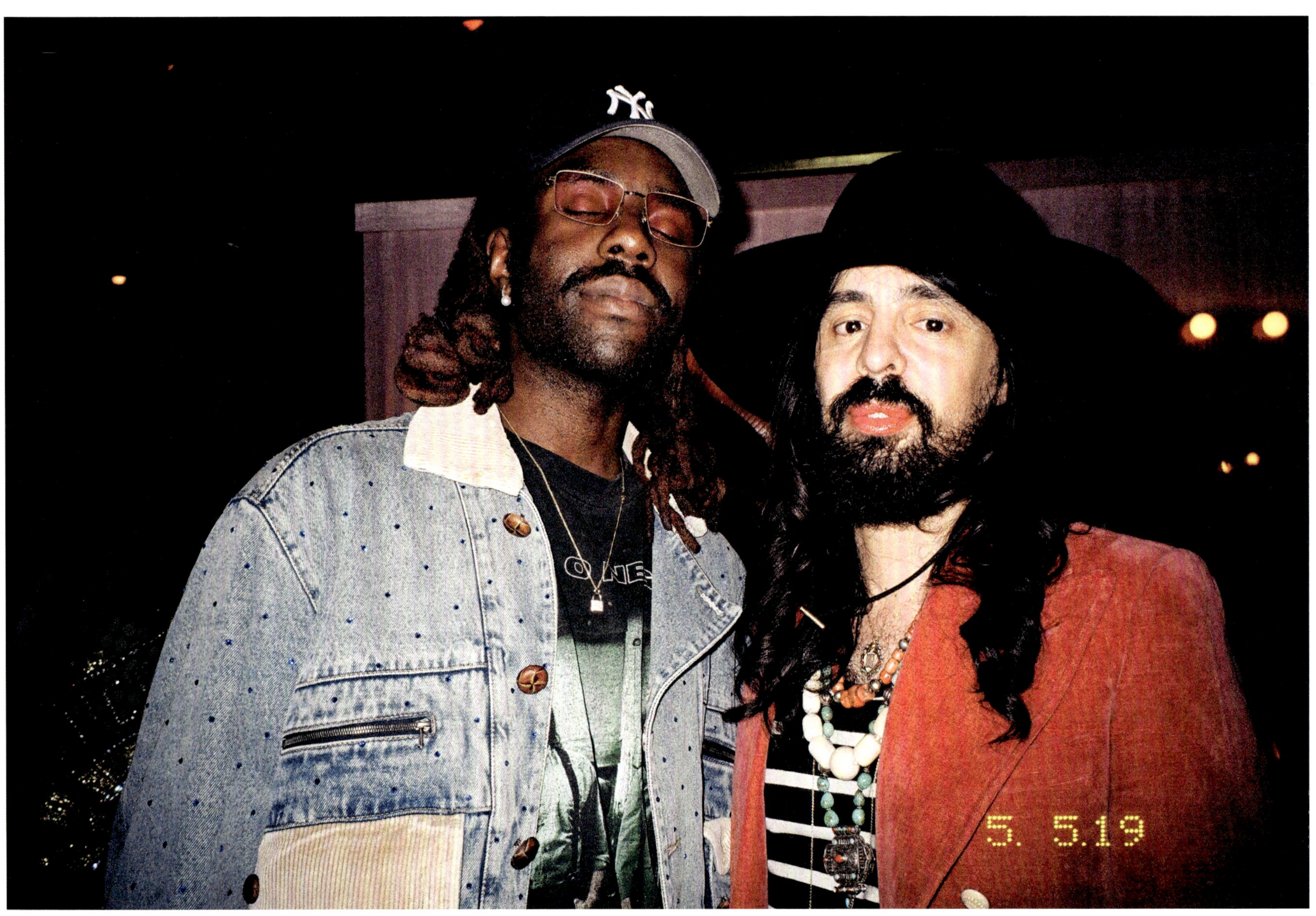
NY
5. 5.19

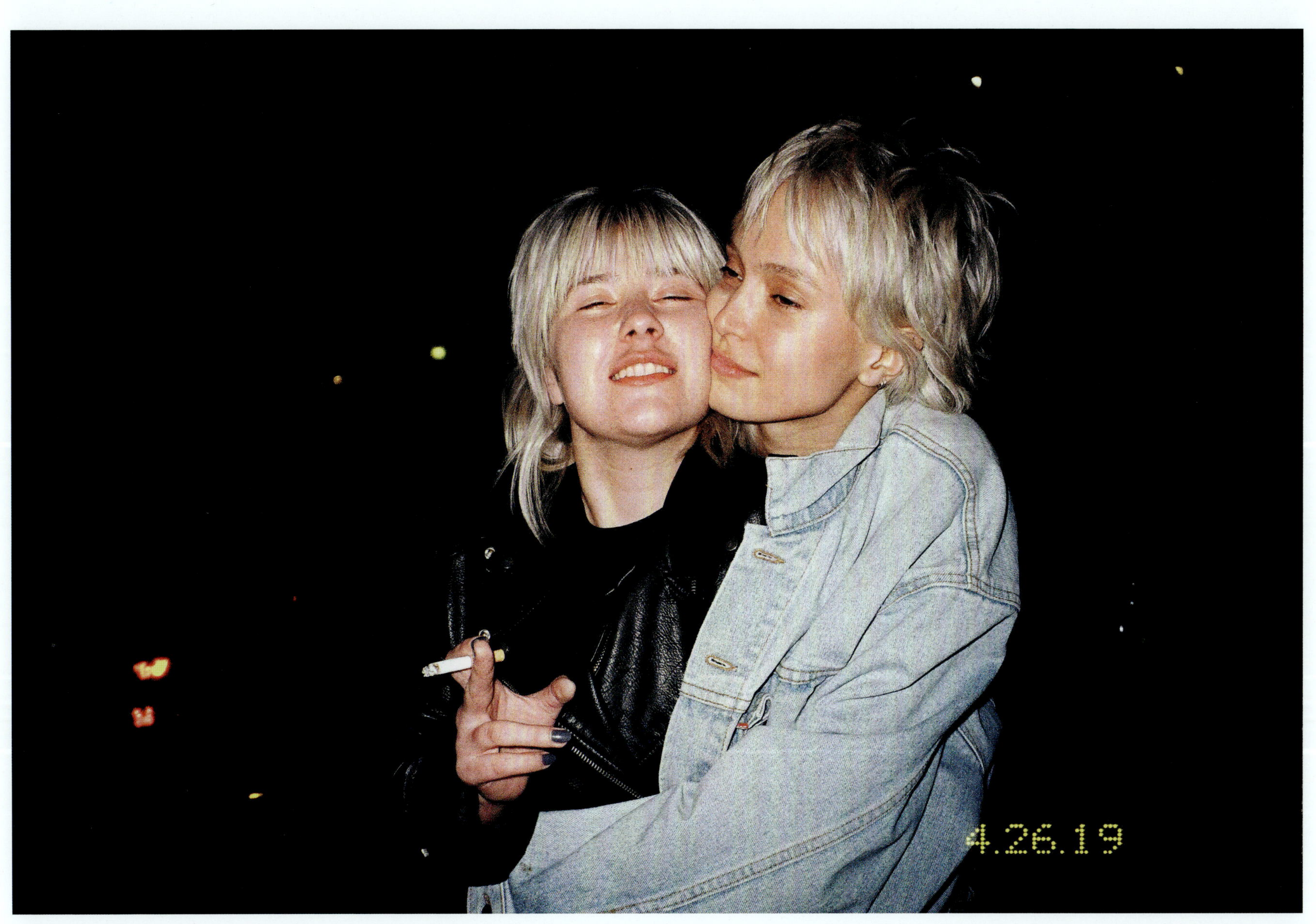
4.26.19

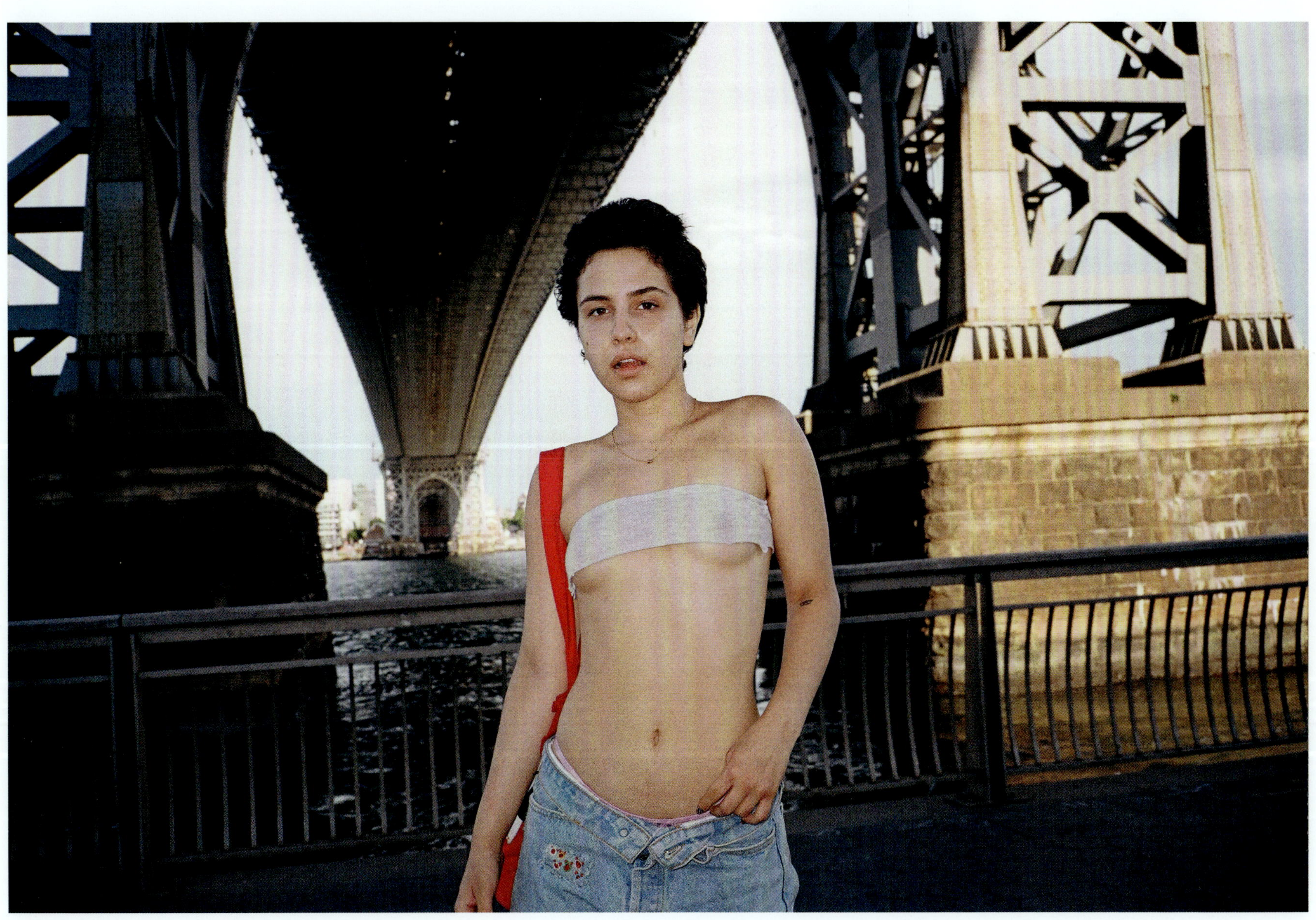

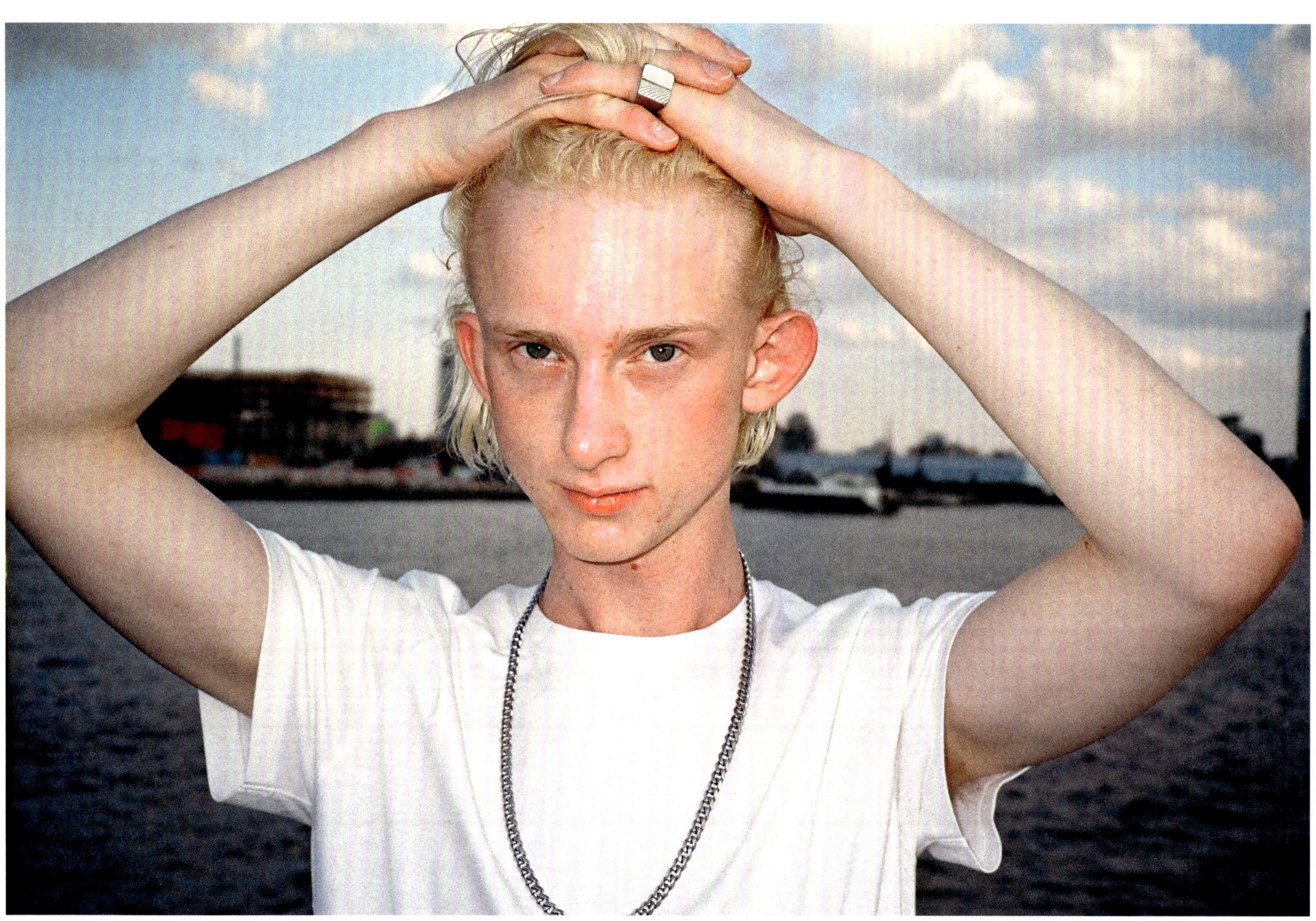

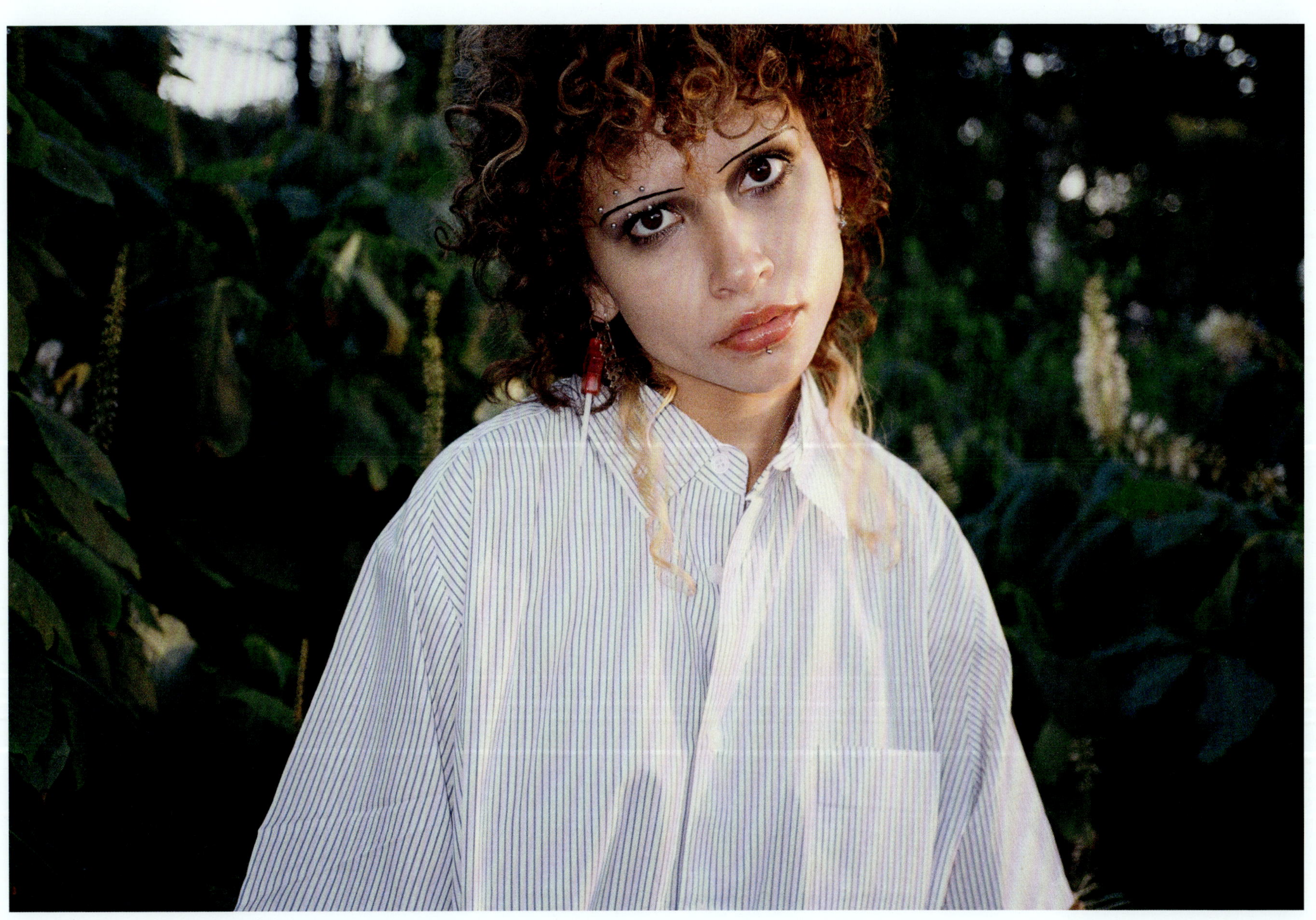

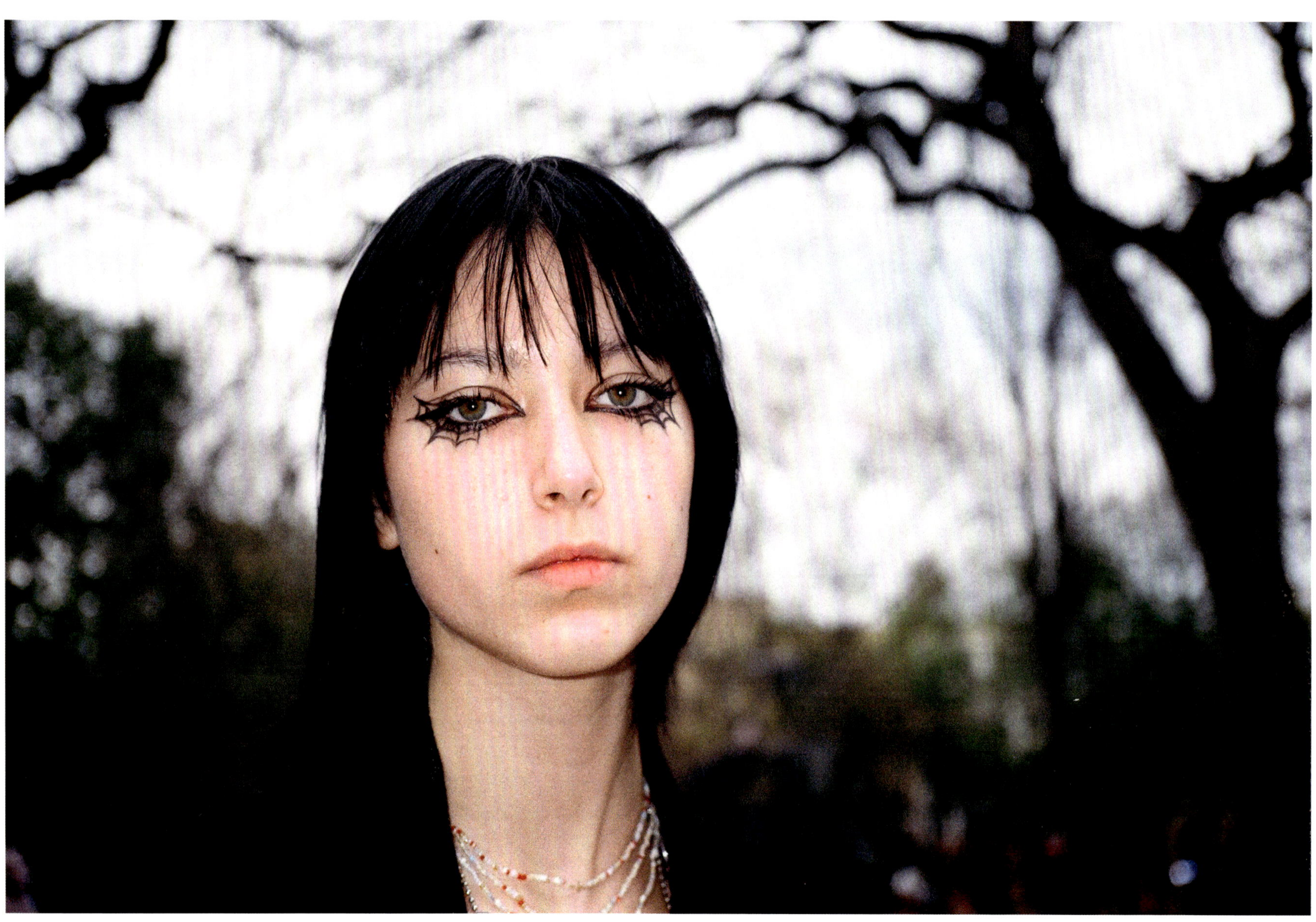

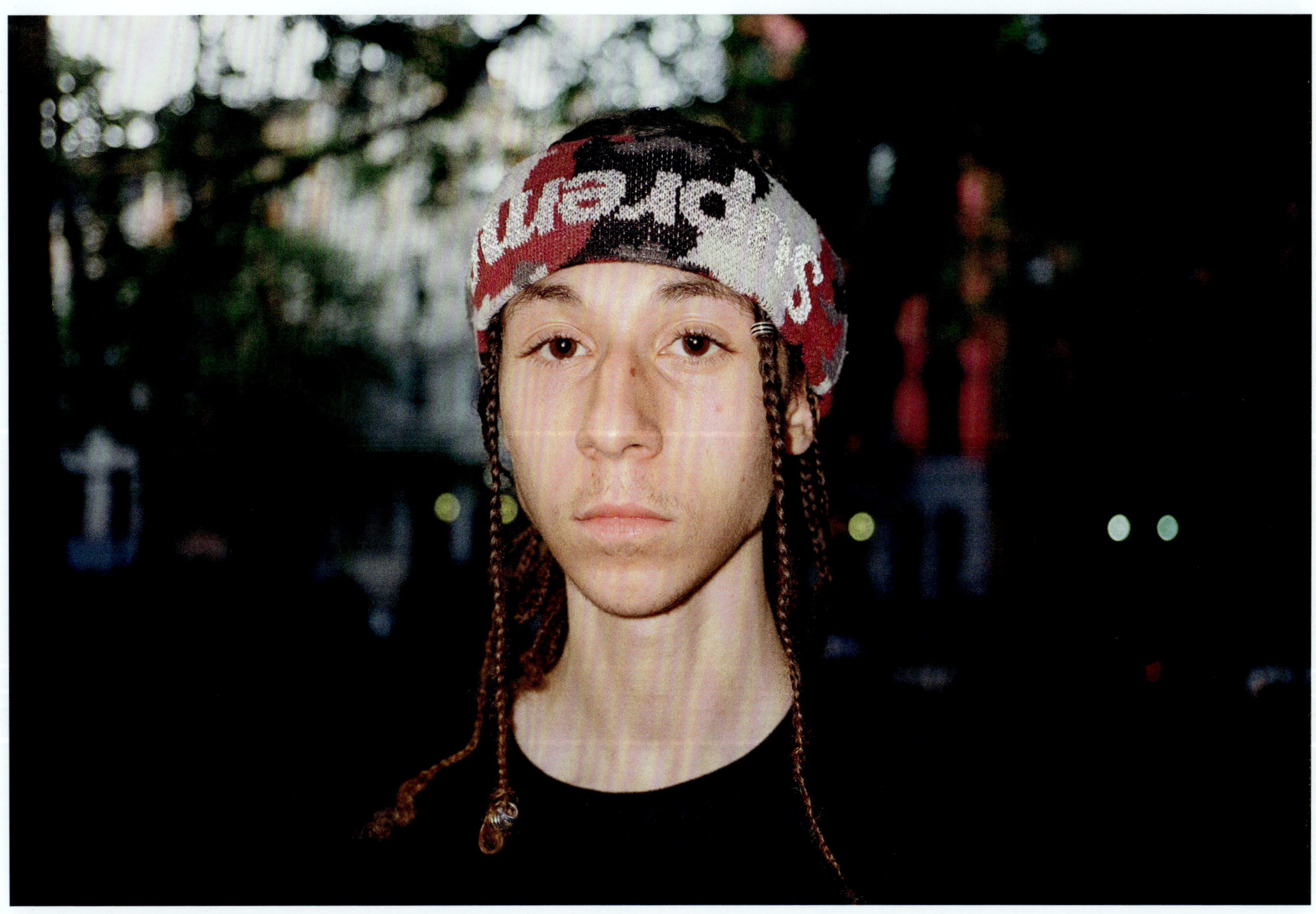

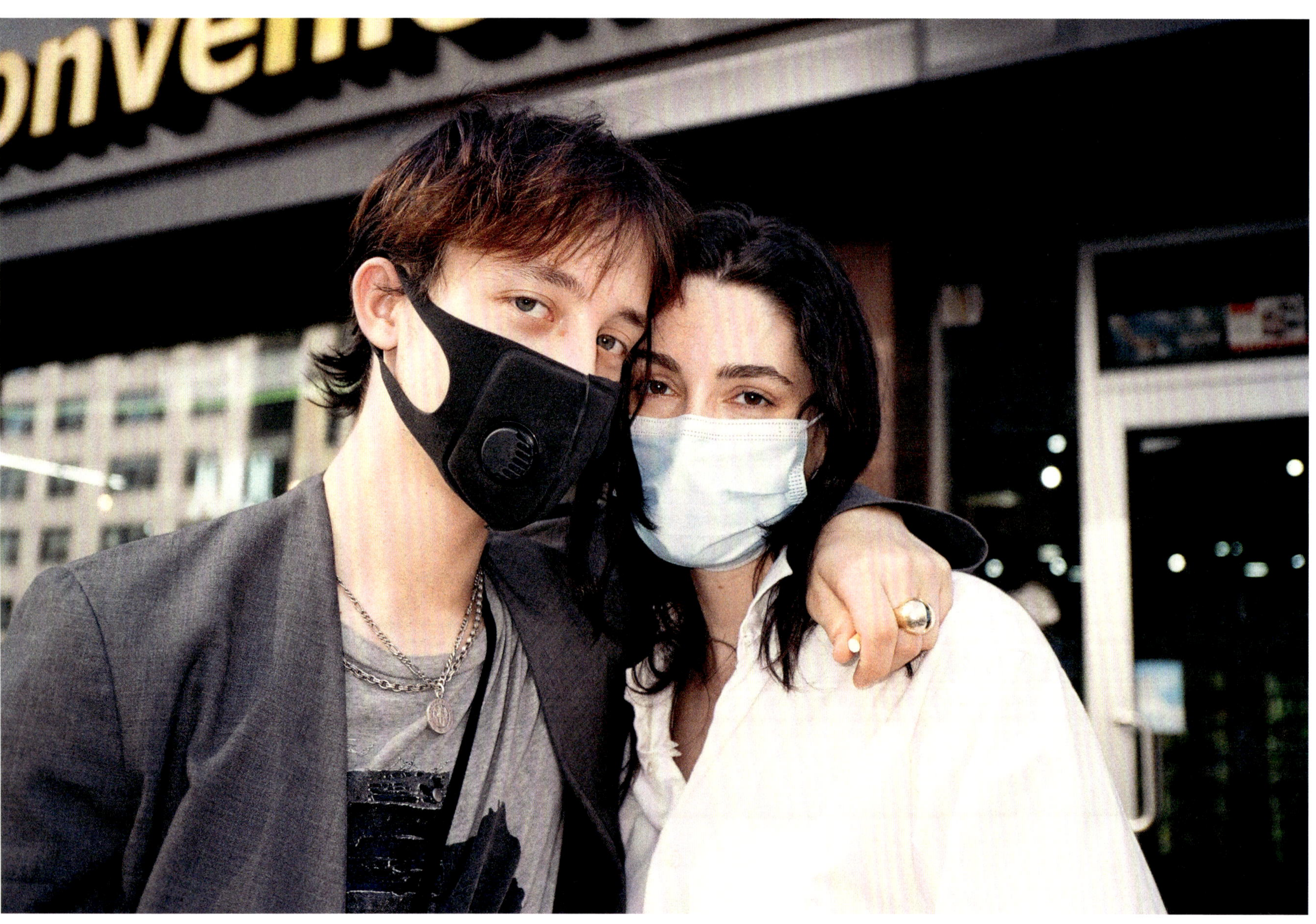

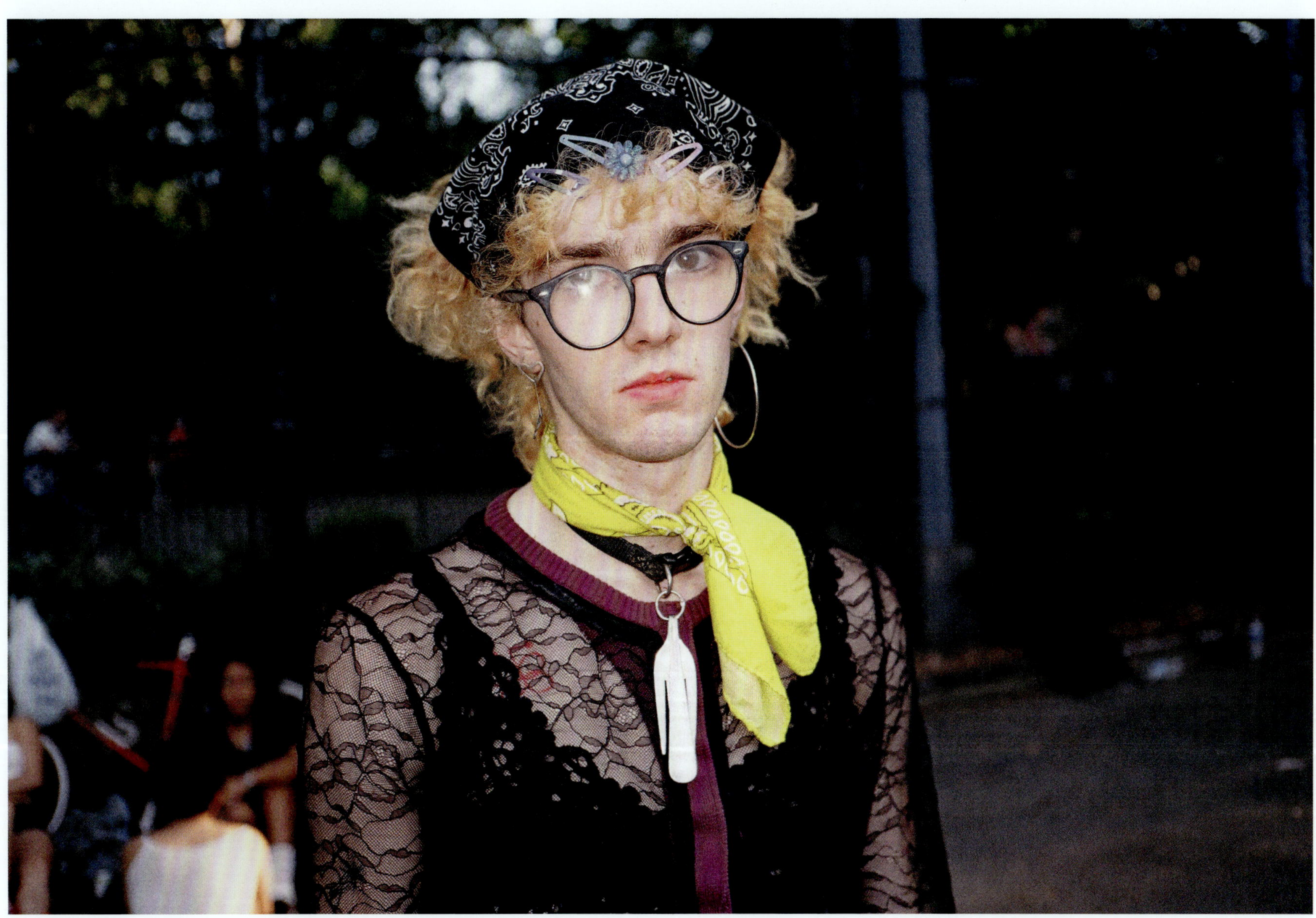

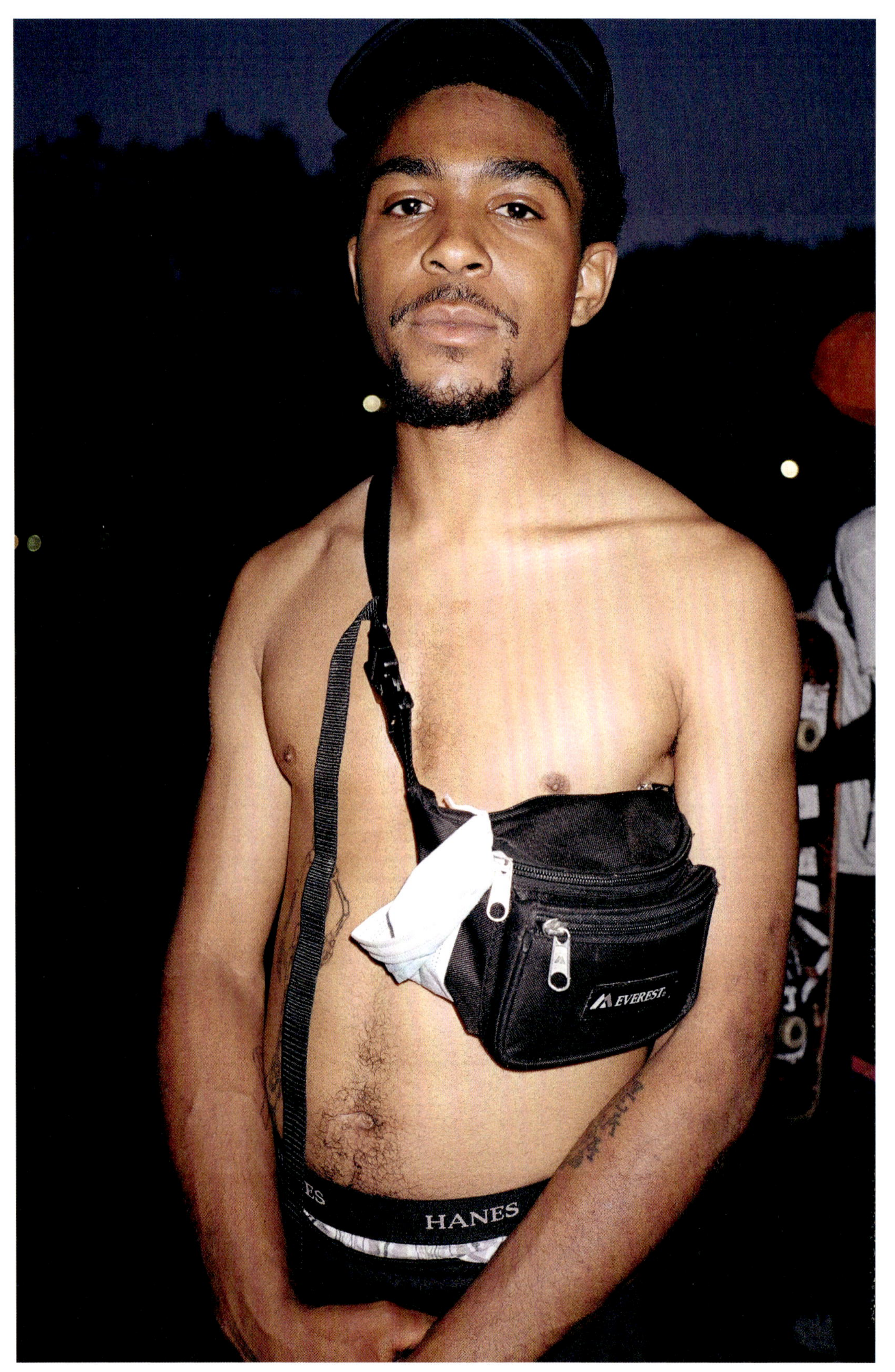
EVEREST
HANES

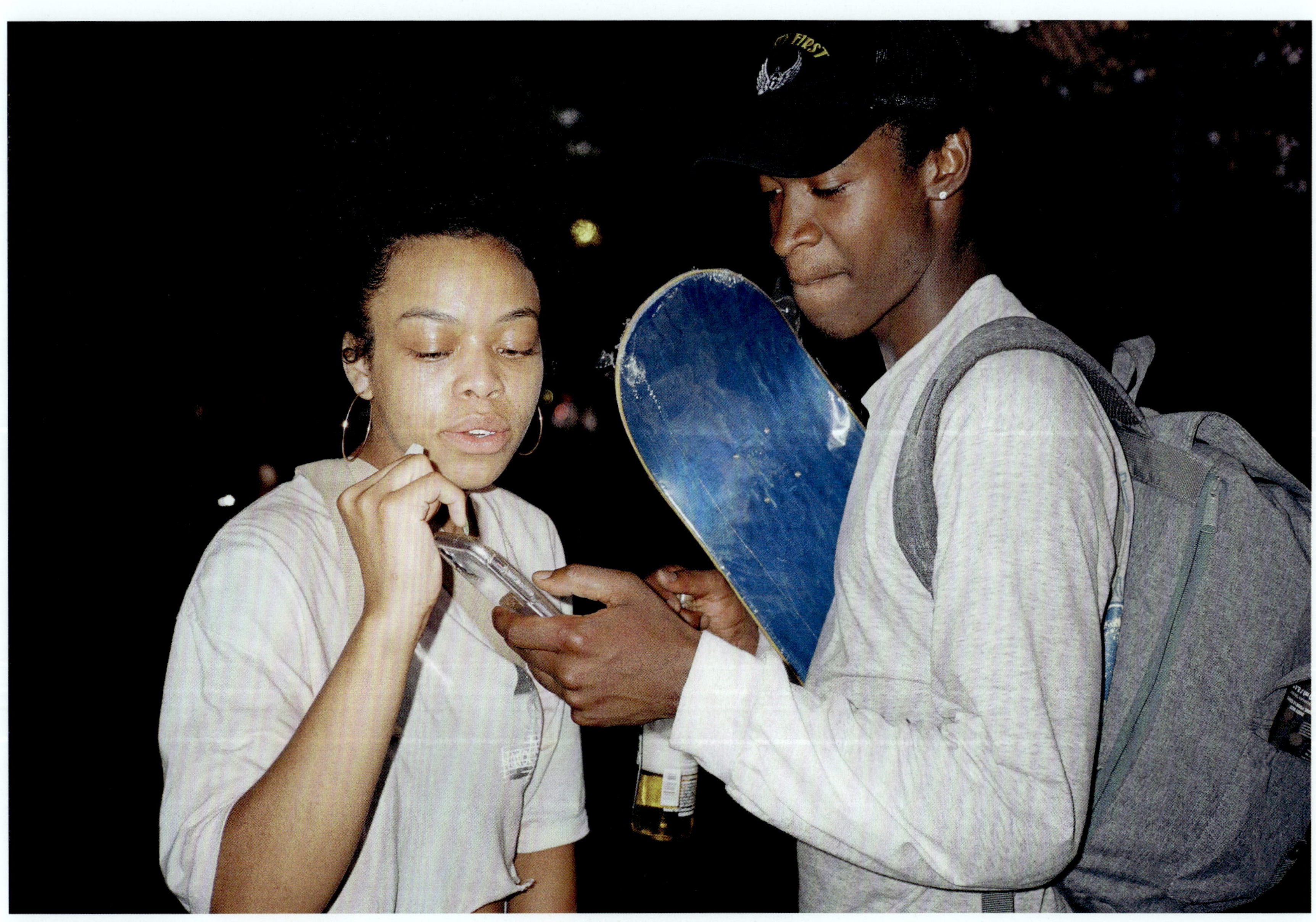
FIRST

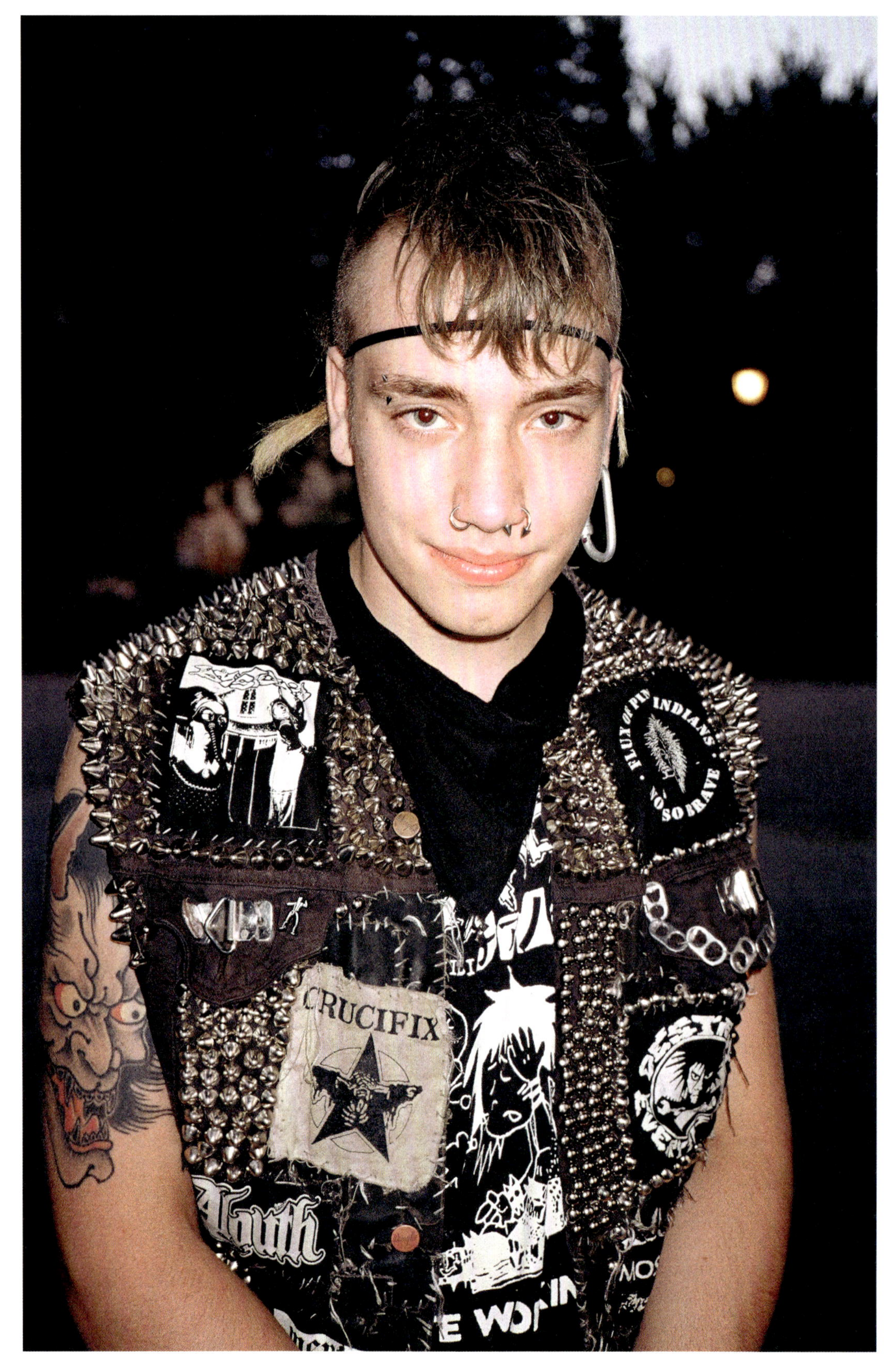
CRUCIFIX

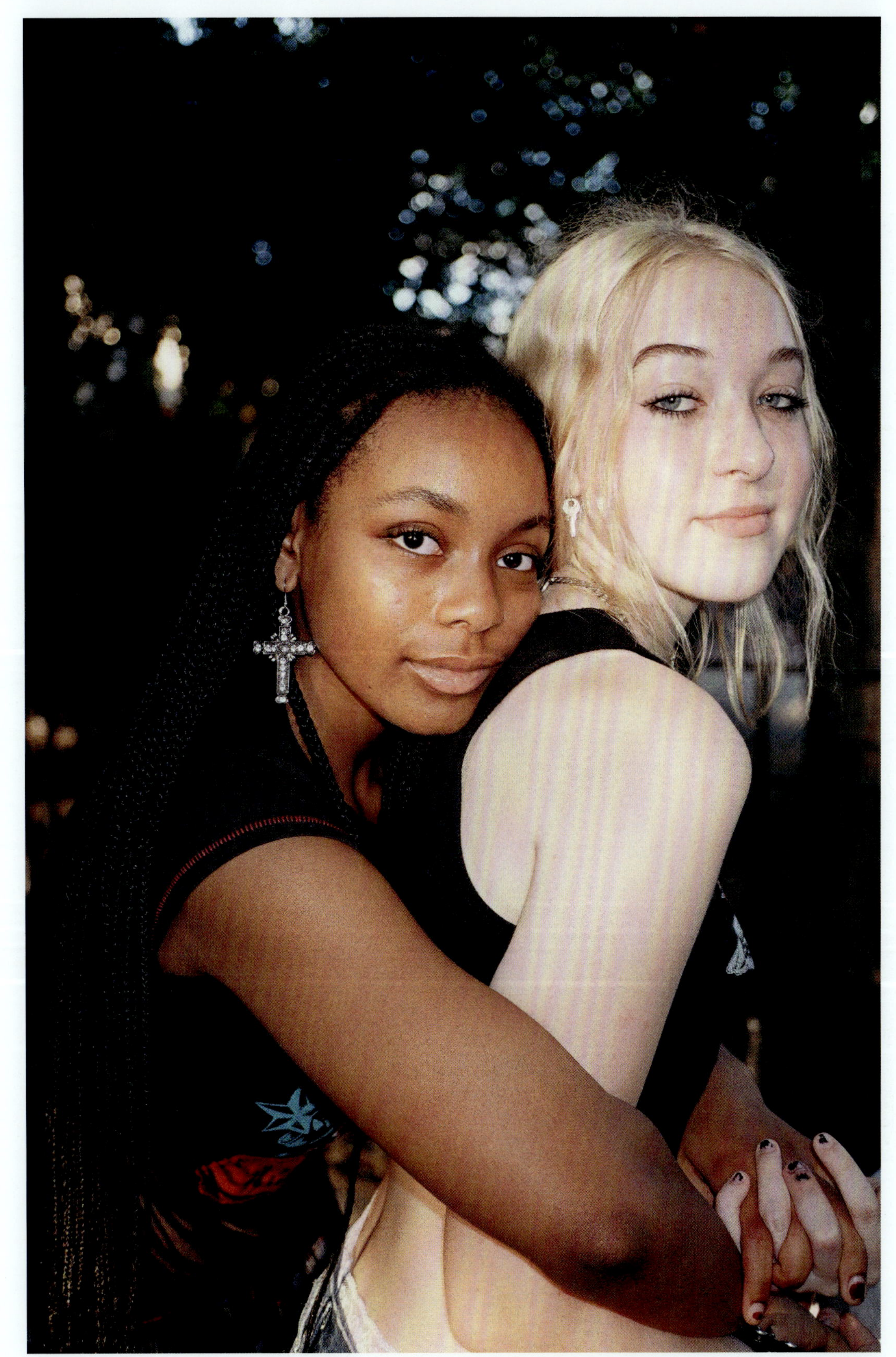

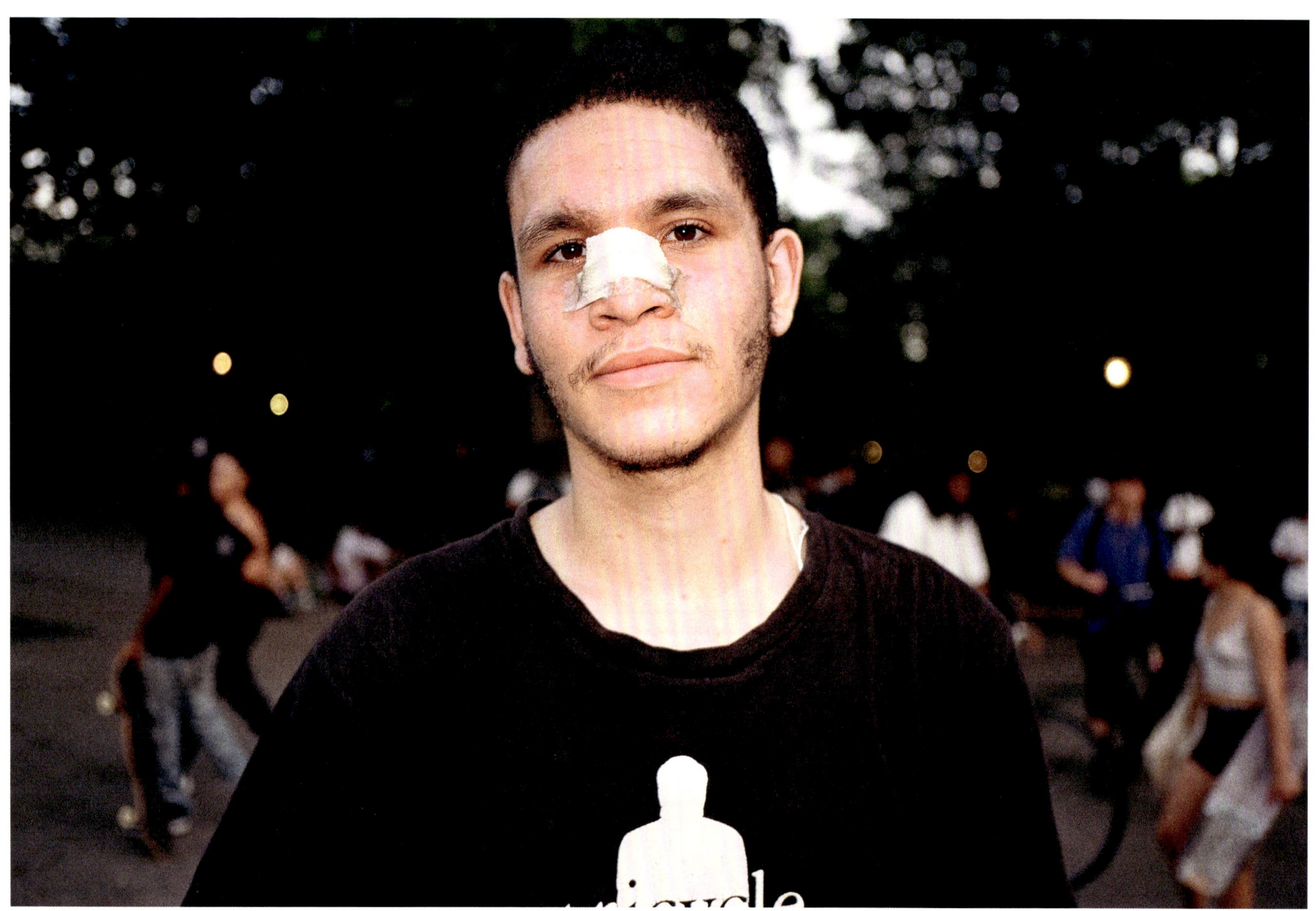

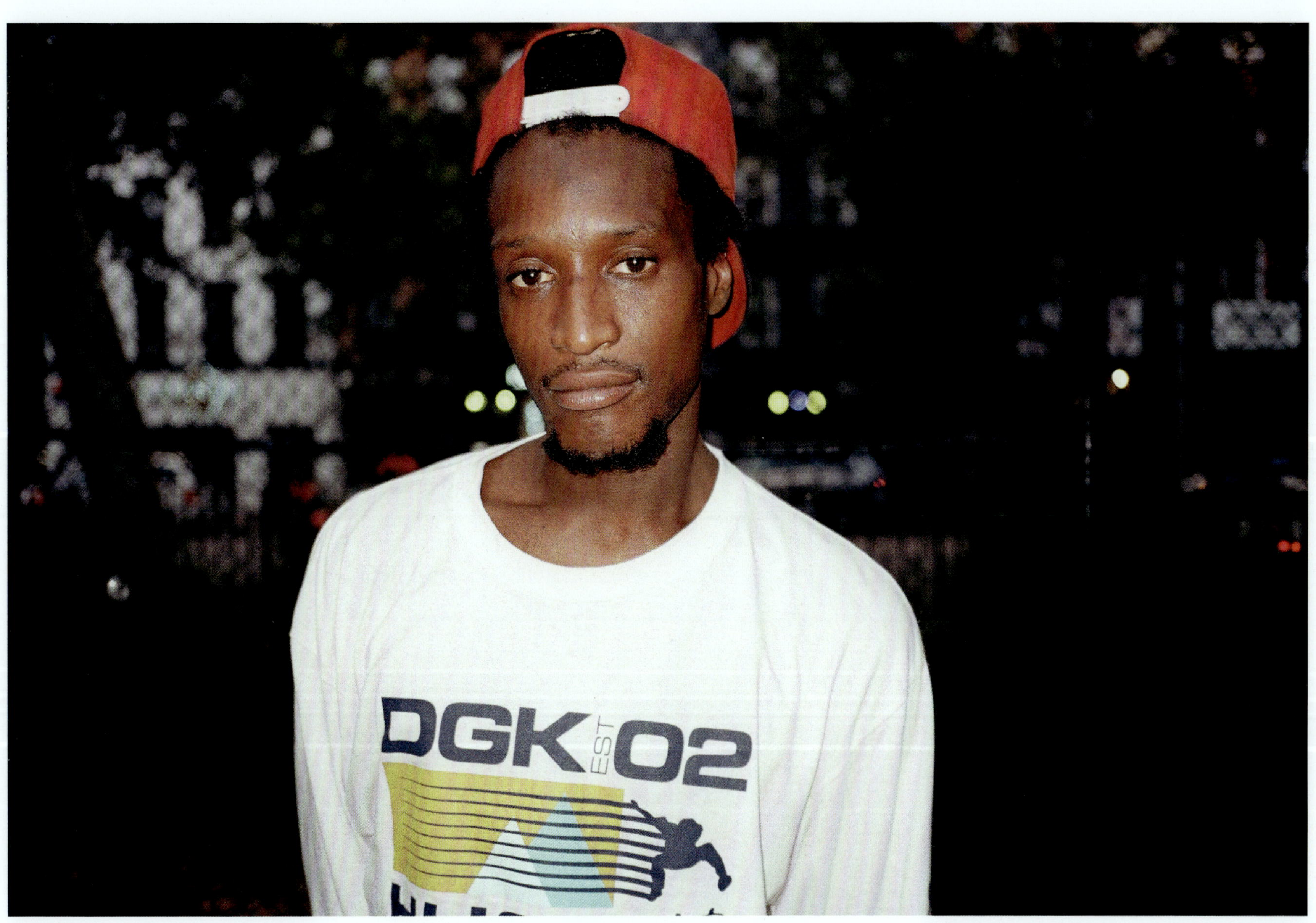
DGK EST 02

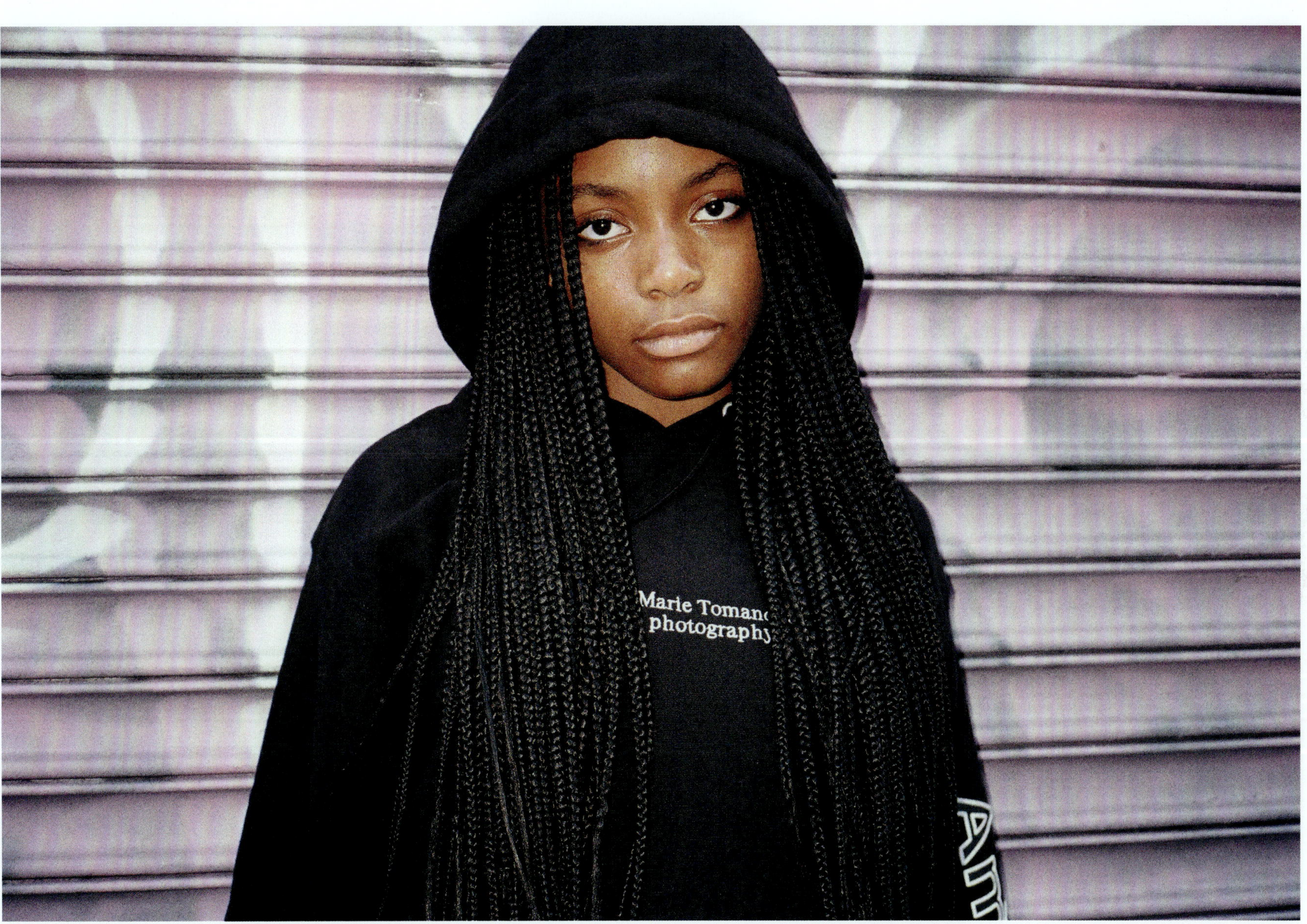
Marie Toman
photography

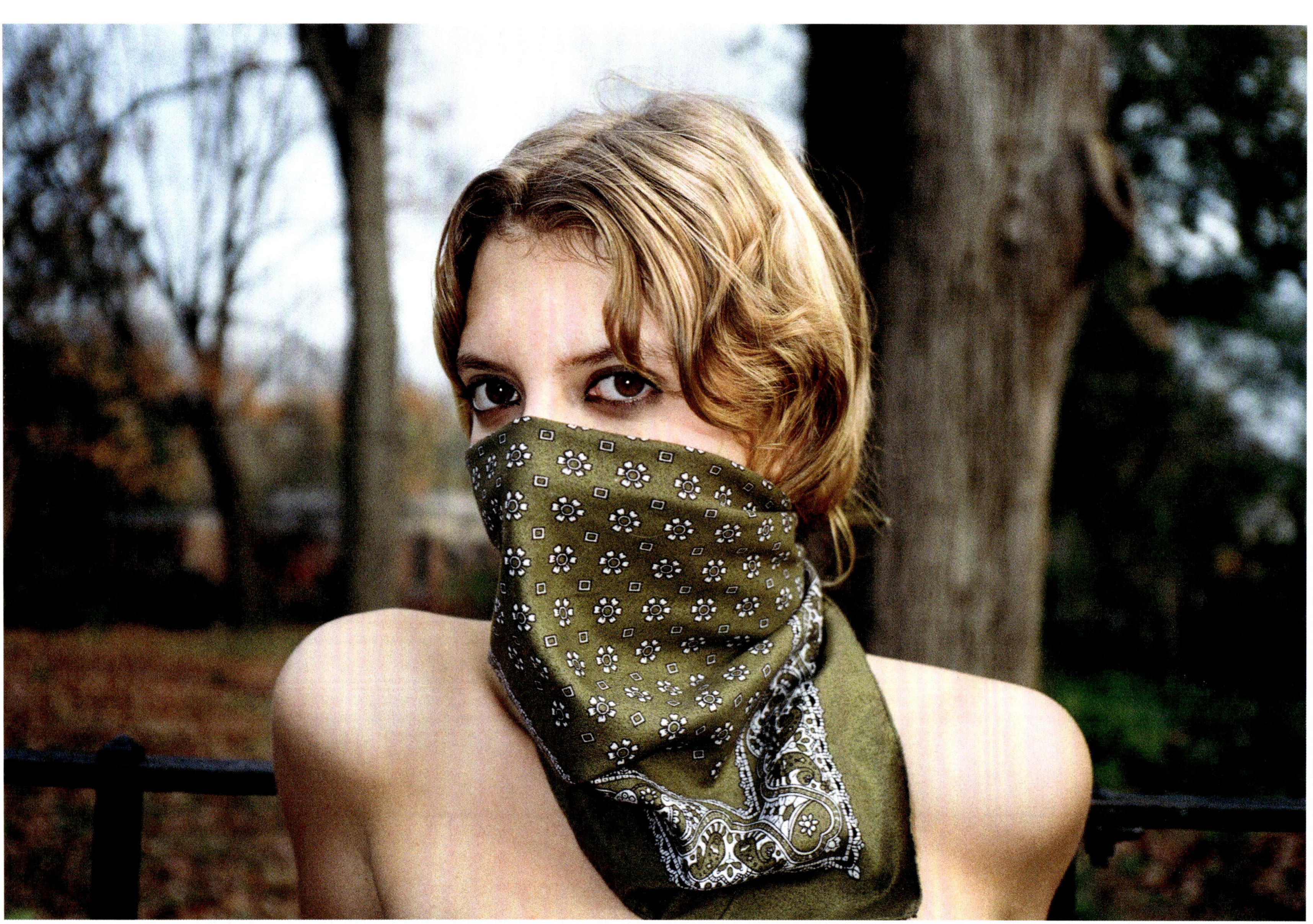

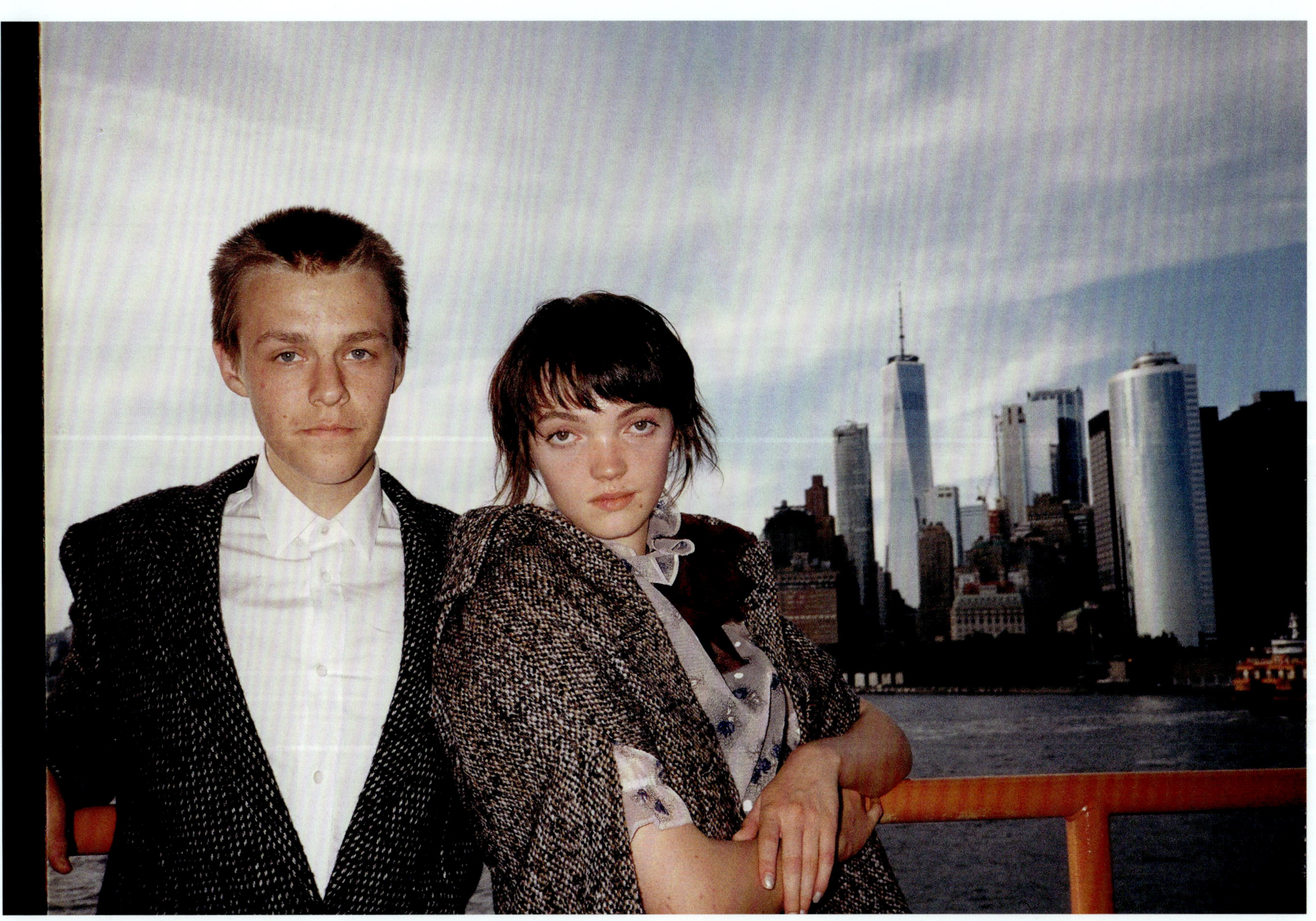

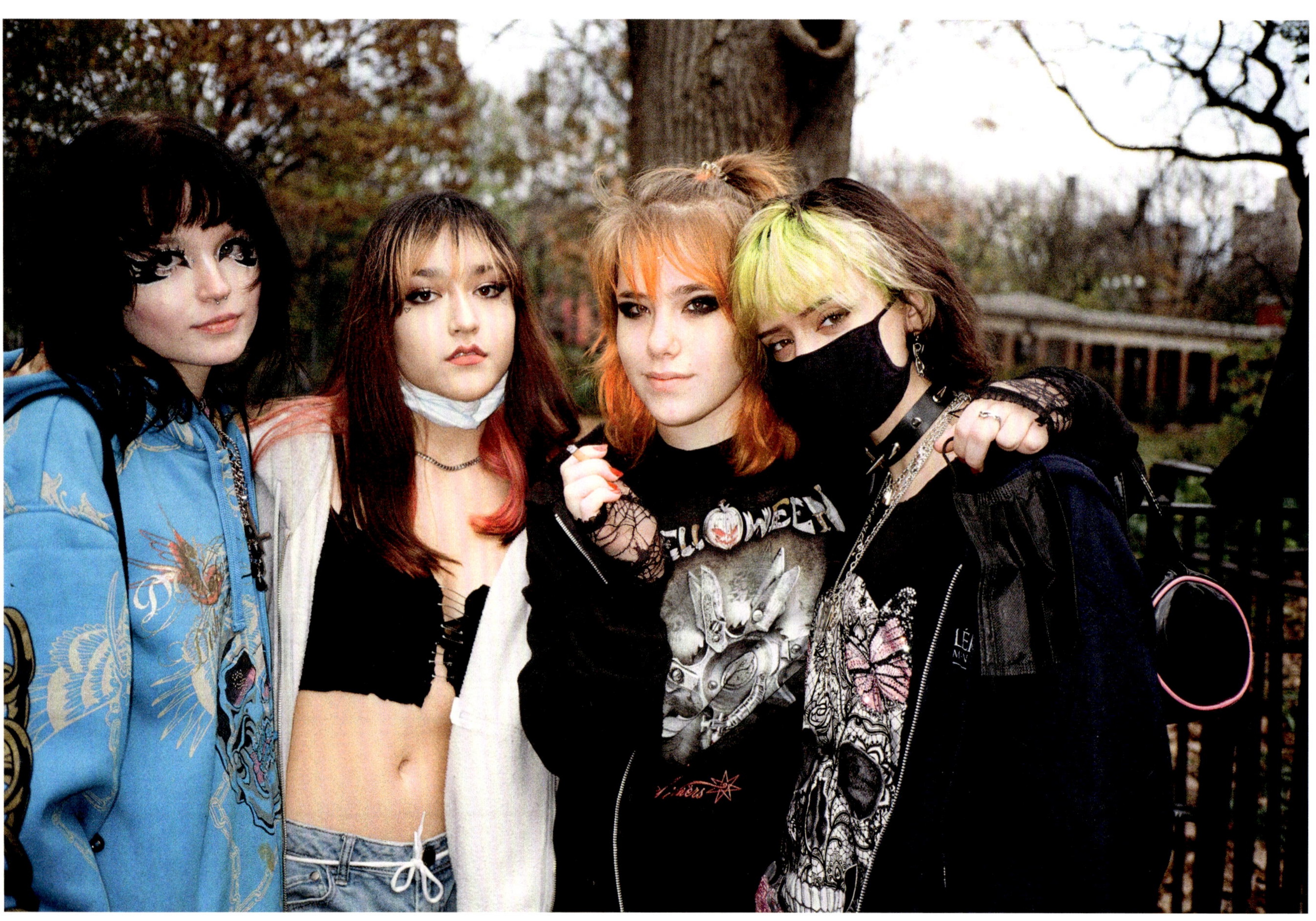

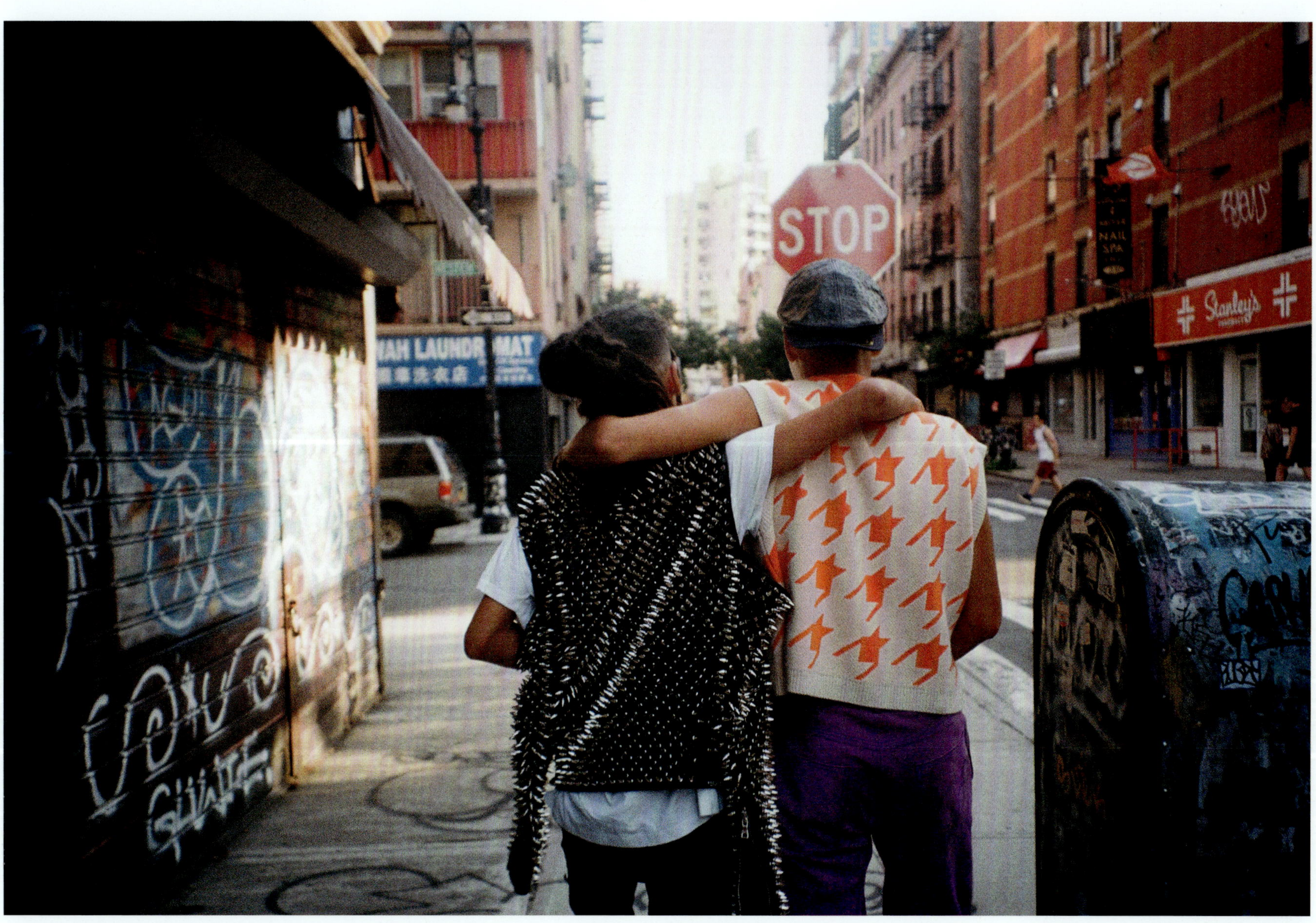
STOP
Stanley's

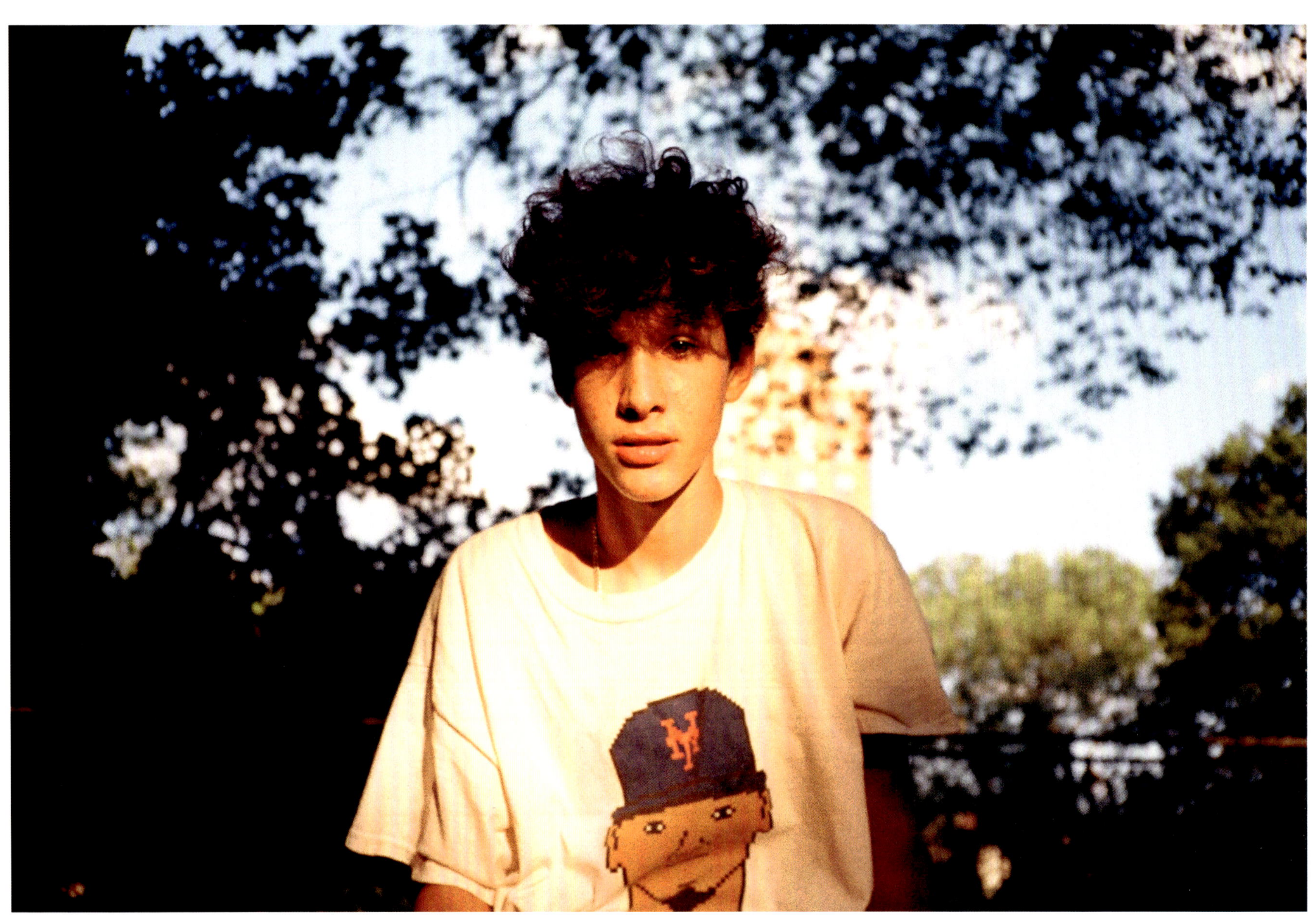

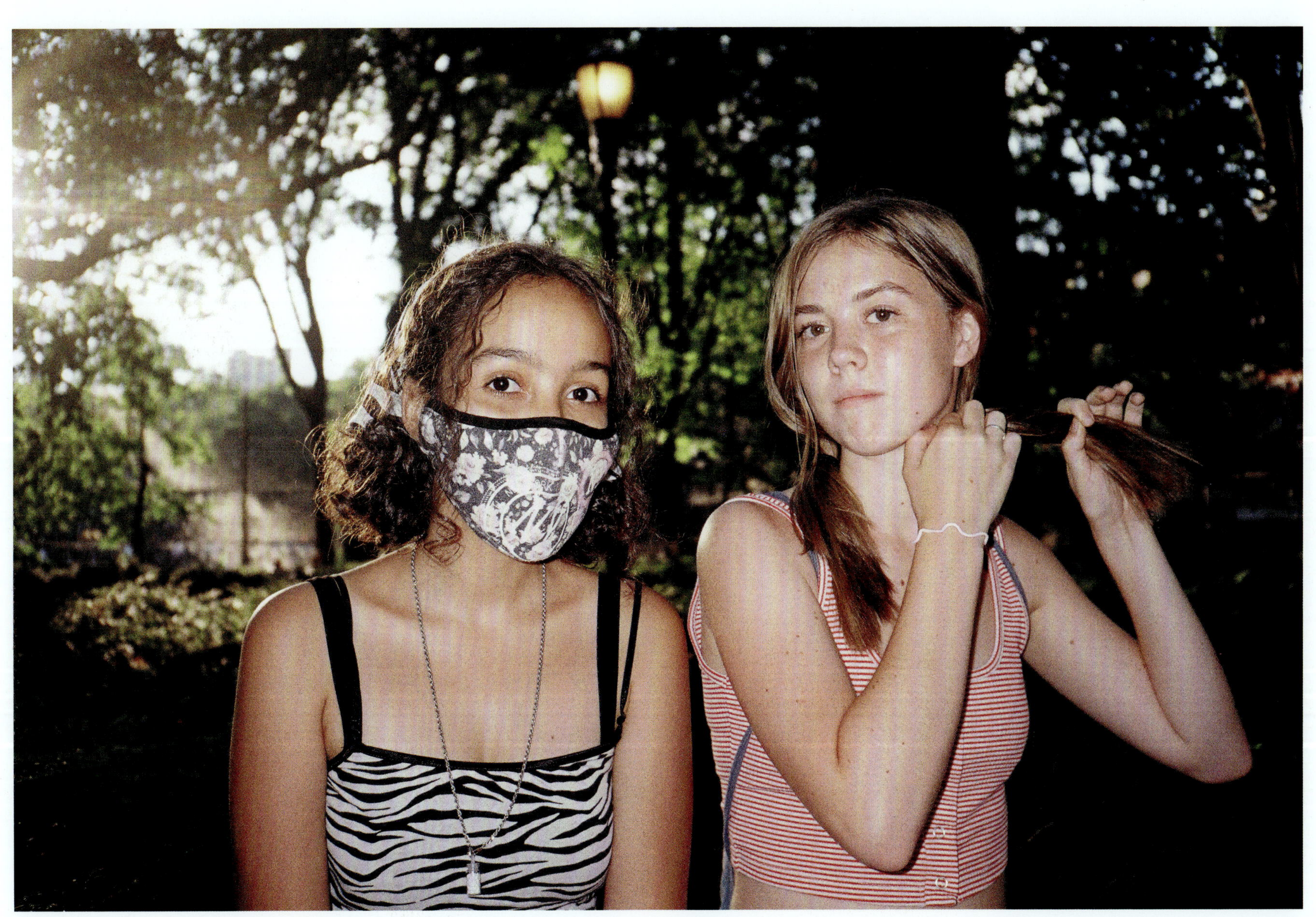

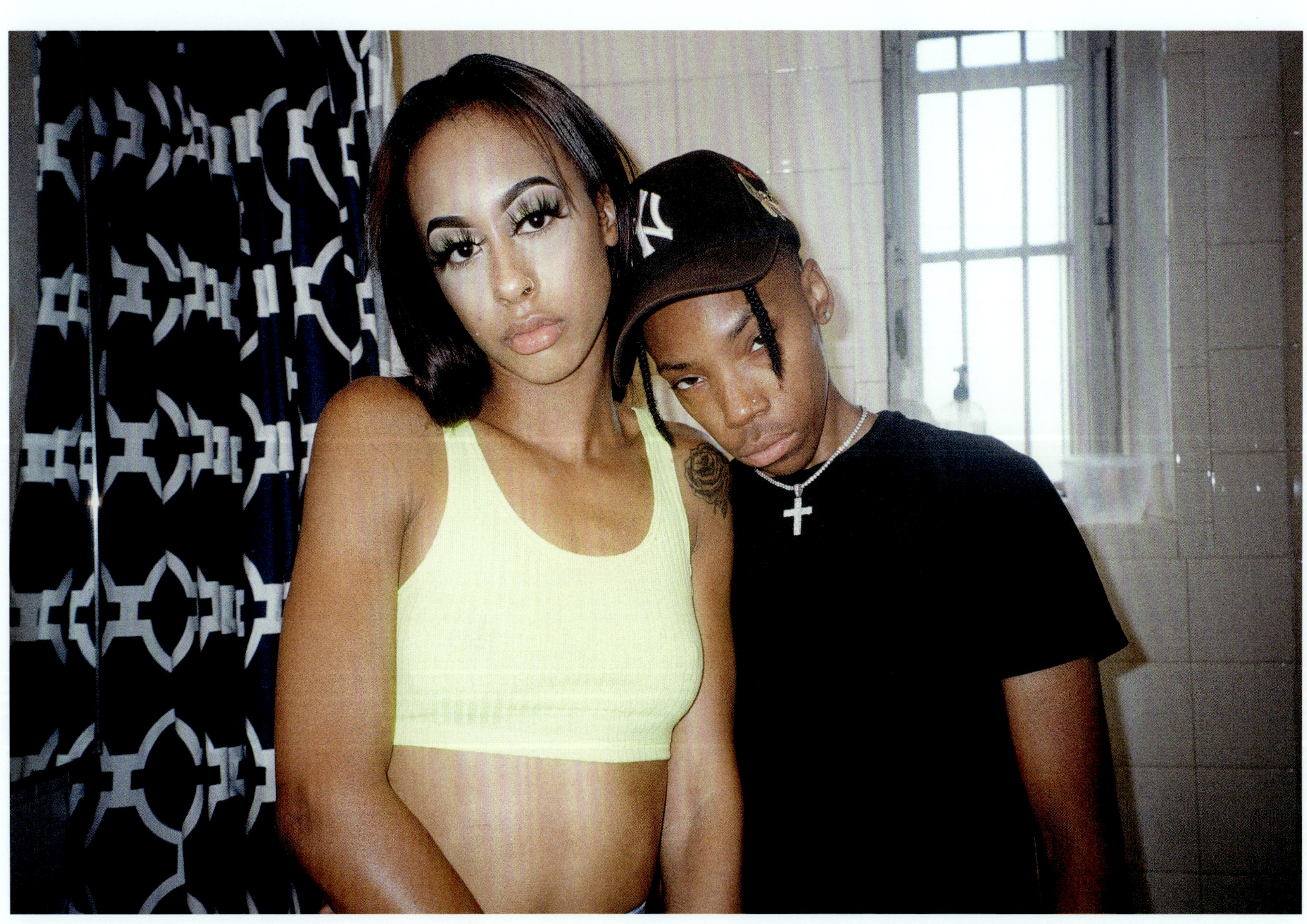

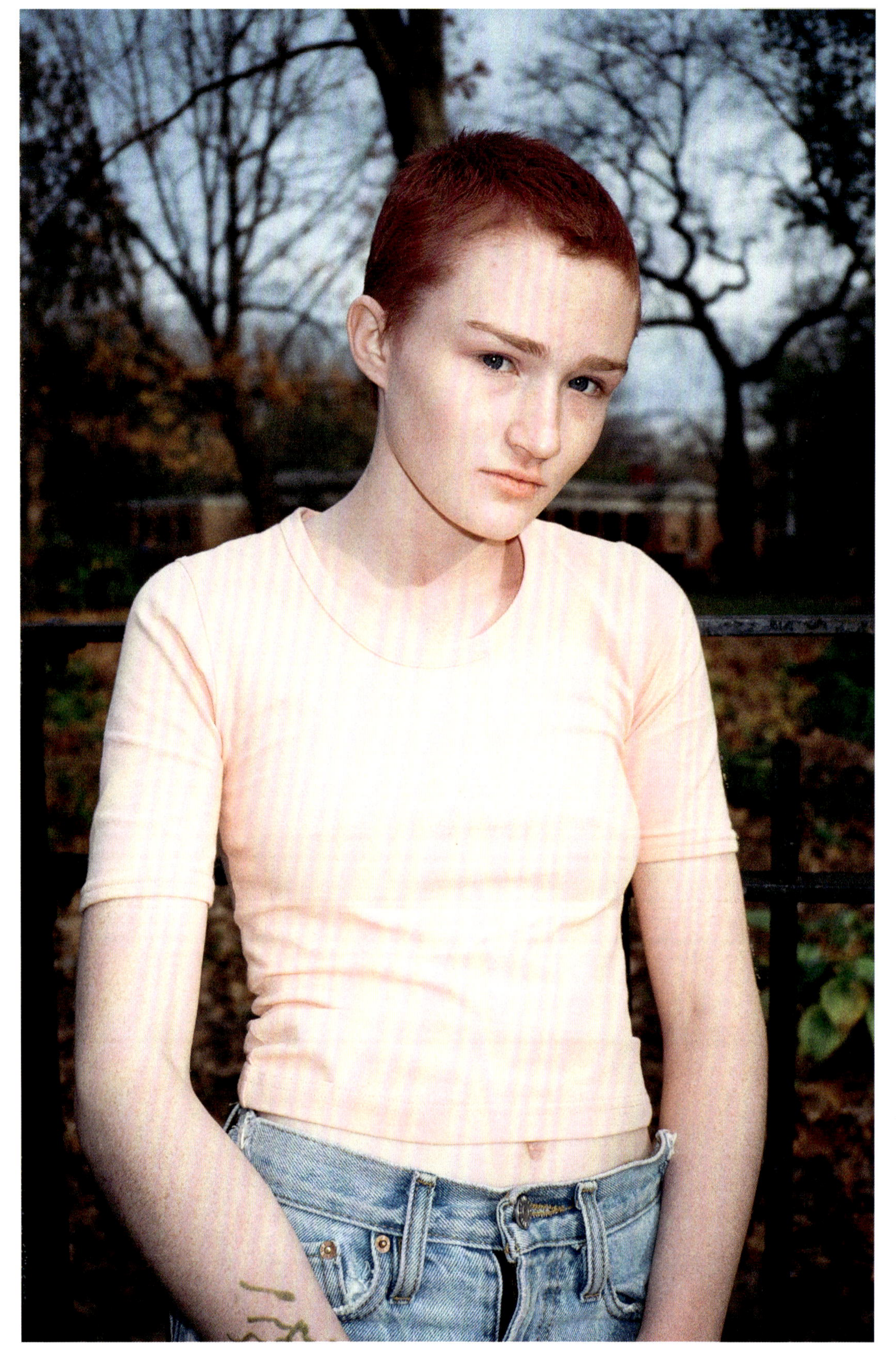

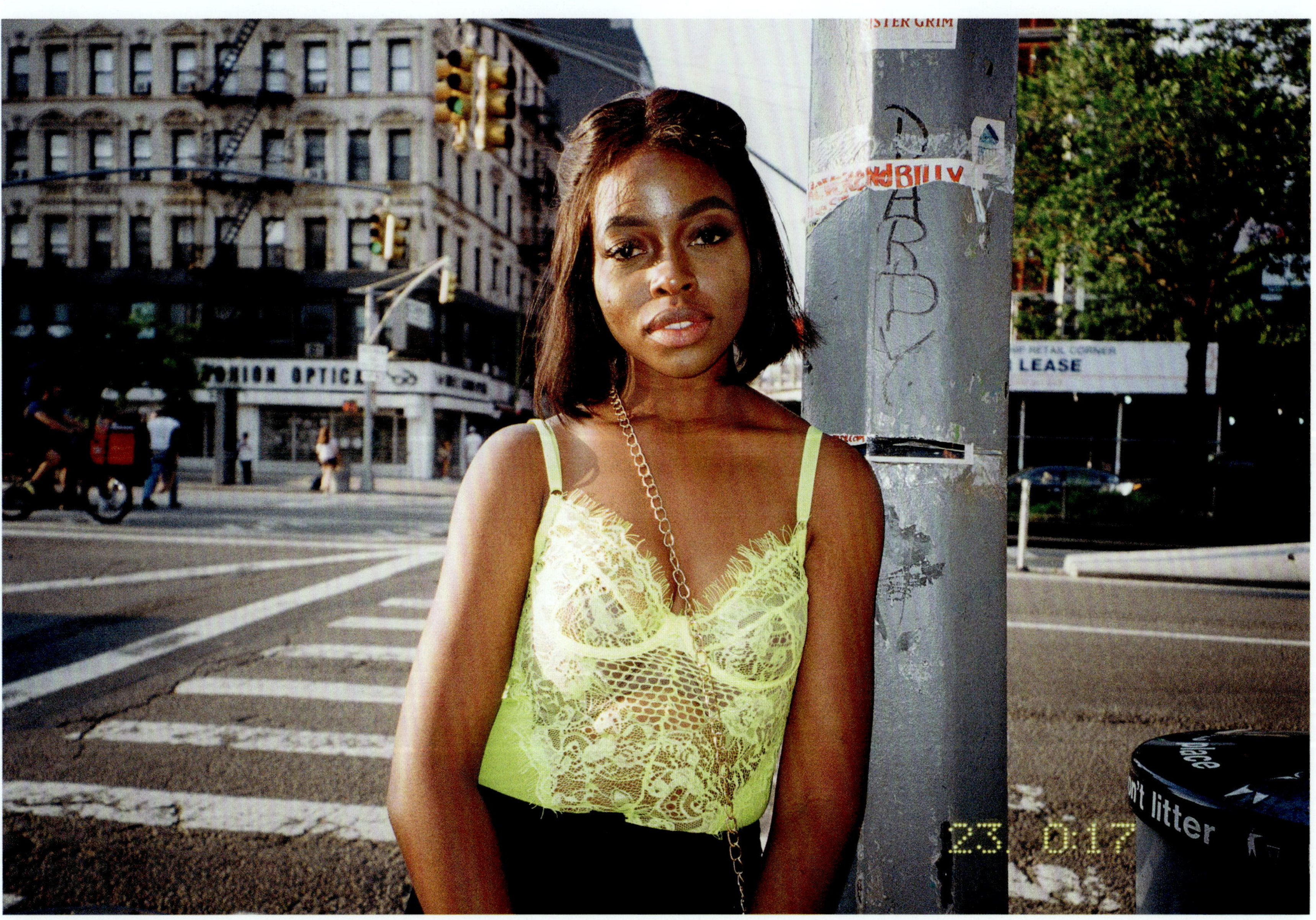

LEASE
23 0:17

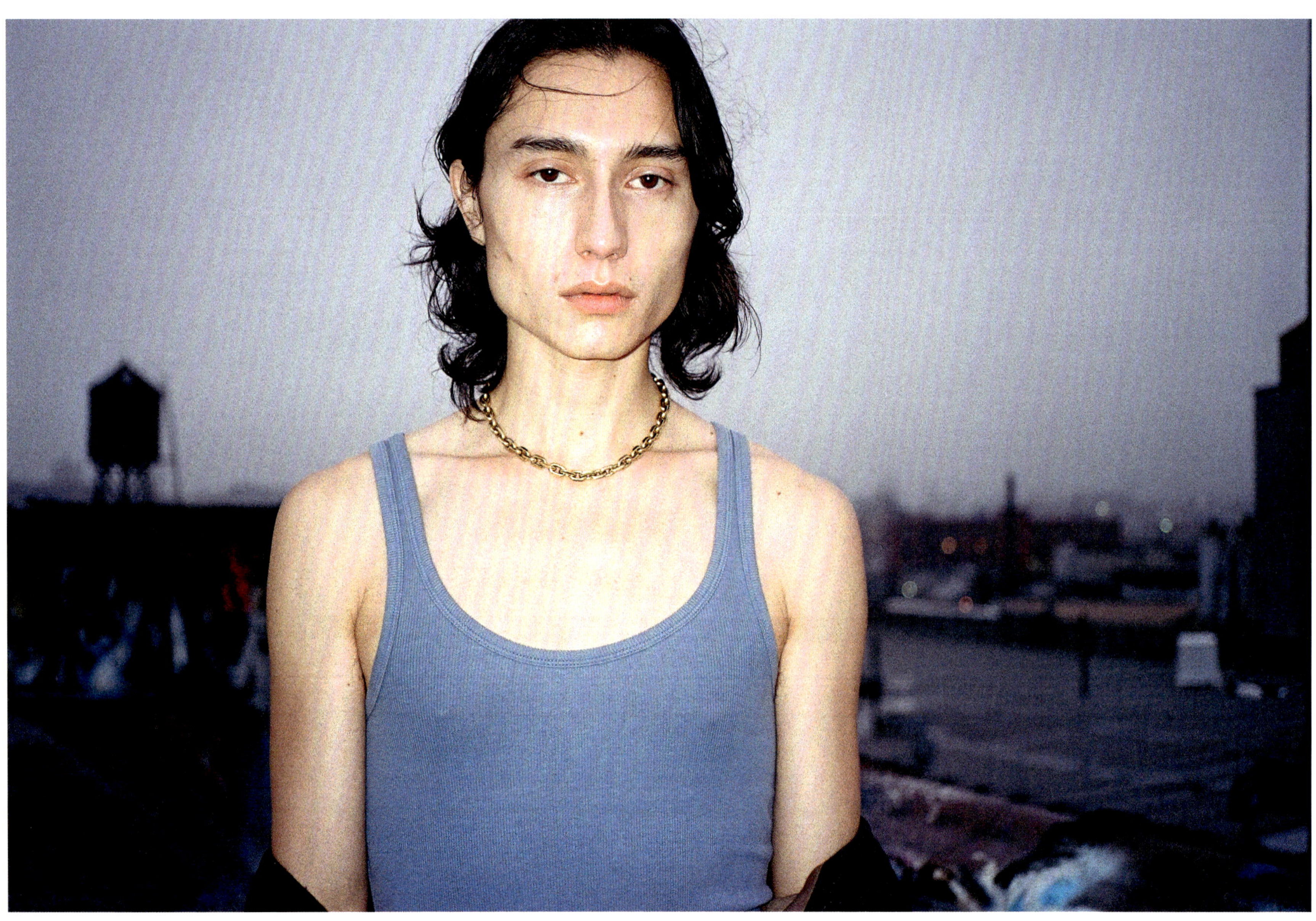

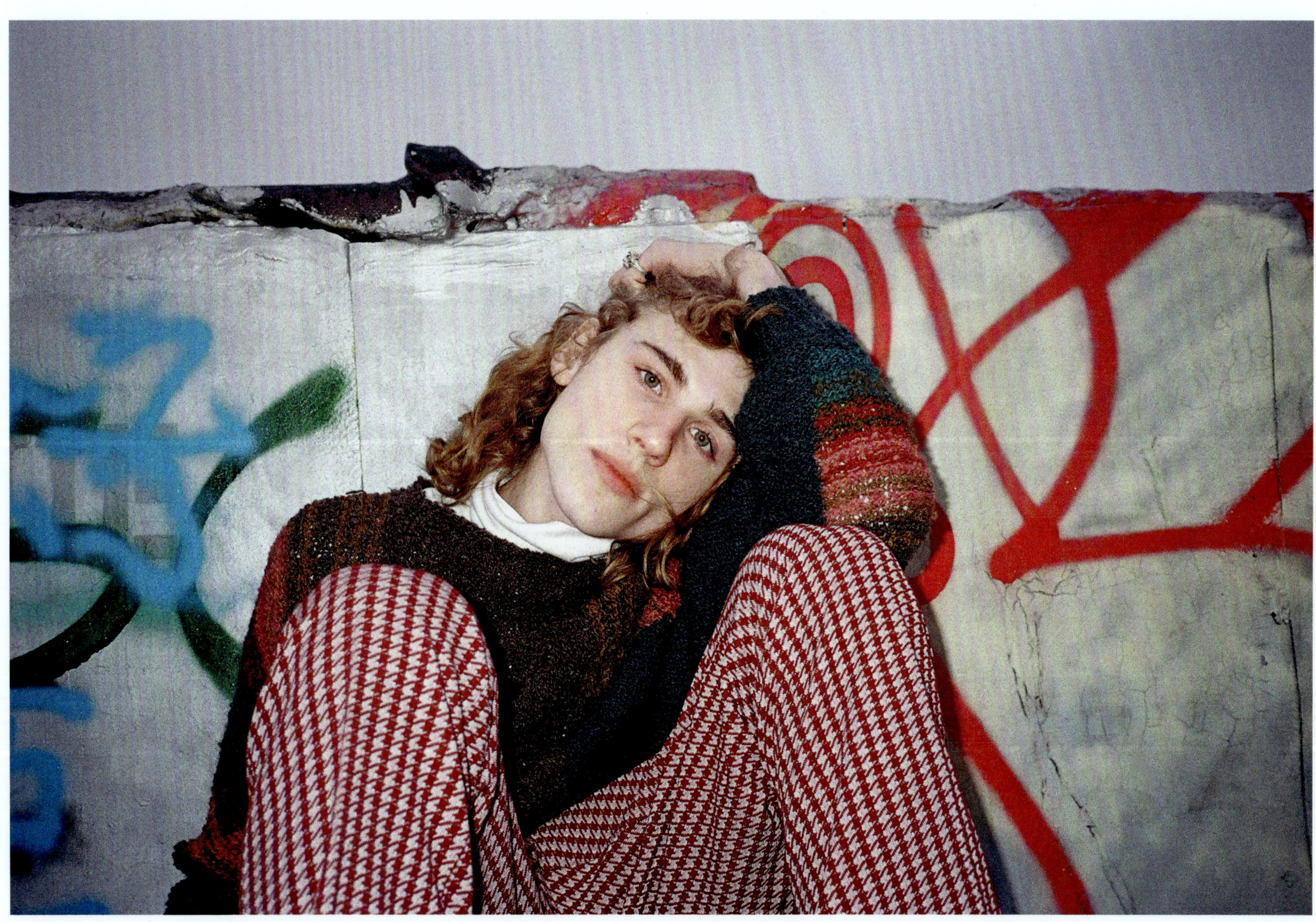

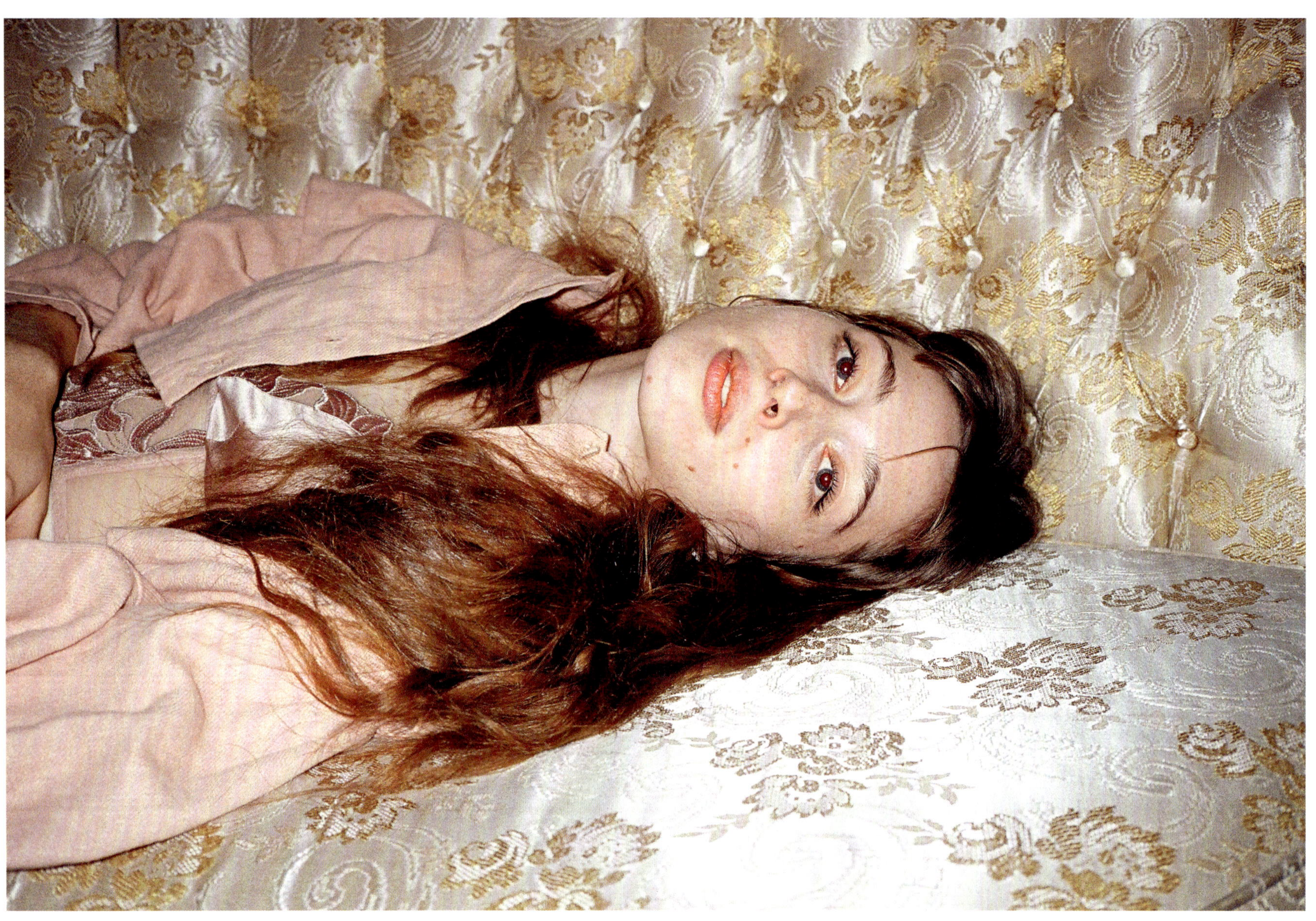

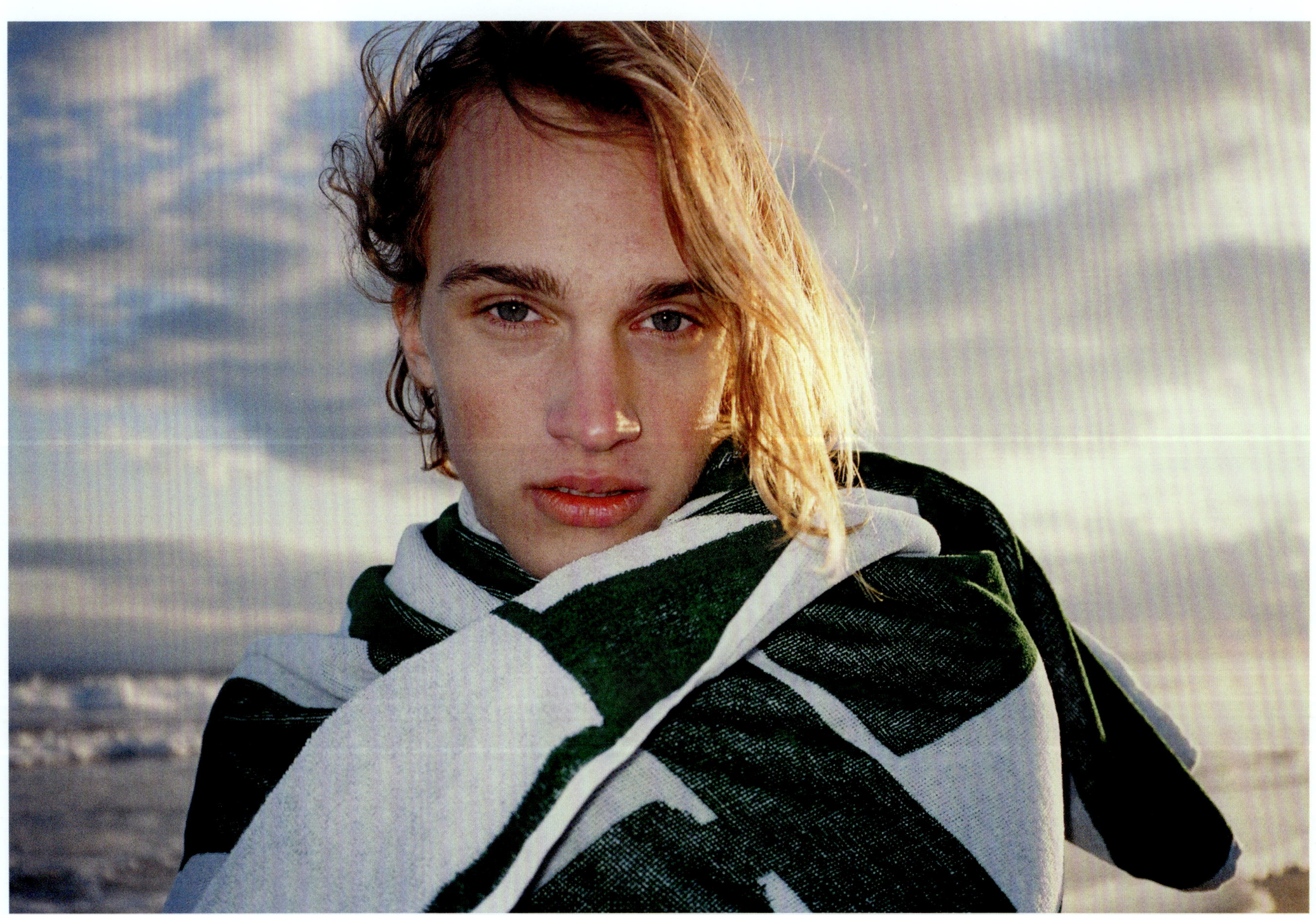

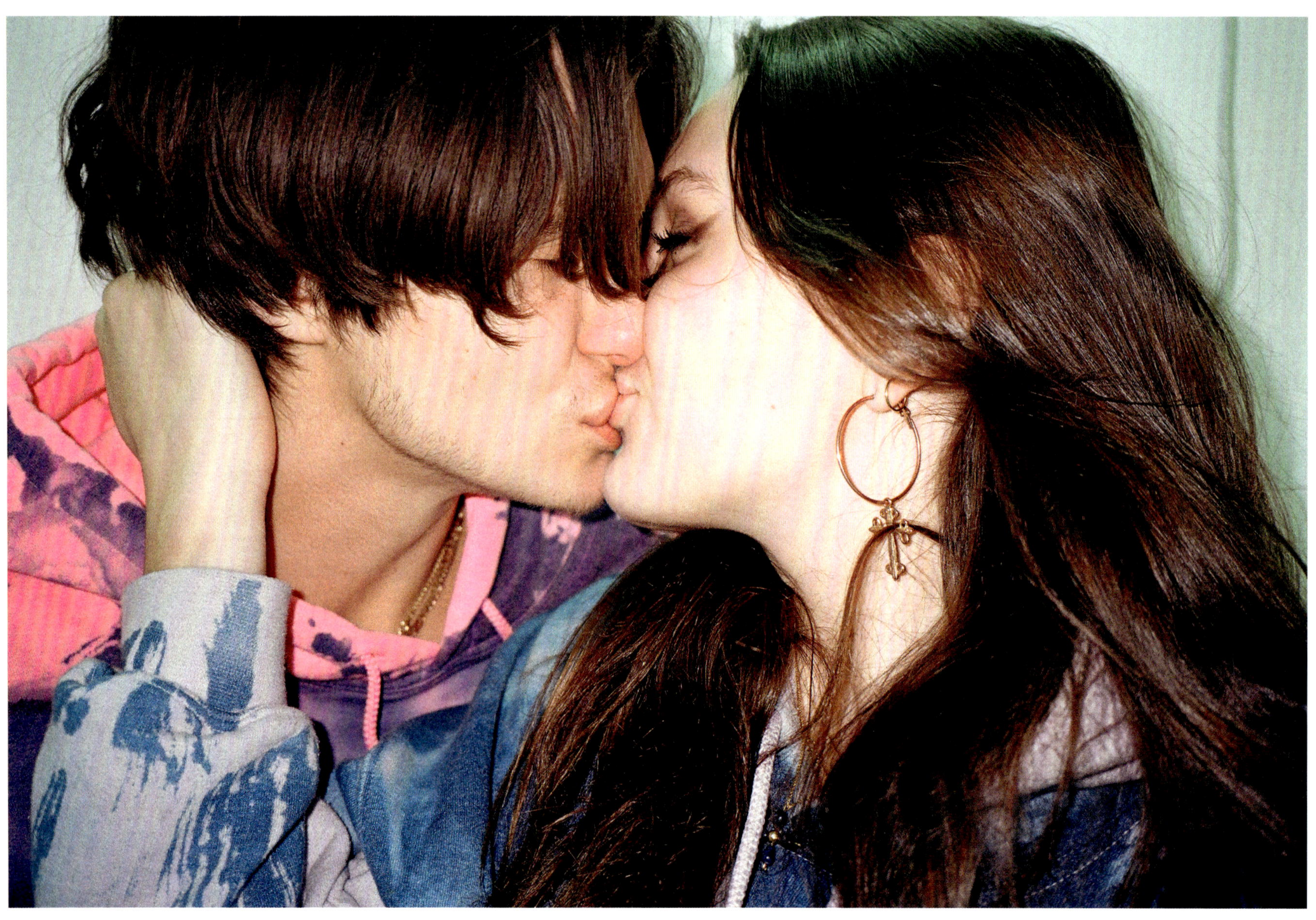

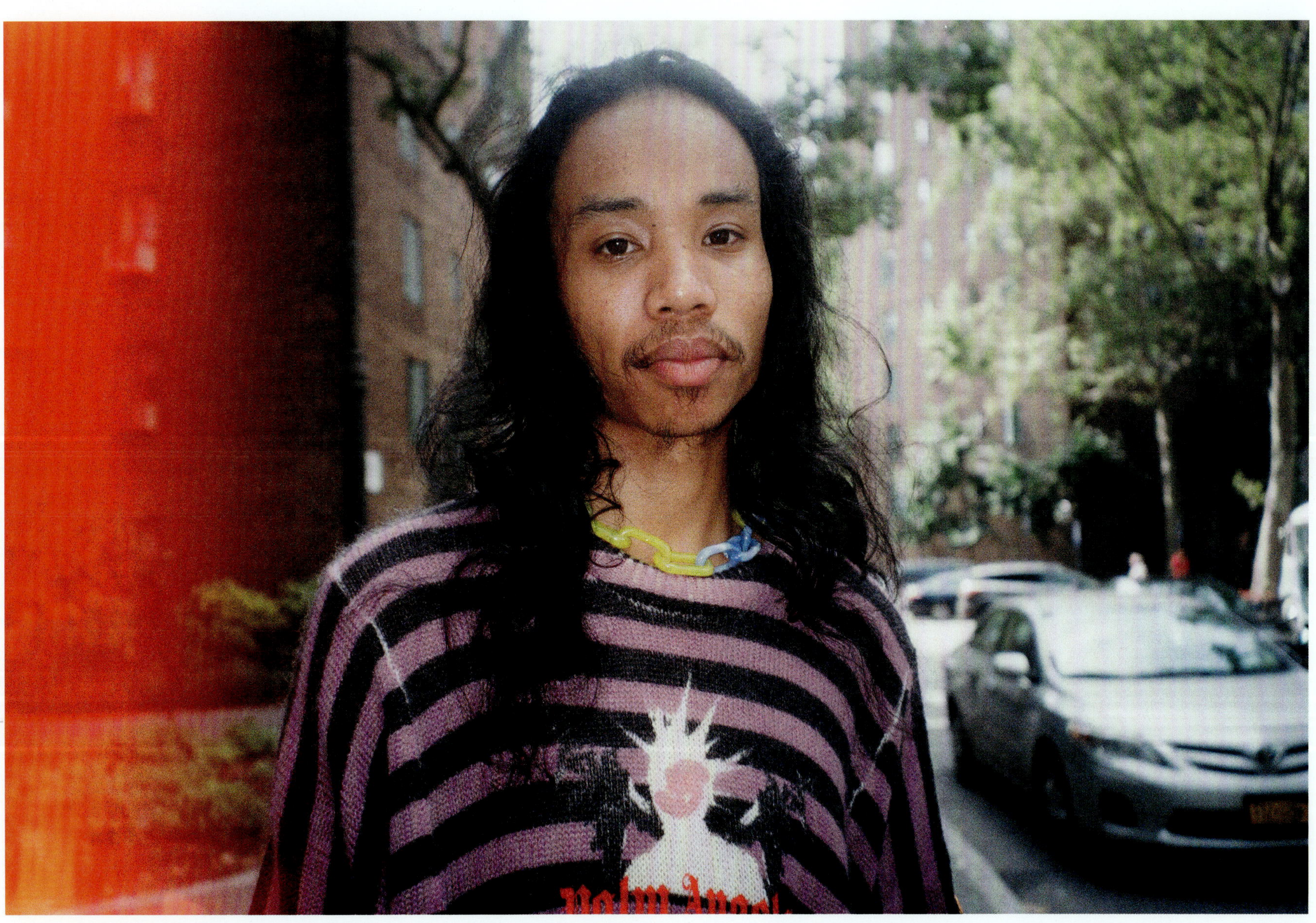

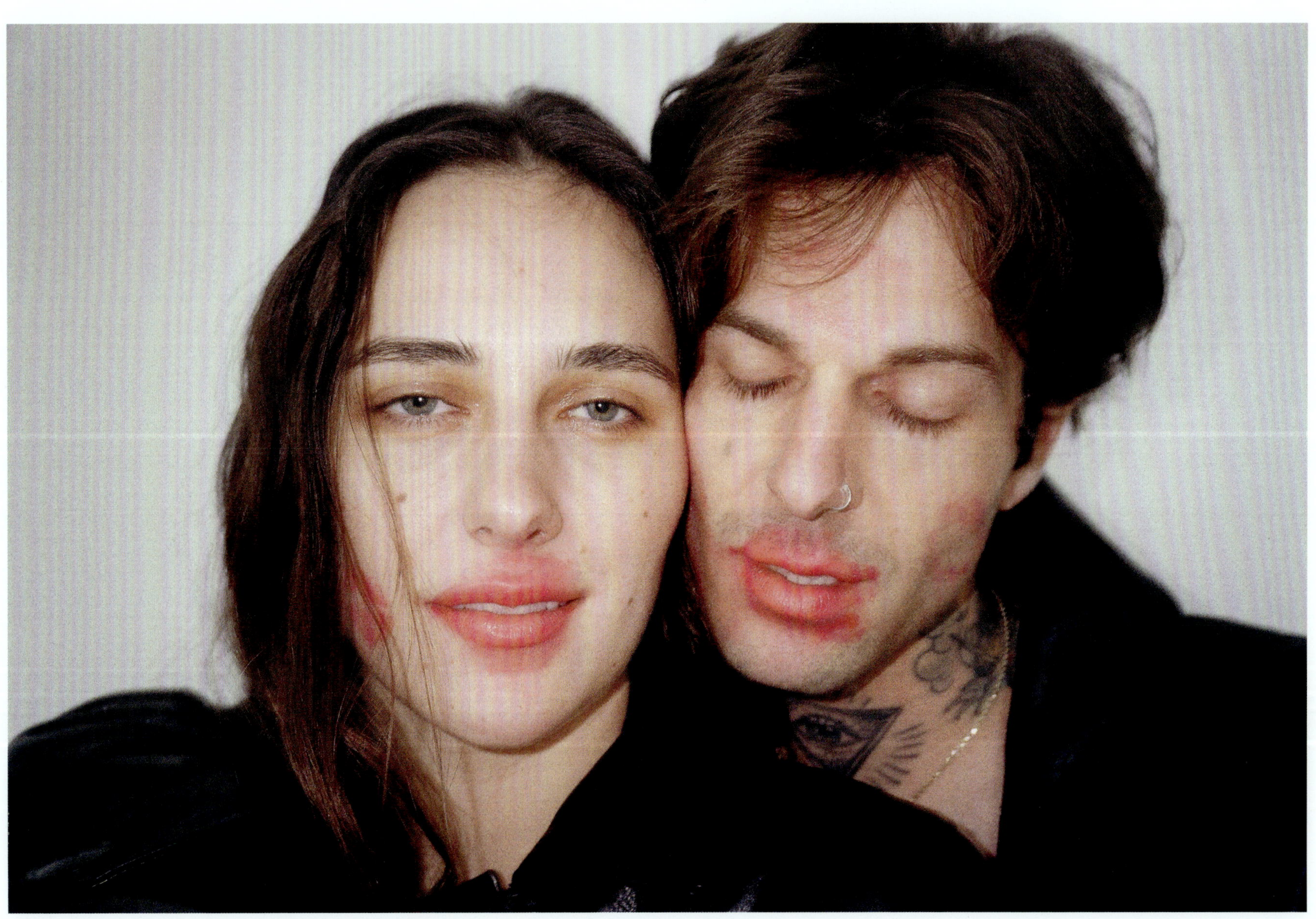

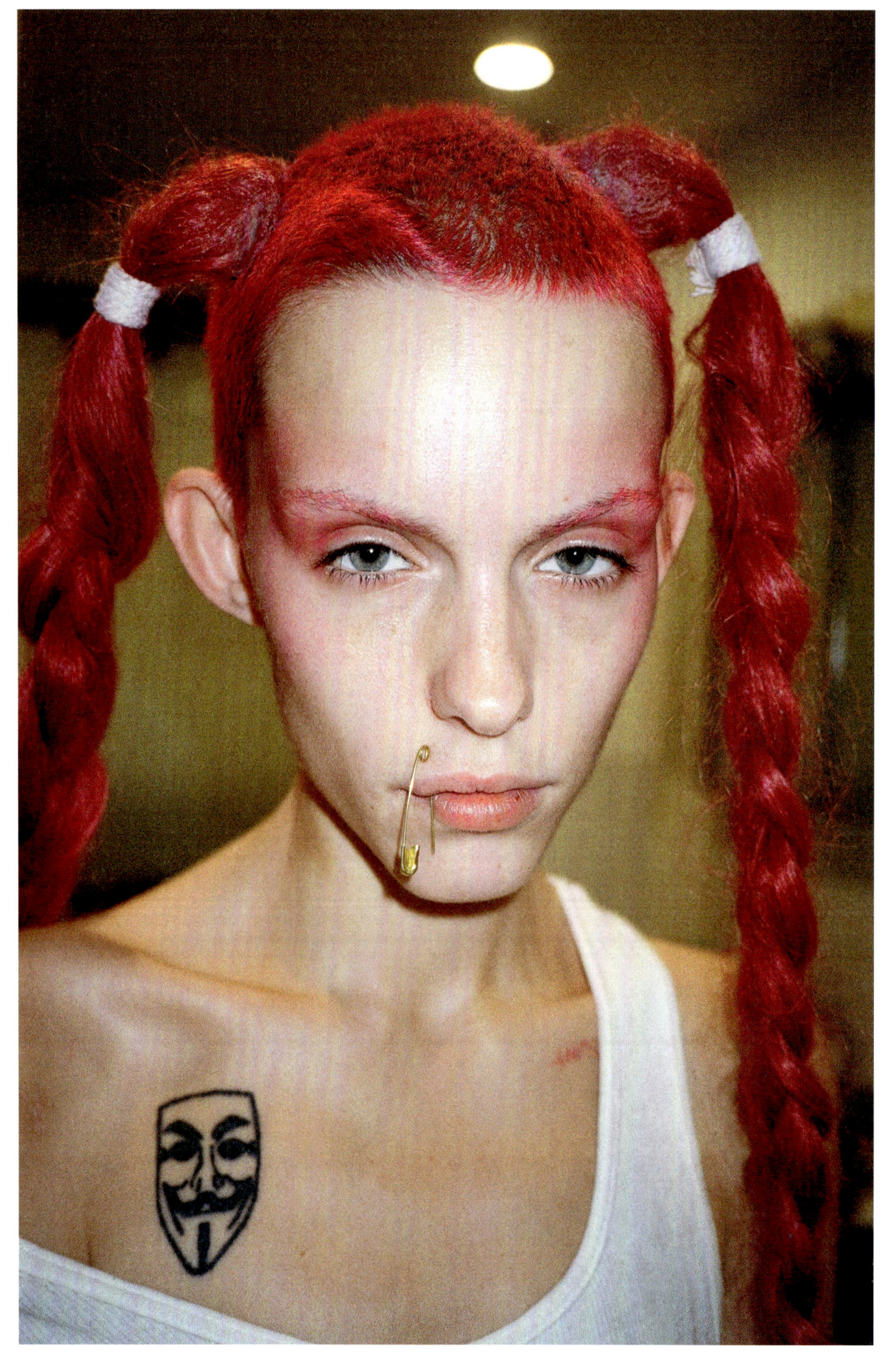

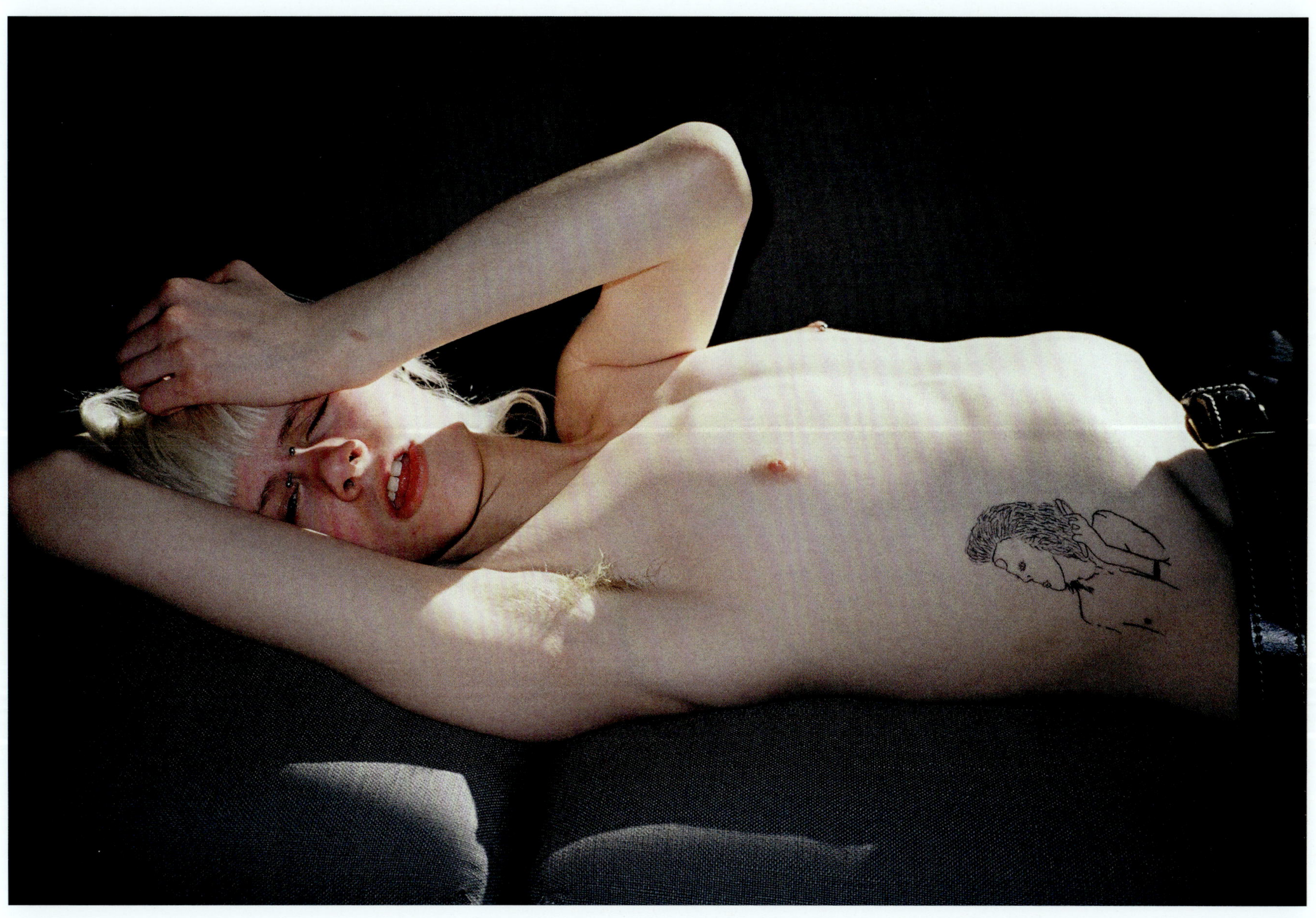

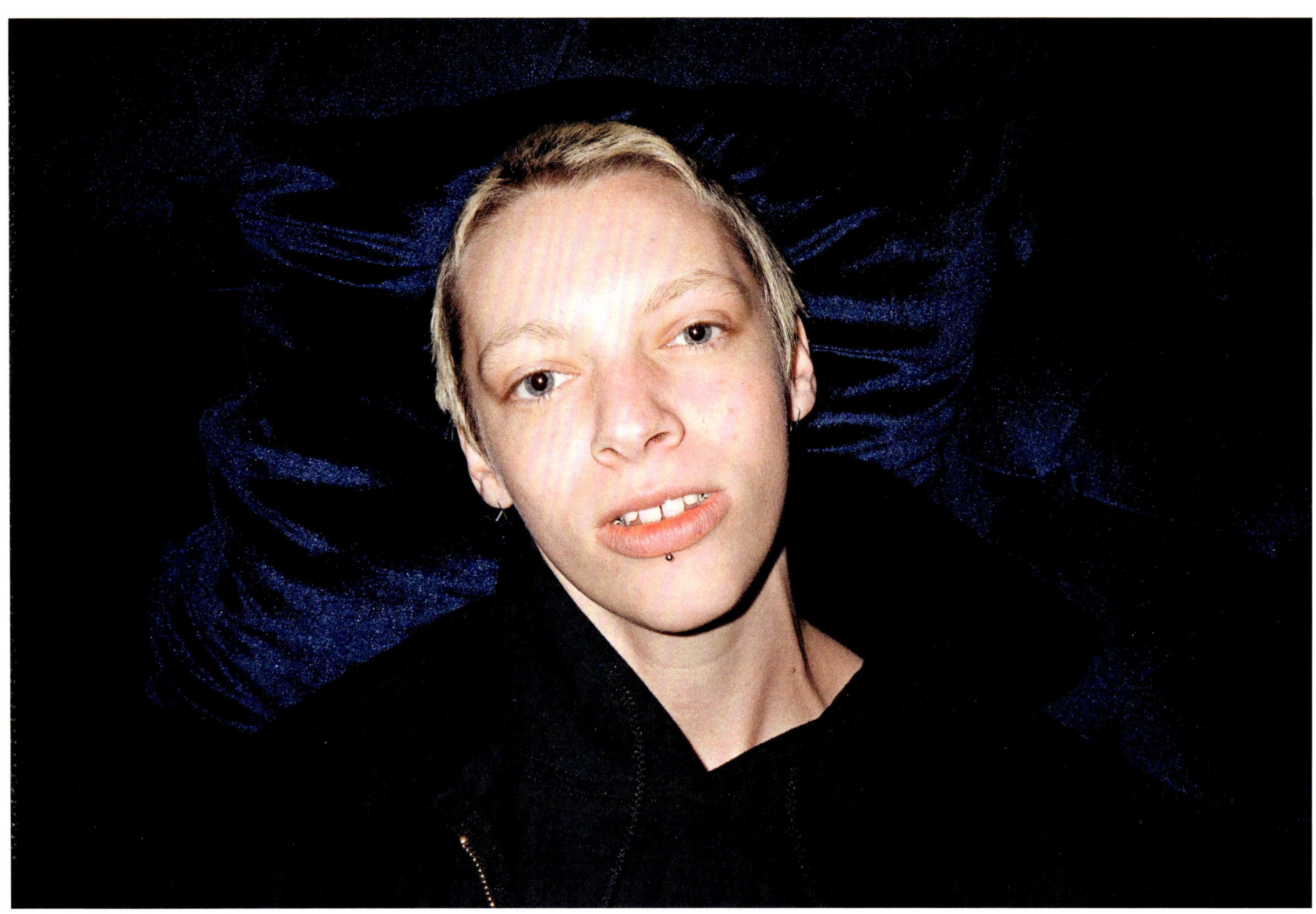

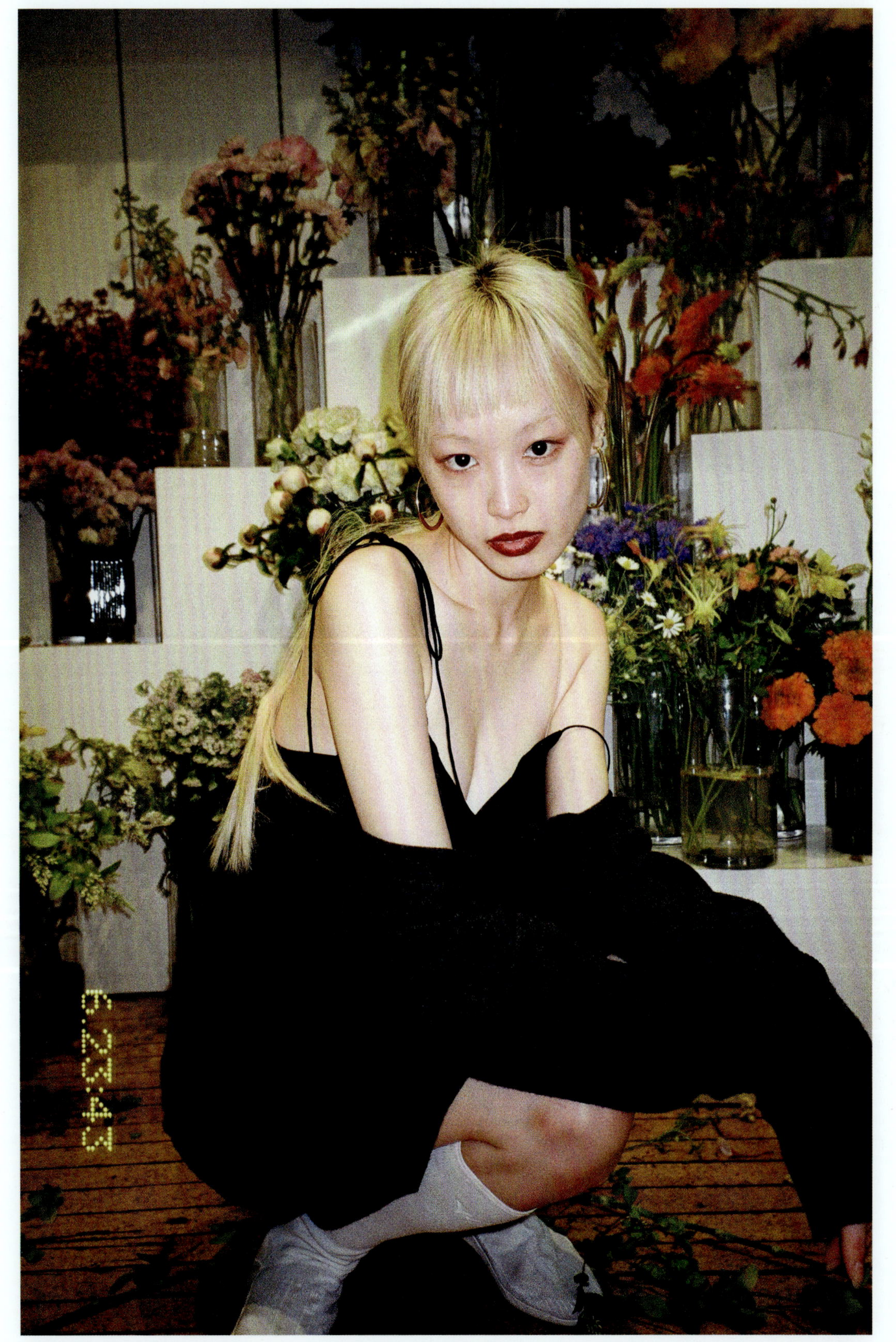
6.23.43

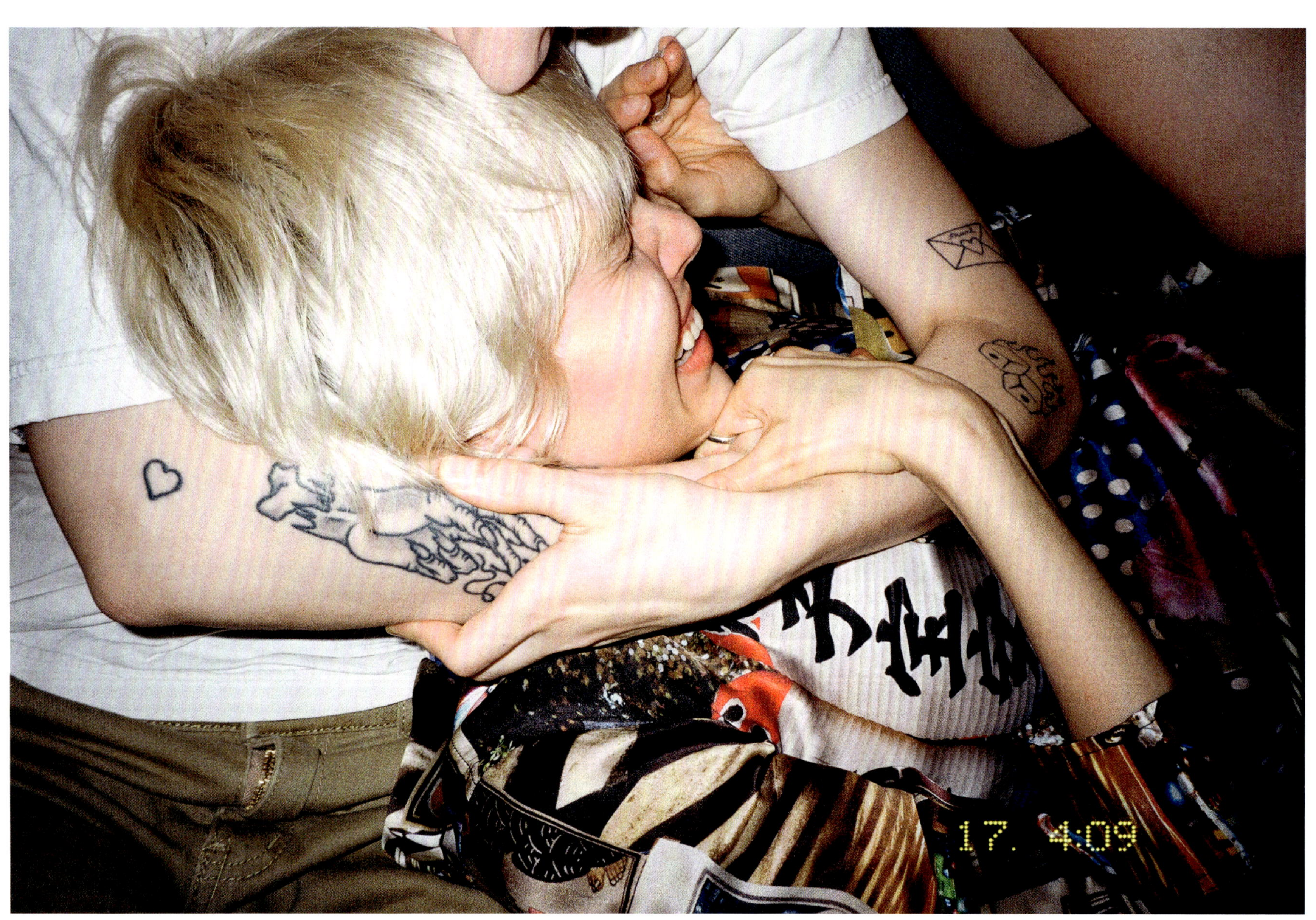
17. 4:09

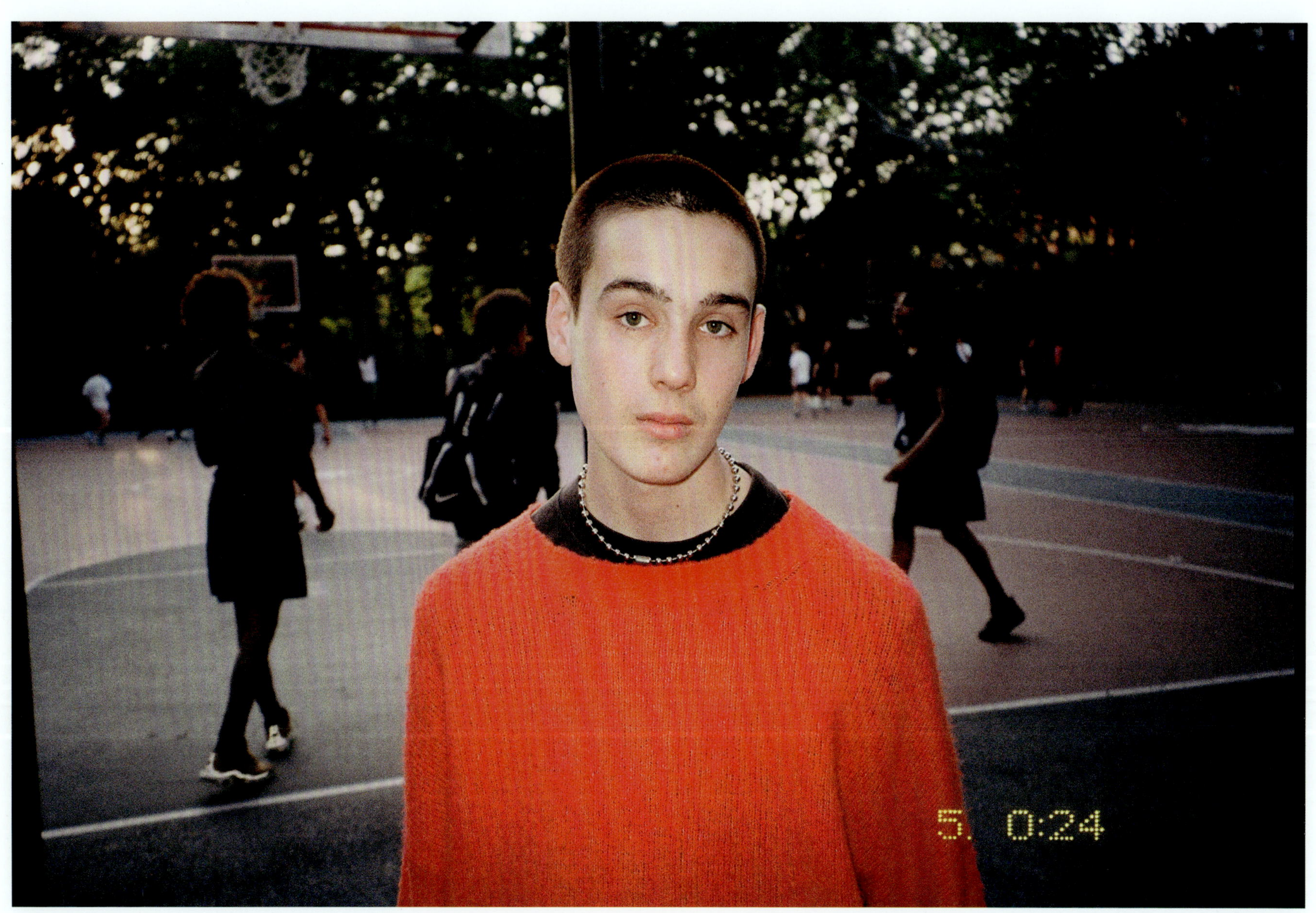
5. 0:24

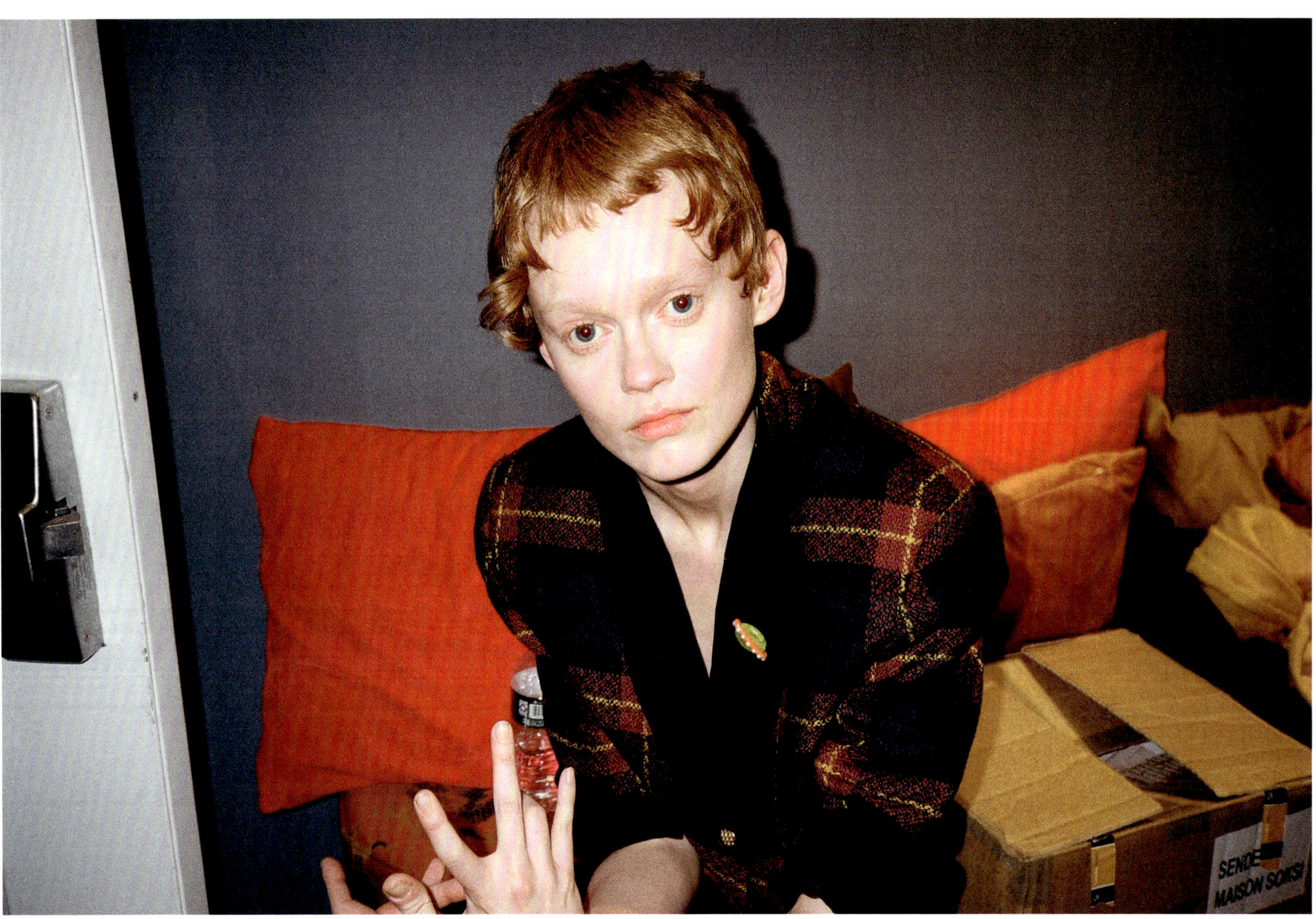
SENDE
MAISON SOKSI

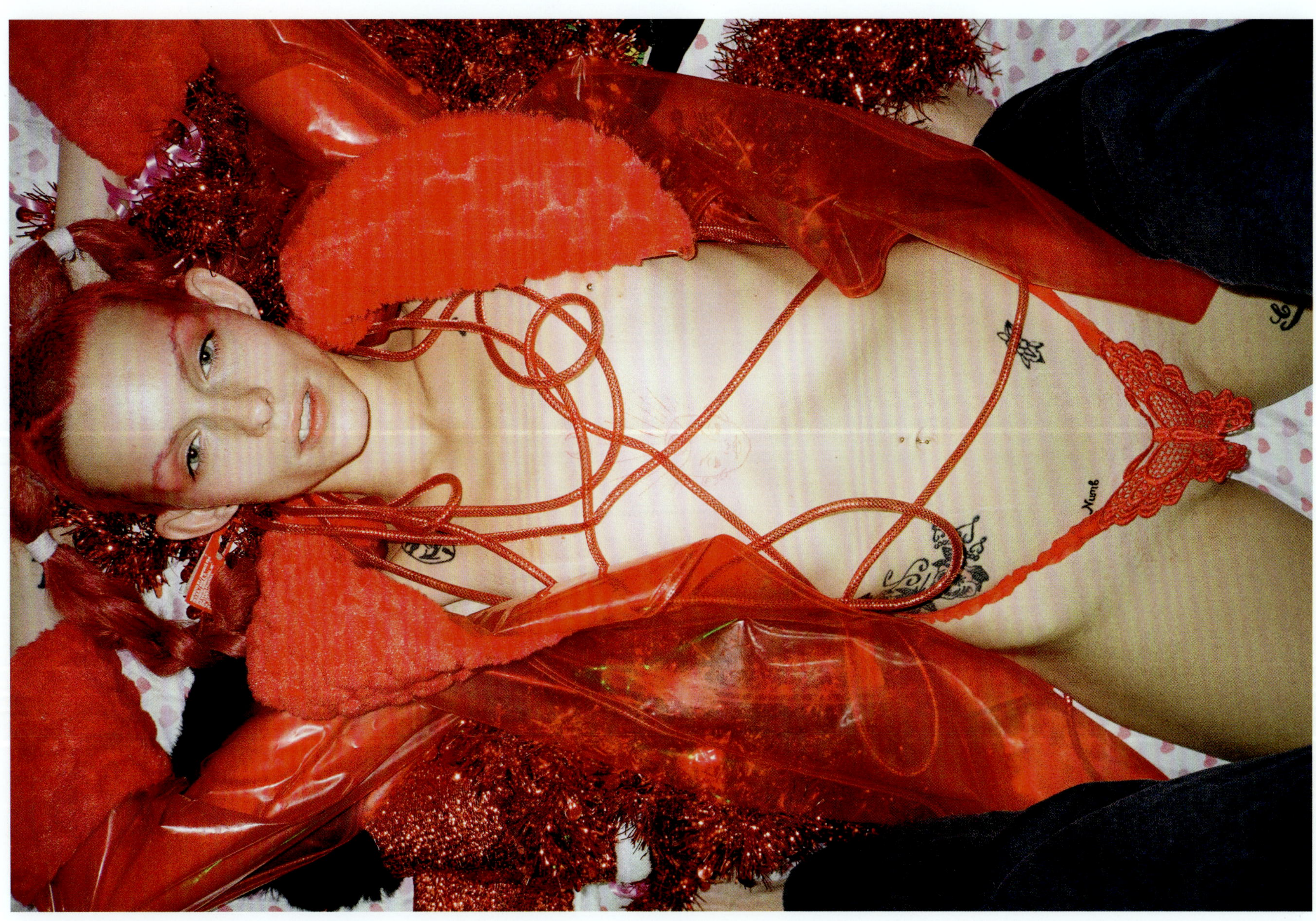

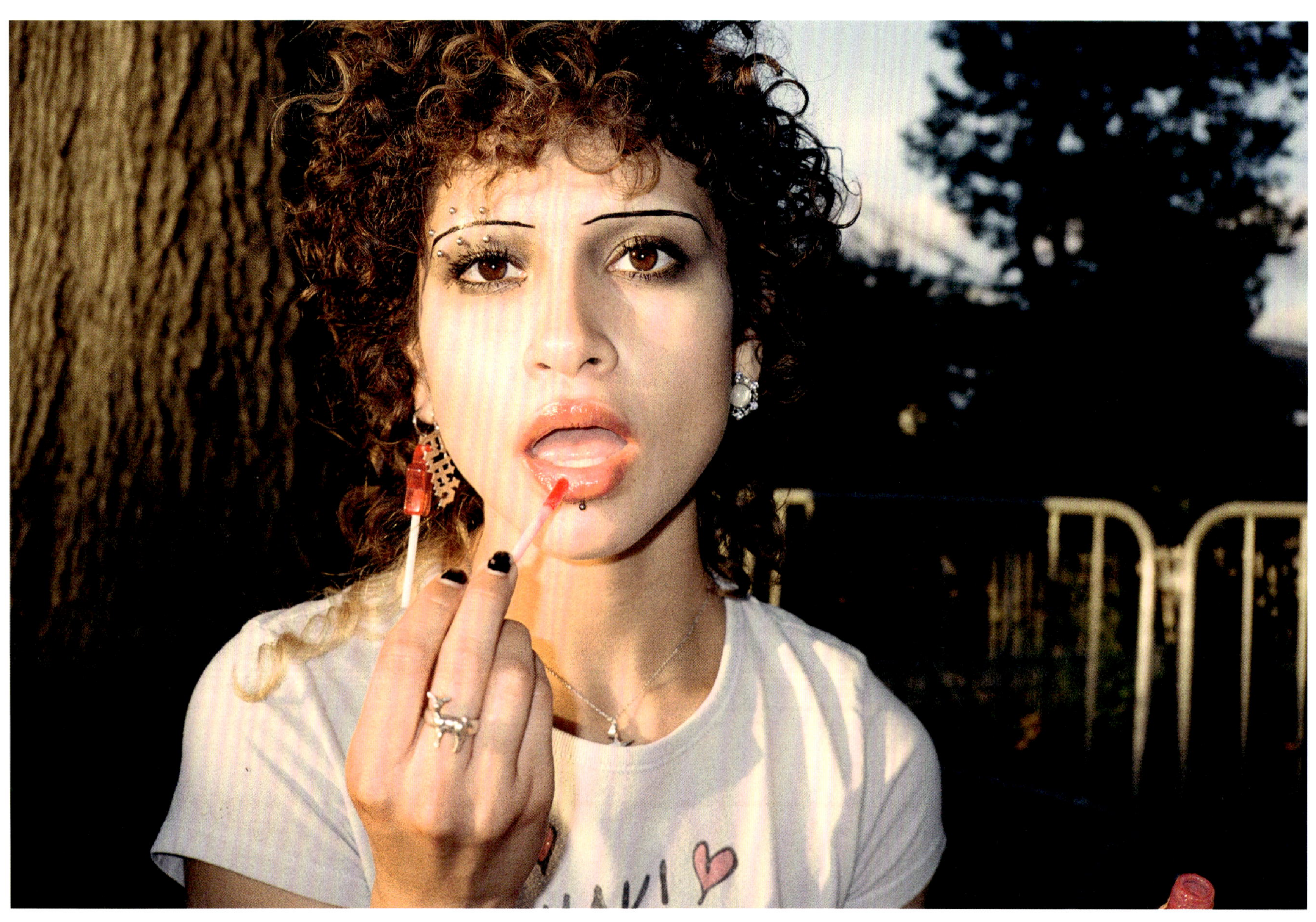

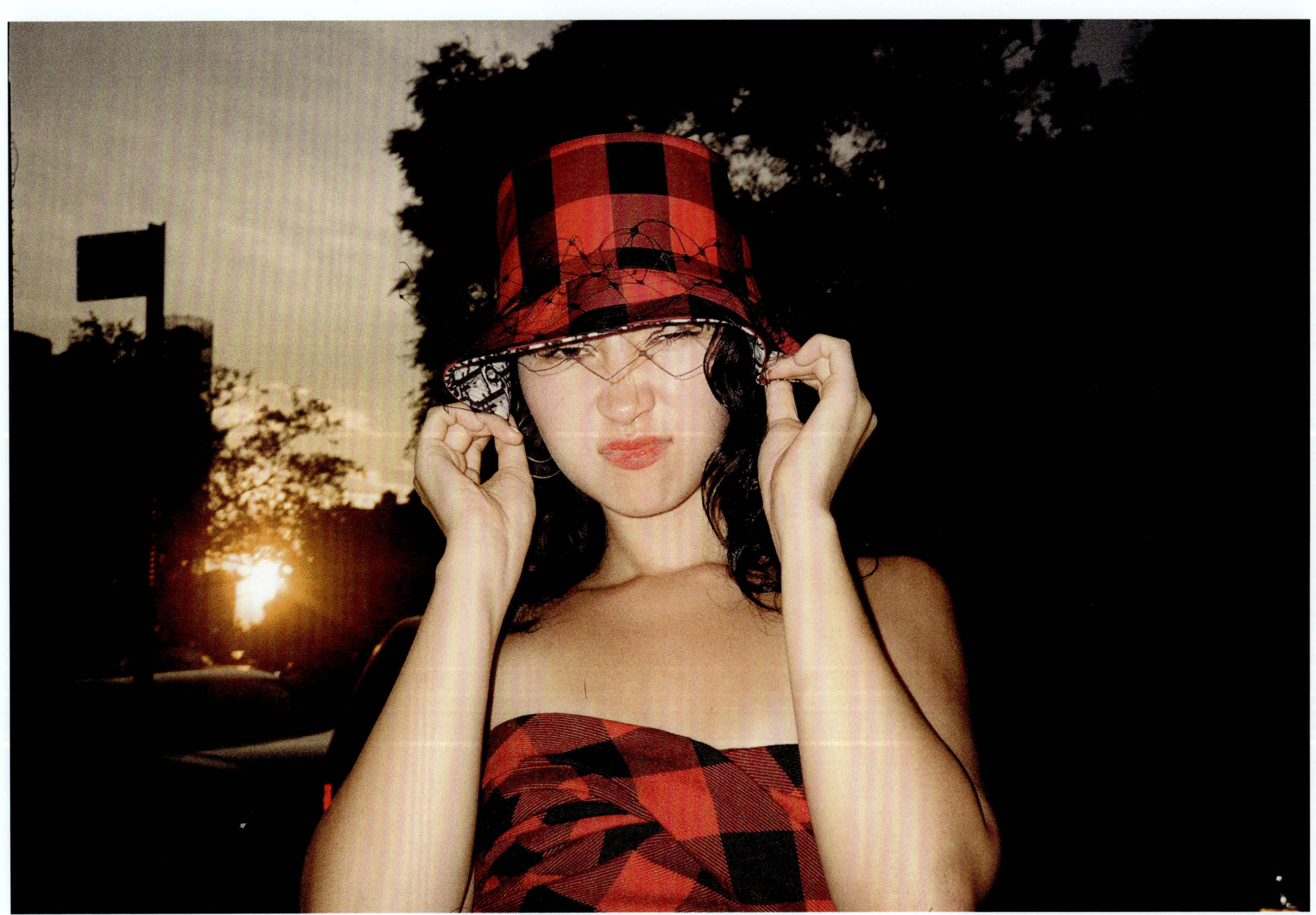

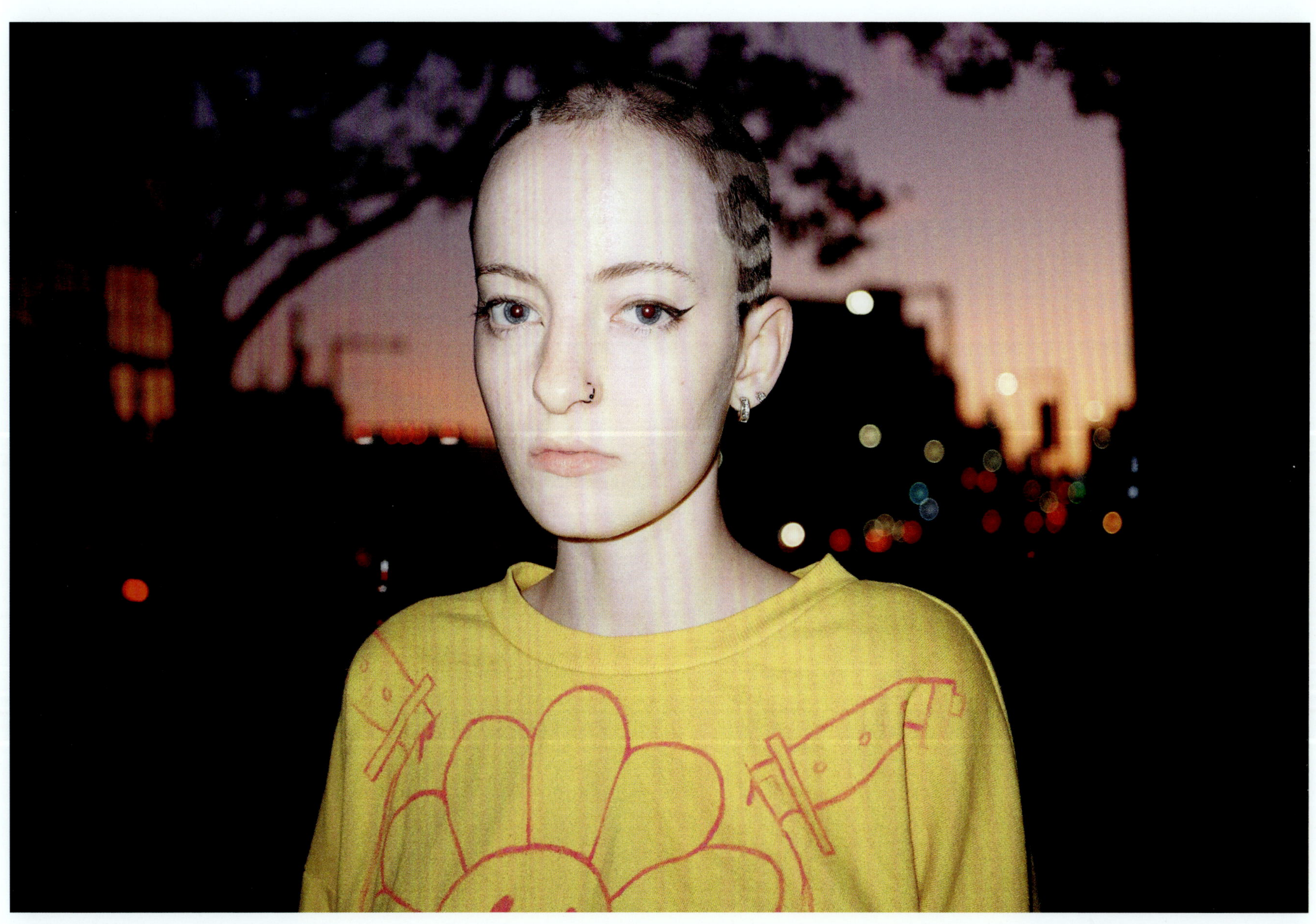

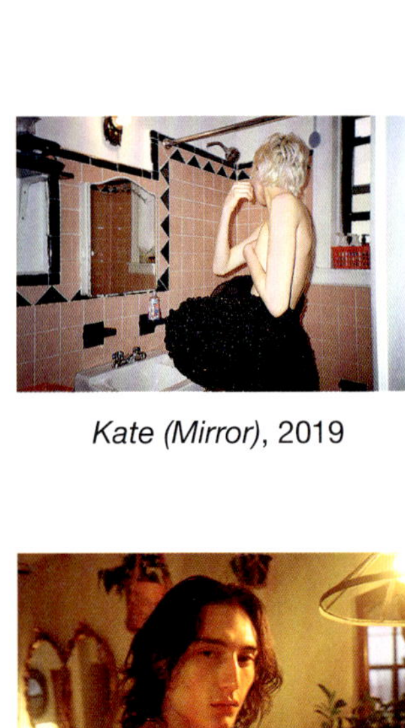

Kate (Mirror), 2019

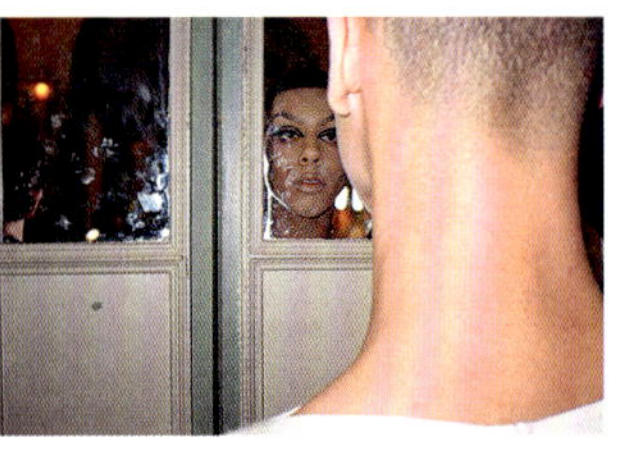

Serena, 2020

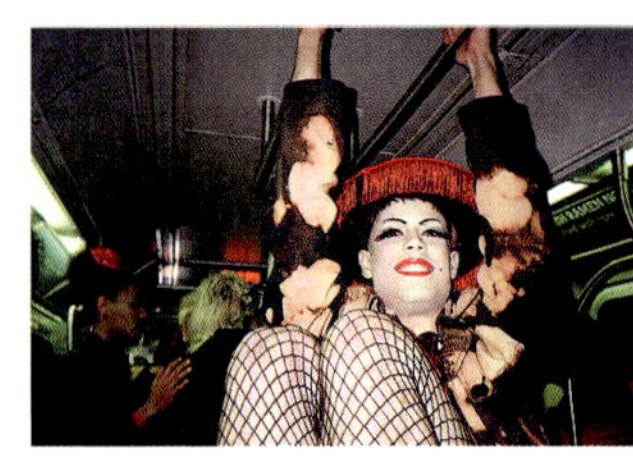

Nicky, 2016

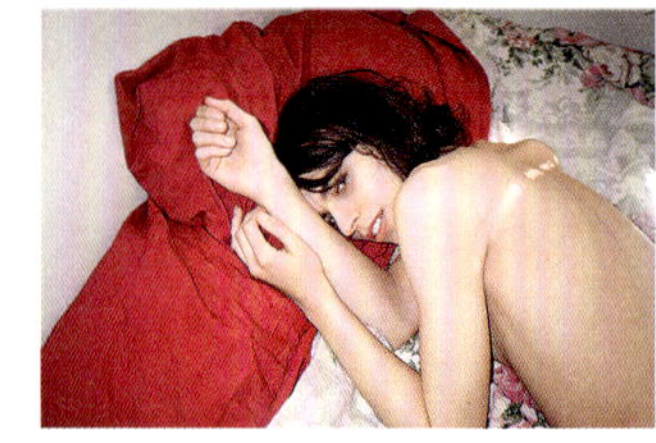

Massima, 2016

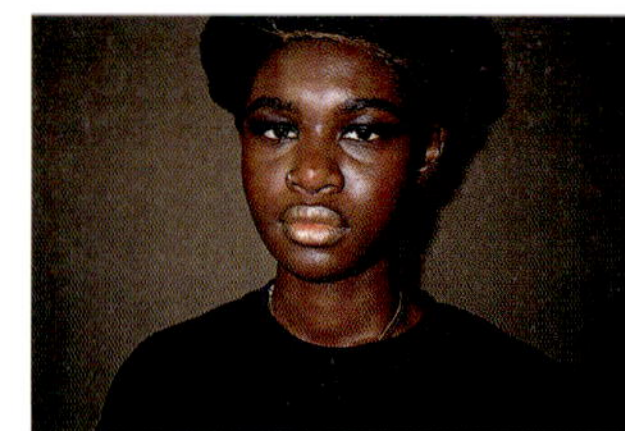

Coumba, 2019

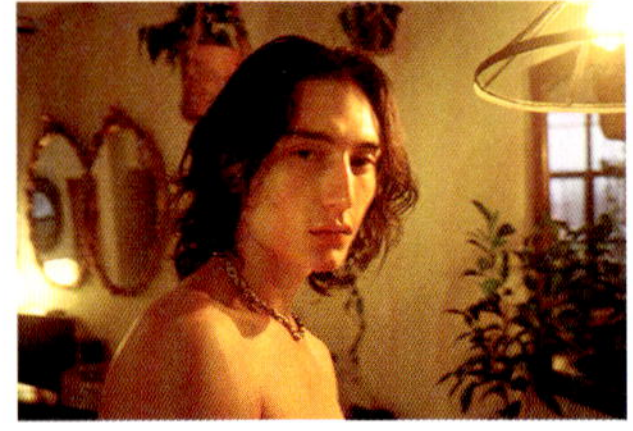

Cameron (Yellow Light), 2019

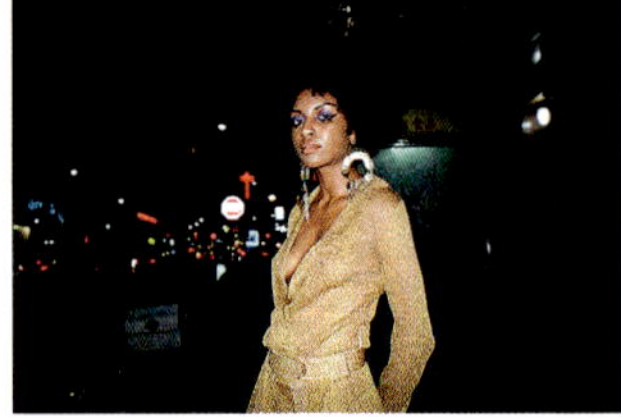

Britney, 2019

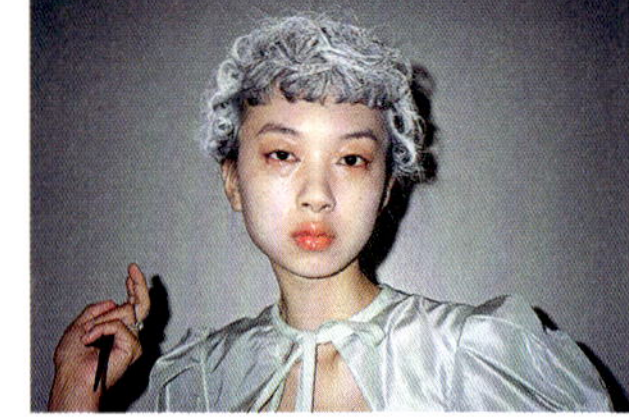

Lynn, 2019

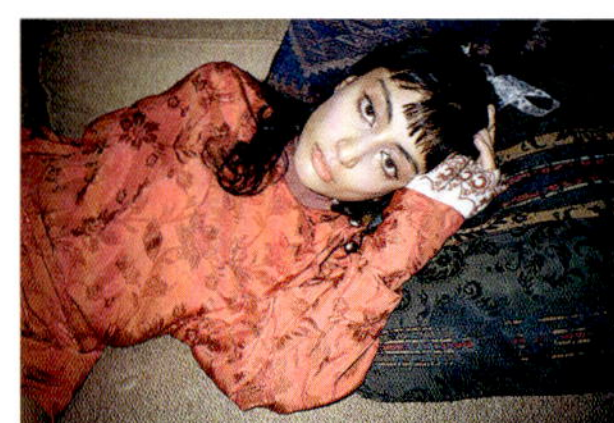

Tash, 2019

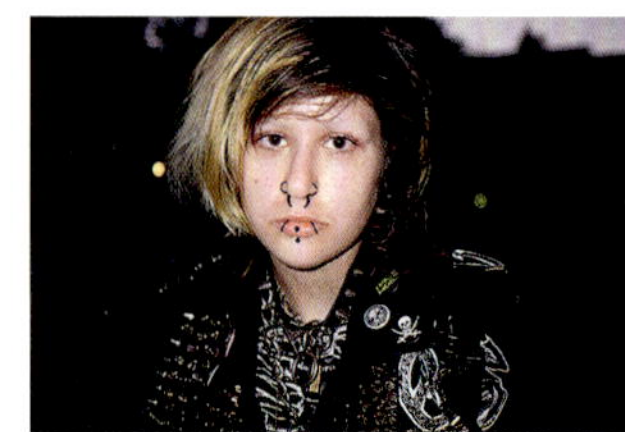

Alex, 2020

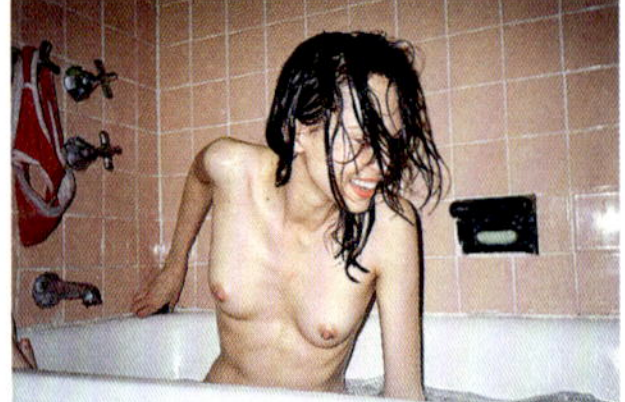

Kate (Bath), 2017

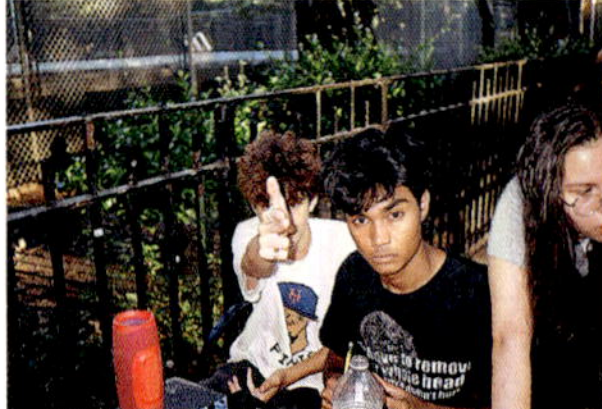

Kids (Tompkins Square Park), 2020

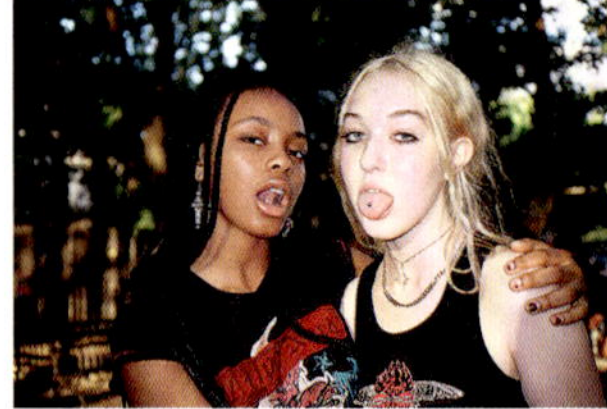

Makenna & Doe, 2020

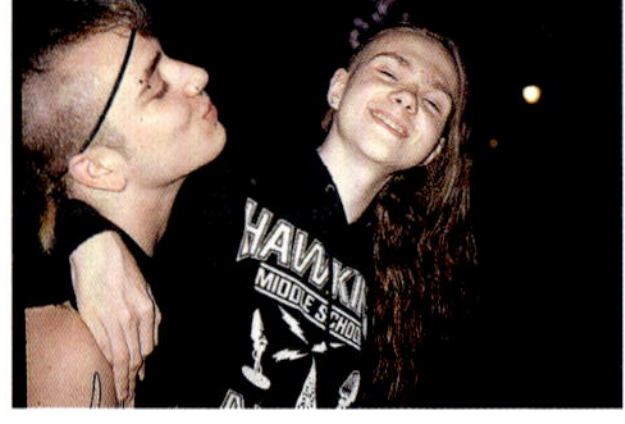

Sharpie & George, 2020

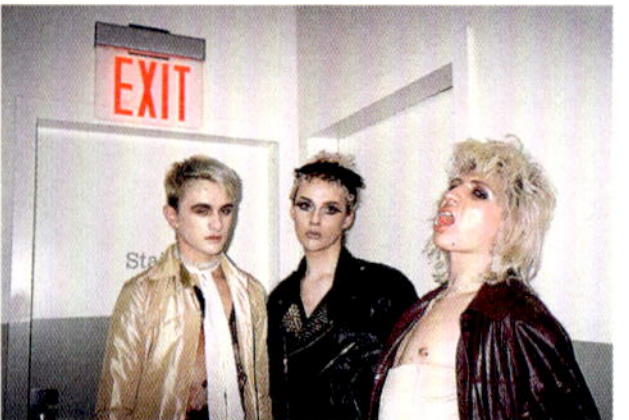

Jordane, Benji & Gia, 2016

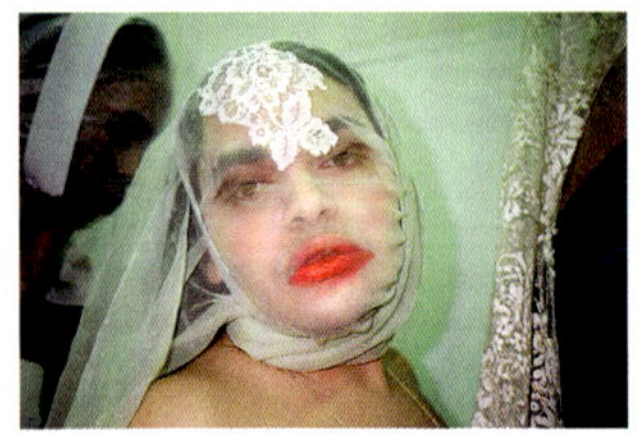

Nico, 2019

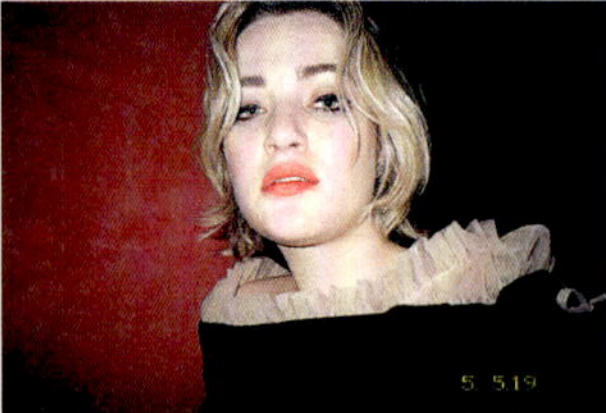

Julia, 2019

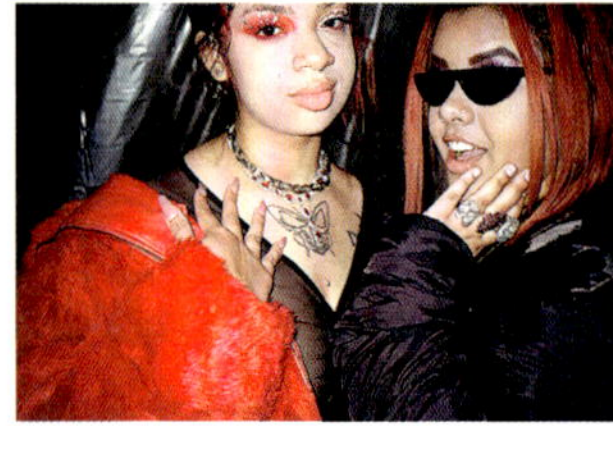

Aaliyah & Nelly, 2020

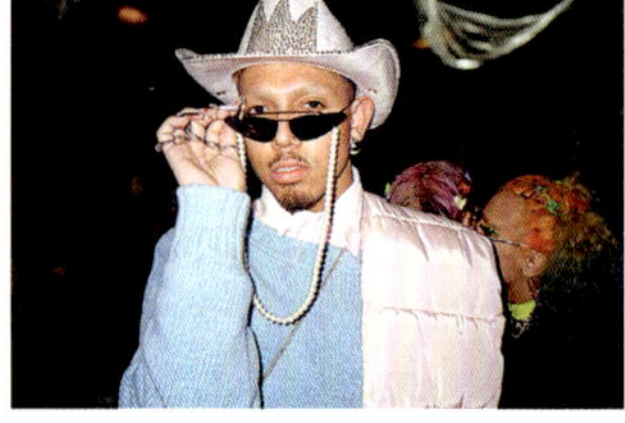

Andy, 2020

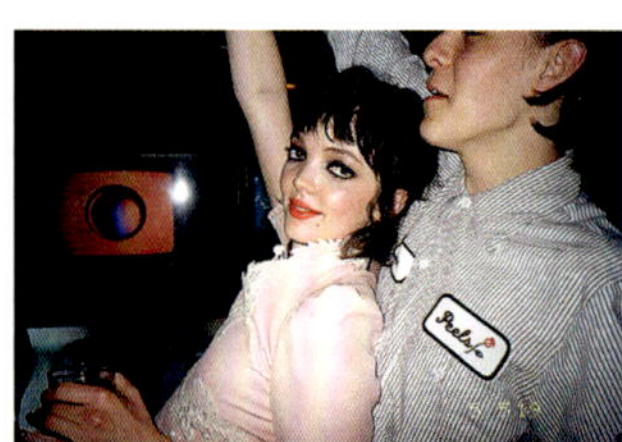

Ellia & Quinn, 2019

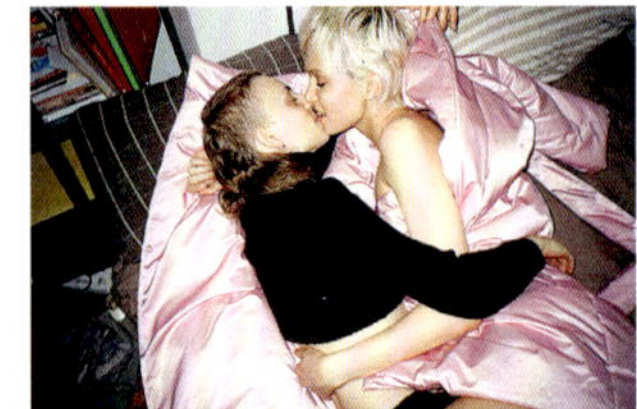

Kate & Odie, 2019

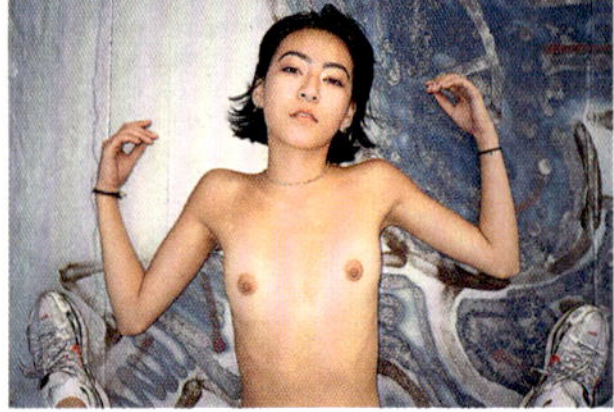

Ayana, 2020

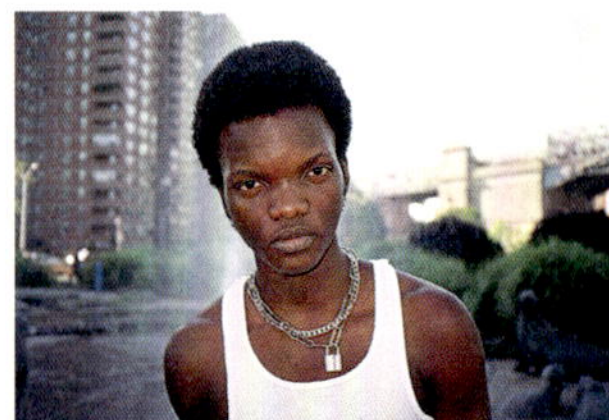

Aheem, 2020

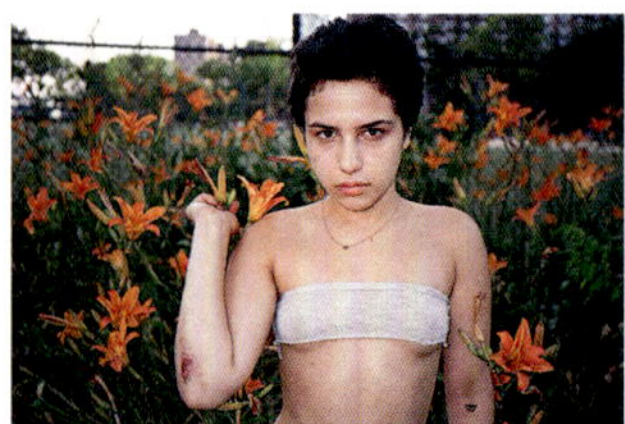

Isabel (Skinned Elbow), 2020

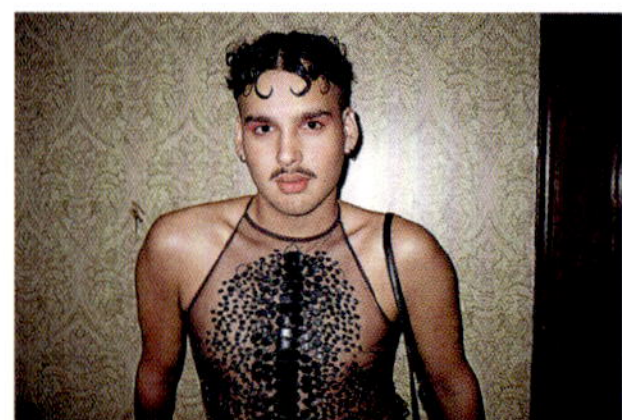

Kiwi, 2020

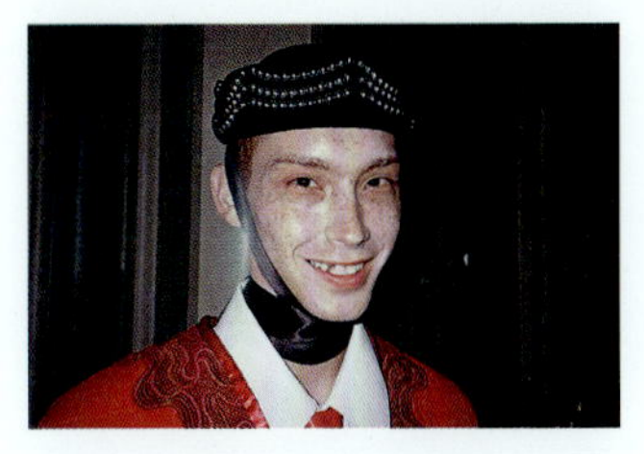
Brandon, 2019

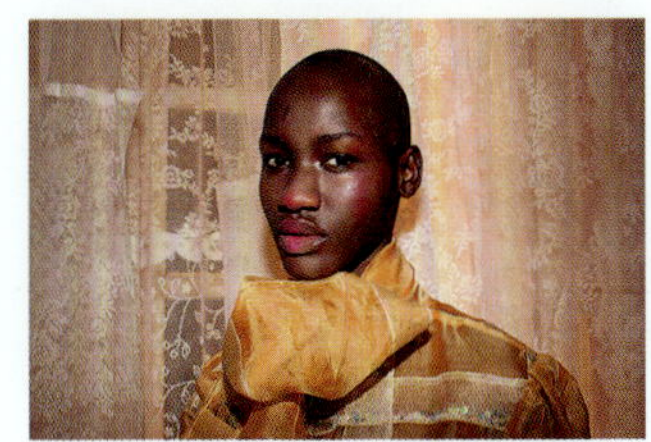
Ayet, 2019

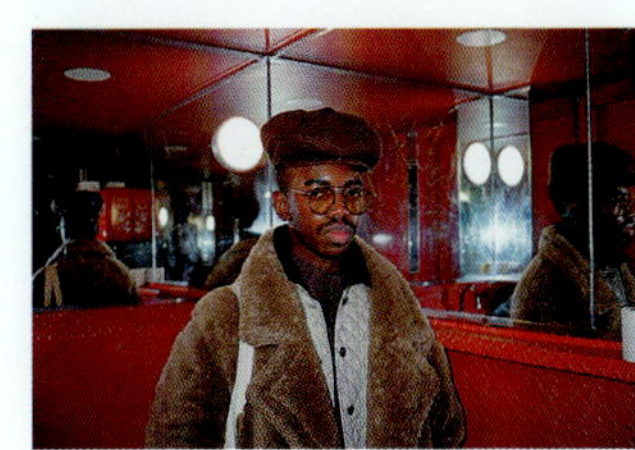
Roberto, 2019

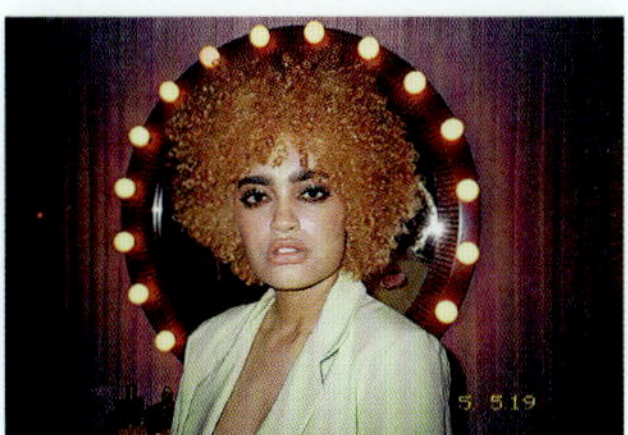
Janibell, 2019

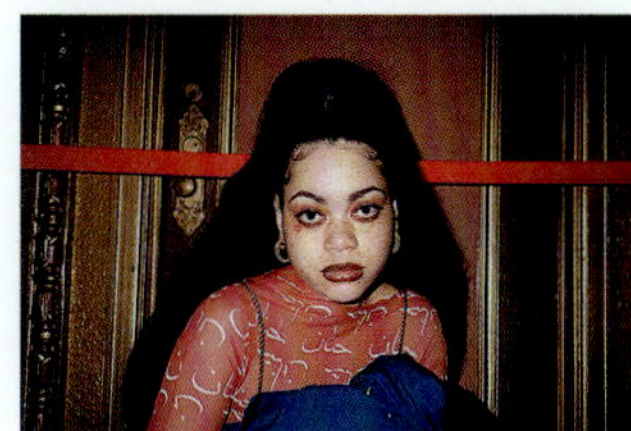
Seashell, 2019

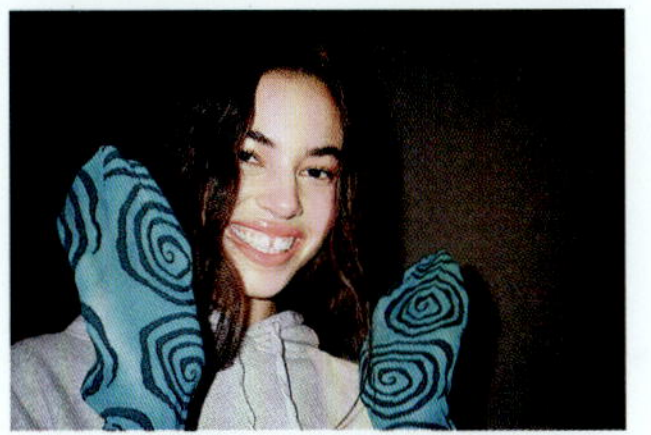
Symone, 2019

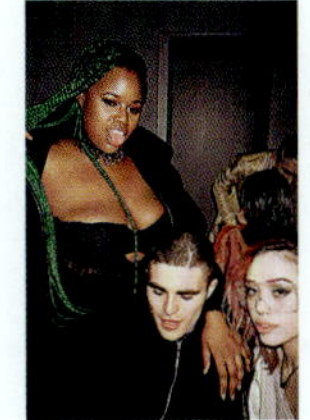
Raisa & Friends, 2016

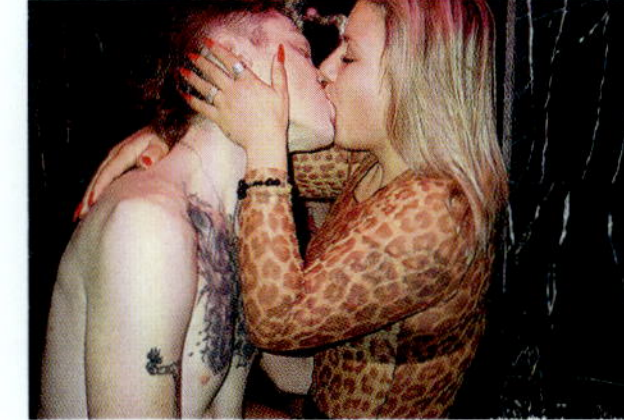
Shane & Luisa, 2021

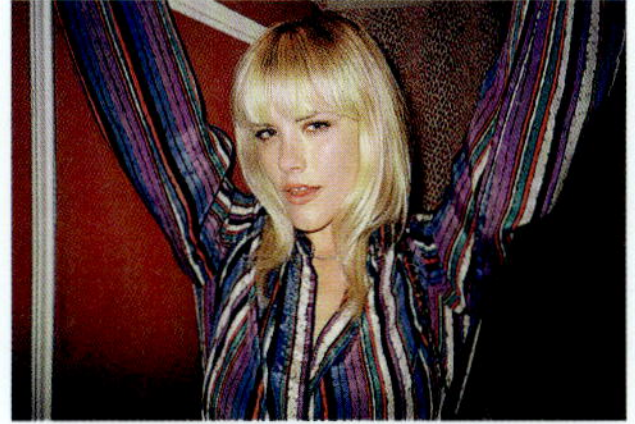
Ashley, 2019

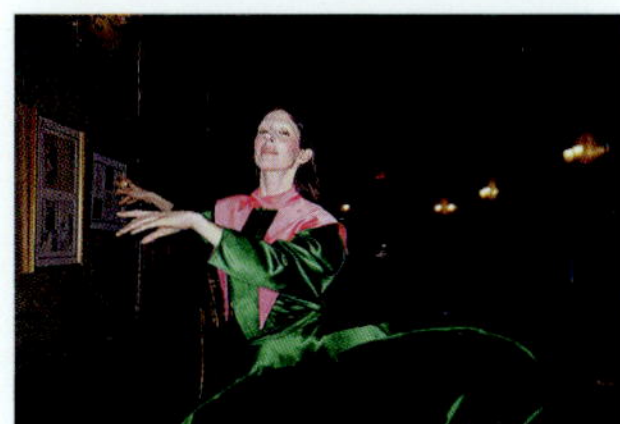
Caroline, 2020

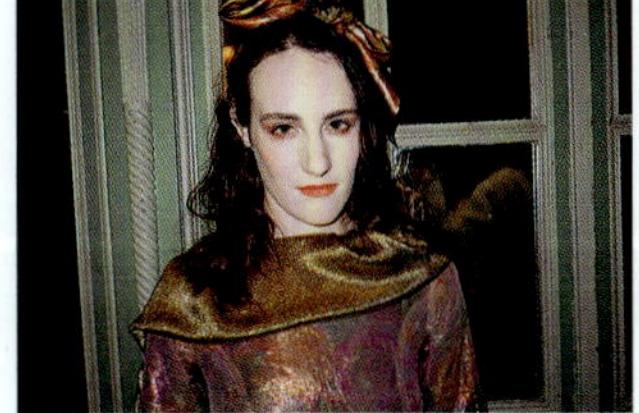
Raffaella, 2020

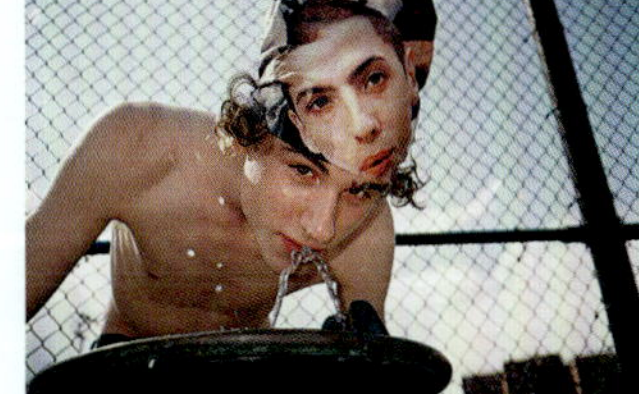
Phineas (Fountain), 2020

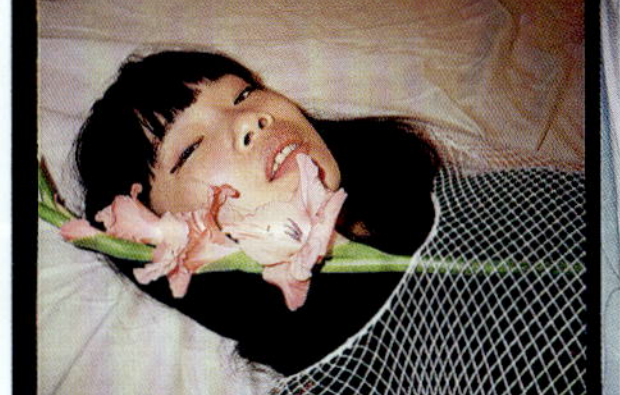
Bei, 2016

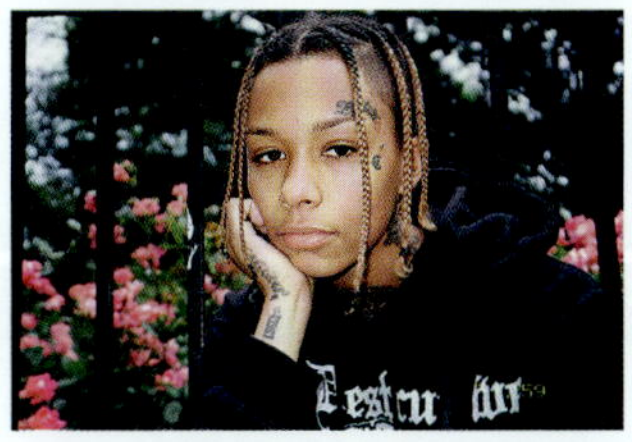
Euro Trilll, 2019

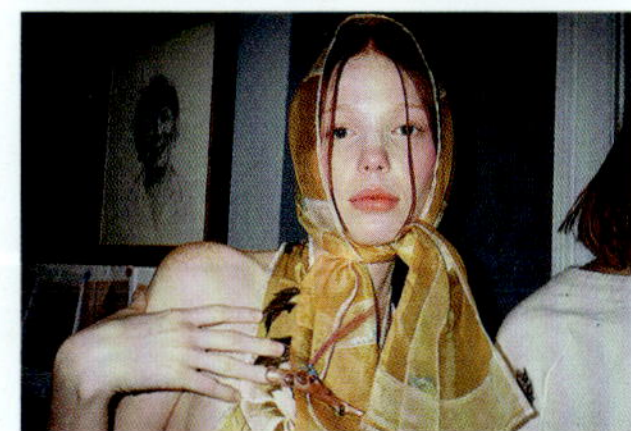
Alina, 2019

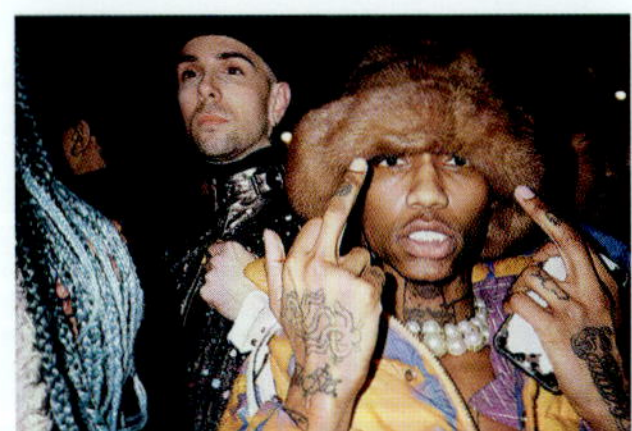
Rico, 2019

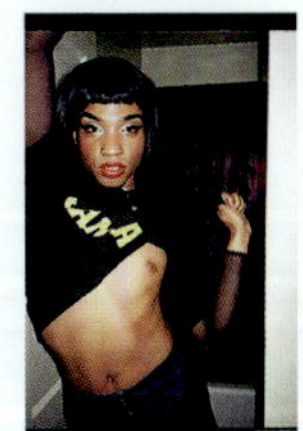
Quay Dash, 2016

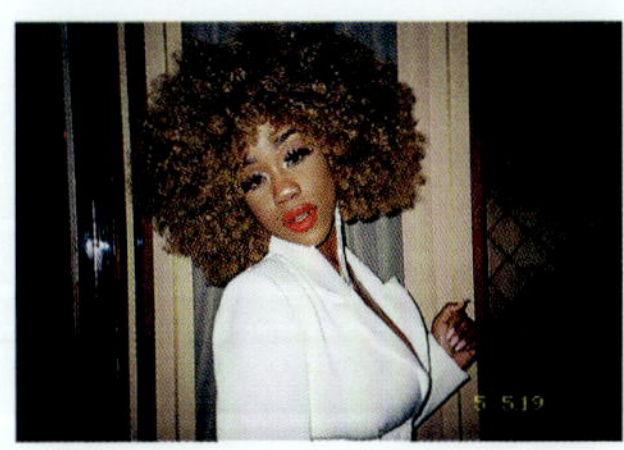
Chidera, 2019

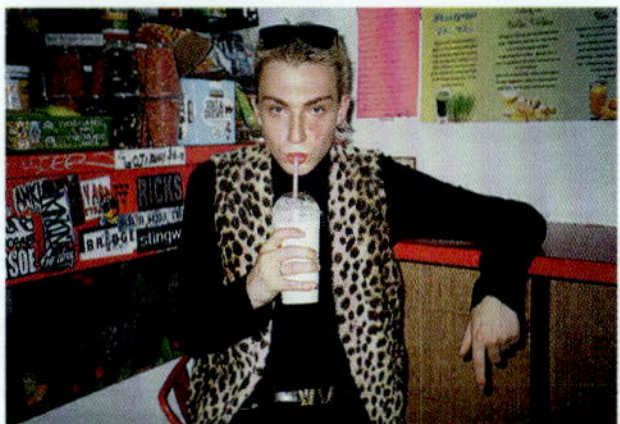
Lil Dallas, 2019

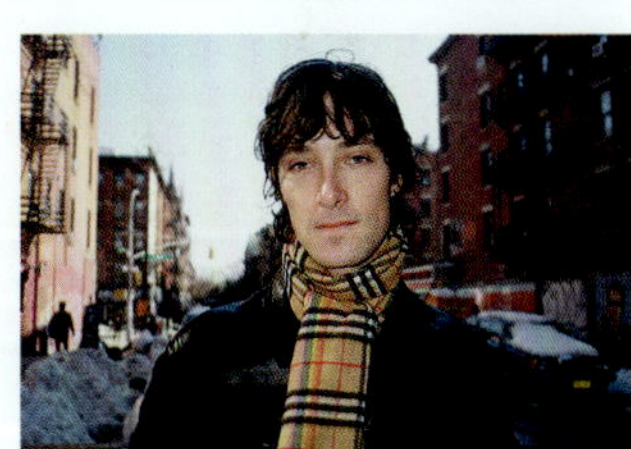
Sam, 2021

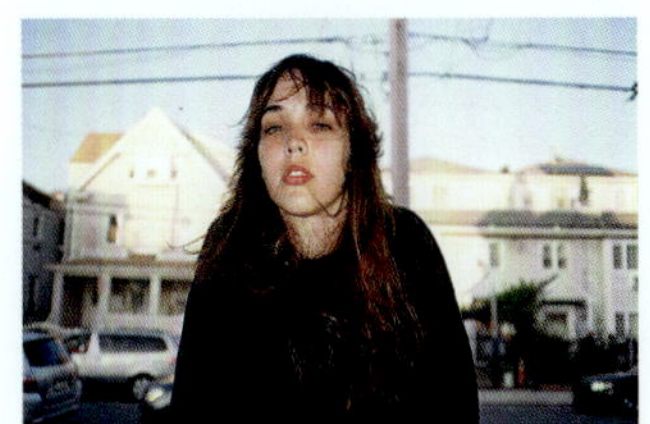
Andromeda, 2020

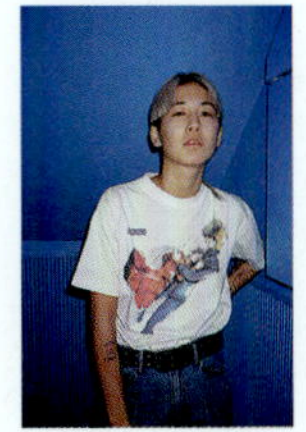
Masami, 2019

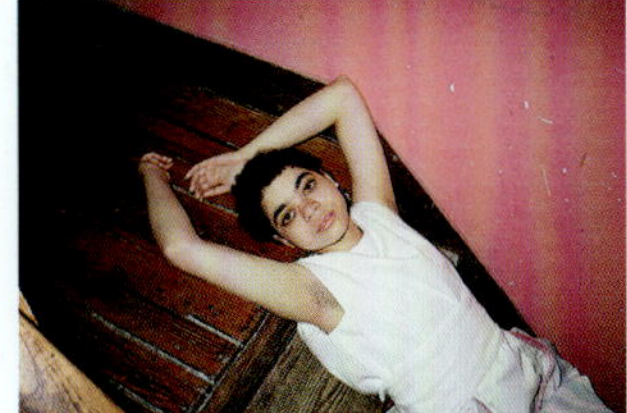
Seashell (Stairs), 2016

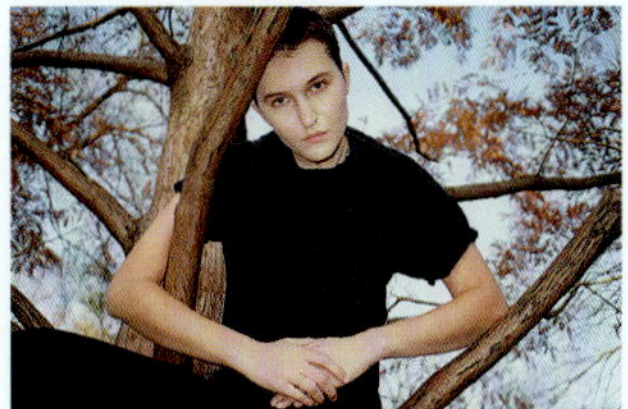
Arta, 2020

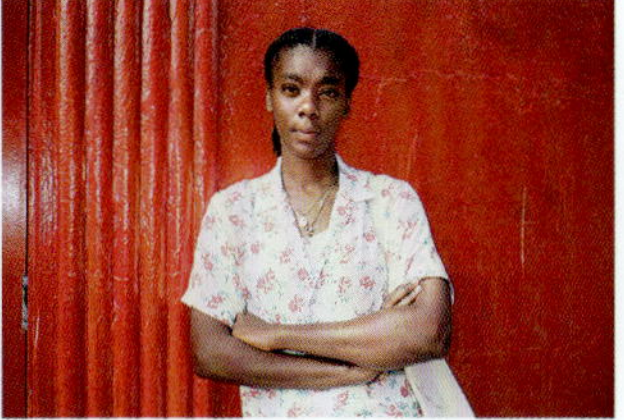
Beatrice, 2020

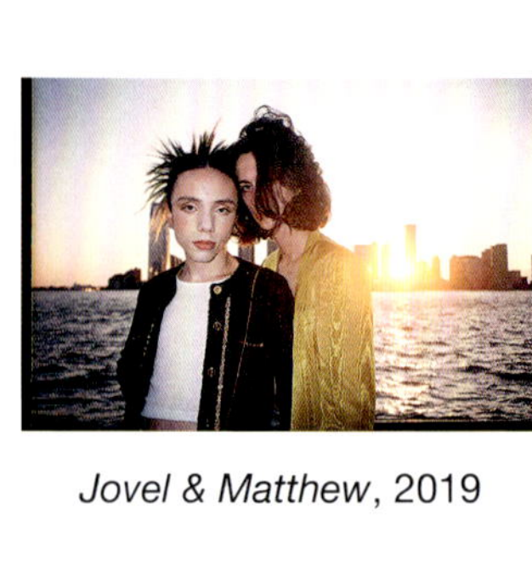

Jovel & Matthew, 2019

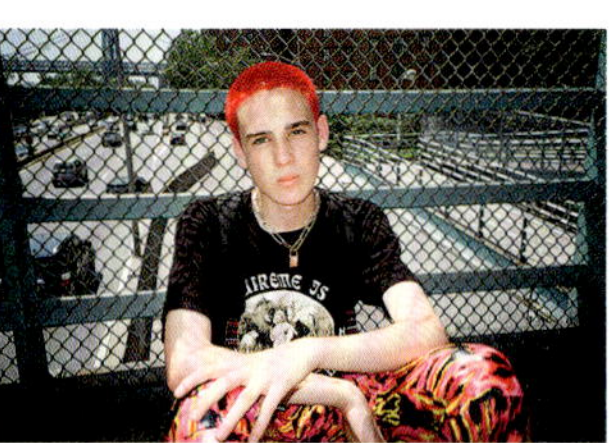

Atticus (Bridge), 2019

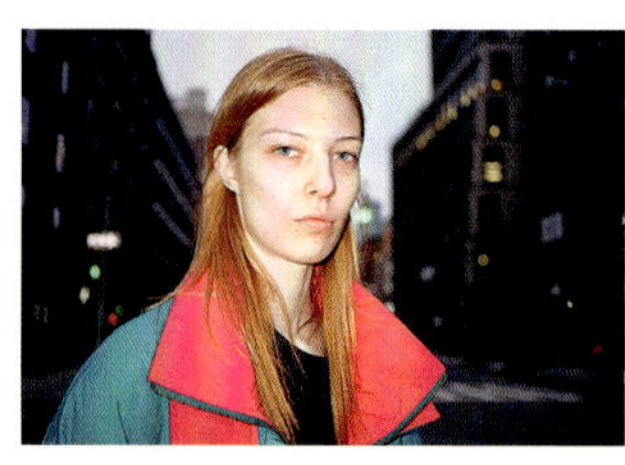

Remington, 2020

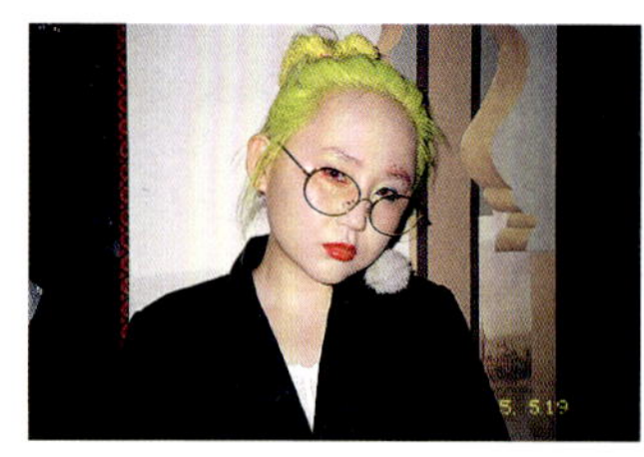

Alice, 2019

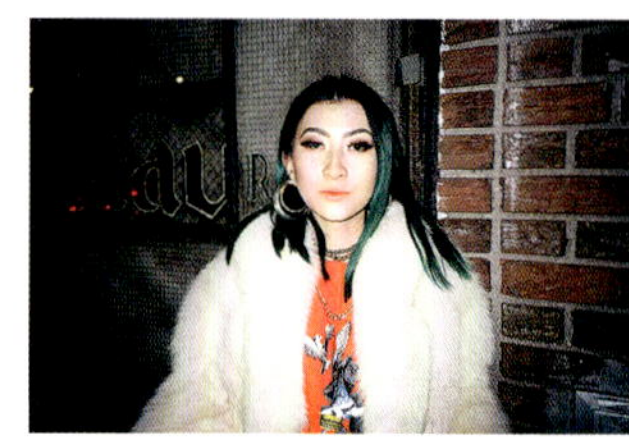

Irene, 2019

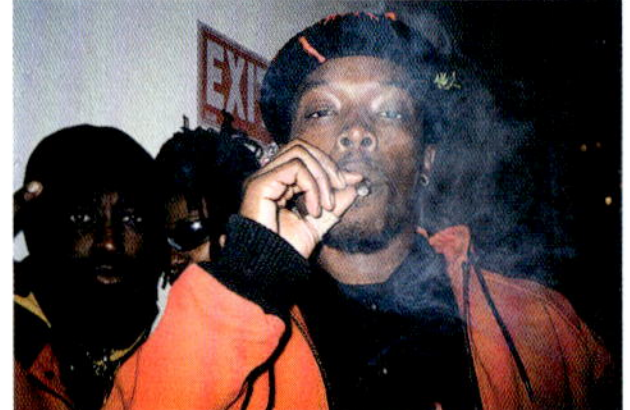

Adante, Slumxweirdo & Zayy, 2019

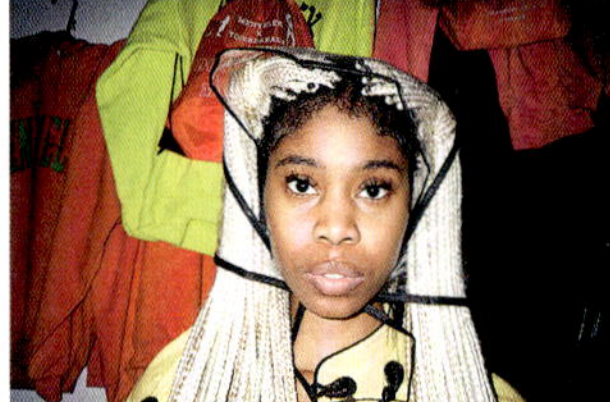

Untitled (Neon), 2019

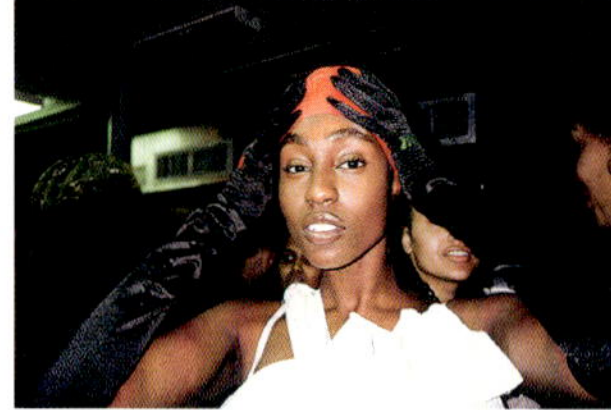

Sika, 2019

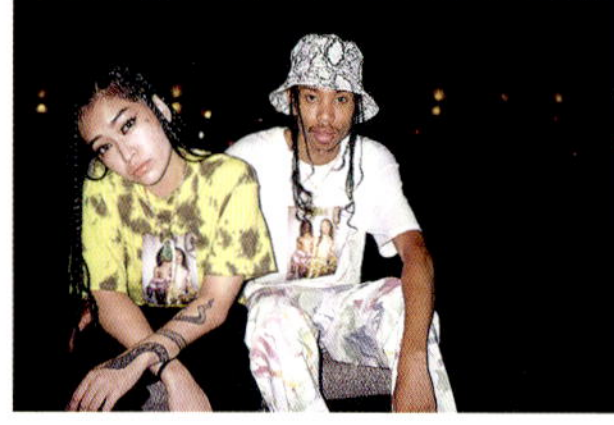

Lean & Zappa, 2020

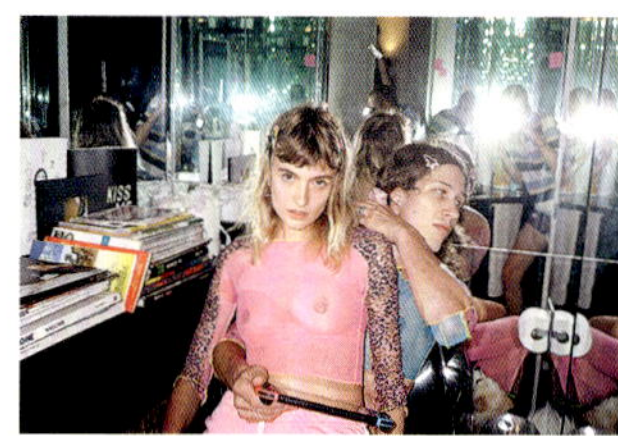

Veronika & Adrian, *2020*

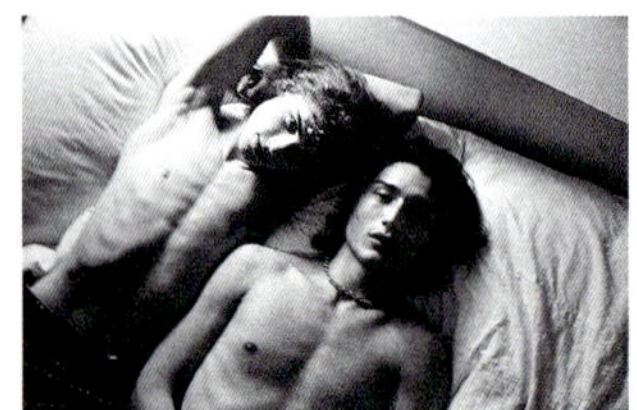

Phineas & Cameron, 2019

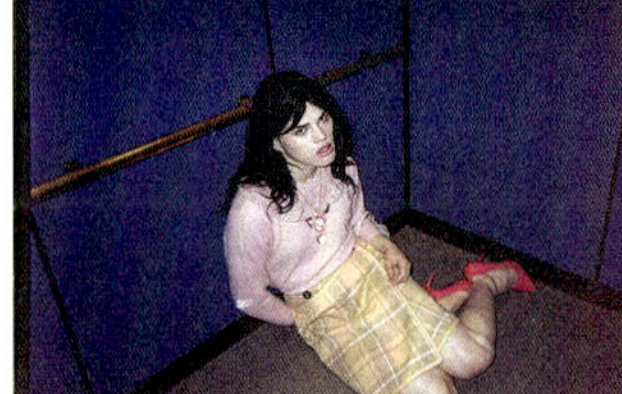

Chloe, 2016

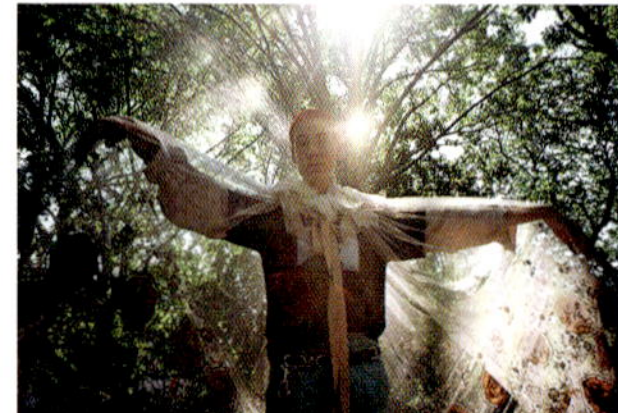

Atticus, 2019

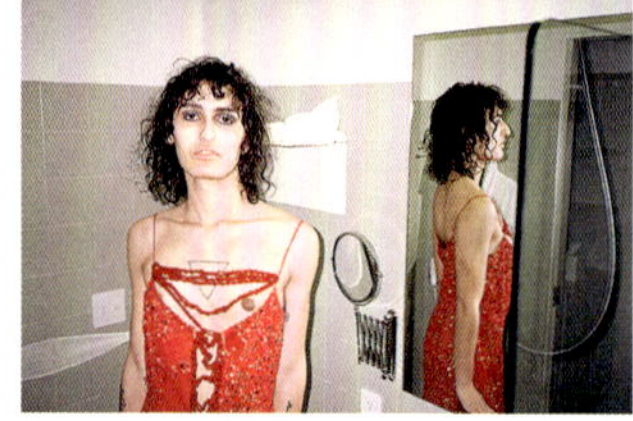

M Zavos, 2016

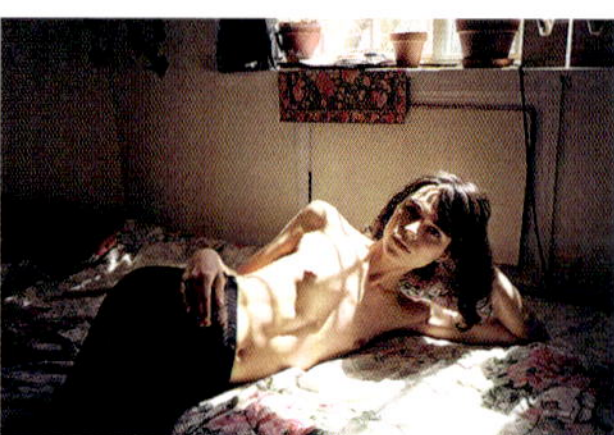

Massima (Sunlight), 2016

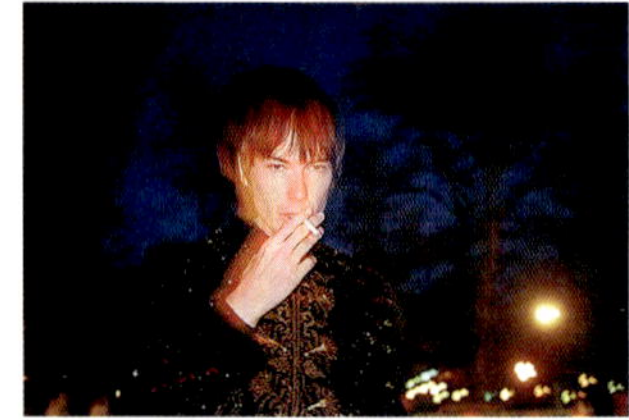

Sid, 2019

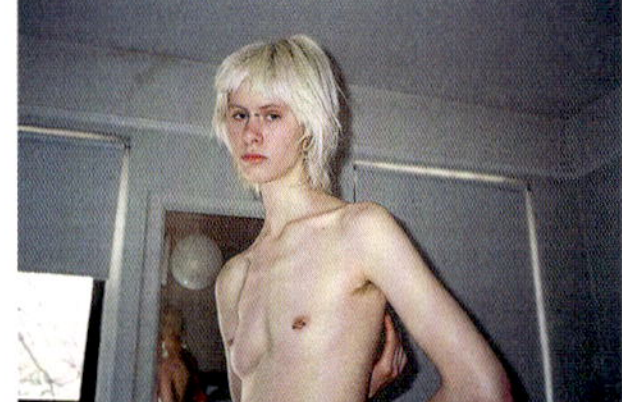

Irene, 2020

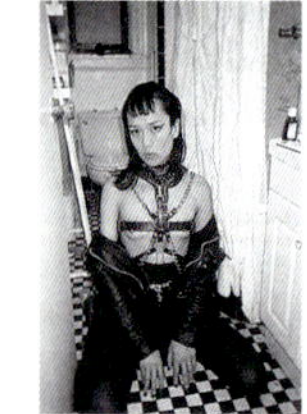

Fashion, 2017

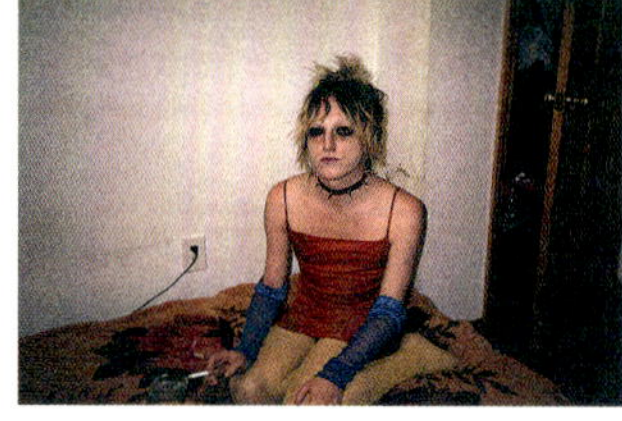

Mae, 2016

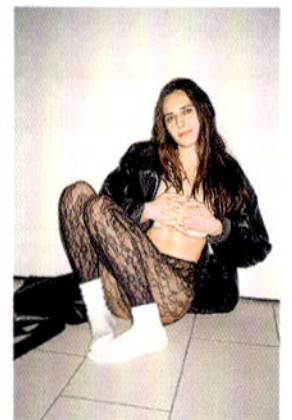

Devon, 2020

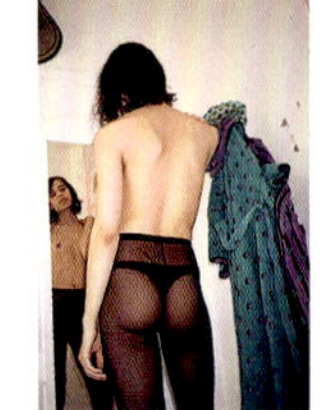

Massima (Mirror), 2016

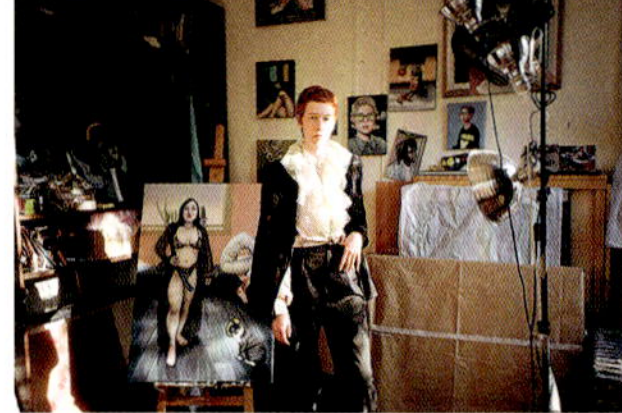

Alannah, 2019

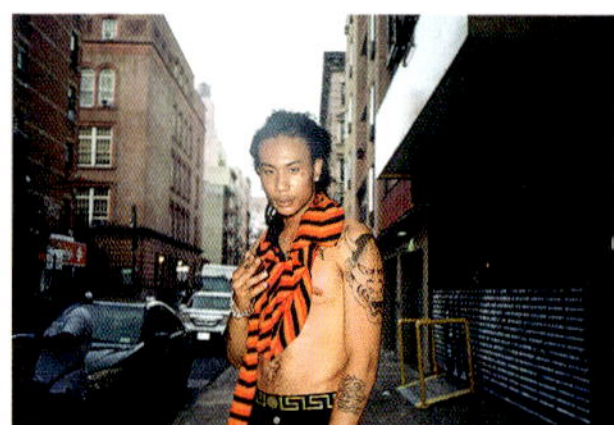

Yoshi, 2019

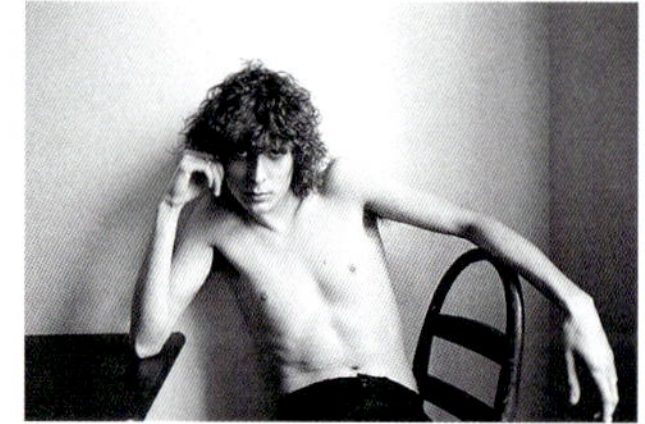

John, 2020

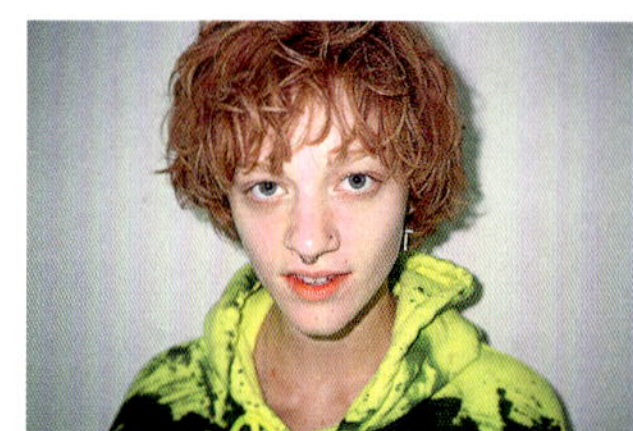

Brick, 2020

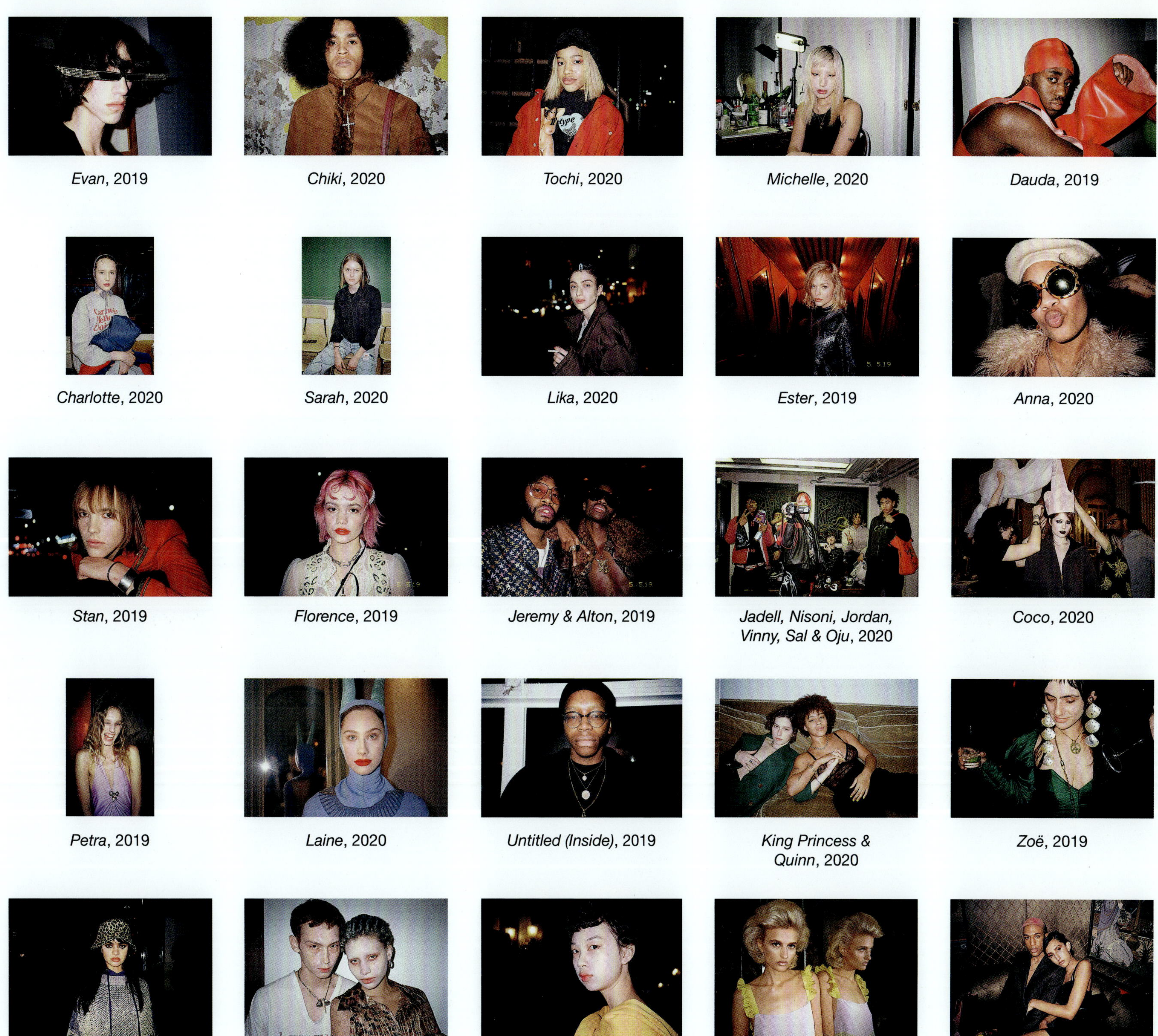

Evan, 2019

Chiki, 2020

Tochi, 2020

Michelle, 2020

Dauda, 2019

Charlotte, 2020

Sarah, 2020

Lika, 2020

Ester, 2019

Anna, 2020

Stan, 2019

Florence, 2019

Jeremy & Alton, 2019

Jadell, Nisoni, Jordan, Vinny, Sal & Oju, 2020

Coco, 2020

Petra, 2019

Laine, 2020

Untitled (Inside), 2019

King Princess & Quinn, 2020

Zoë, 2019

Maria, 2019

Brandon & Neon, 2019

Lynn (Yellow), 2019

Veronika, 2019

Alex & Kayaira, 2019

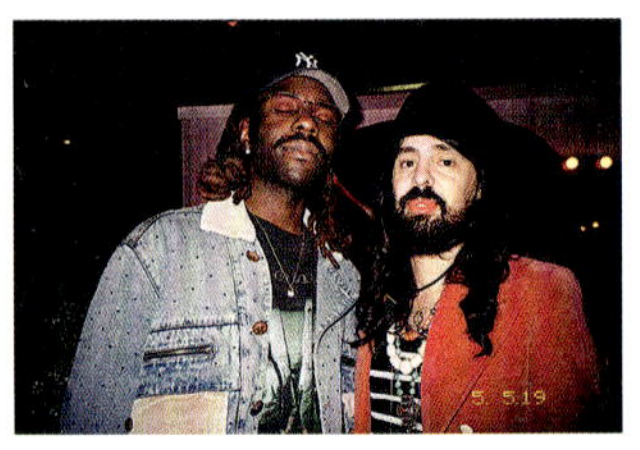

Dev & Alessandro, 2019

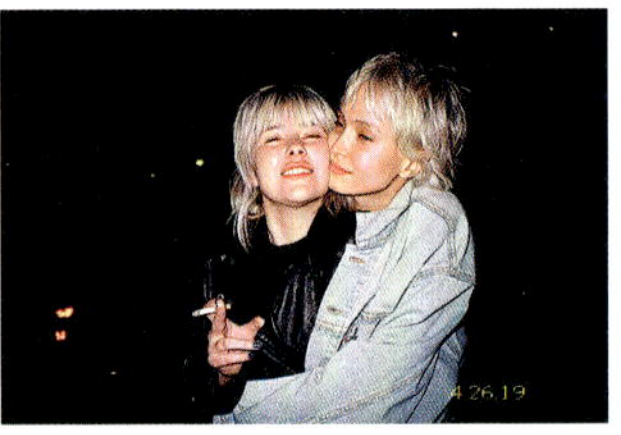

Viktorie & Kate, 2019

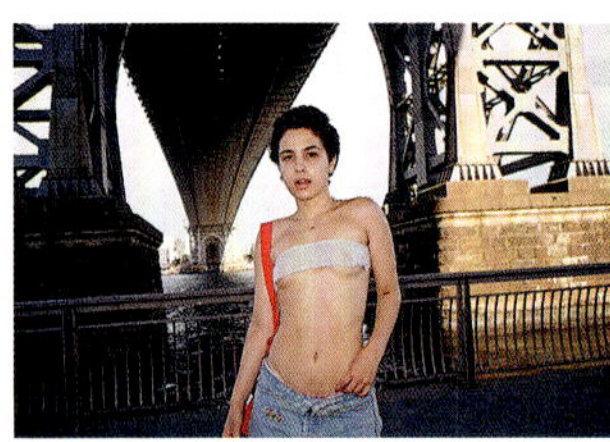

Isabel, 2020

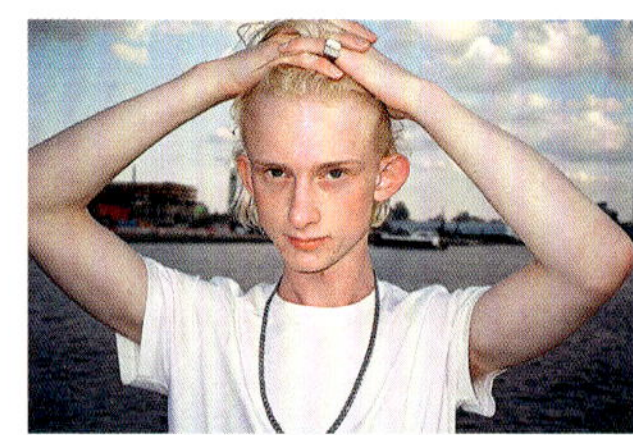

Nikita, 2020

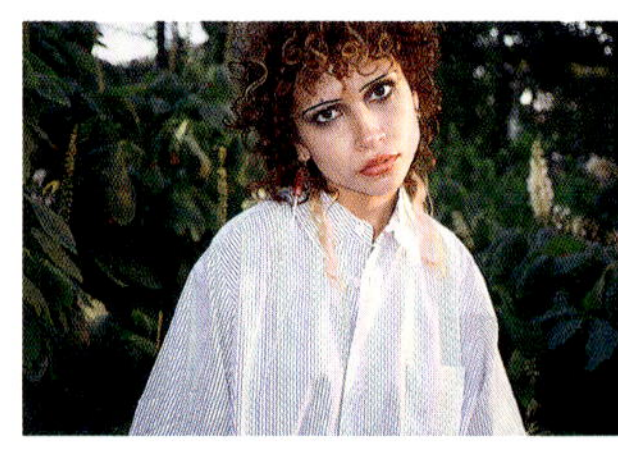

Lexi, 2020

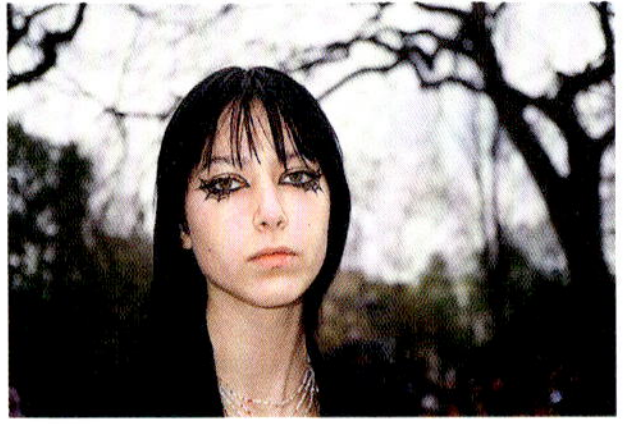

Becky, 2020

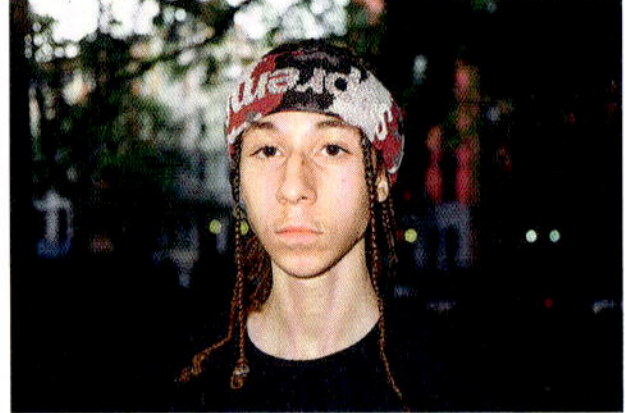

Rocco, 2020

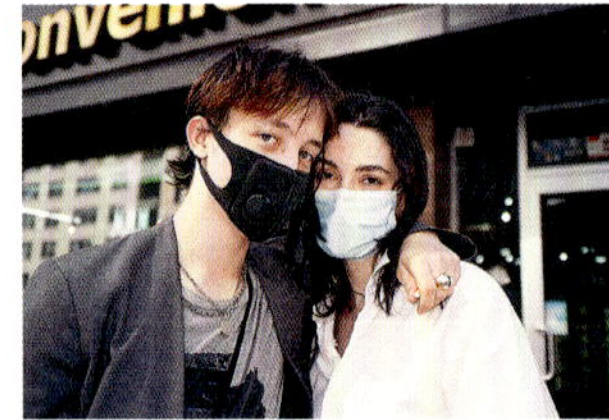

Untitled (Masks), 2020

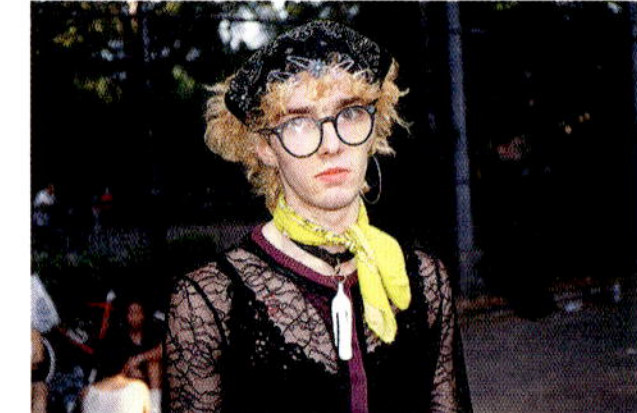

Colleen, 2020

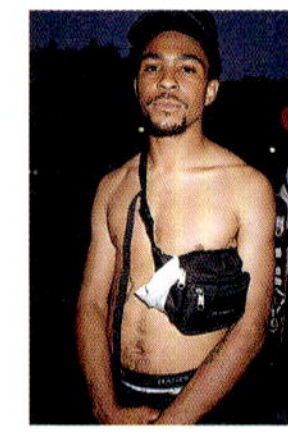

Chris, 2020

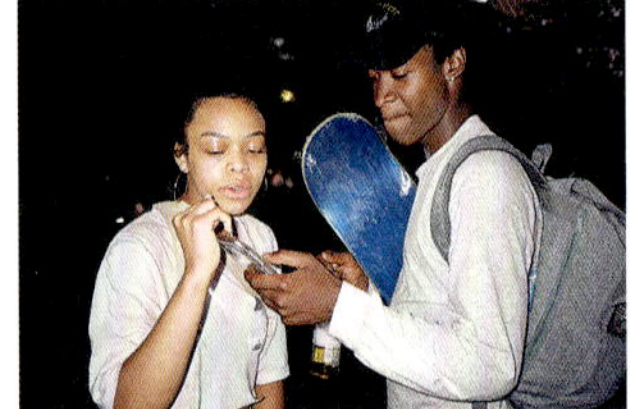

Elle & Jahmali, 2020

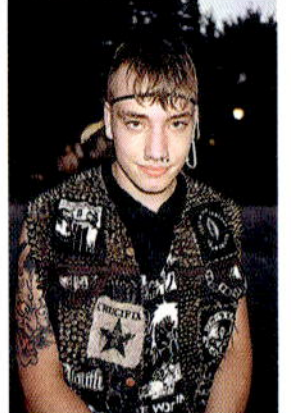

Sharpie, 2020

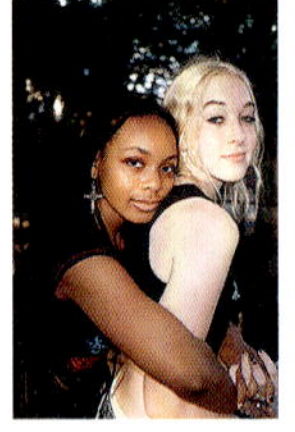

Makenna & Doe (Hugging), 2020

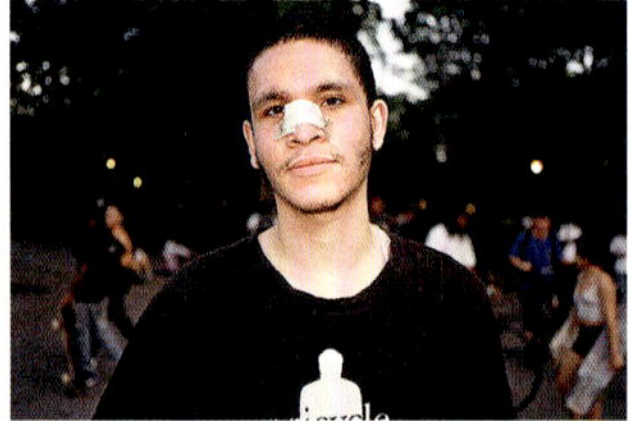

Lenny, 2020

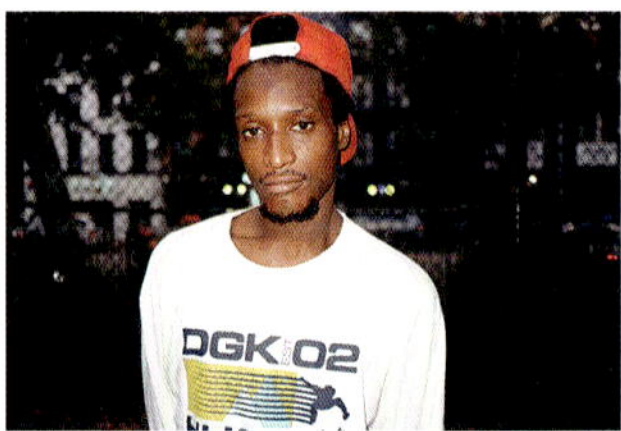

Pat, 2020

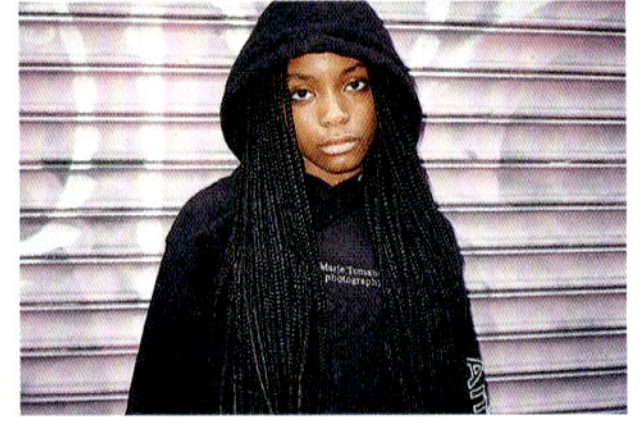

Makenna, 2020

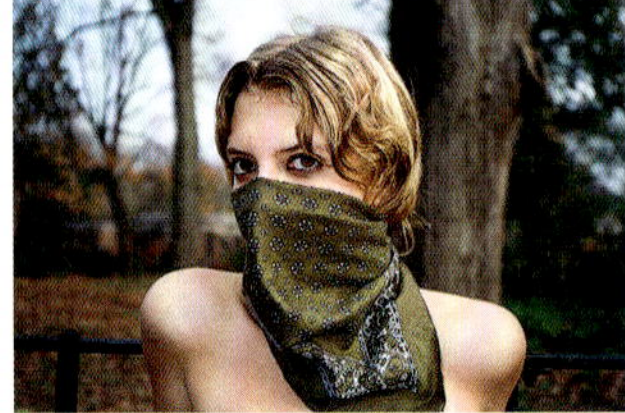

Astrid, 2020

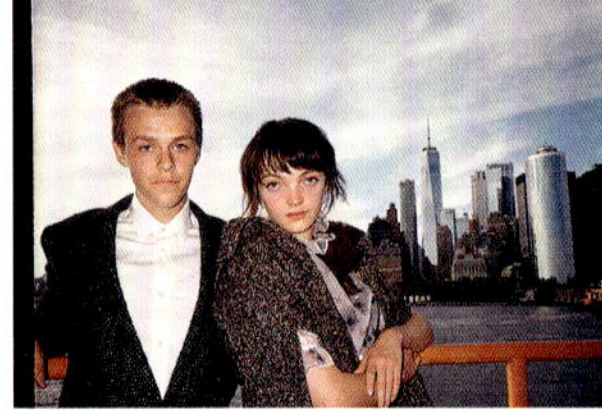

Quinn & Ellia (Ferry), 2019

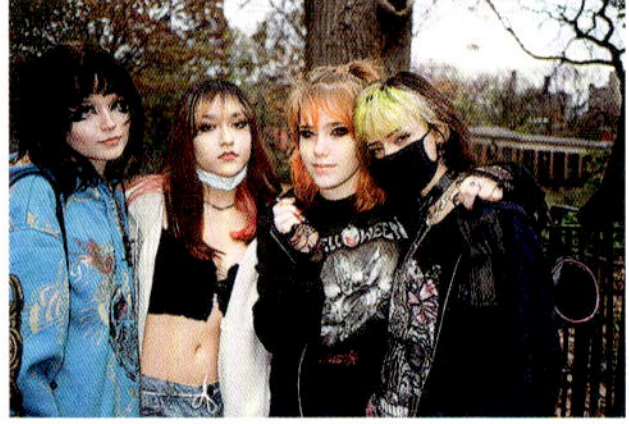

Liv, Angelica, Polly & Eve, 2020

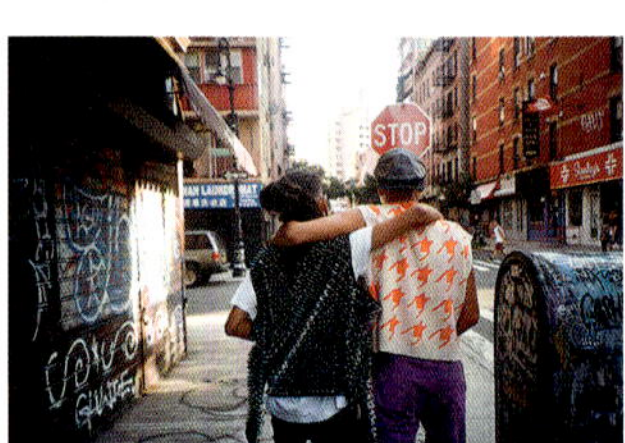

Harley & Poster Boy, 2019

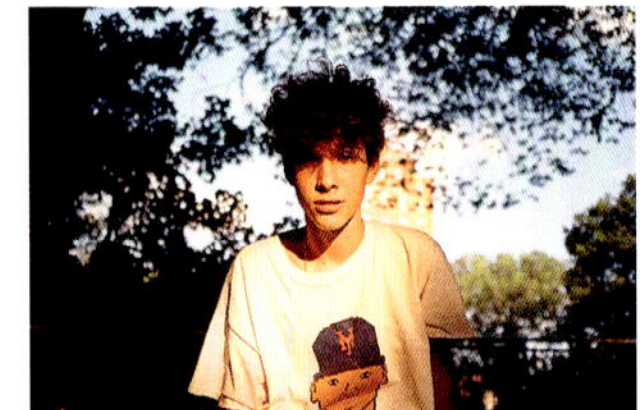

Ari, 2020

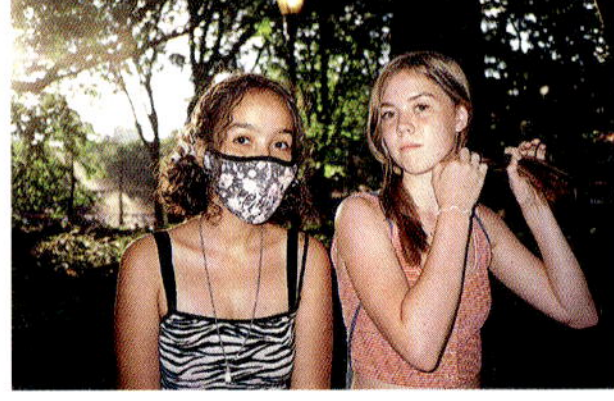

Sophia & Annabel, 2020

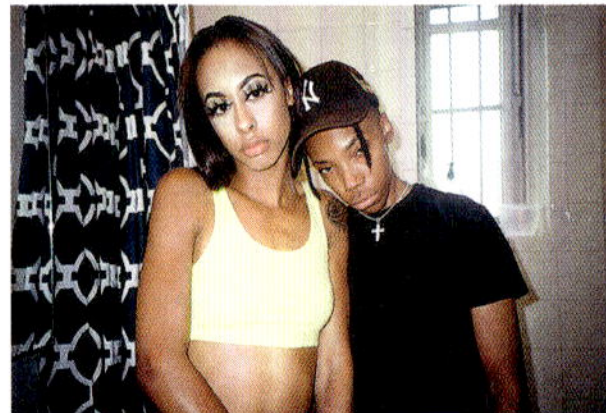

Diamond & Jiggy, 2019

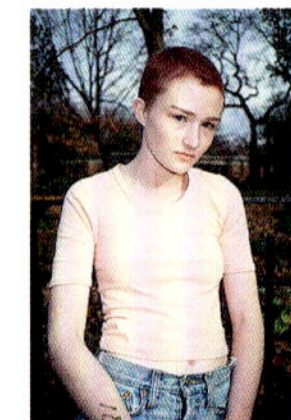

Elena, 2020

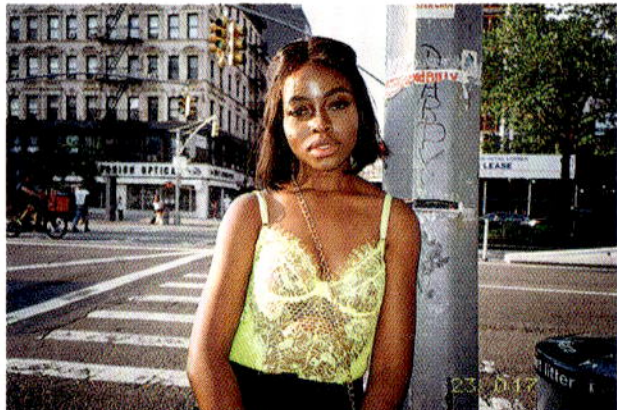

Untitled (Delancey), 2019

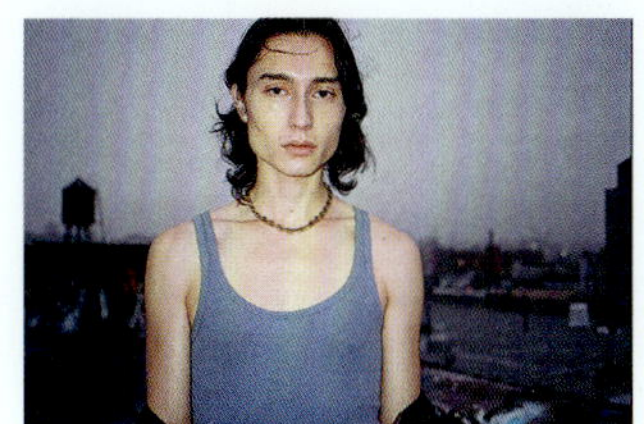
Cameron, 2019

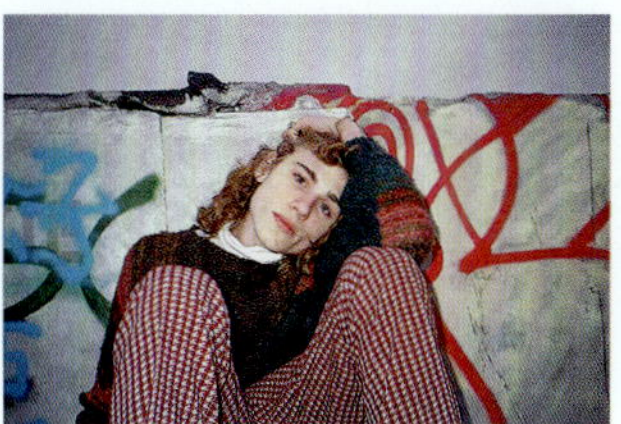
Phineas (Roof), 2019

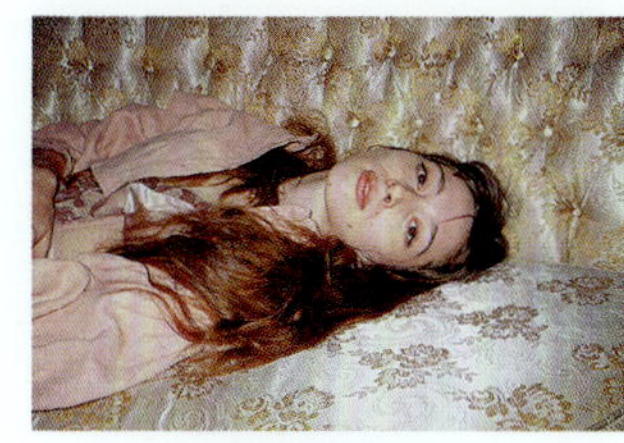
Nika, 2019

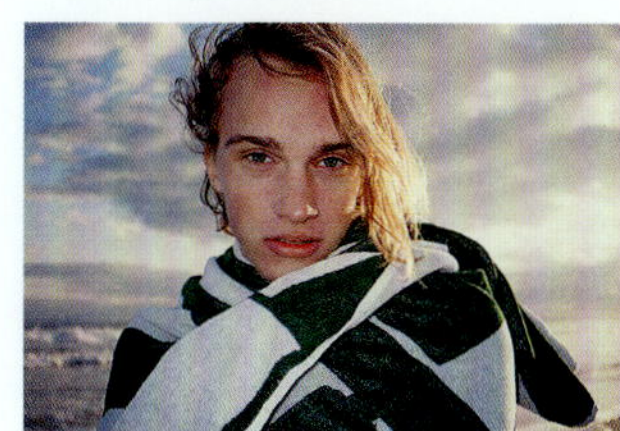
Jass, 2019

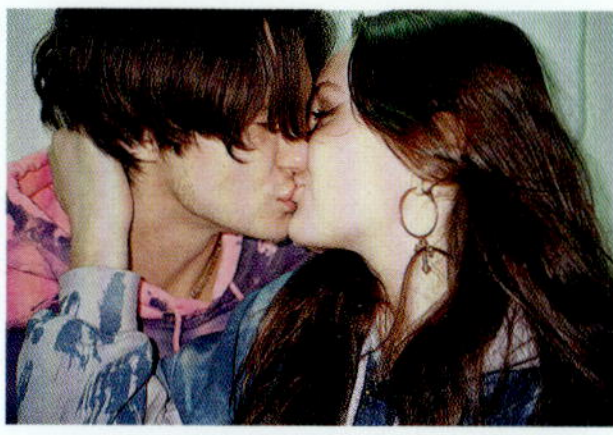
Eli & Madeleine, 2020

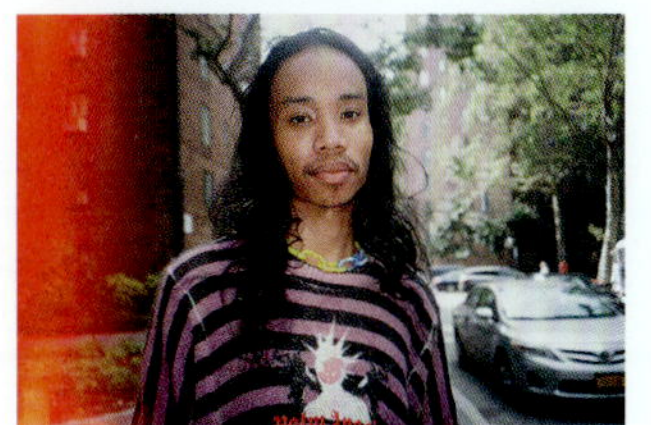
Zappa, 2019

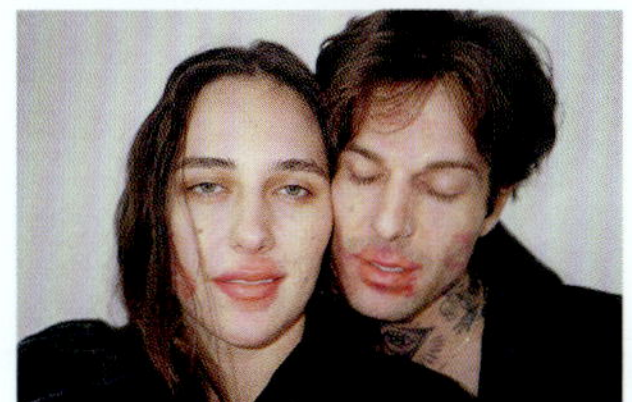
Devon & Jesse, 2020

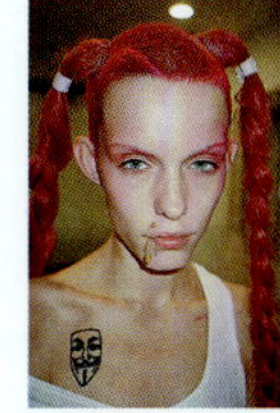
Gracie, 2020

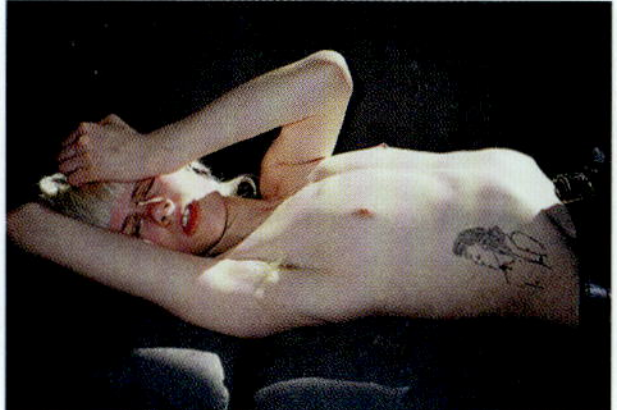
Irene (Couch), 2020

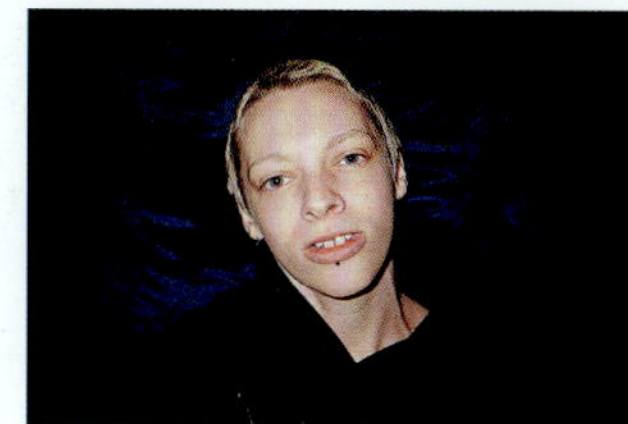
Lou, 2019

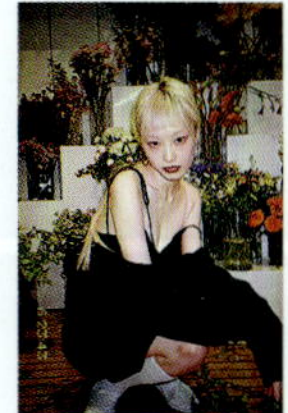
Fernanda, 2019

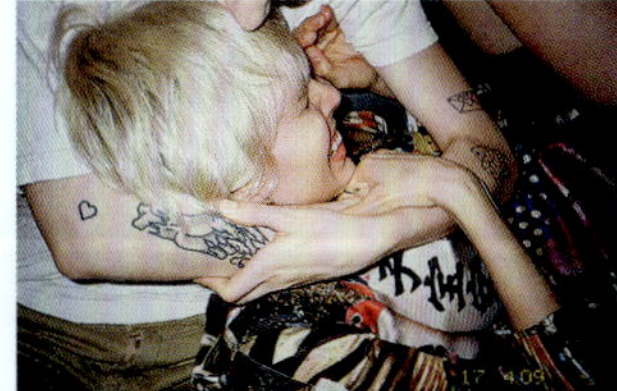
Kate & Odie (Laughing), 2019

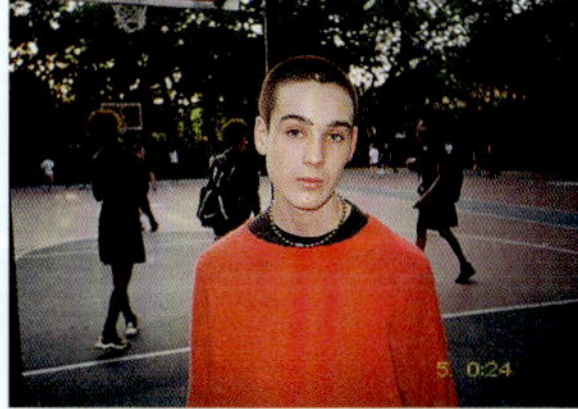
Atticus (Tompkins Square Park), 2019

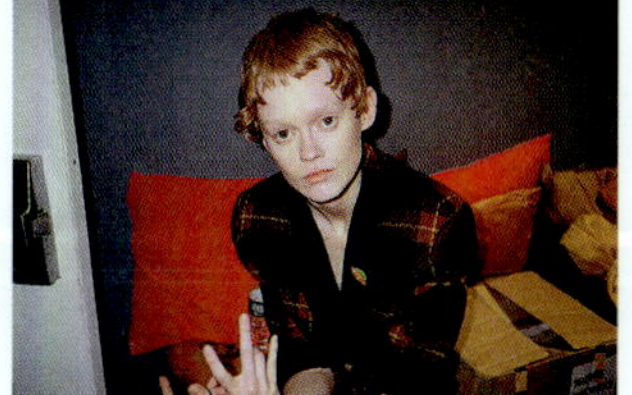
Liz, 2019

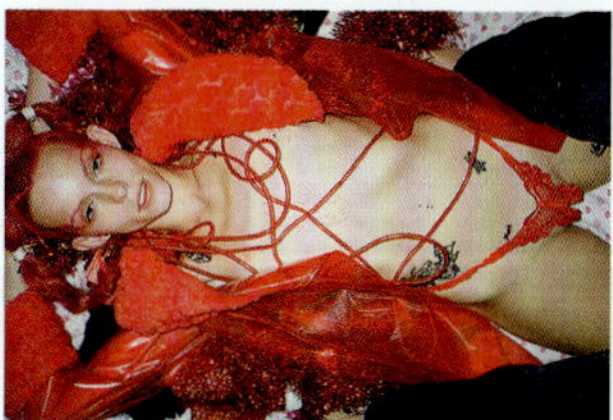
Gracie (Red), 2020

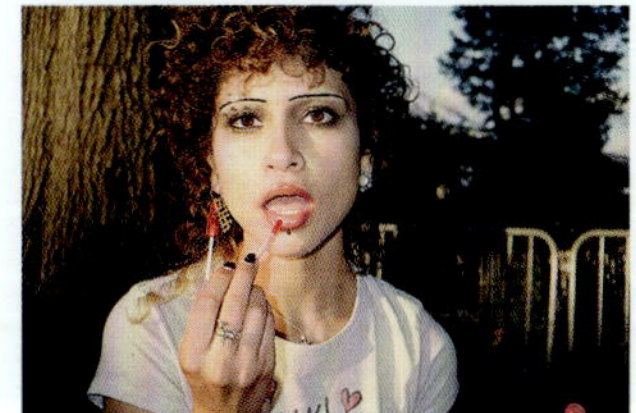
Lexi (Lip Gloss), 2020

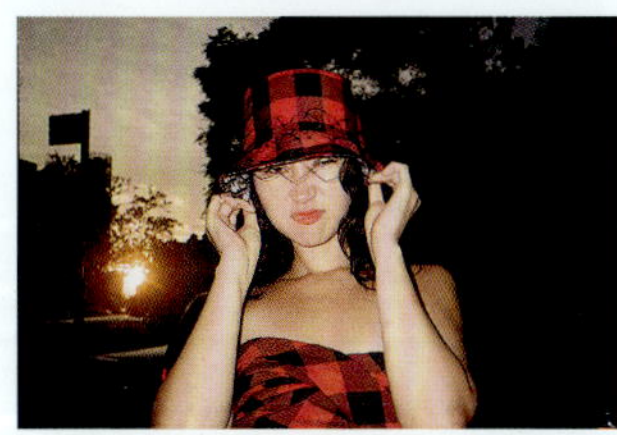
Milk, 2019

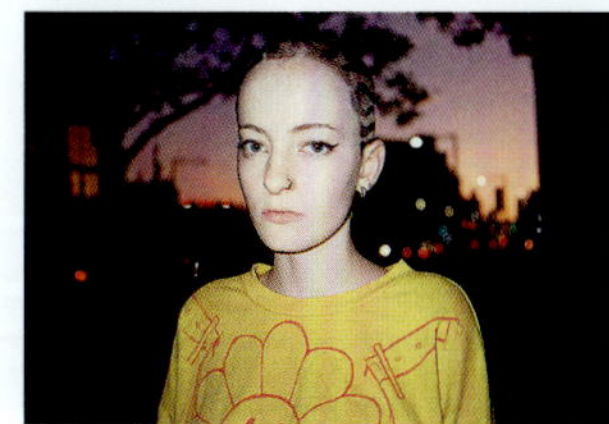
Hannah, 2019

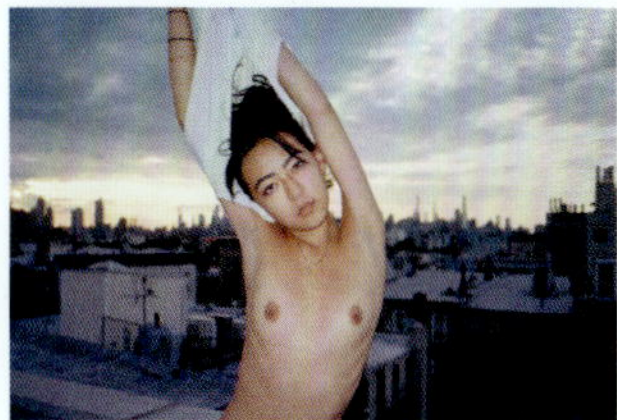
Ayana, 2020
Front cover

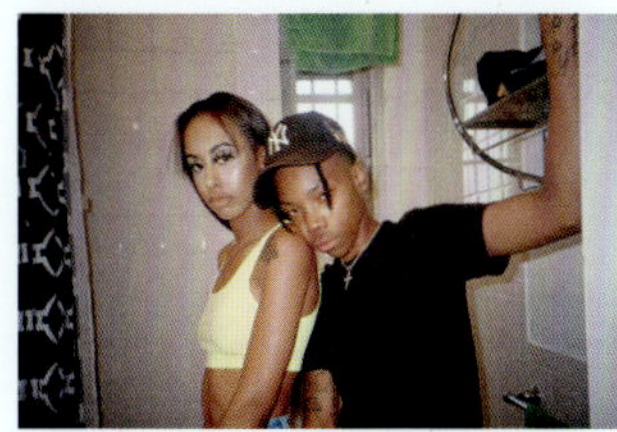
Diamond & Jiggy, 2019
Back cover

Thank you

This book is close to my heart and I would like to thank all the inspiring people in the photographs, people who create the energy of this city, people who made me feel I belong in this new home. This book is for you.

Dedication

I would like to dedicate this book to my mom. She has been my inspiration from early on, though I wasn't fully aware of it until I was older and living so far away. I hadn't seen her for eight years after moving to New York City, except for the one time she came to visit me. It was her first time on a plane, first time in America. It meant so much to me to show her the city I fell in love with. This book is an homage to my dad who wanted to travel the world but passed away before he had the chance to do so. He would have loved New York City—the place that sparked and allowed me to become.

— *Marie Tomanova*

Author: **Thomas Beachdel**
Editor: **Nadine Barth**
Project management: **Tabea Häusler, Hatje Cantz**
Copyediting: **Dawn Michelle d'Atri**
Graphic design: **Vladimíra Pípová**
Typeface: **Helvetica Neue LT Pro**
Production: **Anja Haering, Hatje Cantz**
Reproductions: **Studio Marvil, Prague, Radek Typovský**
Printing and binding: **Printer Trento s.r.l., Italy**
Paper: **Magno Volume, 150 g/m²**

Published by
Hatje Cantz Verlag GmbH
Mommsenstraße 27
10629 Berlin

www.hatjecantz.com
A Ganske Publishing Group Company

ISBN 978-3-7757-5086-8

First edition. Printed in Italy.

Front cover: ***Ayana*, 2020**
Back cover: ***Diamond & Jiggy*, 2019**

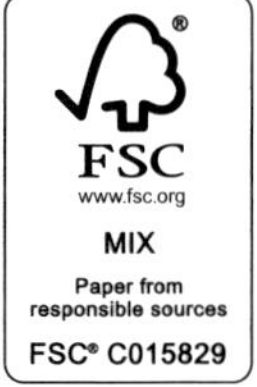